ROBERT SOUTHEY: THE CRITICAL HERITAGE

THE CRITICAL HERITAGE SERIES

GENERAL EDITOR: B.C. SOUTHAM, M.A., B.LITT. (OXON.)
Formerly Department of English, Westfield College, University of London

For a list of books in the series see the back end paper

ROBERT SOUTHEY

THE CRITICAL HERITAGE

Edited by
LIONEL MADDEN

University of Leicester Victorian Studies Centre

LONDON AND BOSTON: ROUTLEDGE & KEGAN PAUL

First published 1972
by Routledge & Kegan Paul Ltd
Broadway House, 68–74 Carter Lane,
London EC4V 5EL and
9 Park Street,
Boston, Mass. 02108, U.S.A.
© *Lionel Madden 1972*

ISBN 0 7100 7375 5

Printed in Great Britain
by Butler & Tanner Ltd, Frome and London

To Mary

General Editor's Preface

The reception given to a writer by his contemporaries and near-contemporaries is evidence of considerable value to the student of literature. On one side we learn a great deal about the state of criticism at large and in particular about the development of critical attitudes towards a single writer; at the same time, through private comments in letters, journals or marginalia, we gain an insight upon the tastes and literary thought of individual readers of the period. Evidence of this kind helps us to understand the writer's historical situation, the nature of his immediate reading-public, and his response to these pressures.

The separate volumes in the *Critical Heritage Series* present a record of this early criticism. Clearly, for many of the highly productive and lengthily reviewed nineteenth- and twentieth-century writers, there exists an enormous body of material; and in these cases the volume editors have made a selection of the most important views, significant for their intrinsic critical worth or for their representative quality—perhaps even registering incomprehension!

For earlier writers, notably pre-eighteenth century, the materials are much scarcer and the historical period has been extended, sometimes far beyond the writer's lifetime, in order to show the inception and growth of critical views which were initially slow to appear.

In each volume the documents are headed by an Introduction, discussing the material assembled and relating the early stages of the author's reception to what we have come to identify as the critical tradition. The volumes will make available much material which would otherwise be difficult of access and it is hoped that the modern reader will be thereby helped towards an informed understanding of the ways in which literature has been read and judged.

B.C.S.

Contents

CONTENTS

Amadis of Gaul (1803)

Madoc (1805)

Metrical Tales and Other Poems (1805)

Specimens of the Later English Poets (1807)

Letters from England (1807)

The Remains of Henry Kirke White (1807, 1822)

The Chronicle of the Cid (1808)

The Curse of Kehama (1810)

The Poet's Pilgrimage to Waterloo (1816)

The Lay of the Laureate. Carmen Nuptiale (1816)

Wat Tyler (1817)

A Letter to William Smith, Esq., M.P. (1817)

The Life of Wesley and the Rise and
Progress of Methodism (1820)

CONTENTS

A Vision of Judgement (1821)

History of the Peninsular War (1823–32)

The Book of the Church (1824)

A Tale of Paraguay (1825)

Sir Thomas More, or, Colloquies on the Progress and Prospects of Society (1829)

Preface

This selection from the extensive body of contemporary writing about Robert Southey is intended as a contribution to our understanding of the Romantic period in English literature. It is hoped that the documents will help to increase our knowledge not only of Southey—himself a writer who has been too little studied—but also of the critical ideals and prejudices of early nineteenth-century reviewers.

There is no need to argue large claims for Southey's literary achievement in order to justify a study of this nature. There is obvious interest and value in examining the judgments of his early reviewers and commentators. His contemporaries saw Southey as a central figure whose work as poet, historian, biographer, social critic, reviewer and novelist demanded serious attention. This selection is designed to illustrate as far as possible the range of his writings and the attitudes adopted by contemporaries to his work and, to a lesser extent, his personality.

The bewildering variety of Southey's writings made any attempt at a balanced assessment particularly difficult during his lifetime. However, the lack of modern estimates of his literary achievement makes any such early assessments especially interesting. It has therefore been decided to include a small selection of important judgments written after his death in 1843. Several of these were inspired by the publication of Southey's *Life and Correspondence* in 1850. A few—notably Carlyle's reminiscences and the evaluation by Edward Dowden which closes this volume—date from the following two decades.

Acknowledgments

I should like to acknowledge permission received from the Clarendon Press, Oxford, for the extracts from *The Collected Letters of Samuel Taylor Coleridge, The Letters of Percy Bysshe Shelley* and *The Letters of William and Dorothy Wordsworth,* and from Messrs J. M. Dent & Sons Ltd for the extracts from *The Letters of Charles and Mary Lamb* and *Henry Crabb Robinson on Books and their Writers.* I am very grateful for financial assistance in the form of a grant from the University of Leicester Research Board.

Like all students of Southey I have derived considerable help from the work of Dr Geoffrey Carnall, Professor Kenneth Curry and Professor Jack Simmons. In the task of identifying contributors to periodicals I have benefited especially from three works: the first volume of *The Wellesley Index to Victorian Periodicals,* edited by Walter Houghton; B. C. Nangle, *The Monthly Review, second series, 1790–1815;* and John O. Hayden, *The Romantic Reviewers, 1802–1824.*

During the preparation of this volume I have received much valuable assistance and kind encouragement, especially from Professor Jack Simmons, Professor Philip Collins, Dr Lois Potter and Mr Edward Rushworth of the University of Leicester and Professor Joel Wiener of the City University of New York. Mrs Win Abell has assisted generously with the typing. As with my previous books my wife Mary has given both general support and the benefit of her own specialized knowledge in the preparation and checking of the manuscript.

Abbreviations

Abbreviations have been kept to a minimum. The following short entries are used for works to which frequent reference is made in notes to the Introduction and in the headnotes.

Curry   *New Letters of Robert Southey*, ed. by Kenneth Curry (2 vols, New York, 1965).

Life   *The Life and Correspondence of the Late Robert Southey*, ed. by his son, the Rev. Charles Cuthbert Southey(6 vols, 1849–50).

Simmons Jack Simmons, *Southey* (1945).

Warter   *Selections from the Letters of Robert Southey*, ed. by his son-in-law, John Wood Warter (4 vols, 1856).

Introduction

> Imagine me in this great study of mine from breakfast till dinner, from dinner till tea, and from tea till supper, in my old black coat, my corduroys alternately with the long worsted pantaloons and gaiters in one, and the green shade, and sitting at my desk, and you have my picture and my history.

This was Southey's description of himself as a professional author in 1804.[1] Nine years later Byron wrote in his journal: 'His appearance is *Epic*; and he is the only existing entire man of letters. All the others have some pursuit annexed to their authorship' (No. 45). Byron proceeded to praise Southey's 'talents of the first order', finding them displayed in his 'perfect' prose and in those passages of his poems which are 'equal to any thing'. To the modern reader this seems high commendation from one who had already gibed at Southey in *English Bards and Scotch Reviewers* and who was later to appear as his most powerful satirist and critic. The contradictions in Byron's attitude to Southey, however, may be seen as indicative of the complex ambiguity of contemporary responses to his work.

For most of the twentieth century Southey has been largely ignored by literary critics, though he has continued to hold an apologetic place in literary histories. For serious readers in the first half of the nineteenth century he was an influential figure whose writings demanded critical assessment. Although he ridiculed 'the absurdity of those critics who have classed together three writers so utterly unlike as [Coleridge] and Wordsworth and myself, for the convenience of abuse',[2] he both suffered and gained as a poet from the determination of critics to assume a convenient conspiracy of intention between the 'Lake Poets'. Even Scott followed the *Edinburgh Review* in thinking that Wordsworth and Southey were engaged in founding a new school of poetry.[3]

After his early outpourings of revolutionary enthusiasm Southey's political position changed under the stress of European experiences. To the younger radicals he became the symbol of the political time-server, willing to surrender his ideals for sordid and selfish motives. His reasons for accepting the Laureateship in 1813 were widely misinterpreted. The fact that his earlier earnest attempts at epic poetry were

I

succeeded by adulatory Tory verses seemed to lend support to the radical attacks. The publication by his enemies of his early unpublished revolutionary *Wat Tyler*, at a time when he was advocating in the *Quarterly Review* repressive measures against revolutionaries, fixed his image as a figure of scorn and contempt among a large section of the population.

It is paradoxical, yet indicative of Southey's immense variety and vitality, that, at the very time when he was being bitterly reviled as Poet Laureate, his strongest energies were being channelled into prose writings. He himself knew that his impulse to write poetry was dying and he had begun consciously to seek fame as a historian. During the early Laureate years he was hard at work on his great *History of Brazil* and full of plans for future historical activities. His *Life of Nelson* was published during the year in which he became Poet Laureate and *The Life of Wesley* appeared shortly before *A Vision of Judgement*. His transition from serious poet to prose-writer posed problems of adjustment for contemporary critics. Certainly the more perceptive of them were quick to recognize the superior claims of Southey's prose over much of his poetry. General opinion reacted slowly, however, and perhaps the dominant impression of Southey as in some way a rival and reflector of Wordsworth has never finally been superseded.

The problem of assessing Southey's importance was made especially severe by the enormous bulk and variety of his output. There is certainly a strong element of fatal facility in Southey's literary career. As a poet he attempted a wide range of short verse forms, ballads, verse-dramas, epics and occasional pieces. He was, too, an inveterate experimenter in versification—a trait which made him a particularly attractive target for parody. As a prose-writer he was an ambitious historian, biographer and social commentator as well as a regular and hard-working periodical reviewer and essayist. In addition, he published a novel and undertook a large amount of work as editor and translator. His more ambitious works were extensively and seriously reviewed, his controversial pieces were satirized and defended with heat, and his editions and translations were evaluated in accordance with the standards of the time. It is therefore not surprising that most contemporaries found it difficult to reach a balanced view of his achievement and that the debate about his merits continued to live on after his death.

As early as 1804 Southey was claiming immunity from the pains inflicted by reviewers: 'as for being vexed at a review—I should as soon be fevered by a flea-bite!'[4] He told his friend John Rickman: 'I look upon the invention of reviews to be the worst injury which literature has received since its revival.'[5] As a regular reviewer himself, however, he could scarcely be totally insensitive to the influence of criticism. Nevertheless, he does seem to have possessed a fundamentally self-contained character, writing his various works with little regard for contemporary opinion under the twin impulses of desire for ultimate fame and immediate financial necessity.

The motive of financial necessity is especially important in Southey's life because he possessed a generous nature which readily recognized the duty to provide for dependants. In 1844, shortly after Southey's death, Wordsworth wrote a penetrating comparison of the poetic achievement of Coleridge and Southey in which he stated (No. 126):

Now I do believe . . . that no man can write verses that will live in the hearts of his Fellow creatures but through an over powering impulse in his own mind, involving him often times in labour that he cannot dismiss or escape from, though his duty to himself and others may require it.

Southey could never absolve himself from his duty to others for the sake of his art. For this reason he undertook much arduous and soul-destroying work which inevitably dulled his imagination and restricted his freedom. In 1807 he wrote of himself, perhaps drawing a contrast with Coleridge: 'No person can be more thoroughly convinced that goodness is a better thing than genius, and that genius is no excuse for those follies and offences which are called its eccentricities.'[6] The sentiment is worthy and Southey's principles were undoubtedly noble. No reader of his letters, indeed, can fail to esteem him very highly as a man. Nevertheless, it is clear that, by deliberately choosing a life of systematic application and by shunning the exhausting excitement of imaginative involvement in favour of calm and dispassionate detachment, Southey effectively crushed his own ambitions of major poetic achievement. The process by which critics gradually assessed the strengths and limitations of his varied activities is traced in the following pages.

EARLY REPUTATION

Southey's earliest ambitions were poetic, his earliest politics revolutionary. His career commenced effectively in the autumn of 1794 when he made his first appearance in the London press with a poem—one of his 'Botany Bay Eclogues'—in the *Morning Chronicle*. In the same year the hastily written verse-drama, *The Fall of Robespierre*, was published at Cambridge under the name of Coleridge, though Southey himself had contributed two of the three acts, and *Poems by Robert Lovell and Robert Southey* was published at Bath. Both volumes received encouraging if temperate praise.

During 1794 Southey also submitted for publication by subscription an epic poem of revolutionary sentiments. The subscription plan was unproductive but in the following year Joseph Cottle, the young Bristol bookseller, heard part of the poem and immediately offered Southey favourable terms for its publication. *Joan of Arc*, published in 1796, brought Southey a modest degree of fame. Its political ideas attracted laudatory reviews from the *Analytical*, *Monthly* and *Critical Reviews*, all of which had revolutionary sympathies. John Aikin, in the *Monthly Review*, found the sentiments 'uniformly noble, liberal, enlightened, and breathing the purest spirit of general benevolence and regard to the rights and claims of human kind' (No. 5). The *Critical Review* predicted for Southey a place 'in the first class of English poets' (No. 6), a judgment echoed by the less politically partisan Charles Lamb, who stated: 'On the whole, I expect Southey one day to rival Milton' (No. 7). Wordsworth, however, found the preface 'a very conceited performance' and the poem 'on the whole of very inferior execution' (No. 4), while Coleridge acutely recognized two basic critical points in any assessment of Southey's poetry, now or later—his 'natural, perspicuous, & dignified' language on the one hand and his lack of 'that *toil* of thinking, which is necessary in order to plan *a Whole*' (No. 10).

If sterner critics expressed their doubts in private correspondence, however, the favourable tone of the reviews ensured that Southey's subsequent poetry would receive serious consideration. The following year saw him busy revising *Joan of Arc* for a new edition. In 1797, too, Cottle published a volume of *Poems by Robert Southey*. Both this and a second volume of *Poems* in 1799 had successful sales. The *Critical Review* and the *Monthly Review* again united to praise Southey, Aikin asserting in the latter that 'Genius is a despotic power, and irresistibly commands homage' (No. 12). Commendation again proved easier to win from the reviews than from Coleridge, who remarked to Cottle that 'Wordsworth complains, with justice, that Southey writes *too much at his ease*', a criticism which Coleridge endorsed in his own analysis of Southey's 'fluency' and 'facility'. The same letter to Cottle contains an interesting early attack upon Southey's tendency to show too strong an interest in the mere mechanics of plot for its own sake (No. 11).

If Coleridge's comments foreshadow later judgments of Southey by literary critics, another attack, launched in 1797, constituted the first in a long series of political offensives. On 20 November 1797 was published the first number of a new periodical, the *Anti-Jacobin, or Weekly Examiner*. The brilliant parody of Southey's poem on the regicide Henry Marten (No. 13) was the prelude to further assaults on his revolutionary political ideas, especially as expressed in his support of the French Revolution and his attack on the monarchy and the aristocracy. For the last of its parodies of Southey, however, the *Anti-Jacobin* left his politics to attack his metrical experiments—in this case his dactylics. Both Southey's politics and his metrical experiments were to prove inviting targets for later parodists, so that in 1810 he could write: 'Every apprentice in satire and scandal for the last dozen years has tried his hand upon me.'[7] However, the very fact that he was chosen as a subject for parody must have brought some consolation in 1797. The *Anti-Jacobin* would scarcely have wasted its ammunition on him if he had not achieved at least some eminence.

THE EPICS

Mr. Southey wades through ponderous volumes of travels and old chronicles, from which he carefully selects all that is false, useless, and absurd, as being essentially poetical; and when he has a commonplace book full of monstrosities, strings them into an epic.[8]

The idea of writing an oriental verse tale had attracted Southey as early as 1796.[9] In 1798 he sketched the first plan of *Thalaba the Destroyer* which was finally completed and revised in October 1800 and published in 1801, Southey receiving £115 in payment. *Thalaba* was the first of a group of epics on which Southey's poetic fame was largely built in his own day. In the epics he revealed a strange delight in exotic and mythological subject matter and a passion for metrical experiments. Worse still he yielded fully to the temptation already identified by Wordsworth and Coleridge of writing too much at his ease. Betrayed by his own fluency and facility he was often guilty in his epics of confusing quantity and quality. Southey himself wrote to Walter Savage Landor: 'Pour out your mind in a great poem, and you will exercise authority over the feelings and opinions of mankind as long as the language lasts in which you write.'[10] The passage provides an admirable statement of the power and influence of Wordsworth's *Prelude* but is sadly inapplicable to *Thalaba* or its successors.

Southey soon ceased to favour the title of epic. He described *Thalaba* as a 'metrical romance'. When Longman in 1804 announced *Madoc* as an epic poem Southey wrote: 'the name, of which I was once over-fond, has nauseated me, and, moreover, should seem to render me amenable to certain laws which I do not acknowledge'.[11] Nevertheless, the term stuck with contemporaries and later critics as a convenient description of *Joan of Arc* and the group of long narrative tales in verse published between 1801 and 1814.

However much critics differed about the merits of *Thalaba* they agreed in condemning the poem's metre. Although later experiments were similarly condemned the criticism never influenced Southey's practice. About the overall merits of the poem critical opinion ranged from William Taylor in the *Critical Review* to Francis Jeffrey in the *Edinburgh Review*. Taylor, a friend of Southey, argued for the signi-ficance of *Thalaba* as a work of promise rather than as a finished achievement: 'Perhaps no work of art so imperfect ever announced such power in the artist—perhaps no artist so powerful ever rested his fame on so imperfect a production—as *Thalaba*' (No. 19). Jeffrey, on the other hand, saw Southey as one of the leaders of a new poetic school, the members of which cultivated 'an affectation of great simplicity and familiarity of language', presenting to their readers 'vulgar manners, in vulgar language' (No. 18).

Jeffrey's famous review, although it is, of course, a *locus classicus* for the student of early attitudes towards English Romantic poetry, is directed much more forcibly against the practices of Wordsworth and Coleridge than those of Southey. Jeffrey certainly overestimated the closeness of Southey's literary relationship with his greater contem-poraries. Nevertheless, his review of *Thalaba* shows considerable acuteness at times. He was, for instance, one of the first critics to note that Southey's imaginative impulse tends to be derived from books rather than from life: 'It is impossible to peruse this poem, with the notes, without feeling that it is the fruit of much reading, undertaken for the express purpose of fabricating some such performance.' Too many of Southey's poems are, indeed, 'little else than his commonplace book versified'. His short poem in praise of books—'My days among the dead are passed'—expressed the truth about a basic aspect of his nature which was evident throughout his life. In 1828 he wrote: 'It is more delightful for me to live with books than with men,

6

even with all the relish that I have for such society as is worth having.'[12]

Jeffrey notes that Southey's real genius 'seems naturally to delight in the representation of domestic virtues and pleasures, and the brilliant delineation of external nature. In both these departments, he is frequently very successful; but he seems to want vigour for the loftier flights of poetry.' The success of some of Southey's more intimate and less ambitious poems has certainly led many later readers to the conclusion that he would have been a better poet if he had written more about domestic scenes and family affections and less about remote and great events. Professor Jack Simmons has remarked justly: 'He was a man of strong and deep affections: the tragedy of his poetry is that he so seldom allowed them to appear.'[13]

Southey himself regarded Jeffrey's 'attempt at Thalabacide' as unfair. However, he expressed himself to his friend and patron C. W. Williams Wynn as 'On the whole . . . fully satisfied with the reception the poem has found, such approbation in private as most gratifies me, and such public censure as attracts attention, and will make the subject remembered when the censure itself is forgotten.'[14] Certainly the censure in the *Edinburgh Review* did help to establish in the eyes of the general reading public an impression of his stature as an important poet.

The composition and revision of Southey's next epic, *Madoc*, was spread over ten years. The poem was begun in 1795 and published in 1805. Although it did not sell well—owing partly, no doubt, to its lavish production and high price—it received considerable praise. The *Imperial Review* (No. 25) ranked it only below *Paradise Lost*. Most critics, whether favourable or hostile, cited as defects the reader's general lack of interest in the strangely-named characters, the often flat style and the eccentric diction. As a hostile critic in the *Eclectic Review* remarked: 'Mr S. seems to be enamoured of any thing either very old, or very new-fashioned, so that it be only out of the common way' (No. 26). Wordsworth, however, made a crucial distinction when he praised Southey's 'beautiful pictures and descriptions' and his 'animation' but found the poem deficient in 'knowledge of human Nature and the human heart' (No. 22). *Madoc*, indeed, like Southey's epics generally, appealed to those critics who were concerned primarily with discovering beautiful and decorative features within a long poem. Critics who considered the total effect of the epics were usually less satisfied, detecting in them a lack of unifying thought and sensibility.

Of *The Curse of Kehama*, published in 1810, Southey wrote: 'No

7

subject could have been devised more remote from human sympathies.'[15] It is, indeed, difficult to imagine what could have attracted him to 'the adoption or creation of so *absurd* a fable', as John Foster described his tale of Hindu mythology (No. 40). The exotic and remote subject, which inevitably recalled *Thalaba*, was made even less palatable by what Southey described as 'a style of versification as unusual as the ground-work of the story'.[16] Several critics expressed their sense of impatience at the mental and imaginative extravagance revealed in the conception of such a work. The *Critical Review* accused Southey of being 'entirely deficient in that high corrective quality of the mind . . . we mean a cool, steady, and comprehensive judgment' (No. 39), while the *Literary Panorama* counselled him to abandon such exotic topics 'and treat us with a subject in which the sympathy of the human heart, the interior of man, may afford a scope to the powers of his genius' (No. 41).

In the criticisms of *The Curse of Kehama* one can sense among responsible and intelligent critics a growing exasperation both with Southey's attempt to secure a poetical reputation by sheer bulk of output and with his evasion of any real emotional involvement with his subjects. He himself frequently referred to his inability to endure the continuous excitement of any composition in which his emotions were involved and he recognized that this 'proceeds from weakness, not from strength'.[17] Nevertheless, he expressed an arrogant confidence about the ultimate success of his epics, though this may well have proceeded from self-doubt rather than self-assurance.

The last of Southey's epics, *Roderick, the Last of the Goths*, published in 1814, was financially the most successful. Charles Lamb felt himself more at home with its subject than with those of the other epics: 'I am at home in Spain and Christendom' (No. 56). Many contemporaries agreed that Southey had at last chosen an appropriate subject for an epic poem written in English. Grosvenor Bedford in the *Quarterly Review* (No. 54) and John Taylor Coleridge in the *British Critic* (No. 55) gave weighty praise to the intensity of passion and the moral tone of the work. Critics obviously felt more at ease with the blank verse than with the irregular metres of earlier epics. Lamb alluded—surely with intentional humour—to the poem's voluminous notes as suitable breakfast reading but some reviewers saw these as yet further evidence of the essentially fabricated nature of the epics (cf. Nos 57 and 58).

The examination of contemporary responses to Southey's epics reveals considerable critical confusion. Many reviewers clearly felt that the very attempt at a long poem was itself a necessary exercise for a writer ambitious for poetic fame. Certainly Southey felt a compulsion on himself to undertake such arduous and inadequately rewarded works in order to establish firmly his reputation within the company of great English poets. Yet the effort and persistence which were so clearly shown in his voluminous works themselves implied a certain lack of judgment and control. The *Theatrical Inquisitor*, reviewing *Roderick*, declared: 'His genius runs to waste in its luxuriance' (No. 52).

There is among contemporary critics a frequent sense of frustration that Southey, while willing to write so much, should usually be so unwilling to involve his deepest mental and emotional impulses in his poetry. Occasionally, indeed, critics glimpse some deeper force within the epics. Thus the *Imperial Review* (No. 25) noted the 'tenderness and humanity' which finally pervade *Madoc*. The *British Review*, on the other hand, perceived more sinister energies in *Roderick* when it pointed to 'the totally unqualified expression of a deeply vindictive spirit . . . the fault lies in the apparent zest and relish with which this is done' (No. 58). Such critical insights pierce the defensive outworks of the epics to discover glimpses of real if contradictory aspects of the poet's personality. It was perhaps unfortunate for Southey that contemporary attention should focus on his epics rather than on the ballads and shorter poems in which he often revealed his strengths more clearly.

THE LAUREATE POEMS AND *Wat Tyler*

Early Laureate Poems
In 1813 Scott refused the office of Poet Laureate (see No. 48) and, at his suggestion, it was offered to Southey who had little hesitation in accepting it. The small salary of £90 a year was of practical benefit to his family and he hoped that the duties could be modified so that he would not be expected to produce birthday and New Year odes with mechanical regularity. As he wrote to John King in September 1813: 'You will please to congratulate, and not condole with me, upon this appointment. I take it upon an understanding that no odes are to be expected from me, and I mean to employ the whole salary in insuring my life.'[18] He was, in fact, somewhat disappointed in his hope of a change in the conditions of the Laureateship. In February 1816 he told Grosvenor Bedford: 'Between ourselves, I have not been well used about the Laureateship. They require task verses from me,—not to

keep up the custom of having them befiddled, but to keep up the task, —instead of putting an end to this foolery in a fair and open manner, which would do the court credit, and save me a silly expense of time and trouble.'[19]

The Laureateship came at a significant point in Southey's career. During the last few years he had increasingly been moving away from poetry towards prose. In 1810 he published the first volume of his extensive *History of Brazil* which was intended as only part of an even more ambitious group of historical works. The *Life of Nelson* was published in 1813. As Southey himself realized, the Laureateship was to turn his attention back to poetry, at least for a short time:[20]

The Laureateship will certainly have this effect upon me, that it will make me produce more poetry than I otherwise should have done. For many years I had written little, and was permitting other studies to wean me from it more and more. But it would be unbecoming to accept the only public mark of honour which is attached to the pursuit, and at the same time withdraw from the profession.

The acceptance of the Laureateship exposed Southey to an enormous amount of public scorn. To his opponents he became the type figure of the revolutionary idealist who abandons his principles and turns courtier for financial and social gain. Reviewing his first Laureate poem, the *Carmen Triumphale for the Commencement of the Year 1814*, the *Critical Review* immediately struck the tone which, often with greater vituperation, was to seem appropriate to many subsequent reviewers (No. 59):

When Mr. Southey, 'in happy hour,' was appointed to the laurel, all the world was astonished. Critics of twenty years standing, with much gravity, expatiated on the operations of time, the mutability of man, and the poetry of the *Anti-jacobin*; while the vast body of people, who read birth day odes, waited with extraordinary impatience for the first courtly effusions of a converted muse.

It must be emphasized at once that the majority of contemporary reviews of Southey's Laureate poems had a political rather than a strictly literary critical intention. The *Eclectic Review* might argue that there was no reason why 'a man of integrity and independence of mind' should not accept the office of Poet Laureate (No. 61), but many of the radical or liberal reviews were adamant that such an action by Southey furnished proof of fundamental dishonesty and dependence of mind. Periodicals such as the *Scourge*, the *Critical Review* and the *Augustan Review* waged their political campaign against the *Carmen*

Triumphale, the *Odes to His Royal Highness the Prince Regent, His Imperial Majesty the Emperor of Russia, and His Majesty the King of Prussia, The Poet's Pilgrimage to Waterloo* and *The Lay of the Laureate*. It is interesting to note that several of the reviewers of *The Poet's Pilgrimage* paid special attention to its attractive Proem in which Southey describes the domestic rejoicing which greeted his home-coming. The *European Magazine and London Review*,[21] for example, quoted a selection of stanzas from the Proem with the comment that it is in this 'exquisitely touching picture of domestic life, that the talents of the poet are most happily exerted'. The *British Critic*,[22] citing the Proem, similarly stated:

Whoever has a true feeling for poetry must delight in domestic associations, and whoever is conversant with Mr. Southey's poetry, knows that he is never on stronger ground than when he paints domestic pictures. The scenes of this sort, which he describes, have a simplicity and verity in them, which shew that he draws what he is well acquainted with.

Faced with such an obviously true analysis of one of Southey's strengths, one is again led to speculate why he did not heed valuable and constructive criticism. About his public writing in general there was a large measure of agreement with Jeffrey, who declared in 1816 that 'his Laureate odes are utterly and intolerably bad' (No. 67). Even the usually sympathetic *Eclectic Review* was often dissatisfied with Southey's achievement as a poet of public events, though, in its review of *Carmen Triumphale*, it argued that 'A good political poem, we think, does not exist' (No. 61). It was in the *Eclectic Review*, however, that Josiah Conder contributed one of the most interesting assessments of Southey's achievement as Poet Laureate (No. 66). Conder chose to review *The Poet's Pilgrimage* with Wordsworth's *Thanksgiving Ode, January 18, 1816*. Although the modern reader would probably wish to register dissent from several of Conder's conclusions, there is no doubt that his review shows considerable sympathetic understanding of Southey's personality:

Mr. Southey . . . is never to be mistaken for any other than a husband, a father, a friend;—a man whose sympathies all link him to his country and his fellow-men; whose errors whether poetical or political, proceed from the warmth of feeling or the force of prejudice, and are never the deliberate sins of a perverse intellect, or the indications of dubious principles.

Conder claims that, as a poet, 'Southey excels in force of dramatic conception, in the development of character, and in the expression of the tender affections'. Certainly, the last of these seems the characteristic which it would have benefited Southey to concentrate upon.

Wat Tyler

In February 1817 there appeared in print a dramatic poem, *Wat Tyler*, written by Southey in three mornings twenty-three years earlier in 1794.[23] The poem's republican sentiments contrasted sharply with Southey's reactionary articles 'On Parliamentary Reform', published in the *Quarterly Review* issue for October of the previous year, and 'On the Rise and Progress of Popular Disaffection' which appeared in the *Quarterly* at almost exactly the same time as *Wat Tyler* was published. Of all Southey's numerous works *Wat Tyler* attracted most attention and brought him the most violent denunciations. It was ironical that this immature piece should prove easily the bestseller of all his works, selling tens of thousands of copies and even being acted.[24] For a short time the subject assumed national importance as Southey was attacked in the House of Commons (No. 74), first by Brougham on 25 February and later, on 14 March, by William Smith, during a debate on the Seditious Meetings Bill. On this latter occasion Southey was defended by his friend C. W. Williams Wynn. The attack by Smith prompted Southey to attempt his own defence in *A Letter to William Smith, Esq., M.P.*

Outside Parliament the radicals were not slow to seize upon *Wat Tyler*. In the *Examiner* Hazlitt pointed the contrast between the youthful advocate of reform and the middle-aged supporter of repressive conservatism as he poured vitriolic scorn on Southey's instability and untrustworthiness (No. 73). For Hazlitt, as for Byron and many other contemporaries, Southey had been finally revealed as a living symbol of apostasy and hypocrisy. If political capital was made out of *Wat Tyler* there was certainly also much genuine indignation that Southey should have become so intolerant in his attitude to those who now held opinions which had formerly been his. As Byron wrote to John Murray (No. 77):

It is no disgrace to Mr. Southey to have written *Wat Tyler*, and afterwards to have written his birthday or Victory odes (I speak only of their *politics*), but it is something, for which I have no words, for this man to have endeavoured to bring to the stake (for such would he do) men who think as he thought, and for no reason but because they think so still, when he has found it convenient to think otherwise.

Wat Tyler and the *Letter to William Smith* found few defenders in public. The *Literary Gazette* (No. 76) and the *New Monthly Magazine* (No. 81) attempted to vindicate Southey. The *Courier* supported him as a Tory patron and also printed letters of defence from Southey himself[25] and from Coleridge.[26] In addition to the violent attacks from the periodical reviewers Southey had also to suffer both the wit of Leigh Hunt in two *Examiner* articles—'Death and Funeral of the Late Mr. Southey' and 'Extraordinary Case of the Late Mr. Southey' (No. 79)—and the cheap satire of such popular effusions as *The Changeling* (No. 78).

A Vision of Judgement

The storm over *Wat Tyler* was succeeded by a period of comparative calm for Southey, during which he occupied himself principally with his edition of *The Byrth, Lyf and Actes of King Arthur*, his *Life of Wesley* and his regular reviewing. The death of George III in 1820, however, was an occasion which clearly demanded a public lament from the Poet Laureate. Undeterred by his previous experiences Southey proceeded to write *A Vision of Judgement*. In January 1821 he wrote to Grosvenor Bedford: 'What a grand bespattering of abuse I shall have when the *Vision* appears.'[27]

Even Southey, perhaps, could scarcely have foreseen just how violent the bespattering would be. The *Literary Gazette*, which had supported him over *Wat Tyler* (No. 76), described the *Vision* as 'a mass of absurdity' (No. 90). Other reviewers were less mild. The *Literary Chronicle and Weekly Review* declared: 'To what extent the debasement of talents, and the prostitution of principle may be carried, Mr. Southey furnishes a memorable instance. We know not which to condemn most, the prosing absurdity of this poem, its wanton political profligacy, or its blasphemy' (No. 91). Reviewers were outraged both by the content of the poem and by Southey's attempt at English hexameters. Dorothy Wordsworth might like the metre (No. 92) but the majority of critics found the hexameters at best extravagant and at worst absurd.

Southey's son and editor of the *Life and Correspondence* stated that abuse of the *Vision* was directed less against the poem itself than against the Preface in which Southey attacked the 'Satanic school' of modern poets.[28] It was this Preface which aroused Byron's anger which he expressed in Canto III of *Don Juan* and in a prose appendix to *The Two Foscari* (No. 94). Southey's reply in a letter to the *Courier*[29] was not conciliatory and led to the composition of Byron's own *Vision of*

Judgment, by far the most effective satire ever written against the Poet Laureate (No. 96).

A Vision of Judgement effectively marked the end of Southey's poetic career except for one final attempt at a long poem, *A Tale of Paraguay*, published in 1825. The low sales and small critical response to this work emphasized the declining contemporary interest in his poetry. Nevertheless, the *Eclectic Review* asserted with surprising obtuseness that Southey was unable to write a good short poem but that 'It is on works like this, which the public will not willingly let die, that his fame must stand' (No. 106). By this time, however, Southey was heavily committed to the composition of prose works. His *History of the Peninsular War* was already in progress and he was making plans which were to lead to the publication of *Colloquies* and *The Doctor*.

PROSE WRITINGS

My rule of writing, whether for prose or verse, is the same, and may very shortly be stated. It is, to express myself, 1st, as perspicuously as possible; 2nd, as concisely as possible; 3rd, as impressively as possible. This is the way to be understood, and felt, and remembered.[30]

Southey often expressed understandable impatience with those who sought advice about style in prose composition. In 1829 he wrote to a correspondent: 'When I have been asked the foolish question, what a young man should do who wishes to acquire a good style, my answer has been that he should never think about it; but say what he has to say as perspicuously as he can, and as briefly as he can, and then the style will take care of itself.'[31] Again, in the following year, he stated: 'of what is called *style*, not a thought enters my head at any time. Look to the matter, and the manner takes care of itself.'[32]

The bewildering variety of Southey's output is nowhere better exemplified than in his prose work. A regular reviewer and essayist for periodicals throughout his life, he also published historical and biographical works, studies in social analysis and criticism, and one of the most curious attempts at a novel in the English language. He also contributed introductions and notes to the many editions and translations which he undertook. As his career progressed several discerning critics turned from their rather doubtful evaluation of his poetry to a much more enthusiastic recognition of his achievement as a prose-writer and praise for his 'style' became an accepted expression of their response.

It is interesting to compare Southey's frequently reiterated insistence that he had no consciously adopted stylistic technique with the generous and acute comments of Hazlitt in *The Spirit of the Age* (No. 104) and *The Plain Speaker* (No. 109). Hazlitt recognizes that Southey's style is a complex mixture of natural and artificial characteristics: 'Mr. Southey's prose-style can scarcely be too much praised. It is plain, clear, pointed, familiar, perfectly modern in its texture, but with a grave and sparkling admixture of *archaisms* in its ornaments and occasional phraseology' (No. 104). The same point was made later, in 1833, by Bulwer-Lytton in *England and the English*: 'No writer blends more happily the academical graces of the style of last century, with the popular vigour of that which distinguishes the present' (No. 116). Hazlitt, however, while he recognizes a certain amount of vigour, also identifies the single weakness in some of Southey's prose writing: 'There is rather a want of originality and even of *impetus*: but there is no want of playful or biting satire, of ingenuity, of casuistry, of learning and of information' (No. 104).

Hazlitt's appreciation of the prose is outstandingly perceptive and surprisingly generous when one considers his virulent hostility to Southey's Laureate poems. Coleridge, in 1817, wrote appreciatively in his *Biographia Literaria* of Southey's periodical reviews and essays (No. 83). Wordsworth, in 1829, described Southey's prose style as 'eminently clear, lively, and unencumbered' (No. 111). Many contemporary critics referred to his conciseness and clarity of expression, though none analysed the complex achievement of his best prose so well as Hazlitt. The following sections consider briefly some contemporary reactions to Southey's varied prose output.

Historical and Biographical Works
In 1810 Southey admitted to Landor that he had begun to find more pleasure in writing history than poetry: 'I have an ominous feeling that there are poets enough in the world without me, and that my best chance of being remembered will be as an historian.'[33] This was no new feeling. As early as 1803 he had stated that he discovered in historical work a continuous and placid satisfaction which suited his temperament better than the emotional demands of poetic composition.[34] Many references in Southey's letters make it clear that he was unable to stand the excitement which resulted from deep imaginative involvement in creative work. He early referred to 'that love of steady and productive employment, which is now grown into a necessary

habit with me'.[35] By nature he was a patient and industrious student of books, though he continued throughout much of his life to delude himself. As late as 1816 he could still write: 'By nature I am a poet, by deliberate choice an historian.'[36]

By September 1804 Southey had devised an enormous plan of historical writing which was to include a three-volume history of Portugal, a two- to three-volume history of the Portuguese Empire in Asia, a history of Brazil, a history of the Jesuits in Japan, a two-volume literary history of Spain and Portugal, and a history of monasticism.[37] The plan, in various forms, fascinated him throughout his life. It came to represent a vision which both inspired and tormented him even when his mind was failing during his last years. The grand design, in fact, was little more than begun. Only *The History of Brazil* was completed—itself a considerable achievement for a man so heavily committed to other forms of writing. By the time it was completed in 1819 he had also published *The Life of Nelson*. *The Life of Wesley* followed in 1820 before he embarked on the three-volume *History of the Peninsular War*, published between 1823 and 1832. His controversial excursions into ecclesiastical history, *The Book of the Church* and *Vindiciae Ecclesiae Anglicanae*, appeared in 1824 and 1826. The *Peninsular War* was followed by *Lives of the British Admirals* in five volumes, published between 1833 and 1840.

The reasons for Southey's failure to pursue his grand design were largely financial. In September 1818 he told John Taylor Coleridge: 'I have not yet received so much for the *History of Brazil* as for a single article in the *Quarterly Review*.'[38] Such enormous labour for small rewards was a luxury he could not afford. As late as 1832 he was still asserting that the history of Portugal was 'the work I have most at heart'[39] but 'this work can only have that time allotted to it which can be won from works of necessity, and that not yet'.[40] The need to provide for his dependants increasingly determined the course of Southey's career and is discussed below.

If his greatest plans were not realized, however, Southey's output as a historian was certainly considerable. How did contemporaries assess his achievement? He himself analysed the three basic requirements for a historian as 'industry, judgment, genius; the patience to investigate, the discrimination to select, the power to infer and to enliven'.[41] No critic could deny his great and patient industry. Reviewers of the first volume of *The History of Brazil* agreed in praising 'his labour in the accumulation of facts' (No. 42) and 'his extensive erudition and indefatigable spirit of research' (No. 43). They were, however, less satisfied with other aspects of his work. The *Eclectic Review* (No. 42) wished that his industry and talent for composition could have been combined with greater depth and originality of thought. Joseph Lowe, in the *Monthly Review* (No. 43), found the work lacking in general reflections and in selectivity. Although his style was admitted to be admirably concise his accumulation of detailed facts produced an impression of prolixity. A writer in the *British Critic*,[42] reviewing the first two volumes of *The History of Brazil*, asserted that the historian's duty is not merely to record events but to select, classify, compare and evaluate them so that 'moral lessons are enforced, and principles of human conduct deduced'. The charge that Southey included too much detail and made too little attempt at comparison and interpretation was repeated by the *Eclectic Review* thirteen years later in its review of the first volume of the *History of the Peninsular War*: 'We seldom find that dexterity in detecting the secret motives and springs of action, which is so indispensable a faculty in the historian. There is but little profound or vigorous political discussion' (No. 99).

If the critics had reservations about Southey's achievement as a historian in these large detailed works there was considerable enthusiasm for his short *Life of Nelson*. This work grew out of an article on Nelson published in the *Quarterly Review* in February 1810. Murray was so delighted with the piece that he commissioned Southey to turn it into a small book. Although the work achieved its greatest popularity with the general public after Southey's death[43] it was well received by critics at the time of publication. The *Critical Review* praised Southey's impartiality and his straightforward and uncomplicated narrative (No. 49). The *British Critic*, similarly, noted his factual accuracy and vigorous 'plain narrative' (No. 50). The *Antijacobin Review & Magazine*[44] criticized the publication of the work in two volumes instead of a single pocket volume—an unfortunate printer's error which had a bad effect on the book's sale. The reviewer, however, described the work favourably as 'a valuable compilation, drawn up with care, exhibiting every material fact which marked the eventful life of Nelson, and interspersed with observations, many of which are highly pertinent and judicious'.

Later writers frequently praised *The Life of Nelson* as one of Southey's outstanding achievements as a historian and biographer. Lockhart, in 1824, described it as 'truly a masterpiece;—a brief animated—glowing —straightforward—manly English work' (No. 89). Macaulay thought it the best of all Southey's works. In his review of *Colloquies* in 1830 he described *The Life of Nelson* as 'beyond all doubt, the most perfect and the most delightful of his works' (No. 113). Macaulay claimed that, because Southey was 'by no means so skilful in designing, as in filling up', he found the writing of biography a particularly congenial occupation. In Southey's work generally Macaulay found the same lack of analytic power noted by earlier critics of his historical books. For a writer with such a limitation the biography of Nelson was an ideal task: 'There were no fine riddles of the human heart to read—no theories to found—no hidden causes to develope—no remote consequences to predict. . . . The subject did not require the exercise of those reasoning powers the want of which is the blemish of his prose.'

According to Macaulay, Southey failed in his *Life of Wesley* because this was a subject which demanded not merely an adequate narrative technique but 'all the qualities of a philosophic historian'. Southey himself, writing in March 1820, predicted that the book would obtain 'a moderate sale, and a durable reputation'.[45] When Lockhart reviewed *The Life of Wesley* in 1824 he asked: 'Who but Southey would ever have dreamt that it was possible for a man that was not a Methodist, and that had never seen John Wesley's face, nor even conversed with any one of his disciples, to write two thumping volumes under the name of a *Life of Wesley*, without turning the stomach of the Public?' (No. 89). Lockhart's review, however, like many others, displayed much less sympathetic understanding of Methodist ideas than Southey's book. The official Methodist reply by Richard Watson (No. 88) paid tribute to Southey's genuine attempt at candour and impartiality.

Southey's attempts to secure fame as a historian were certainly sincerely and seriously undertaken. Only the ill-judged *Book of the Church* and the *Vindiciae Ecclesiae Anglicanae* were obviously propaganda works which could appeal only to those who were already committed. It is ironic that Southey, who planned so many ambitious historical projects, should be best remembered for one of his slightest and least pretentious works, *The Life of Nelson*. As his career progressed he certainly appeared to contemporaries too much as 'a Laureate of all trades' (No. 101) and a man who 'has run through every stage of literature' (No. 103). Perceptive critics had found in his poetry the defect of too much learning and too little observation and reflection. Those who most closely analysed his historical works discerned weaknesses of the same kind which were concisely enumerated by Hazlitt in *The Spirit of the Age*: 'His mind is after all rather the recipient and transmitter of knowledge, than the originator of it. He has hardly grasp of thought enough to arrive at any great leading truth' (No. 104).

Social Commentary

In the introduction to his edition of Letters from England[46] Jack Simmons advances convincing reasons for Southey's decision to publish the book under a pseudonym and briefly discusses its contemporary reception. The book received favourable notices in the Courier and the Morning Post and Southey wrote to Coleridge in February 1808: 'I verily believe, half the sale must be attributed to the puffs in the Courier.'[47] The disguise of the author as a Spaniard failed to mislead most critics who generally agreed with the Universal Magazine: 'That this is the production of a Spaniard we firmly disbelieve. It has too many internal evidences of being a home made article, a London manufacture, to pass current as a translation from the Spanish.'[48] The work gained generally favourable reviews, though most of these were more concerned with paraphrasing the ideas expressed in the Letters than with analysis. The emphasis on religion in the book was an open invitation to reviewers to pander to the prejudices of their own readers and to avoid a serious discussion of the value of the writer's opinions and arguments. Francis Jeffrey, in the Edinburgh Review, launched a substantial attack upon the Letters, which in some ways anticipated Macaulay's later criticism of Colloquies, in which, while he acknowledged the evident stylistic merits of the work, he found the author deficient in his knowledge of political economy and weak in the power of reasoning (No. 32).

Simmons aptly indicates ideological affinity between Jeffrey's review of Letters from England and Macaulay's attack on Colloquies: 'What lay behind both was the eternal antagonism between the Liberal, the convinced believer in progress, unchecked and unlimited, and the Tory who saw at the same time a little of the suffering it caused.'[49] Sir Thomas More, or, Colloquies on the Progress and Prospects of Society, published in 1829, was Southey's most ambitious attempt at social commentary and analysis. Although most of the contemporary reviews of the book are of little interest, the Edinburgh Review included the most concentrated attack ever made upon Southey's outlook and abilities as a rational critic of society. Macaulay's review is of major importance in any study of Southey and is reprinted in full in the present volume (No. 113). Like other critics—such as the Quarterly Review[50] and Samuel O'Sullivan in Blackwood's Edinburgh Magazine[51]

—Macaulay used Southey's work as a springboard from which to advance his own opinions. Geoffrey Carnall has described Macaulay's review as 'a monument of nineteenth-century optimism'.[52] Nevertheless, the review contains both an interesting survey of Southey's literary achievement to date and much valid criticism of illogicalities in his thought.

Despite all the modern reader's sense of Macaulay's greater intellectual power, however, the course of historical events has brought an increasing sympathy with Southey's viewpoint. His comparison of the characteristic products of manufacturing and agricultural systems is certainly open to Macaulay's objection that he has not studied 'bills of mortality and statistical tables'—that his judgments, in fact, are impressionistic rather than logical. There is, too, about Southey, as Geoffrey Carnall has noted, the air of 'a benevolent gentleman viewing the lower orders from a considerable social distance'.[53] Nevertheless, Macaulay's contempt for 'Rose-bushes and poor-rates, rather than steam-engines and independence' may seem very two-edged to the modern reader.

No other contemporary review of *Colloquies* displayed the serious intelligence of Macaulay and no attempt at a more balanced assessment of the value of the book, indeed, was made until a century later.

Reviews and Essays

Throughout his life Southey derived his regular income from his activities as a periodical reviewer and essayist. He was at once dependent on such support and resentful of its claims upon his time and energies. In 1803 he wrote to William Taylor in a characteristic tone of complaint about the drudgery of reviewing: 'Do you know Quarles's emblem of the soul that tries to fly, but is chained by the leg to the earth? For myself I could do easily, but not easily for others, and there are more claims than one upon me.'[54]

His letters make it clear that he was an earnest and painstaking reviewer who took his duties seriously even though he found them irksome. In 1815 he declared that his reviews 'cost me more time than they would any other person, for upon every subject, I endeavour to read all such books relating to it, as I had before left unread'.[55]

For twentieth-century readers Southey the reviewer is best remembered as the author of the first review of *Lyrical Ballads*, which appeared anonymously in the *Critical Review*.[56] His descriptions of 'The Ancient Mariner' as 'a Dutch attempt at German sublimity' and of 'The Idiot

Boy'—'It resembles a Flemish picture in the worthlessness of its design and the excellence of its execution'—have often been quoted. However, as Jack Simmons has observed, such sentences, which have achieved 'a wretched immortality', do not fairly represent the whole review which 'is less unfavourable and unjust than has often been supposed'.[57]

The review of *Lyrical Ballads* seems to have had little effect upon the young Southey's reputation. He continued to contribute regular reviews to a variety of periodicals, thus providing himself with sufficient financial means to allow him to publish his more ambitious works. In 1809 he began his long connection with the *Quarterly Review*, contributing a paper to its first number in February. In so far as contemporaries noticed his reviewing activities—and it was an aspect of his work to which they paid little regard—it was his symbolic status as one of the mainstays of the Tory *Quarterly Review* towards which they directed their attention. Southey had frequent differences of opinion with the editor, William Gifford, of whom he wrote in July 1837: 'He was a man with whom I had no literary sympathies; perhaps there was nothing upon which we agreed, except great political questions.'[58] In particular, he often complained of Gifford's mutilation of his articles, describing him to Grosvenor Bedford in 1818 as 'a butcherly review-gelder'.[59] Nevertheless, hostile critics were happy to present Southey as a representative of the *Quarterly* type of mind—'the prop of the *Quarterly Review*' as Byron described him (No. 86).

The publication of *Wat Tyler* in 1817 afforded the ideal opportunity for a contrast between Southey's early revolutionary politics and his present position as Tory reviewer and Laureate. Hazlitt, especially, painted the contrast in striking colours, using Southey's article 'On Parliamentary Reform' to illustrate his political position (No. 73). In the same year, however, Coleridge, in his *Biographia Literaria*, paid just and deserved tribute to Southey's skill as an essayist-reviewer (No. 83):

When I regard him as a popular essayist, (for the articles of his compositions in the reviews are for the greater part essays on subjects of deep or curious interest rather than criticisms on particular works) I look in vain for any writer, who has conveyed so much information, from so many and such recondite sources, with so many just and original reflections, in a style so lively and poignant, yet so uniformly classical and perspicuous; no one in short who has combined so much wisdom with so much wit; so much truth and knowledge with so much life and fancy.

The Doctor

Southey's appearance, towards the end of his life, as a novelist excited only a limited amount of critical attention. *The Doctor* was published anonymously and there was some speculation about the author's identity, though Henry Crabb Robinson, after reading the first volume, had 'no doubt, whatever, that it is by Southey' (No. 118). Perhaps such a relaxed and rambling book did not seem to contemporaries to deserve much serious attention, while its occasional bitterness and intolerance marked it, as Lockhart noted, as 'the work of a man who stands more in need of physic than of criticism' (No. 117).

Editions and Translations

During his career Southey produced many editions and translations. His editions include works by Thomas Chatterton (1803), Henry Kirke White (1807, 1822), Malory (1817), Bunyan (1830), John Jones (1831), Isaac Watts (1834) and Cowper (1835–7). He translated French, Spanish and Portuguese works. Many of these projects included the writing of an introduction. Most of this work was well received although, in general, critics preferred to discuss the merits of the works themselves rather than Southey's particular contribution as editor or translator. Scott, in the *Edinburgh Review*, gave generous praise to the translation of *Amadis of Gaul*, 'which appears to us marked with the hand of a master' (No. 20), while Coleridge found *The Chronicle of the Cid* full of interest, though he criticized the introduction as 'shallow, flippant, and *ipse dixitish*' (No. 35). Most of Southey's editions and translations, indeed, were executed with care and skill, revealing his considerable scholarly impulse at its most attractive. Jack Simmons provides an interesting description of Southey's methods of work when compiling his fifteen-volume edition of Cowper,[60] which may be taken as an example of his customarily painstaking attitude to such projects.

The most serious criticisms were reserved for *Specimens of the Later English Poets* which Southey ill-advisedly edited jointly with Grosvenor Bedford in 1807. The text was badly corrected and appeared full of printers' errors. The *Annual Review* praised the Preface and the biographical sketches[61] but most reviewers were critical of the principles of selection and the methods of editing and annotation. The *Monthly Magazine* found that the whole compilation showed signs of too great haste.[62] The *Universal Magazine* accused the editors of a 'radical defect of plan' and stated that 'Mr. Southey has shewn neither taste nor judgment in his selections' (No. 31).

REPUTATION ABROAD

Most of the items in the present selection illustrate the progress of Southey's reputation in Britain. The inclusion of comments by George Ticknor (Nos 82 and 120) and Nathaniel Hawthorne (No. 135), however, serves to indicate the existence of interest in his writings abroad. Although it is difficult to discover much serious foreign criticism of Southey's works there can be no doubt that he enjoyed some American popularity during his lifetime. *Joan of Arc* and the early volume of *Poems* were both published in Boston shortly after their appearance in England. All the epics were quickly published in American editions and several of Southey's other volumes of verse received American publication. His own ten-volume edition of his *Poetical Works* was published in New York in 1839 and was followed by a succession of one-volume American editions of his poetry. A further ten-volume edition of the *Poetical Works* with a memoir of Southey by Henry Theodore Tuckerman was published in Boston in 1860. Of the prose works, the *Letters from England* seems to have enjoyed the greatest popularity, although *The Life of Nelson*, *The Life of Wesley*, *The Book of the Church* and *The Doctor* all appeared in American editions soon after their initial publication in England.

In Europe Southey seems to have achieved only limited popularity. Of the epics, part of *Thalaba* was translated into German in 1837 and *Roderick* was translated into French in 1820 and Dutch in 1823/4. *Letters from England* appeared in French in 1817 and in German in the following year, while *The Life of Wesley* was translated into German in 1828. A one-volume edition of Southey's poetry was published in Paris in 1829.

Any clear estimate of Southey's American and European reputation must depend upon future research. Fortunately, the influence of his *History of Brazil* within Portugal itself has been interestingly surveyed by J. de Sousa-Leão.[63] Work on a Portuguese translation of *The History of Brazil* was commenced by Henry Koster, a friend of Southey. Koster never completed his translation and died in 1820. The fact that Southey's work received only a limited reputation among contemporaries in Portugal was clearly due largely to the lack of a published translation. When a Portuguese translation by Fernandes Pinheiro was

ALBRIGHT COLLEGE LIBRARY 171647

finally published in 1862 the value of Southey's pioneering contribution had already to some extent been obscured by subsequent historical work. Nevertheless, *The History of Brazil* was sufficiently highly regarded for Southey to be honoured by the Queen of Portugal when she created him a Knight of the Order of the Tower and Sword in February 1839. Since his death he has been kindly remembered by the Portuguese and his grave in Crosthwaite churchyard was recently restored by the generosity of the Brazilian Government.

SOUTHEY'S FINANCES

For much of his life Southey supported himself and his dependants almost wholly by his writing. His generous nature made him accept numerous claims upon his income. He assisted all his brothers in turn and made himself responsible for Coleridge's family. His letters reveal frequent acts of charity, as when, in 1821, he gave his entire savings to his friend John May who had suffered financial misfortune. As Wordsworth said: 'Southey has a little world dependent upon his industry.'[64] With such heavy commitments it was unlikely that Southey would ever make his fortune from writing. There is, indeed, no indication that he ever became affluent though he certainly achieved a comfortable income late in life. Throughout most of his career, however, his letters reveal a constant concern with the problems of balancing income and expenditure.

The most regular and reliable source of Southey's income was periodical reviewing. When he began to write for the *Monthly Magazine* in 1796 he received a fee of 5 gns for a sheet of sixteen closely printed pages.[65] In 1797 the *Critical Review* paid him 3 gns a sheet, which he described as 'a very acceptable addition to my straitened income'.[66] In the following year he also contracted to supply verses to be published anonymously in the *Morning Post* at 1 gn per poem. His letters make it clear that he found reviewing tedious. In 1804 he described himself as 'yawning over tiresome work'.[67] However, the proceeds from his early books were small and offered little hope of relief. For the first edition of *Joan of Arc* he received 50 gns from Cottle. For *Thalaba* Longman paid £115. *Amadis of Gaul* sold more quickly but his next epic, *Madoc*, which was expensively produced, yielded only £3. 17s. 1d. on the first year's sale. By 1807 his total profits from *Madoc* were only £25.

Until 1807 Southey was assisted by an annuity of £160 from his friend C. W. Williams Wynn. He relinquished this in 1807 when he was granted a pension of £200 per annum. Since £56 of this was deducted for tax his financial position was not improved by the pension. Furthermore, payment was extremely irregular.[68] Although he described his affairs as 'not in a bad train' his total income in 1808 barely exceeded £300. It was ironical that the first two volumes of *Remains of Henry Kirke White*, published in the autumn of 1807, proved very popular and the first edition was sold in less than three months. This provided no benefit for Southey who had made over all the profits to White's family.

Realizing that 'St. Cecilia herself could not have played the organ if there had been nobody to blow the bellows for her',[69] Southey resolved to take on still more work as a reviewer, even at the expense of his more ambitious plans. His dislike of Francis Jeffrey and his lack of sympathy with the periodical's point of view led him to reject Scott's proposal that he should contribute to the *Edinburgh Review*[70] but in 1809 he became responsible for all the historical part of the *Edinburgh Annual Register* at a salary of £400 per year.[71] This work was abandoned in the winter of 1812/13 because of the difficulties he experienced in securing his salary. In February 1809 he contributed his first paper to the first number of the *Quarterly Review*, for which he received a fee of £21. 13s. 0d.[72] During the next few years his fee for work for the *Quarterly* rose from 10 gns per sheet in 1810 to a standard fee of £100 per article in 1816. For the next twenty-three years this brought him an average yearly income of £275.[73]

Southey's work for the *Quarterly Review* helped him towards economic security, while the acceptance of the Laureateship in 1813 enabled him to use the stipend of £90 per year to insure his life for £3,000.[74] In a letter of December 1822 he estimated his needs and his income:[75]

My establishment requires £600 a-year, exclusive of other calls. The average produce of my account with Longman is about £200; what I derive from the Exchequer you know; the rest must come from the grey goose quill; and the proceeds of a new book have hitherto pretty generally been anticipated. They may float me for a second year perhaps. *Roderick* did for three years, with the help of the *Pilgrimage*—then the tide ebbs, and so I go on.

Few of his books were outstandingly successful. *The Life of Nelson* had a steady sale but in 1818 he stated that he had not yet received as much for *The History of Brazil* as for a single article in the *Quarterly Review*.[76] Of his epics *Roderick* was easily the most successful, bringing him £700 by 1818. *The Poet's Pilgrimage to Waterloo* brought a profit of £215 within two months of publication.[77]

As he grew older the sale of most of his earlier works inevitably declined. In 1828 the proceeds from all his books published by Longman amounted only to £26 and he was still relying heavily on his reviewing.[78] He had now begun to write also for the *Foreign Quarterly Review* at the same rate as for the *Quarterly*. His professional reputation had also enabled him to secure an outright fee of 1,000 gns for the *History of the Peninsular War*, the publisher retaining copyright.

Constant worry about the family's variable income must certainly have contributed to his wife's mental illness. Sadly, however, when she was placed in a lunatic asylum in October 1834 Southey had for the first time achieved real financial security. He had contracted with the publishers Baldwin & Cradock to prepare an edition of Cowper for 1,000 gns—though, in fact, he never received full payment for this due to the publishers' bankruptcy—and had secured good terms from Murray for his *Lives of the British Admirals*. In 1835 Sir Robert Peel offered him a baronetcy which he refused because he felt he could not afford to support the honour. Peel then raised his pension to a total of £500 per year, of which £300 was free of tax.

At the end of his career as a writer, then, Southey had achieved an income sufficient to cover his expenses and to afford him a measure of comfort. He had fully emancipated himself from the poverty which in his younger days had often led him to walk 'the streets at dinner time for want of a dinner'.[79] His career as a whole offers an interesting and often sad example of conflict between personal generosity and literary ambition. Few men, perhaps, have worked so hard and so selflessly to support their own and others' dependants and so resolutely committed their energies to tedious tasks at the expense of more attractive projects.

POSTHUMOUS REPUTATION TO 1879

Although Southey became Queen Victoria's first Poet Laureate his literary career effectively ended in the year of her accession, 1837, with the publication in ten volumes of *The Poetical Works of Robert Southey, Collected by Himself*. In November 1837 his first wife died. When he married Caroline Bowles in June 1839 his mind had begun to fail. He lived on until March 1843 in a state of increasing insensibility and weakness.

Neither the publication of the *Poetical Works* nor Southey's death occasioned much critical comment, though the former event did inspire one very sensitive and intelligent review of his poetic career by Herman Merivale (No. 122). In 1850 Southey's son, Charles Cuthbert, published *The Life and Correspondence of the Late Robert Southey* in six volumes. The work received considerable attention from reviewers, many of whom took this opportunity of reassessing Southey's achievement. For a few years Southey was a living subject of critical debate before he again passed into increasing obscurity.

Reviewers of the *Life and Correspondence* pointed clearly to Southey's faults. One criticism was that his inspiration was too bookish. John Anster noted in the *North British Review*: 'We feel that he is writing in the midst of his books' (No. 128). Many critics found that he wrote too much and deleted too little, falling into the danger of confusing quality and quantity. As J. G. Lockhart and Whitwell Elwin wittily observed in the *Quarterly Review*: 'He was never sufficiently sensible that in the currency of Parnassus two-and-forty sixpences are not equivalent to a guinea' (No. 132). Southey's writing, further, showed too little emotion, 'passion and Southey being irreconcilable terms', as W. B. Donne claimed (No. 133). It was Donne, too, in his article in the *Edinburgh Review*, who described Southey with outstanding accuracy as having 'a mind averse from introversion, and strenuous rather than susceptible'.

If Southey's prolixity harmed his poetry it also reduced the impact and readability of much of his prose. W. B. Donne might assert that 'in prose the more men write, the better probably they will write' (No. 133) but few of Southey's readers, perhaps, would agree with him. Lockhart and Elwin perceived justly that in his prose Southey was usually 'more diffuse in what he told than in his manner of telling it' (No. 132). They recognized the value of the periodical review for a writer of Southey's temperament since 'It was for his advantage to be confined within narrow limits.' An anonymous contributor to *Bentley's Miscellany* in 1856 referred ironically to Southey's belief that time spent in reviewing represented time lost—'lost from those colossal poems which, in his heart of hearts (truly the heart is deceitful above all things), he believed to contain a full solution of the problem' of his literary immortality (No. 137).

In contrast to the temperate assessments of the reviewers and the privately expressed praises of Newman (No. 129) and Charlotte Brontë (No. 130), there were those such as Walter Bagehot who found little or no merit in Southey's works. Bagehot clearly regarded Southey as a bore—'an industrious and caligraphic man . . . who might have earned money as a clerk' (No. 134). The description is close to Nathaniel Hawthorne's picture of Southey as blameless but lacking colour and warmth (No. 135). For Thackeray, writing in 1860, it was not Southey's writings but his life that was important: 'Southey's private letters are worth piles of epics' (No. 138).

The interest in Southey aroused by the *Life and Correspondence* was followed inevitably by a period of increasing neglect in which, however, two evaluations stand out as of major significance. In 1867 Carlyle wrote his account of Southey which was later published in the appendix to his *Reminiscences* (No. 141). The description of Southey's physical presence and Carlyle's remarkable insight into the passionate nature which was always threatening to tear him apart have never been equalled. The account remains as one of the most illuminating guides to Southey's personality. The assessment by Edward Dowden in the final chapter of his study of Southey in the English Men of Letters Series closes the present volume (No. 144). Dowden's analysis of Southey's epics as mainly 'the outcome of his moral nature' indicates a useful approach for their understanding. For Dowden, however, Southey's best work is in prose. His historical writing is 'narrative rendered spiritual by moral ardour', worth reading but less successful than his biographical works and especially his *Life of Nelson*.

REPUTATION AFTER 1879

A recent writer on Wordsworth has described Southey as 'an unfairly neglected member of the Lake Poets'.[80] How far recent neglect of Southey has been unfair is open to debate. Certainly, he has received relatively little serious critical attention since the publication of Dowden's study. The scholarly output on Southey has been surveyed in masterly fashion by Kenneth Curry.[81] As Curry notes: 'Southey has often been the target for depreciatory criticism whose purpose has been to enhance at his expense another author or group of authors.' Despite his assertion that 'Southey has not been well served by his biographers' it seems clear that the twentieth century has undertaken much more serious and valuable work on Southey's life and ideas than on the strictly literary assessment of his achievement.

Three contributions to Southey's biography are of major importance.

William Haller's study of his early life[82] is particularly valuable for its account of his poetic development and his personal and literary relationships with Wordsworth and Coleridge before 1803. Jack Simmons's *Southey* (1945) is the standard biography, covering the whole of Southey's life. This gracefully written work provides an admirably clear and sympathetic account of his career and of the historical background against which his ideas evolved. The most recent major addition to our biographical knowledge is Kenneth Curry's two-volume edition of *New Letters*.[83] These letters make available much material for the interpretation of Southey's career, while Curry's notes provide extensive information about many of Southey's correspondents.

If nineteenth-century commentators often overestimated the merit of Southey's creative writing they tended equally to undervalue his significance as a critic of society. Twentieth-century social historians, by contrast, have found much to praise in his support for human dignity and individual freedom, his attacks upon the materialism of industrial society and his agitation for factory reform. A. V. Dicey,[84] Crane Brinton,[85] Alfred Cobban[86] and Bernard N. Schilling[87] have praised the humanitarian viewpoint of *Colloquies* and, to a lesser degree, of *Letters from England* and the *Quarterly* essays, finding beneath Southey's rather cold exterior a warm concern for the improvement of social conditions. More recently Raymond Williams has described Southey, in his social thought, as 'an influential if unacknowledged figure', a sympathizer with Robert Owen and, with him, an influence on Christian Socialism.[88] Williams rightly emphasizes that the interest of Southey's thought lies less in his detailed proposals for reform than in his general affirmation of the need for an active and responsible government against the *laissez-faire* doctrine of the political economists. In a different field, A. M. Allchin has found in *Colloquies* 'the most interesting pre-Tractarian discussion of the idea of women's communities'.[89]

The most thorough study of Southey's ideas is contained in Geoffrey Carnall's *Robert Southey and his Age* (1960). This study is specially concerned with the development of Southey's political attitudes. In its fine analysis of his periodical contributions, however, it provides considerable insight into many aspects of his thought, especially on social and religious questions. Where previous writers have merely referred to Southey in the course of wider discussions, Carnall has subjected his ideas to intensive but sympathetic scrutiny to produce the most important assessment yet undertaken of his moral and intellectual stature.

While interest in Southey's social thought has increased steadily since 1879 his reputation as a creative writer—and especially as a poet—has suffered a severe decline. Even George Saintsbury, who admired his variety, learning and industry and praised *The Curse of Kehama* as a 'long poem which goes near to, if it does not attain, absolute greatness', recognized the irony that Southey's very virtues as a man—his sense of duty and his extensive charity—combined to prevent the highest achievement.[90]

Later critics have tended to be less kind to the poetry. Leslie Stephen[91] admired the character revealed in Southey's letters but emphasized his poetic inadequacy, his inability to pause from literary toil in order to reflect on his experiences. For Stephen, as for many readers, Southey's failure was in part explicable by his over-conscientious and business-like approach to authorship. He was too completely a professional man of letters and too much of a scholarly researcher to succeed as a creative writer.

For literary historians Southey has remained significant for his friendships with the first generation of Romantics and his position in the contemporary literary scene. S. C. Chew has observed that as a poet 'he was early in many fields of romance and in some led the way followed by greater poets'.[92] While his historical interest has been generally acknowledged, however, few critics have sought to interpret Southey's poetry on its own terms. Probably the best attempt was made by Ernest Bernbaum in his *Guide through the Romantic Movement*.[93] Most notably, Bernbaum points out that, despite their antiquarian interest, Southey's epics were concerned with asking significant questions about the nature and characteristics of leadership and the best form of civilization. Geoffrey Carnall, in his British Council pamphlet on Southey,[94] finds the epics 'above all, poems of violence'. Southey's characteristic buoyancy, however, 'finds its most natural expression in many of his shorter poems' and he is often at his best in playful works such as The Story of the Three Bears in *The Doctor*. His prose is 'vigorous, direct, and covers much ground in little time'.

A few of Southey's prose works have been reprinted since the Second World War. Apart from *The Life of Nelson*, which has been reprinted frequently, there have been modern editions of *Letters from England*,[95] *Journals of a Residence in Portugal*[96] and *Omniana*.[97] Recently, Geoffrey Grigson has attempted to produce an acceptable selection of

Southey's verse for the modern reader.[98] In the introduction to his slim volume Grigson argues that most of Southey's best verse was composed in a brief period of one year between the summers of 1798 and 1799 during which he was living at Westbury-on-Trym in Gloucestershire. In these poems and in a few verses in praise of domestic pleasures later in life Southey displays his particular talents.

While Grigson allows that Southey's impulse is essentially bookish and lacking in emotional intensity he finds in his best poems clarity, humour, satire and a spice of agreeable morbidity. A re-reading of such poems as 'The Battle of Blenheim', 'The Holly Tree' and 'God's Judgement on a Wicked Bishop'—described by Grigson as Southey's masterpiece—may not establish Southey as a major poet but certainly serves to modify the commonly received view, expressed by Robert Gittings in his edition of *Omniana*, that his genius 'was not truly literary, not truly creative, but almost purely academic and factual'. As man and artist Southey remains something of an enigma: beneath his conscientious virtue the reader senses a savage violence lurking, yet is puzzled by the lack of artistic vitality necessary to bring to life the works of his enormous industry.

NOTES

1 *Life*, ii, p. 262.
2 Curry, ii, p. 52.
3 *The Letters of Sir Walter Scott*, ed. Sir H. J. C. Grierson (1932–7), i, pp. 287–9.
4 *Life*, ii, p. 276.
5 *Ibid.*
6 *Life*, iii, p. 67.
7 *Life*, iii, p. 278.
8 Thomas Love Peacock, *The Four Ages of Poetry* (1820). Reprinted from *The Halliford Edition of the Works of Peacock*, ed. H. F. B. Brett-Smith and C. E. Jones (1924–34), viii, p. 19.
9 Simmons, p. 64.
10 *Life*, iii, p. 144.
11 *Life*, ii, pp. 274–5.
12 *Life*, v, p. 333.
13 Simmons, p. 148.
14 Curry, i, p. 306.
15 *Life*, iii, p. 286.
16 *Ibid.*

17 *Life*, iii, p. 300.
18 Curry, ii, p. 73.
19 *Life*, iv, p. 148.
20 *Life*, iv, p. 72.
21 *European Magazine and London Review*, November 1816, lxx, 438–9.
22 *British Critic*, July 1816, series 2, vi, 27–40.
23 For an interesting discussion of the reception of *Wat Tyler* see Frank Taliaferro Hoadley, 'The controversy over Southey's *Wat Tyler*', *Studies in Philology*, 1941, xxxviii, 81–96. See also Geoffrey Carnall, *Robert Southey and His Age* (1960), pp. 61–5.
24 Cf. Carnall, *loc. cit.*
25 *Courier*, 17 March 1817.
26 *Courier*, 17, 18, 27 March; 2 April 1817.
27 *Life*, v, p. 61.
28 *Life*, v, p. 67.
29 *Courier*, 5 January 1822.
30 *Life*, iii, p. 275.
31 *Life*, vi, p. 53.
32 *Life*, vi, p. 99.
33 *Life*, iii, p. 283.
34 *Life*, ii, p. 214.
35 *Life*, ii, p. 221.
36 *Life*, iv, p. 215.
37 *Life*, ii, pp. 305–6.
38 *Life*, iv, p. 312.
39 *Life*, vi, p. 158.
40 *Life*, vi, p. 191.
41 *Life*, ii, p. 242.
42 *British Critic*, March 1818, series 2, ix, 225–45; April 1818, series 2, ix, 369–91.
43 Cf. Simmons, pp. 142–3 for an account of the growth in popularity of *The Life of Nelson*.
44 *Antijacobin Review & Magazine*, July 1813, xlv, 72–89; August 1813, xlv, 138–60.
45 *Life*, v, p. 34.
46 Southey, *Letters from England*, ed. with an introduction by Jack Simmons (1951).
47 *Life*, iii, p. 134.
48 *Universal Magazine*, January 1808, series 2, ix, 42–3.
49 *Letters from England*, ed. Simmons, xxiii.
50 *Quarterly Review*, July 1829, xli, 1–27.
51 *Blackwood's Edinburgh Magazine*, October 1829, xxvi, 611–30.
52 Geoffrey Carnall, *Robert Southey and His Age* (1960), p. 180.
53 *Ibid.*, p. 151.

54 *Life*, ii, p. 199.
55 *Life*, iv, pp. 102–3.
56 *Critical Review*, October 1798, xxiv, 197–204.
57 Simmons, p. 76.
58 *Life*, vi, p. 336.
59 Warter, iii, p. 87.
60 Simmons, p. 196.
61 *Annual Review*, 1808, vi, 557–60.
62 *Monthly Magazine*, 30 July 1807, xxiii, 640–1.
63 J. de Sousa-Leão, 'Southey and Brazil', *Modern Language Review*, July 1943, xxxviii, 181–91.
64 Simmons, p. 191.
65 *Life*, i, p. 283.
66 Simmons, p. 71.
67 *Life*, ii, p. 250.
68 Warter, ii, p. 3.
69 *Life*, iii, p. 117.
70 Warter, ii, pp. 29–32.
71 *Life*, iii, pp. 271–2.
72 Simmons, p. 129.
73 Simmons, p. 151.
74 Curry, ii, p. 80; Warter, ii, p. 337.
75 *Life*, v, p. 130.
76 *Life*, iv, p. 312.
77 Warter, iii, pp. 46–7.
78 *Life*, v, p. 336.
79 *Life*, ii, p. 206.
80 John Purkis, *A Preface to Wordsworth* (1970), p. 180.
81 Kenneth Curry, 'Robert Southey' in *The English Poets and Essayists: A Review of Research and Criticism*, revised edn, ed. Carolyn Washburn Houtchens and Lawrence Huston Houtchens (New York, 1966).
82 William Haller, *The Early Life of Robert Southey* (New York, 1917).
83 *New Letters of Robert Southey*, ed. Kenneth Curry (New York, 1965).
84 A. V. Dicey, *Lectures on the Relation between Law and Public Opinion in England during the Nineteenth Century* (1905).
85 Crane Brinton, *Political Ideas of the English Romanticists* (1926).
86 Alfred Cobban, *Edmund Burke and the Revolt against the Eighteenth Century* (1929).
87 Bernard N. Schilling, *Human Dignity and the Great Victorians* (New York, 1946).
88 Raymond Williams, *Culture and Society 1780–1950* (1958).
89 A. M. Allchin, *The Silent Rebellion: Anglican Religious Communities 1845–1900* (1958).
90 George Saintsbury, *Essays in English Literature, 1780–1860: 2nd Series* (1895).

91 Leslie Stephen, *Studies of a Biographer* (1902).
92 *A Literary History of England*, ed. Albert C. Baugh (1950).
93 Ernest Bernbaum, *Guide through the Romantic Movement* (2nd edn, New York, 1949).
94 Geoffrey Carnall, *Robert Southey* (1964).
95 *Letters from England*, ed. Jack Simmons (1951).
96 *Journals of a Residence in Portugal 1800–1801 and a Visit to France 1838*, ed. Adolfo Cabral (1960).
97 *Omniana, or Horae Otiosiores*, ed. Robert Gittings (1969).
98 *A Choice of Robert Southey's Verse*, ed. Geoffrey Grigson (1970).

The materials included in this volume follow the original texts in all important respects. Omissions are clearly indicated. Obvious misprints have been silently corrected but mis-spellings of proper names are often interesting and illuminating and have usually been retained. Titles of books and periodicals have been italicized throughout. The editor's footnotes are indicated with arabic numerals; those integral to the original texts are marked with asterisks.

THE FALL OF ROBESPIERRE

1794

This verse drama in three acts was hastily written and published at Cambridge under the name of Samuel Taylor Coleridge. Coleridge himself wrote only the first act, the second and third acts being contributed by Southey.

1. Unsigned review, *Critical Review*

November 1794, 2nd series, xii, 260–2

The fall of Robespierre was an event of the greatest importance to the affairs of France, and is a very proper subject for the tragic muse. It may, however, be thought by some to be too recent an event to admit of that contrivance which is essentially necessary in unravelling the plot of the drama. Indeed, we have been informed, that the work before us was the production of a few hours exercise, and must, therefore, not be supposed to smell very strongly of the lamp. Several parts too being necessarily made up of such reports of the French convention, as have already been collected through the medium of newspapers, may be expected to have little of the charms of novelty.

By these free remarks, we mean not to under-rate Mr. Coleridge's historical drama. It affords ample testimony, that the writer is a genuine votary of the Muse, and several parts of it will afford much pleasure to those who can relish the beauties of poetry. Indeed a writer who could produce so much beauty in so little time, must possess powers that are capable of raising him to a distinguished place among the English poets. [Quotes from Act 1.]

This drama consists only of three acts, of which the first is by far the most finished. The third act closes beautifully:
[Quotes conclusion of Act III.]

2. Unsigned notice, *British Critic*

May 1795, v, 539-40

Mr. Coleridge has aimed at giving a dramatic air to a detail of Conventional speeches, which they were scarcely capable of receiving. The sentiments, however, in many instances are naturally, though boldly conceived, and expressed in language, which gives us reason to think the Author might, after some probation, become no unsuccessful wooer of the tragic muse.

3. A Bristol view of Southey

1795(?)

From *The Observer, Part 1st. Being a transient glance at about forty youths of Bristol. Enumerating what are the prominent traits in their characters, whether they be worthy of imitation, or otherwise*, published anonymously in Bristol probably in 1795. The sketch of Southey is followed by a depiction of Coleridge, whose slovenly appearance and monotonous delivery clearly produced a less favourable impression on his audiences.

> Example is a living Law whose sway
> Men more than all the written Laws obey.
>   S. C. SEDLEY

ROBERT SOUTH*Y.

In him may be seen a pattern for imitation; his natural genius is far above mediocrity; his classical acquisitions render that genius of a superior class: his poetical writings breathe a fire of imagination that my pen is totally insufficient to the task of describing; his bosom glows with that philanthropy alone felt by the advocates in the cause of the liberation of their fellow-men; his principles are the result of conviction. Not the prospects of a large fortune at an Aunt's demise, or any other pecuniary consideration could make him act derogatory to what were his opinions. He was educated at Oxford, where he made such rapid strides in the school of literature, as not to be followed by his fellow-scholars. He has lately delivered some Lectures in this City, which ought to draw from all men their most warm approbation; the language was that of truth, it was the language of Liberty! I must here observe, that his gesticulation and attitude when he is speaking in Public is not the most pleasing, his body is always too stiff, his features are apt to be distorted; they are faults which he can easily obviate; if he do, I am bold to say, that he will possess Demosthenean or Ciceronian abilities. From what has been adduced it is almost unnecessary to say, that he is really the man of virtue according to the present state of Society. He has produced many pieces which would do credit to a Pope or a Dryden, he has a Work about to be published entitled *Joan of Arc* an 'Epic Poem' the vast number of subscribers to it, plead strongly in its favour.

JOAN OF ARC

1796

Southey commenced *Joan of Arc* in July 1793 and completed the first version within six weeks. In the following year he unsuccessfully attempted to publish the poem by subscription. In 1795 he read part of the work to Joseph Cottle, the young Bristol bookseller, who offered terms of 50 gns and fifty free copies which Southey could sell at his own profit. After further revision, carried out with some assistance from Coleridge, the poem was published by Cottle in 1796. It was generally favourably received, although Southey expressed dissatisfaction with its slow sale in London (*Life*, i, p. 291). He continued to revise it and a second edition was published by Longman in 1798.

---

4. Wordsworth, from a letter to William Matthews

21 March 1796

Reprinted from *The Letters of William and Dorothy Wordsworth, 1787–1805*, 2nd edn revised by C. L. Shaver (1967), p. 169.

You were right about Southey, he is certainly a coxcomb, and has proved it completely by the preface to *his Joan of Arc*, an *epic* poem which he has just published. This preface is indeed a very conceited performance and the poem though in some passages of first-rate excellence is on the whole of very inferior execution.

5. John Aikin, unsigned review, *Monthly Review*

April 1796, n.s. xix, 361–8

Aikin (1747–1822), doctor and author, originally contributed reviews of medical works to the *Monthly Review* but later concentrated increasingly on literary topics. His enthusiastic assessment of Southey's *Poems* (1797) is reprinted below (No. 12).

We were sorry to observe, in the preface to this work, certain facts stated in order to display the extreme rapidity with which it was written. An epic poem in 12 books finished in six weeks, and, on its improved plan in 10 books, almost entirely recomposed during the time of printing! Is it possible that a person of classical education can have so slight an opinion of (perhaps) the most arduous effort of human invention, as to suffer the fervour and confidence of youth to hurry him in such a manner through a design which may fix the reputation of a whole life? Though it may be that a work seldom gains much by remaining long in the bureau, yet is it respectful to the public to present to it a performance of bulk and pretension, bearing on its head all the unavoidable imperfections of haste? Does an author do justice to himself, by putting it out of his power to correct that which he will certainly in a few years consider as wanting much correction? To *run a race with the press, in an epic poem*, is an idea so extravagant, that Mr. S. must excuse us if it has extorted from us these animadversions. We now proceed to the work itself.

[Outlines plot.]

To proceed to the *execution* of the design: we do not hesitate to declare our opinion that the poetical powers displayed in it are of a very superior kind, and such as, if not wasted in premature and negligent exertions, promise a rich harvest of future excellence. Conceptions more lofty and daring, sentiments more commanding, and language more energetic, than some of the best passages in this poem afford, will not easily be found:—nor does scarcely any part of it sink to languor; as the glow of feeling and genius animates the whole. The language is, for the most part, modelled on that of Milton, and not unfrequently it has a strong relish of Shakspeare: but there are more defective and discordant lines than might be wished, either owing to carelessness, or to that piece of false taste, as we think it, the copying of harsh sounds or images in harsh versification. Indeed, the author, in his preface, expressly imputes his defects of this kind to design: but surely the loose prosody of English blank verse is neither too difficult, nor too melodious, to render a close adherence to its rules an indispensable law of poetry. Another frequent cause of halting measure is the false pronunciation of French proper names, which the writer commonly accents on the first syllable, after the English manner. We confess that we are also offended with the frequency of alliteration, often when the repeated sound is most harsh and unmusical. Nor can we praise the licentious coinage of new verbs out of nouns, in which our poet, in common with many other modern lovers of novelty, too much indulges. Indeed, there are few pages in which there is not somewhat to be mended in the diction or versification,—clearly accusing the hurry with which so great a work has been completed.

With respect to the *sentiments*, they are less adapted to the age in which the events took place, than to that of the writer; being uniformly noble, liberal, enlightened, and breathing the purest spirit of general benevolence and regard to the rights and claims of human kind. In many parts, a strong allusion to later characters and events is manifest; and we know not where the ingenuity of a crown lawyer would stop, were he employed to make out a list of innuendos. In particular, War, and the lust of conquest, are every where painted in the strongest colours of abhorrence.—Far be it from us to check or blame even the excesses of generous ardour in a youthful breast! Powerful antidotes are necessary to the corrupt selfishness and indifference of the age.

[Quotes several passages from the poem.]

6. From an unsigned review, *Critical Review*

June 1796, 2nd series, xvii, 182–92

This favourable review appeared in two parts. The first, published
in February 1796, 2nd series, xvi, 191–5, was primarily devoted to quotations from the Preface and opening of the poem.
The following extracts are from the second part of the review.

We are sorry to have been so long detained by unforeseen and unavoidable business, from further attention to the present work, which
has been already announced in our Review for February: we then presented our readers with some judicious observations of Mr. Southey's,
from the Preface, and an extract from the poem, as a specimen of its
merit.

That passage, we doubt not, afforded our readers pleasure, and led
them to form a favourable opinion of Mr. Southey's poetical talents.
We proceed to lay before them a few more extracts, and to intersperse
some occasional observations.

When the character of the Maid of Orleans, and the part taken by
her against the English, are considered, together with the manner in
which the history has been treated by other writers, some suspicion
may at first arise, that Mr. Southey has chosen a subject scarcely suited
to the dignity of epic poetry. His prudence at least may be called in
question. How can he expect to interest the English nation in the fortunes of a heroine who was an active champion against his own
countrymen, or be hardy enough to felicitate those successes that
involved the English in disgrace? Many of his readers will undoubtedly
ask these questions,—and, at a time when the course of public opinion
is more than ordinarily influenced by recent occurrences, will not be
over forward to compliment his patriotism.

As to ourselves, we profess to accord in sentiment with those who
think the cause of truth of higher importance than any particular
interest,—that national claims may be ill-founded, and that patriotism
is something worse than enthusiasm, unless guided by moderation, and

43

settling in justice.—That the English, in the instance before us, pursued measures that cannot, on any principles of justice, be vindicated, we scruple not to assert: and that man's time would be misemployed, who should turn their apologist. We do not wholly challenge for Charles the right to the crown of France, on the ground of his being the true and undoubted heir, but of his being the person on whom that part of the French nation reposed, who wished to preserve the independence of their country. In truth, Charles was not only the heir to the crown according to the usual acceptation of the word, but obtained the approbation of his countrymen; his exclusion from the crown proceeding from the weakness of his father, and the spirit of faction;—while the English, at best, sought but to make the French people bend to their yoke. A regard to truth produces the true sublime; and to sacrifice, on the altar of justice, a national prejudice that engenders many follies, and leads to the perpetration of many crimes, takes nothing from the dignity of the epic, but adds to it considerably; though it is contrary to the method pursued by Homer and Virgil.

An epic poem should be founded in true history, though it admits the additional embellishments of fiction. One law of it is, that it be distinguished by some illustrious action, and terminate in some splendid event, calculated to give importance and dignity to moral principle, and to inspire the breast with the love of heroic undertakings.

Joan of Arc, in many instances, possesses these qualities. We have here an amiable prince unjustly deprived of the throne of his ancestors, and under circumstances not only disgraceful to himself, but likely to involve his country in subjection to a foreign yoke. The threatening calamities are successfully warded off; and the means by which the deliverance of the prince is brought about, and the country preserved from foreign power, are no less extraordinary in the effects produced, than simple in their operations. The matter is such as naturally to call forth generous sentiments; and the morality is pure and correct. . . .

Mr. Southey sometimes uses quaint and antiquated expressions. We allow that a word, not in general use, may sometimes be safely adopted in poetry; and that an old word which has been disused, may sometimes be happily restored, more particularly when (as in England) though it is lost in one part of the country, it may be preserved in another. It may be allowed a poet also, to possess a consciousness of his own powers, and to enrich his verse by new expressions, formed on the principles of his own language, or fairly derived from others. This practice, however, requires judgment, and, by a young writer, should be followed with caution. Frequent instances occur throughout this poem, of receding, and sometimes we think not happily, from the customary language,—as in the frequent use of the word '*aye*,' for '*always*,' and particularly when the same monosyllable is compounded with an adjective, as it is sometimes used, in the manner of Spencer, both by Mr. Southey and Mr. Coleridge. Compound adjectives also require a prudent use; for though sometimes they give stateliness to verse,—if not skilfully introduced, they rather inflate than dignify it. Several instances of this kind of inflation might be pointed out. . . .

The poetical powers of Mr. Southey are indisputably very superior, and capable, we doubt not, of producing a poem that will place him in the first class of English poets. He is at present, he tells his readers, engaged in the execution of *Madoc*, an epic poem, on the discovery of America by that prince. We cannot, therefore, help expressing our wish, that he would not put his future poem to so hazardous an experiment as he has this, by assigning himself so little time for its completion.

7. Lamb, from a letter to Coleridge

10 June 1796

Reprinted from *The Letters of Charles and Mary Lamb*, ed. E. V. Lucas (1935), i, pp. 13–15.

With *Joan of Arc* I have been delighted, amazed. I had not presumed to expect any thing of such excellence from Southey. Why the poem is alone sufficient to redeem the character of the age we live in from the imputation of degenerating in Poetry, were there no such beings extant as Burns and Bowles, Cowper and——fill up the blank how you please, I say nothing. The subject is well chosen. It opens well. . . . On the whole, considering the celerity wherewith the poem was finish'd,

I was astonish'd at the infrequency of weak lines. I had expected to find it verbose. Joan, I think, does too little in Battle—Dunois, perhaps, the same—Conrade too much. The anecdotes interspersed among the battles refresh the mind very agreeably, and I am delighted with the very many passages of simple pathos abounding throughout the poem —passages which the author of 'Crazy Kate' might have written. Has not Master Southey spoke very slightingly in his preface and disparagingly of Cowper's Homer?—what makes him reluctant to give Cowper his fame? And does not Southey use too often the expletives 'did' and 'does?' they have a good effect at times, but are too inconsiderable, or rather become blemishes, when they mark a style. On the whole, I expect Southey one day to rival Milton. I already deem him equal to Cowper, and superior to all living Poets besides. What says Coleridge?

8. Unsigned notice, *Monthly Magazine*

July 1796, ii, 487

[*Joan of Arc*] is certainly entitled to the first wreathe of honour among our late poetical productions. To 'run a race with the press,' in an epic poem, as Mr. Southey appears to have done, was juvenile presumption, of which the necessary consequence has been many defective and faulty passages: but, viewed as a whole, the performance has singular merit. It abounds in lofty conceptions, vigorous sentiments, rich imagery, and all the sublimer graces of poetry. The author possesses uncommon powers of poetic invention; and with that diligence of study, and severity of correction, to which genius so reluctantly submits, may become a poet of the first order.

9. From an unsigned review,
Analytical Review

1796, xxiii, 170-7

Among the classes of poetry, the epic has commonly been allowed the first place. Without attempting to define it, or to analyse its characters, the very small number of successful productions, which have ever appeared under this denomination, will be admitted as a proof, that this, if not the most excellent, is at least the most difficult of all poetical compositions. When we read that Virgil, after devoting eleven years to his *Æneid*, left it at last unfinished, and that an interval of about twelve years passed between the commencement and the completion of the *Paradise Lost*, we learn with astonishment, that *Joan of Arc*, in its first form, in twelve books, was, except the first three hundred lines, finished in *six weeks*; and that, afterwards, when the author, upon receiving the first proof from the printer, seeing its faults, formed a resolution to new-model the work, although, with the exception of the first three hundred and forty lines, the plan of the whole was changed, and not a thousand lines remained as they were originally written, the rest was composed while the printing went on. We feel ourselves little disposed, we must acknowledge, to concur with the author of this poem in the contempt which, in relating these particulars, he casts upon the Horatian precept, *Nonum prematur in annum*;[1] or to flatter an ill-placed vanity by applauding the rapidity with which this poem was written. Nevertheless, we would by no means allow a circumstance so perfectly adventitious any weight in the scale of criticism against the merit of the work. We thought it right to mention a fact on which the author, by detailing it in the beginning of his preface, appears to lay some stress; but we wish entirely to forget it in our examination of the poem, and request our readers to do the same.

The story, upon which this poem is founded, is one of the most interesting in the history of France, and is, in several respects, happily adapted to epic representation. The heroine exhibits a character vested in a kind of obscurity, which gives it sublimity. Though, in this

---

[1] 'Let it be kept quiet till the ninth year.' (Horace, *Ars Poetica*.)

incredulous age, it will not be commonly believed that she was really inspired, it must at least be admitted, that she thought herself so, and that this was the common opinion among the vulgar at the time when she performed her great exploit; and this furnishes a sufficient ground for those supernatural incidents, which may be called the machinery of the poem. The events, being of the heroic kind, are adapted to excite strong and elevated emotions. The story turns upon one great incident, and is comprised within a moderate compass both with respect to time and place; it therefore admits of unity of action. Lastly, the moral lesson, which the story teaches, is of universal importance, that unjust ambition and tyranny must expect punishment: and it is no objection, that this lesson is taught at the expense of the author's native country; for he who wishes success to injustice because his countrymen support it, is a traitor to human kind.

[Outlines plot with quotations.]

The general result of the impression which the perusal of this poem has made upon our minds is this: that, although the poem has some redundancies, which the chastised taste of maturer years would have struck out; though a manifest incongruity runs through the piece, in ascribing to characters of the fifteenth century the politics and metaphysics of an enlightened philosopher of the eighteenth; and though allegorical personages, dreams and visions, but ill supply the place of that grand machinery, which produced so powerful an effect in those epic poems, which have obtained the glorious meed of immortality; we, nevertheless, admire, the noble spirit of freedom, which is evidently the poet's inspiring muse; the ready invention, which has enabled him to embellish an historical narrative of narrow extent, with all the charms of fiction; the fertile fancy, which has enriched his piece with every kind of poetical ornament; the learning, which has furnished him with a great variety of historical and mythological illustrations; and the correct and elegant taste in versification, which has qualified him to produce, with the exception of very few lines, an harmonious poem. Mr. S. will, we have no doubt, meet with sufficient encouragement, in the approbation which his *Joan of Arc* will obtain, to induce him to present the public with a *more elaborate* production in his *Madoc*, an epic poem, on the discovery of America by that prince, on which he is at present employed.

10. Coleridge, from three letters

November and December 1796, March 1797

Reprinted from *Collected Letters of Samuel Taylor Coleridge*, ed. E. L. Griggs (1956–).

(a) To John Thelwall, 19 November 1796
Of course, you have read the *Joan of Arc*. Homer is the Poet for the Warrior—Milton for the Religionist—Tasso for Women—Robert Southey for the Patriot. The first & fourth books of the *Joan of Arc* are to me more interesting than the same number of Lines in any poem whatsoever. [i, p. 258.]

(b) To John Thelwall, 31 December 1796
I entirely accord with your opinion of Southey's *Joan*—the 9th book is execrable—and the poem tho' it frequently reach the *sentimental*, does not display, the *poetical, Sublime*. In language at once natural, per-spicuous, & dignified, in manly pathos, in soothing & sonnet-like description, and above all, in character, & *dramatic* dialogue, Southey is unrivalled; but as certainly he does not possess opulence of Imagi-nation, lofty-paced Harmony, or that *toil* of thinking, which is necessary in order to plan *a Whole*. Dismissing mock humility, & hanging your mind as a looking-glass over my Idea-pot, so as to image on the said mind all the bubbles that boil in the said Idea-pot, (there's a damn'd long-winded Metaphor for you) I think, that an admirable Poet might be made by *amalgamating him & me*. I *think* too much for a *Poet*; he too little for a *great* Poet. But he abjures *thinking*— & lays the whole stress of excellence—on *feeling*.—Now (as you say) they must go together. [i, pp. 293–4.]

(c) To Joseph Cottle, 10 March 1797
I have heard from Sheridan, desiring me to write a Tragedy——I have no genius that way—Robert Southey has—and highly as I think of his

Joan of Arc, I cannot help prophesying, that he will be known to posterity as Shakespear's great Grandson, and only as Milton's great great grand nephew-in-law.—I think, that he will write a Tragedy; and Tragedies.——[i, p. 313.]

POEMS BY ROBERT SOUTHEY

1797, 1799

The two volumes of *Poems* published in 1797 and 1799 included a selection of new and reprinted pieces. The volumes sold well and were quickly reprinted, though Southey's royalties were not large.

---

11. Coleridge, from two letters

December 1796 and April 1797

Reprinted from *Collected Letters of Samuel Taylor Coleridge*, ed. E. L. Griggs (1956–).

(a) Letter to Southey, 27 December 1796

I thank you, Robert Southey! for your poems; and by way of return present you with a collection of (what appear to me) the faults.— 'The Race of Banquo' and 'To the Genius of Africa' ought to have rescued the ode from your very harsh censure. The latter is perfect, saving the last line, which is one of James Jennings's *new thoughts*; and besides, who after having been whirled along by such a tide of enthusiasm can endure to be impaled at last on the needle-point of an Antithesis? Of the Inscriptions I like the first and last the least: all the rest almost equally, and each very much. In the spirited & most original Lines to your own Miniature 'wrong'—*rhymes* with—'solitary song.'— You, I doubt not, have associated feelings dear to you with the ideas— 'this little picture was for ornament design'd' &c——and therefore do right in retaining them. To me &, I suppose, to most strangers the four last lines appear to drag excrementitiously——the Poem would conclude more satisfactorily at 'Spirit of Spenser! was the Wanderer

51

wrong?' The fault of the four Lines *seems* to be that having digressed you do not *lead* yourself to your subject, but without ceremony take a huge *leap* back again. Now tho' it is always well to *leave* the subject on the mind, yet rather than use such means I would forego it.——'The poem on the Death of an old Spaniel' will, I doubt not, be set to music by angelic & archangelic Dogs in their state of exaltation. It is a poem which will do good—and that is saying a great deal.—In the ode to Contemplation 'the smoke long shadowing play' is scarcely accurate— 'the smoke's long shadow' would surely be more natural & perspicuous?—

'The Musings on a Landscape' is a delicious poem.——The words To HIM begin the Line awkwardly, to *my* ear.——The final pause at the end of the first two Syllables of a line is seldom tolerable, except when the first two Syllables form a trochee—the reason, I apprehend, is, that to the ear they with the line foregoing make an Alexandrine.

—I have animadverted on those poems only which are my particular favorites—and now for the Penates, which if I were to abandon my judgment to the impulse of present Feelings, I should pronounce the most interesting poem of it's length in our Language.—I have detected two faults only, that a Man amid the miseries of a struggling Life should look back on the quiet happiness of childhood bears no resemblance to a Persian Monarch leaving the Luxuries of a Palace to revisit the cot where he had been a shepherd—.——But the *five first Lines* of the Poem—they are very, very *beautiful*; but (pardon my obtuseness) have they any *meaning*? 'The Temple of Paean' does not, I presume, mean any real temple—but is only an allegorical building— expressing Poesy—either ancient or modern. If modern, how is it's wall ruined? If ancient, how do *you* hang up your silent harp on it? Does it allude to ancient Poetry, as expressing the subject of the Present Poem? yet you say, that you shall strike that 'high and solemn strain' *ere* you hang it up. (—Besides, is *Paean* the God of *Poetry*?—I think, that the ancients religiously confined the name to Apollo in his capacity of *Healer & Python-killer*: but of this I am not certain.) However, whether ancient or modern poesy be indicated, or whatever may be the import of each distinct image, your general meaning is clear— namely, that after this Song you will intermit the writing of Poetry / yet in the next lines you say, there may its strings make melancholy music——i.e. This one song, and then I will *discontinue* verse-writing— during which discontinuance I will write verses!—Is all this only my obtuseness & frigidity? or have you not faultily mixed spiritual with corporeal, allegorical meanings with meanings predictable only of catgut & rosin, bricks & mortar?—A Tempest may shake an aged pile— but what has a tempest to do with ancient poetry?—If there were any respectable God with a respectable name who presided over the Law, or the affairs of active Life in general, you would have acted wiselier (I speak not dogmatically, but merely say, I think, you would have acted wiselier) if you had hung up your harp on the walls of his Temple—& added—yet shall it's strings, (if any ruder storm is abroad) make melancholy music. i.e. Tho' I intermit my poetry in consequence of the calls of Business, yet if any particular occasion arise, I will *unhang* my harp.—What if you *left* the harp in the fane of Vacuna? If these observations strike you as just, I shall be sorry, they did not strike me when you *read* the poem! But indeed the lines sound so sweet, and *seem* so much like sense, that it is no great matter. 'Tis a handsome & finely-sculptur'd Tomb——& few will break it open with the sacrilegious spade & pick-ax of Criticism to discover, whether or no it be not a *Cenotaph*. [i, pp. 290–2.]

(b) Letter to Joseph Cottle, early April 1797

I see they have reviewed Southey's *Poems* and my *Ode*[1] in the *Monthly Review*. Notwithstanding the Reviews, I, who in the sincerity of my heart am *jealous* for Robert Southey's fame, regret the publication of that volume. Wordsworth complains, with justice, that Southey writes *too much at his ease*—that he seldom 'feels his burthened breast

Heaving beneath th' incumbent Deity.'

He certainly will make literature more *profitable to him* from the fluency with which he writes, and the facility with which he pleases himself. But I fear, that to posterity his wreath will look unseemly— here an ever living amaranth, and close by its side some weed of an hour, sere, yellow, and shapeless—his exquisite beauties will lose half their effect from the bad company they keep. Besides I am fearful that he will begin to rely too much on *story* and *event* in his poems, to the neglect of those *lofty imaginings*, that are peculiar to, and definitive of, the poet. The *story* of Milton might be told in two pages—it is this which distinguishes an *Epic Poem* from a *Romance in metre*. [i, p. 320.]

---

[1] *Ode on the Departing Year.*

12. John Aikin, unsigned review, *Monthly Review*

March 1797, n.s. xxii, 297–302

See also No. 5.

No one who possesses a true relish for poetry, we conceive, will open with indifference a volume by the author of *Joan of Arc*. He will, perhaps, be prepared to expect somewhat of negligence and inequality, but he will certainly look for examples of that vivid force of imagination, and that warm colouring of expression, which essentially distinguish the POET from the artificial measurer of syllables. Nor will such a reader be disappointed by the publication before us. It contains abundant variety of style and subject, and consists of pieces very differently valued by the author himself. Of the lyric compositions, (which, indeed, are not numerous,) he speaks in terms of disparagement which may lead us to wonder that they should have been admitted; nor can we forbear to repeat a hint which we formerly ventured to give this youthful writer,—that a little more deference for the public, and a greater sensibility towards his own permanent fame, would be useful in directing the efforts of his genius. The poetical character, surely, is not that slight and trivial thing which is not worth the pains of acquiring or keeping. If poetry be not the first of all the energies of the human mind, as some of its votaries have deemed it, there is, at least, enough in it to found an immortal name, and to afford delight and instruction to whole ages and nations. Neither is it probable that a truly poetical genius can, with much advantage, substitute another pursuit as a basis for reputation and profit. Poetry is a trifle to trifling poets and trifling readers:—but no one ever excelled in it who treated it as a trifle.

[Quotes from several poems.]

It can scarcely be necessary for us, after the quotations which we have made, and the general view that we have given, formally to recommend this volume to the notice of our poetical readers, and its author to their esteem. Genius is a despotic power, and irresistibly commands homage.

13. Parodies in the *Anti-Jacobin*

November and December 1797

The *Anti-Jacobin, or Weekly Examiner* included in its early numbers four very effective parodies of poems by Southey. In these the metres and ideas of Southey's poems were cleverly ridiculed. In the first number Southey's poem was also printed before the parody. Although this practice was not repeated in later numbers it has been followed here for each poem.

The *Anti-Jacobin* was edited by William Gifford. Some uncertainty surrounds the authorship of the parodies but they certainly owed much to George Canning and John Hookham Frere (cf. *Poetry of the Anti-Jacobin*, ed. L. Rice-Oxley, Oxford, 1924).

(a) 20 November 1797, no. 1, 8:

INSCRIPTION

FOR THE APARTMENT IN CHEPSTOW CASTLE, WHERE HENRY MARTEN, THE REGICIDE, WAS IMPRISONED THIRTY YEARS.

For thirty years secluded from mankind
Here MARTEN linger'd. Often have these walls
Echoed his footsteps, as with even tread
He pac'd around his prison; not to him
Did Nature's fair varieties exist;
He never saw the Sun's delightful beams;
Save when thro' yon high bars he pour'd a sad
And broken splendour. Dost thou ask his crime?

He had REBELL'D AGAINST THE KING, AND SAT
IN JUDGMENT ON HIM; for his ardent mind
Shap'd goodliest plans of happiness on earth,
And Peace and Liberty. Wild dreams! but such
As PLATO lov'd; such as with holy zeal
Our MILTON worshipp'd. Blessed hopes! a while
From man with-held, even to the latter days
When CHRIST shall come, and all things be fulfill'd!

(IMITATION.)

INSCRIPTION

FOR THE DOOR OF THE CELL IN NEWGATE WHERE MRS. BROWNRIGG, THE
'PRENTICE-CIDE, WAS CONFINED PREVIOUS TO HER EXECUTION.

For one long Term, or e'er her trial came,
Here BROWNRIGG linger'd. Often have these cells
Echoed her blasphemies, as with shrill voice
She scream'd for fresh Geneva. Not to her
Did the blithe fields of Tothill, or thy street,
St. Giles, its fair varieties expand;
Till at the last in slow-drawn cart she went
To execution. Dost thou ask her crime?
SHE WHIPP'D TWO FEMALE 'PRENTICES TO DEATH,
AND HID THEM IN THE COAL-HOLE. For her mind
Shap'd strictest plans of discipline. Sage Schemes!
Such as LYCURGUS taught, when at the shrine
Of the Orthyan Goddess he bade flog
The little Spartans; such as erst chastised
Our MILTON, when at College. For this act
Did BROWNRIGG swing. Harsh Laws! But time shall come,
When France shall reign, and Laws be all repealed!

(b) 27 November 1797, no. 2, 15–16:

THE WIDOW.

SAPPHICS.

Cold was the night wind, drifting fast the snow fell,
Wide were the downs and shelterless and naked,

When a poor Wanderer struggled on her journey,
    Weary and way-sore.

Drear were the downs, more dreary her reflections;
Cold was the night-wind, colder was her bosom:
She had no home, the world was all before her,
    She had no shelter.

Fast o'er the heath a chariot rattled by her,
'Pity me!' feebly cried the lonely wanderer;
'Pity me, strangers! lest with cold and hunger
    Here I should perish.

'Once I had friends,—though now by all forsaken!
Once I had parents,—they are now in Heaven!
I had a home once—I had once a husband—
    Pity me, strangers!

'I had a home once—I had once a husband—
I am a widow, poor and broken-hearted!'
Loud blew the wind, unheard was her complaining,
    On drove the chariot.

(IMITATION.)

SAPPHICS.

THE FRIEND OF HUMANITY AND THE KNIFE-GRINDER.

FRIEND OF HUMANITY.

'Needy Knife-grinder! whither are you going?
Rough is the road, your Wheel is out of order—
Bleak blows the blast;—your hat has got a hole in't,
    So have your breeches!

'Weary Knife-grinder! little think the proud ones,
Who in their coaches roll along the turnpike-
road, what hard work 'tis crying all day "Knives and
    "Scissars to grind O!"

'Tell me, Knife-grinder, how you came to grind knives?
Did some rich man tyrannically use you?
Was it the 'Squire? or Parson of the Parish?
    Or the Attorney?

'Was it the 'Squire for killing of his Game? or
Covetous Parson for his Tythes distraining?
Or roguish Lawyer made you lose your little
    All in a law-suit?

'(Have you not read the Rights of Man, by TOM PAINE?)
Drops of compassion tremble on my eye-lids,
Ready to fall, as soon as you have told your
    Pitiful story.'

KNIFE-GRINDER.

'Story! God bless you! I have none to tell, Sir,
Only last night a-drinking at the Chequers,
This poor old hat and breeches, as you see, were
    Torn in a scuffle.

'Constables came up for to take me into
Custody; they took me before the Justice;
Justice OLDMIXON put me in the Parish-
    Stocks for a Vagrant.

'I should be glad to drink your Honour's health in
A Pot of Beer, if you will give me Sixpence;
But for my part, I never love to meddle
    With Politics, Sir.'

FRIEND OF HUMANITY.

'*I* give thee Sixpence! I will see thee damn'd first—
Wretch! whom no sense of wrongs can rouse to vengeance—
Sordid, unfeeling, reprobate, degraded,
    Spiritless outcast!'

(*Kicks the Knife-grinder, overturns his Wheel, and exit in a transport of
republican enthusiasm and universal philanthropy.*)

(c) 11 December 1797, no. 5, 39:

THE SOLDIER'S WIFE.

DACTYLICS.

Weary way-wanderer, languid and sick at heart,
Travelling painfully over the rugged road,
Wild-visaged Wanderer! God help thee wretched one!

Sorely thy little one drags by thee bare-footed,
Cold is the baby that hangs at thy bending back,
Meagre and livid and screaming for misery.

Woe-begone mother, half anger, half agony,
As over thy shoulder thou lookest to hush the babe,
Bleakly the blinding snow beats in thy hagged face.

Ne'er will thy husband return from the war again,
Cold is thy heart and as frozen as Charity!
Cold are thy children.—Now God be thy comforter!

(IMITATION.)

THE SOLDIER's FRIEND.

DACTYLICS.

Come, little Drummer Boy, lay down your knapsack here:
I am the Soldier's Friend—here are some Books for you;
Nice clever Books, by TOM PAINE the Philanthropist.

Here's Half-a-crown for you—here are some Hand-bills too—
Go to the Barracks, and give all the Soldiers some.
Tell them the Sailors are all in a Mutiny.
[*Exit Drummer Boy, with Hand-bills and Half-a-crown.—Manet*
Soldier's Friend.

Liberty's friends thus all learn to amalgamate,
Freedom's volcanic explosion prepares itself,
Despots shall bow to the Fasces of Liberty,
   Reason, philosophy, 'fiddledum diddledum,'
   Peace and Fraternity, higgledy, piggledy,
   Higgledy, piggledy, 'fiddledum diddledum.'
               Et cetera, et cetera, et cetera.

(d) 18 December 1797, no. 6, 46. Further parody of 'The Soldier's
Wife':

DACTYLICS,

Being the quintessence of all the Dactylics that ever were, or ever
will be written.

SOUTHEY

HUMBLY ADDRESSED TO THE AUTHOR OF THE SAME.

Wearisome Sonnetteer, feeble and querulous,
Painfully dragging out thy demo-cratic lays—
Moon-stricken Sonnetteer, 'ah! for thy heavy chance!'

Sorely thy Dactylics lag on uneven feet:
Slow is the Syllable which thou would'st urge to speed,
Lame and o'erburthen'd, and 'screaming its wretchedness!'

† ⋆ ⋆ ⋆ ⋆ ⋆ ⋆ ⋆ ⋆ ⋆ ⋆

Ne'er talk of Ears again! look at thy Spelling-book;
Dilworth and *Dyche* are both mad at thy quantities—
DACTYLICS, call'st thou 'em?—'God help thee, silly one!'

† My worthy friend, the Bellman, had promised to supply an additiona lStanza; but the business of assisting the Lamp-lighter, Chimney-sweeper, &c. with Complimentary Verses for their worthy Masters and Mistresses, pressing on him at this Season, he was obliged to decline it.

60

14. Lamb, letter to Southey

15 March 1799

This letter was written by Lamb on receipt of the second volume of *Poems*. Reprinted from *The Letters of Charles and Mary Lamb*, ed. E. V. Lucas (1935), i, pp. 150–2.

I have received your little volume, for which I thank you, though I do not entirely approve of this sort of intercourse, where the presents are all one side. I have read the last Eclogue again with great pleasure. It hath gained considerably by abridgment, and now I think it wants nothing but enlargement. You will call this one of tyrant Procrustes' criticisms, to cut and pull so to his own standard; but the old lady is so great a favourite with me, I want to hear more of her; and of 'Joanna' you have given us still less. But the picture of the rustics leaning over the bridge, and the old lady travelling abroad on a summer evening to see her garden watered, are images so new and true, that I decidedly prefer this 'Ruin'd Cottage' to any poem in the book. Indeed I think it the only one that will bear comparison with your 'Hymn to the Penates' in a former volume.

I compare dissimilar things, as one would a rose and a star, for the pleasure they give us, or as a child soon learns to choose between a cake and a rattle; for dissimilars have mostly some points of comparison. The next best poem, I think, is the First Eclogue; 'tis very complete, and abounding in little pictures and realities. The remainder Eclogues, excepting only the 'Funeral,' I do not greatly admire. I miss *one*, which had at least as good a title to publication as the 'Witch,' or the 'Sailor's Mother.' You call'd it the 'Last of the Family.' The 'Old Woman of Berkeley' comes next; in some humours I would give it the preference above any. But who the devil is Matthew of Westminster? You are as familiar with these antiquated monastics, as Swedenborg, or, as his followers affect to call him, the Baron, with his invisibles. But you have raised a very comic effect out of the true narrative of Matthew of Westminster. 'Tis surprising with how little addition you have been able to convert with so little alteration his incidents, meant for terror, into circumstances and food for the spleen. The Parody is *not* so successful; it has one famous line indeed, which conveys the finest death-bed image I ever met with:

> The doctor whisper'd the nurse, and the surgeon knew what he said.

But the offering the bride three times bears not the slightest analogy or proportion to the fiendish noises three times heard! In 'Jaspar,' the circumstance of the great light is very affecting. But I had heard you mention it before. The 'Rose' is the only insipid piece in the volume; it hath neither thorns nor sweetness, and, besides, sets all chronology and probability at defiance.

'Cousin Margaret,' you know, I like. The allusions to the *Pilgrim's Progress* are particularly happy, and harmonise tacitly and delicately with old cousins and aunts. To familiar faces we do associate familiar scenes and accustomed objects; but what hath Apollidon and his sea-nymphs to do in these affairs? Apollyon I could have borne, though he stands for the devil; but who is Apollidon? I think you are too apt to conclude faintly, with some cold moral, as in the end of the poem called 'The Victory'—

> Be thou her comforter, who art the widow's friend;

a single common-place line of comfort, which bears no proportion in weight or number to the many lines which describe suffering. This is to convert religion into mediocre feelings, which should burn, and glow, and tremble. A moral should be wrought into the body and soul, the matter and tendency, of a poem, not tagged to the end, like a 'God send the good ship into harbour,' at the conclusion of our bills of lading. The finishing of the 'Sailor' is also imperfect. Any dissenting minister may say and do as much.

These remarks, I know, are crude and unwrought; but I do not lay claim to much accurate thinking. I never judge system-wise of things, but fasten upon particulars. After all, there is a great deal in the book that I must, for time, leave *unmentioned*, to deserve my thanks for its own sake, as well as for the friendly remembrances implied in the gift. I again return you my thanks.

THALABA THE DESTROYER

1801

Southey first outlined the plan of *Thalaba* in 1798. The poem was completed by October 1800, when Southey was in Portugal, and was despatched to his friend John Rickman who had agreed to act as his agent. It was published by Longman in an edition of 1,000 copies, for which Southey received £115. The poem sold slowly and by spring 1804 only 500 copies had been sold. The second edition, heavily revised, did not appear until 1809. Southey, while admitting *Thalaba*'s faults, claimed: 'I know of no poem which can claim a place between it and the *Orlando*' (*Life*, ii, p. 134).

15. Unsigned review, *British Critic*

September 1801, xviii, 309–10

The process of *writing himself down* is here fully performed by Mr. Southey, if it be allowed that he had ever written himself up. A more complete monument of vile and depraved taste no man ever raised. In his Preface he has the absurdity to speak of the verse of Dryden and Pope, that is, the English heroic couplet, in the following ridiculous terms: 'Verse is not enough favoured by the English reader; perhaps this is owing to the obtrusiveness, the regular *Jews-harp twing twang*, of what has been foolishly called heroic measure.' He has, therefore, given a rhapsody of Twelve Books in a sort of irregular lyric, so unlike verse or sense, that if it were worth while to present our readers with a tissue of so coarse a texture, we could fill whole pages with specimens of its absurdity. We will have mercy, and give only a single example, which may be taken at random, for no part seems to be better than the rest.

> In the eve he arrived at a well,
> The acacia bent over its side,

SOUTHEY

Under whose long light-hanging boughs
He chose his night's abode.
There due ablutions made and prayers performed,
The youth his mantle spread,
And silently produced
His solitary meal.
The silence and the solitude recalled
Dear recollection; and with folded arms
Thinking of other days, he sate, till thought
Had left him, and the acacia's moving shade
Upon the sunny sand
Had caught his idle eye,
And his awakened ear,
Heard the grey Lizard's chirp,
The only sound of life.   Book IV.

This is really *chirping like a Lizard!*—and the writer of this wretched
stuff has the vanity to censure the approved verse of his country; this
unharmonious stuff—which, were not the lines divided by the printer,
no living creature would suspect to be even intended for verse; for this
execrable performance, loaded with notes, often brought in without
necessity, often as nonsensical as the text itself, the purchaser is modestly
required to pay 14s. We can only say that, if fourteen copies are sold,
and thirteen of the buyers do not repent their bargain, the world is
more foolish than we could imagine. The work may be characterized
in five words, 'Tales of Terror, run mad.'

16. Unsigned review, *Monthly Mirror*

October 1801, xii, 243–7

It is a matter to be lamented, that, in times like the present, a work of
letters can rarely be reviewed upon the ground of its own proper merits.
Report, equally industrious to spread truth and falsehood, flies with some
tale of an author's political or religious opinions, and with it assails the
vaunted impartiality of a reviewer.—The combat between integrity

64

and prejudice is soon at an end—the latter possesses the full power of magic, and soon shifts into the resemblance of the former, and mighty indeed is the mischief that follows. We do not boast of candour that is *not* to be conquered—but, with opinions decidedly adverse to those *attributed* to the present author, we shall try if it be not possible to review a work of fancy in the spirit of justice, and the language of gentlemen.

We shall not dwell upon the light expressions, which occur in the preface to this romance. Mr. Southey's adversaries may *rejoice* at them, and his friends will *regret* them:—we deeply *censure*, and leave them. In the consideration of this romance, the judicious critic cannot but feel that one rule of good writing has been studiously observed. His work will not incur the censure passed by the late Mr. Collins upon his Persian Eclogues, namely, that, from erroneous manners, they were 'Irish.' He has read every thing which could inform him upon the subject, and his notes are not only illustrations—they were the *materials* of his poem. We had at first designed an examination of the story, but it is in truth too slight for analysis—it is a work of ornament, and he who should attempt it would succeed like the man who would criticise the mere form of a gothic shrine, regardless of its clustered ornaments, and its gilded tracery—the surface of grotesque art and profuse expence. Leaving the tale to the author's mode of telling it, we now come to consider what that mode is. He tells us it is *metrical*: certainly, and so is every line that comes from a human mouth. Yes, but it is in the measures of *poetry*. He will excuse our ears, but we cannot agree with him. Among the sins of our youth, we, like him, have traded in desultory versification, but have long been brought back to lyrical *rhyme*, and heroic *blank verse*. The reasons are obvious. Accent alone (we have little *quantity*) in our language will not support the ode, and no human patience can endure an epic of 10,000 lines in rhyme. What, therefore, are our wishes as to the present poem? Why, that the descriptive and narrative parts had been in blank verse, and the speeches lyrical rhyme. The reasons for these wishes are not only grounded upon our principles, but our actual feelings. Mr. Southey rarely succeeds in this romance, except when he writes in these modes.

[Quotes extensively from the poem.]

We are now compelled to execute the less pleasing part of our task The desire to preserve a real poet from affectation, puerility, and false English, will be our justification, and may be our sole reward.

Yet we hope a cultivated and feeling mind will be also ingenuous: the author may yield to our decision. He may, and probably does, despise most of the remarks he may hear; but we will venture to try his own eye and ear, now the hurry of composition is over. What does he think of such expressions as the following?—*Deathy* dark—more *fiendishness*—mingle *deathiness*—*bluey* pale—*tort* vibration (from the Latin *tortus*, we suppose)—*crunching* snow—and a thousand *repetitions* of them—favourites, like disorderly brats. But we will not dwell upon *spots* like these. The spunge! the spunge! by the sacred adjurations of good sense and poetry.

Two or three beauties, as atonements for these deformities, and we close our labour.

> And kindred plants, that, with unwatered root,
> *Fed in the burning sand.*

> Woe to him! he hath laid his toils
> To take the Antelope;
> *The* LION *is come in.*

> When the blast is loud,
> When the waters *fill*
> *The traveller's tread in the sands.*
> When the door-curtain *hangs in heavier folds.*

And instances numberless of a poet's notice, and a poet's language. We recommend his beauties to the esteem, and his faults to the forgetfulness, of every reader. Upon the whole, he has our thanks for much amusement, and some information.

17. From an unsigned review, *Monthly Magazine*

January 1802, xii, 581–4

To those who have been long accustomed to the swing of rime and the
see-saw of couplets, the irregular verse, or measured prose, in which
this very poetical poem is composed, will appear to have been adopted
rather for the accommodation of the writer than of the reader—rather
to elude the abecedary drudgery of spelling *ban, can, dan, fan,* &c. *bare,
care, dare, fare,* &c. till the desiderated syllable arrives, than to invite
from the second gate of the palace of pleasure a new charmer of the
ear. . . .

But those who delight in the narrative odes of Pindar, or the descriptive odes of Stolberg, will perceive that ages have sanctioned and
nations have admired a similar structure of metre.

The fable or story of *Thalaba* is perhaps too marvellous: every
incident is a miracle; every utensil, an amulet; every speech, a spell;
every personage, a god, or rather a talismanic statue; of which destiny
and magic overrule the movements, not human hopes and fears—not
human desires and passions, which always must excite the vivid
sympathy of men. It offers, however, scope beyond other metrical
romances, for a splendid variety of description, which, as in *Alexander's
Feast*, as in the *Progress of Poesy*, as in the *Operas* of Quinault, shifts,
with the cameleon capriciousness of lyric inspiration, and with the
versatile instantaneity of pantomime scenery, from the blasted wilderness, to caverns of flame; from bowers of paradise, to cities of jewelry;
from deserts of snow, to aromatic isles; and from the crush of worlds,
to the bliss of heaven. As in shuffling tarocco-cards, figures, motley,
new, and strange, causing palpitation, dance before the eye, and thwart
the anxious grasp; so here portentous and alarming forms glare on the
wonder, without enabling the spectator to form any guess about their
approaching influence over the play, by any speculation of probability.
Whatever loss of interest this poem may sustain, as a whole, by an apparent driftlessness of the events and characters, is compensated by the busy
variety, the picturesque imagery, and striking originality of the parts.

18. Francis Jeffrey, unsigned review, *Edinburgh Review*

October 1802, i, 63–83

Jeffrey (1773–1850) was a founder and first editor of the *Edinburgh Review*. Southey expressed strong dissatisfaction with this notable attack upon *Thalaba* (see Introduction, p. 7). When he first met Jeffrey in 1805 he described him as 'a man of ready wit, no taste and so little knowledge that it would have been scarcely inaccurate to have said none' (Curry, i, pp. 407–8). In treating Southey as a major representative of a new movement in poetry, however, Jeffrey's review helped to further his reputation by bringing him to the notice of a wider public.

Poetry has this much, at least, in common with religion, that its standards were fixed long ago, by certain inspired writers, whose authority it is no longer lawful to call in question; and that many profess to be entirely devoted to it, who have no *good works* to produce in support of their pretensions. The catholic poetical church, too, has worked but few miracles since the first ages of its establishment; and has been more prolific, for a long time, of Doctors, than of Saints: it has had its corruptions and reformation also, and has given birth to an infinite variety of heresies and errors, the followers of which have hated and persecuted each other as cordially as other bigots.

The author who is now before us, belongs to a *sect* of poets, that has established itself in this country within these ten or twelve years, and is looked upon, we believe, as one of its chief champions and apostles. The peculiar doctrines of this sect, it would not, perhaps, be very easy to explain; but, that they are *dissenters* from the established systems in poetry and criticism, is admitted, and proved indeed, by the whole tenor of their compositions. Though they lay claim, we believe, to a creed and a revelation of their own, there can be little doubt, that their doctrines are of *German* origin, and have been derived from some of the great modern reformers in that country. Some of their leading principles, indeed, are probably of an earlier date, and seem to have been borrowed from the great apostle of Geneva. As Mr Southey is the first author, of this persuasion, that has yet been brought before us for judgment, we cannot discharge our inquisitorial office conscientiously, without premising a few words upon the nature and tendency of the tenets he has helped to promulgate.

The disciples of this school boast much of its originality, and seem to value themselves very highly, for having broken loose from the bondage of antient authority, and reasserted the independence of genius. Originality, however, we are persuaded, is rarer than mere alteration; and a man may change a good master for a bad one, without finding himself at all nearer to independence. That our new poets have abandoned the old models, may certainly be admitted; but we have not been able to discover that they have yet created any models of their own; and are very much inclined to call in question the worthiness of those to which they have transferred their admiration. The productions of this school, we conceive, are so far from being entitled to the praise of originality, that they cannot be better characterized, than by an enumeration of the sources from which their materials have been derived. The greater part of them, we apprehend, will be found to be composed of the following elements: 1. The antisocial principles, and distempered sensibility of Rousseau—his discontent with the present constitution of society—his paradoxical morality, and his perpetual hankerings after some unattainable state of voluptuous virtue and perfection. 2. The simplicity and energy (*horresco referens*)[1] of Kotzebue and Schiller. 3. The homeliness and harshness of some of Cowper's language and versification, interchanged occasionally with the *innocence* of Ambrose Philips, or the quaintness of Quarles and Dr Donne. From the diligent study of these few originals, we have no doubt that an entire art of poetry may be collected, by the assistance of which, the very *gentlest* of our readers may soon be qualified to compose a poem as correctly versified as *Thalaba*, and to deal out sentiment and description, with all the sweetness of Lambe, and all the magnificence of Coleridge.

The authors, of whom we are now speaking, have, among them, unquestionably, a very considerable portion of poetical talent, and have, consequently, been enabled to seduce many into an admiration of the false taste (as it appears to us) in which most of their productions are composed. They constitute, at present, the most formidable conspiracy that has lately been formed against sound judgment in matters

1 'I shudder at the recollection.'

poetical; and are entitled to a larger share of our censorial notice, than could be spared for an individual delinquent. We shall hope for the indulgence of our readers, therefore, in taking this opportunity to inquire a little more particularly into their merits, and to make a few remarks upon those peculiarities which seem to be regarded by their admirers as the surest proofs of their excellence.

Their most distinguishing symbol, is undoubtedly an affectation of great simplicity and familiarity of language. They disdain to make use of the common poetical phraseology, or to ennoble their diction by a selection of fine or dignified expressions. There would be too much *art* in this, for that great love of nature with which they are all of them inspired; and their sentiments, they are determined shall be indebted, for their effect, to nothing but their intrinsic tenderness or elevation. There is something very noble and conscientious, we will confess, in this plan of composition; but the misfortune is, that there are passages in all poems, that can neither be pathetic nor sublime; and that, on these occasions, a neglect of the embellishments of language is very apt to produce absolute meanness and insipidity. The language of passion, indeed, can scarcely be deficient in elevation; and when an author is awanting in that particular, he may commonly be presumed to have failed in the truth, as well as in the dignity of his expression. The case, however, is extremely different with the subordinate parts of a composition; with the narrative and description, that are necessary to preserve its connexion; and the explanation, that must frequently prepare us for the great scenes and splendid passages. In these, all the requisite ideas may be conveyed, with sufficient clearness, by the meanest and most negligent expressions; and, if magnificence or beauty is ever to be observed in them, it must have been introduced from some other motive than that of adapting the style to the subject. It is in such passages, accordingly, that we are most frequently offended with low and inelegant expressions; and that the language, which was intended to be simple and natural, is found oftenest to degenerate into mere slovenliness and vulgarity. It is in vain, too, to expect that the meanness of those parts may be redeemed by the excellence of others. A poet, who aims at all at sublimity or pathos, is like an actor in a high tragic character, and must sustain his dignity throughout, or become altogether ridiculous. We are apt enough to laugh at the mock-majesty of those whom we know to be but common mortals in private; and cannot permit Hamlet to make use of a single provincial intonation, although it should only be in his conversation with the grave-diggers.

The followers of simplicity are, therefore, at all times in danger of occasional degradation; but the simplicity of this new school seems intended to ensure it. *Their* simplicity does not consist, by any means, in the rejection of glaring or superfluous ornament,—in the substitution of elegance to splendour, or in that refinement of art which seeks concealment in its own perfection. It consists, on the contrary, in a very great degree, in the positive and *bonâ fide* rejection of art altogether, and in the bold use of those rude and negligent expressions, which would be banished by a little discrimination. One of their own authors, indeed, has very ingenuously set forth, (in a kind of manifesto that preceded one of their most flagrant acts of hostility), that it was their capital object 'to adapt to the uses of poetry, the ordinary language of conversation among the middling and lower orders of the people.' What advantages are to be gained by the success of this project, we confess ourselves unable to conjecture. The language of the higher and more cultivated orders may fairly be presumed to be better than that of their inferiors: at any rate, it has all those associations in its favour, by means of which, a style can ever appear beautiful or exalted, and is adapted to the purposes of poetry, by having been long consecrated to its use. The language of the vulgar, on the other hand, has all the opposite associations to contend with; and must seem unfit for poetry, (if there were no other reason), merely because it has scarcely ever been employed in it. A great genius may indeed overcome these disadvantages; but we can scarcely conceive that he should court them. We may excuse a certain homeliness of language in the productions of a ploughman or a milkwoman; but we cannot bring ourselves to admire it in an author, who has had occasion to indite odes to his college bell, and inscribe hymns to the Penates.

But the mischief of this new system, is not confined to the depravation of language only; it extends to the sentiments and emotions, and leads to the debasement of all those feelings which poetry is designed to communicate. It is absurd to suppose, that an author should make use of the language of the vulgar, to express the sentiments of the refined. His professed object, in employing that language, is to bring his compositions nearer to the true standard of nature; and his intention to copy the sentiments of the lower orders, is implied in his resolution to make use of their style. Now, the different classes of society have each of them a distinct character, as well as a separate idiom; and the names of the various passions to which they are subject respectively, have a signification that varies essentially, according to the condition of the persons to whom they are applied. The love, or grief, or indignation of an enlightened and refined character, is not only expressed in a different language, but is in itself a different emotion from the love, or grief, or anger of a clown, a tradesman, or a market-wench. The things themselves are radically and obviously distinct; and the representation of them is calculated to convey a very different train of sympathies and sensations to the mind. The question, therefore, comes simply to be—which of them is the most proper object for poetical imitation? It is needless for us to answer a question, which the practice of all the world has long ago decided irrevocably. The poor and vulgar may interest us, in poetry, by their *situation*: but never, we apprehend, by any sentiments that are peculiar to their condition, and still less by any language that is characteristic of it. The truth is, that it is impossible to copy their diction or their sentiments correctly, in a serious composition; and this, not merely because poverty makes men ridiculous, but because just taste and refined sentiment are rarely to be met with among the uncultivated part of mankind; and a language, fitted for their expression, can still more rarely form any part of their 'ordinary conversation.' The low-bred heroes, and interesting rustics of poetry, have no sort of affinity to the real vulgar of this world; they are imaginary beings, whose characters and language are in contrast with their situation; and please those, who can be pleased with them, by the marvellous, and not by the nature of such a combination. In serious poetry, a man of the middling or lower order *must necessarily* lay aside a great deal of his ordinary language; he must avoid errors in grammar and orthography; and steer clear of the cant of particular professions, and of every impropriety that is ludicrous or disgusting: nay, he must speak in good verse, and observe all the graces in prosody and collocation. After all this, it may not be very easy to say how we are to find him out to be a low man, or what marks can remain of the ordinary language of conversation in the inferior orders of society. If there be any phrases that are not used in good society, they will appear as blemishes in the composition, no less palpably, than errors in syntax or quantity; and, if there be no such phrases, the style cannot be characteristic of that condition of life, the language of which it professes to have adopted. All approximation to that language, in the same manner, implies a deviation from that purity and precision, which no one, we believe, ever violated spontaneously.

It has been argued, indeed, (for men will argue in support of what they do not venture to practise), that as the middling and lower orders of society constitute by far the greater part of mankind, so, their feelings and expressions should interest more extensively, and may be taken, more fairly than any other, for the standards of what is natural and true. To this, it seems obvious to answer, that the arts that aim at exciting admiration and delight, do not take their models from what is ordinary, but from what is excellent; and that our interest in the representation of any event does not depend upon our familiarity with the original, but on its intrinsic importance, and the celebrity of the parties it concerns. The sculptor employs his art in delineating the graces of Antinous or Apollo, and not in the representation of those ordinary forms that belong to the crowd of his admirers. When a chieftain perishes in battle, his followers mourn more for him, than for thousands of their equals that may have fallen around him.

After all, it must be admitted, that there is a class of persons (we are afraid they cannot be called *readers*), to whom the representation of vulgar manners, in vulgar language, will afford much entertainment. We are afraid, however, that the ingenious writers who supply the hawkers and ballad-singers, have very nearly monopolized that department, and are probably better qualified to hit the taste of their customers, than Mr Southey, or any of his brethren, can yet pretend to be. To fit them for the higher task of original composition, it would not be amiss if they were to undertake a translation of Pope or Milton into the vulgar tongue, for the benefit of those children of nature.

There is still another disagreeable effect of this affected simplicity, which, though of less importance than those which have been already noticed, it may yet be worth while to mention: This is, the extreme difficulty of supporting the same tone of expression throughout, and the inequality that is consequently introduced into the texture of the composition. To an author of reading and education, it is a style that must always be assumed and unnatural, and one from which he will be perpetually tempted to deviate. He will rise, therefore, every now and then, above the level to which he has professedly degraded himself; and make amends for that transgression, by a fresh effort of descension. His composition, in short, will be like that of a person who is attempting to speak in an obsolete or provincial dialect; he will betray himself by expressions of occasional purity and elegance, and exert himself to efface that impression, by passages of unnatural meanness or absurdity.

In making these strictures on the perverted taste for simplicity, that seems to distinguish our modern school of poetry, we have no particular allusion to Mr Southey, or the production now before us: On the contrary, he appears to us, to be less addicted to this fault than most of his fraternity; and if we were in want of examples to illustrate the preceding observations, we should certainly look for them in the effusions of that poet who commemorates, with so much effect, the chattering of Harry Gibbs' teeth; tells the tale of the one-eyed huntsman 'who had a cheek like a cherry;' and beautifully warns his studious friend of the risk he ran of 'growing double.'

At the same time, it is impossible to deny that the author of the *English Eclogues* is liable to a similar censure; and few persons, we believe, will peruse the following verses (taken almost at random from the *Thalaba*), without acknowledging that he still continues to deserve it.

> At midnight Thalaba started up,
> For he felt that the ring on his finger was moved.
> He called on Allah aloud,
> And he called on the Prophet's name.
> Moath arose in alarm,
> 'What ails thee, Thalaba?' he cried,
> 'Is the robber of night at hand?'
> 'Dost thou not see,' the youth exclaimed,
> 'A spirit in the Tent?'
> Moath looked round, and said,
> 'The moon-beam shines in the Tent,
> I see thee stand in the light,
> And thy shadow is black on the ground.'
> Thalaba answered not.
> 'Spirit!' he cried, 'what brings thee here?' &c.

> WOMAN.
> Go not among the Tombs, Old Man!
> There is a madman there.

> OLD MAN.
> Will he harm me if I go?

> WOMAN.
> Not he, poor miserable man!
> But 'tis a wretched sight to see
> His utter wretchedness.
> For all day long he lies on a grave,
> And never is he seen to weep,
> And never is he heard to groan,
> Nor ever at the hour of prayer

Bends his knee, nor moves his lips.
I have taken him food for charity,
And never a word he spake;
But yet so ghastly he looked
That I have awakened at night, &c.

Now, this style, we conceive, possesses no one character of excellence; it is feeble, low, and disjointed; without elegance, and without
dignity; the offspring, we should imagine, of mere indolence and
neglect; or the unhappy fruit of a system that would teach us to
undervalue that vigilance and labour which sustained the loftiness of
Milton, and gave energy and direction to the pointed and fine propriety
of Pope.

The *style* of our modern poets, is that, no doubt, by which they are
most easily distinguished: but their genius has also an internal character;
and the peculiarities of their taste may be discovered, without the
assistance of their diction. Next after great familiarity of language,
there is nothing that appears to them so meritorious as perpetual
exaggeration of thought. There must be nothing moderate, natural, or
easy, about their sentiments. There must be a 'qu'il mourut,'[1] and a
'let there be light,' in every line; and all their characters must be in
agonies and ecstasies, from their entrance to their exit. To those who
are acquainted with their productions, it is needless to speak of the
fatigue that is produced by this unceasing summons to admiration, or
of the compassion which is excited by the spectacle of these eternal
strainings and distortions. Those authors appear to forget, that a whole
poem cannot be made up of striking passages; and that the sensations
produced by sublimity, are never so powerful and entire, as when they
are allowed to subside and revive, in a slow and spontaneous succession.
It is delightful, now and then, to meet with a rugged mountain, or a
roaring stream; but where there is no sunny slope, nor shaded plain, to
relieve them—where all is beetling cliff and yawning abyss, and the
landscape presents nothing on every side but prodigies and terrors—
the head is apt to grow giddy, and the heart to languish for the repose
and security of a less elevated region.

The effect even of genuine sublimity, therefore, is impaired by the
injudicious frequency of its exhibition, and the omission of those
intervals and breathing-places, at which the mind should be permitted
to recover from its perturbation or astonishment: but where it has

[1] 'Let him die.

75

been summoned upon a false alarm, and disturbed in the orderly course of its attention, by an impotent attempt at elevation, the consequences are still more disastrous. There is nothing so ridiculous (at least for a poet) as to fail in great attempts. If the reader foresaw the failure, he may receive some degree of mischievous satisfaction from its punctual occurrence; if he did not, he will be vexed and disappointed; and, in both cases, he will very speedily be disgusted and fatigued. It would be going too far, certainly, to maintain, that our modern poets have never succeeded in their persevering endeavours at elevation and emphasis; but it is a melancholy fact, that their successes bear but a small proportion to their miscarriages; and that the reader who has been promised an energetic sentiment, or sublime allusion, must often be contented with a very miserable substitute. Of the many contrivances they employ to give the appearance of uncommon force and animation to a very ordinary conception, the most usual is, to wrap it up in a veil of mysterious and unintelligible language, which flows past with so much solemnity, that it is difficult to believe it conveys nothing of any value. Another device for improving the effect of a cold idea, is, to embody it in a verse of unusual harshness and asperity. Compound words, too, of a portentous sound and conformation, are very useful in giving an air of energy and originality; and a few lines of scripture, written out into verse from the original prose, have been found to have a very happy effect upon those readers to whom they have the recommendation of novelty.

The qualities of style and imagery, however, form but a small part of the characteristics by which a literary faction is to be distinguished. The subject and object of their compositions, and the principles and opinions they are calculated to support, constitute a far more important criterion, and one to which it is usually altogether as easy to refer. Some poets are sufficiently described as the flatterers of greatness and power, and others as the champions of independence. One set of writers is known by its antipathy to decency and religion; another, by its methodistical cant and intolerance. Our new school of poetry has a moral character also; though it may not be possible, perhaps, to delineate it quite so concisely.

A splenetic and idle discontent with the existing institutions of society, seems to be at the bottom of all their serious and peculiar sentiments. Instead of contemplating the wonders and the pleasures which civilization has created for mankind, they are perpetually brooding over the disorders by which its progress has been attended.

They are filled with horror and compassion at the sight of poor men spending their blood in the quarrels of princes, and brutifying their sublime capabilities in the drudgery of unremitting labour. For all sorts of vice and profligacy in the lower orders of society, they have the same virtuous horror, and the same tender compassion. While the existence of these offences overpowers them with grief and confusion, they never permit themselves to feel the smallest indignation or dislike towards the offenders. The present vicious constitution of society alone is responsible for all these enormities: the poor sinners are but the helpless victims or instruments of its disorders, and could not possibly have avoided the errors into which they have been betrayed. Though they can bear with crimes, therefore, they cannot reconcile themselves to punishments; and have an unconquerable antipathy to prisons, gibbets, and houses of correction, as engines of oppression, and instruments of atrocious injustice. While the plea of moral necessity is thus artfully brought forward to convert all the excesses of the poor into innocent misfortunes, no sort of indulgence is shown to the offences of the powerful and rich. Their oppressions, and seductions, and debaucheries, are the theme of many an angry verse; and the indignation and abhorrence of the reader is relentlessly conjured up against those perturbators of society, and scourges of mankind.

It is not easy to say, whether the fundamental absurdity of this doctrine, or the partiality of its application, be entitled to the severest reprehension. If men are driven to commit crimes, through a certain moral necessity; other men are compelled, by a similar necessity, to hate and despise them for their commission. The indignation of the sufferer is at least as natural as the guilt of him who makes him suffer; and the good order of society would probably be as well preserved, if our sympathies were sometimes called forth in behalf of the former. At all events, the same apology ought certainly to be admitted for the wealthy, as for the needy offender. They are subject alike to the over-ruling influence of necessity, and equally affected by the miserable condition of society. If it be natural for a poor man to murder and rob, in order to make himself comfortable, it is no less natural for a rich man to gormandize and domineer, in order to have the full use of his riches. Wealth is just as valid an excuse for the one class of vices, as indigence is for the other. There are many other peculiarities of false sentiment in the productions of this class of writers, that are sufficiently deserving of commemoration. But we have already exceeded our limits in giving these general indications of their character, and must now hasten back to the consideration of the singular performance which has given occasion to all this discussion.

The first thing that strikes the reader of *Thalaba*, is, the singular structure of the versification, which is a jumble of all the measures that are known in English poetry, (and a few more), without rhyme, and without any sort of regularity in their arrangement. Blank odes have been known in this country about as long as English sapphics and dactylics; and both have been considered, we believe, as a species of monsters, or exotics, that were not very likely to propagate, or thrive, in so unpropitious a climate. Mr Southey, however, has made a vigorous effort for their naturalization, and generously endangered his own reputation in their behalf. The melancholy fate of his English sapphics, we believe, is but too generally known; and we can scarcely predict a more favourable issue to the present experiment. Every combination of different measures is apt to perplex and disturb the reader who is not familiar with it; and we are never reconciled to a stanza of a new structure, till we have accustomed our ear to it by two or three repetitions. This is the case, even where we have the assistance of rhyme to direct us in our search after regularity, and where the definite form and appearance of a stanza assures us that regularity is to be found. Where both of these are wanting, it may be imagined that our condition will be still more deplorable; and a compassionate author might even excuse us, if we were unable to distinguish this kind of verse from prose. In reading verse, in general, we are guided to the discovery of its melody, by a sort of preconception of its cadence and compass; without which, it might often fail to be suggested by the mere articulation of the syllables. If there be any one, whose recollection does not furnish him with evidence of this fact, he may put it to the test of experiment, by desiring any of his illiterate acquaintances to read off some of Mr Southey's dactylics, or Sir Philip Sydney's hexameters. It is the same thing with the more unusual measures of the antient authors. We have never known any one who fell in, at the first trial, with the proper rhythm and cadence of the *pervigilium Veneris*,[1] or the choral lyrics of the Greek dramatists. The difficulty, however, is virtually the same, as to every new combination; and it is an unsurmountable difficulty, where such new combinations are not repeated with any degree of uniformity, but are multiplied, through the whole composition, with an unbounded license of variation. Such, however,

[1] An anonymous Latin poem to love and springtime, probably written between the second and the fifth centuries A.D.

is confessedly the case with the work before us; and it really seems unnecessary to make any other remark on its versification.

The author, however, entertains a different opinion of it. So far from apprehending that it may cost his readers some trouble to convince themselves that the greater part of the book is not mere prose, written out into the form of verse, he is persuaded that its melody is more obvious and perceptible than that of our vulgar measures. 'One advantage,' says Mr Southey, 'this metre *assuredly* possesses; the dullest reader cannot distort it into discord: he may read it with a *prose mouth*, but its flow and fall will still be perceptible.' We are afraid, there are duller readers in the world than Mr Southey is aware of. We recommend the following passages for experiment.

> 'The Day of the Trial will come,
> When I shall understand how profitable
> It is to suffer now.'

> Hodeirah groaned and closed his eyes,
> As if in the night and the blindness of death
> He would have hid himself.

> 'Blessed art thou, young man,
> Blessed art thou, O Aswad, for the deed!
> In the day of visitation,
> In the fearful hour of judgment,
> God will remember thee!'

> 'It is the hour of prayer, . .
> My children, let us purify ourselves
> And praise the Lord our God!'
> The boy the water brought;
> After the law they purified themselves,
> And bent their faces to the earth in prayer.

> Azure and yellow, like the beautiful fields
> Of England, when amid the growing grass
> The blue-bell bends, the golden king-cup shines,
> In the merry month of May!

> But Thalaba took not the draught,
> For rightly he knew had the Prophet forbidden
> That beverage the mother of sins.

> The blinded multitude
> Adored the Sorcerer,
> And bent the knee before him,

And shouted out his praise,
'Mighty art thou, the Bestower of joy,
The Lord of Paradise!'

Dizzy with the deafening strokes,
In blind and interrupted course,
Poor beast, he struggles on;
And now the dogs are nigh!
How his heart pants! you see
The panting of his heart;
And tears like human tears
Roll down, along the big veins——

—————————— they perished all,
All in that dreadful hour: but I was saved
To remember and revenge.

Like the flowing of a Summer gale he felt
Its ineffectual force;
His countenance was not changed,
Nor a hair of his head was singed.

'Aye! look and triumph!' he exclaimed,
'This is the justice of thy God!
A righteous God is he, to let
His vengeance fall upon the innocent head!
Curse thee, curse thee, Thalaba!'

With what a thirst of joy
He should breathe in the open gales of heaven!

Vain are all spells! the Destroyer
Treads the Domdaniel floor.

'Thou hast done well, my Servant!
Ask and receive thy reward!'

Mr Southey must excuse us for doubting, whether even a *poet's
mouth* could turn these passages into good verse; and we are afraid, the
greater part of his readers will participate in our scepticism.

The subject of this poem is almost as ill chosen as the diction; and
the conduct of the fable as disorderly as the versification. The corporation of magicians, that inhabit 'the Domdaniel caverns, under the roots
of the ocean,' had discovered, that a terrible *destroyer* was likely to rise
up against them from the seed of Hodeirah, a worthy Arab, with eight
fine children. Immediately the murder of all those innocents is resolved
on; and a sturdy assassin sent with instructions to destroy the whole

family (as Mr Southey has it) 'root and branch.' The good man, accordingly, and seven of his children are despatched: But a cloud comes over the mother and the remaining child; and the poem opens with the picture of the widow and her orphan, wandering, by night, over the deserts of Arabia. The old lady, indeed, might as well have fallen under the dagger of the Domdanielite; for she dies without doing any thing for her child, in the end of the first book; and little Thalaba is left crying in the wilderness. Here he is picked up by a good old Arab, who takes him home, and educates him like a pious mussulman; and he and the old man's daughter fall in love with each other, according to the invariable custom in all such cases. The magicians, in the mean time, are hunting him over the face of the whole earth; and one of them gets near enough to draw his dagger to stab him, when a providential *simoom* lays him dead on the sand. From the dead sorcerer's finger, Thalaba takes a ring, inscribed with some unintelligible characters, which he is enabled to interpret by the help of some other unintelligible characters that he finds on the forehead of a locust; and soon after takes advantage of an eclipse of the sun, to set out on his expedition against his father's murderers, whom he understands (we do not very well know how) he has been commissioned to exterminate. Though they are thus seeking him, and he seeking them, it is amazing what difficulty they find in meeting: they do meet, however, every now and then, and many sore evils does the Destroyer suffer at their hands. By faith and fortitude, however, and the occasional assistance of the magic implements he strips them of, he is enabled to baffle and elude their malice, till he is conducted, at last, to the Domdaniel cavern, where he finds them assembled, and pulls down the roof of it upon their heads and his own; perishing, like Samson, in the final destruction of his enemies.

From this little sketch of the story, our readers will easily perceive, that it consists altogether of the most wild and extravagant fictions, and openly sets nature and probability at defiance. In its action it is not an imitation of any thing; and excludes all rational criticism, as to the choice and succession of its incidents. Tales of this sort may amuse children, and interest, for a moment, by the prodigies they exhibit, and the multitude of events they bring together: but the interest expires with the novelty; and attention is frequently exhausted, even before curiosity has been gratified. The pleasure afforded by performances of this sort, is very much akin to that which may be derived from the exhibition of a harlequin farce; where, instead of just imitations of nature and human character, we are entertained with the transformation of cauliflowers and beer-barrels, the apparition of ghosts and devils, and all the other magic of the wooden sword. Those who can prefer this eternal sorcery to the just and modest representation of human actions and passions, will probably take more delight in walking among the holly griffins and yew sphinxes of the city gardener, than in ranging among the groves and lawns which have been laid out by a hand that feared to violate nature, as much as it aspired to embellish her; and disdained the easy art of startling by novelties, and surprising by impropriety.

Supernatural beings, though easily enough raised, are known to be very troublesome in the management, and have frequently occasioned much perplexity to poets and other persons, who have been rash enough to call for their assistance. It is no very easy matter to preserve consistency in the disposal of powers, with the limits of which we are so far from being familiar; and when it is necessary to represent our spiritual persons as ignorant, or suffering, we are very apt to forget the knowledge and the powers with which we had formerly invested them. The antient poets had several unlucky encounters of this sort with Destiny and the other deities; and Milton himself is not a little hampered with the material and immaterial qualities of his angels. Enchanters and witches may, at first sight, appear more manageable; but Mr Southey has had difficulty enough with them; and cannot be said, after all, to have kept his fable quite clear and intelligible. The stars had said, that the Destroyer might be cut off in that hour when his father and brethren were assassinated; yet he is saved by a special interposition of heaven. Heaven itself, however, had destined him to extirpate the votaries of Eblis; and yet, long before this work is done, a special message is sent to him, declaring, that, if he chooses, the Death-angel is ready to take him away instead of the sorcerer's daughter. In the beginning of the story, too, the magicians are quite at a loss where to look for him; and Abdaldar only discovers him by accident, after a long search; yet, no sooner does he leave the old Arab's tent, than Lobaba comes up to him, disguised and prepared for his destruction. The witches have also a decoy ready for him in the desart; yet he sups with Okba's daughter, without any of the sorcerers being aware of it; and afterwards proceeds to consult the simorg, without meeting with any obstacle or molestation. The simoom kills Abdaldar, too, in spite of that ring which afterwards protects Thalaba from lightning, and violence, and magic. The Destroyer's arrow then falls blunted from

Lobaba's breast, who is knocked down, however, by a shower of sand of his own raising; and this same arrow, which could make no impression on the sorcerer, kills the magic bird of Aloadin, and pierces the rebellious *spirit* that guarded the Domdaniel door. The whole infernal band, indeed, is very feebly and heavily pourtrayed. They are a set of stupid, undignified, miserable wretches, quarrelling with each other, and trembling in the prospect of inevitable destruction. None of them even appears to have obtained the price of their self-sacrifice in worldly honours and advancement, except Mohareb; and he, though assured by destiny that there was one death-blow appointed for him and Thalaba, is yet represented, in the concluding scene, as engaged with him in furious combat, and aiming many a deadly blow at that life on which his own was dependent. If the innocent characters in this poem were not delineated with more truth and feeling, the notoriety of the author would scarcely have induced us to bestow so much time on its examination.

Though the tissue of adventures through which Thalaba is conducted in the course of this production, be sufficiently various and extraordinary, we must not set down any part of the incidents to the credit of the author's invention. He has taken great pains, indeed, to guard against such a supposition; and has been as scrupulously correct in the citation of his authorities, as if he were the compiler of a true history, and thought his reputation would be ruined by the imputation of a single fiction. There is not a prodigy, accordingly, or a description, for which he does not fairly produce his vouchers, and generally lays before his readers the whole original passage from which his imitation has been taken. In this way, it turns out, that the book is entirely composed of scraps, borrowed from the oriental tale books, and travels into the Mahometan countries seasoned up for the English reader with some fragments of our own ballads, and shreds of our older sermons. The composition and harmony of the work, accordingly, is much like the pattern of that patchwork drapery that is sometimes to be met with in the mansions of the industrious, where a blue tree overshadows a shell-fish, and a gigantic butterfly seems ready to swallow up Palemon and Lavinia. The author has the merit merely of cutting out each of his figures from the piece where its inventor had placed it, and stitching them down together in these judicious combinations.

It is impossible to peruse this poem, with the notes, without feeling that it is the fruit of much reading, undertaken for the express purpose of fabricating some such performance. The author has set out with a resolution to make an oriental story, and a determination to find the materials of it in the books to which he had access. Every incident, therefore, and description,—every superstitious usage, or singular tradition, that appeared to him susceptible of poetical embellishment, or capable of picturesque representation, he has set down for this purpose, and adopted such a fable and plan of composition, as might enable him to work up all his materials, and interweave every one of his quotations, without any *extraordinary* violation of unity or order. When he had filled his commonplace book, he began to write; and his poem is little else than his commonplace book versified.

It may easily be imagined, that a poem constructed upon such a plan, must be full of cumbrous and misplaced description, and overloaded with a crowd of incidents, equally unmeaning and ill assorted. The tedious account of the palace of Shedad, in the first book—the description of the Summer and Winter occupations of the Arabs, in the third—the ill-told story of Haruth and Maruth—the greater part of the occurrences in the island of Mohareb—the paradise of Aloadin, &c. &c.—are all instances of disproportioned and injudicious ornaments, which never could have presented themselves to an author who wrote from the suggestions of his own fancy; and have evidently been introduced, from the author's unwillingness to relinquish the corresponding passages in D'Herbelot, Sale, Volney, &c. which appeared to him to have great capabilities for poetry.

This imitation, or admiration of Oriental imagery, however, does not bring so much suspicion on his taste, as the affection he betrays for some of his domestic models. The former has, for the most part, the recommendation of novelty; and there is always a certain pleasure in contemplating the *costume* of a distant nation, and the luxuriant landscape of an Asiatic climate. We cannot find the same apology, however, for Mr Southey's partiality to the drawling vulgarity of some of our old English ditties. Here is what he has been pleased to present to his readers (in a note), as 'one of the most beautiful of our old ballads, so full of beauty.' The heroine is an old *mare* belonging to John Poulter.

> At length old age came on her
>   And she grew faint and poor,
> Her master he fell out with her
>   And turned her out of door,
> Saying, if thou wilt not labour,
>   I prithee go thy way,—

And never let me see thy face
Until thy dying day.
These words she took unkind,
And on her way she went,
For to fulfil her master's will
Always was her intent.
The hills were very high,
The vallies very bare,
The Summer it was hot and dry—
It starved Old Poulter's mare.

There are three stanzas more; but we shall only add the last. Old Poulter repents, and sends his man Will to bring the mare back. Will, at first, cannot find her; but, as he is thinking of giving up the search,

He went a little farther
And turned his head aside,
And just by goodman Whitfield's gate
Oh there the Mare he spied.
He asked her how she did,
She stared him in the face,
Then down she laid her head again,—
She was in wretched case.

These three last lines, Mr Southey seriously considers as the *ne plus ultra* of purity and pathos.

The text certainly is not, by any means, so bad as might have been expected from such a note; though there are some passages, in which a patriotic zeal for neglected English authors has made him copy their style a little too faithfully. Could the great master of *Namby Pamby* have lisped out his repetitions in blank verse, with more amiable simplicity than in the following passage? The author is describing a certain spring, that, he says, 'tossed and heaved strangely up and down.'

And yet the depths were clear,
And yet no ripple wrinkled o'er
The face of that fair Well.

And on that Well so strange and fair
A little boat there lay,
Without an oar, without a sail:
One only seat it had, one seat
As if for only Thalaba.
And at the helm a Damsel stood,
A Damsel bright and bold of eye;

Yet did a maiden modesty
Adorn her fearless brow.
She seemed sorrowful, but sure
More beautiful for sorrow.

From the extracts and observations which we have hitherto presented to our readers, it will be natural for them to conclude, that our
opinion of this poem is very decidedly unfavourable; and that we are
not disposed to allow it any sort of merit. This, however, is by no
means the case. We think it written, indeed, in a very vicious taste, and
liable, upon the whole, to very formidable objections: But it would
not be doing justice to the genius of the author, if we were not to add,
that it contains passages of very singular beauty and force, and displays
a richness of poetical conception, that would do honour to more
faultless compositions. There is little of human character in the poem,
indeed; because Thalaba is a solitary wanderer from the solitary tent
of his protector: But the home group, in which his infancy was spent,
is pleasingly delineated; and there is something irresistibly interesting
in the innocent love and misfortunes, and fate of his Oneiza. The
catastrophe of her story is given, it appears to us, with great spirit and
effect, though the beauties are of that questionable kind, that trespass
on the border of impropriety, and partake more of the character of
dramatic, than of narrative poetry. After delivering her from the
polluted paradise of Aloadin, he prevails on her to marry him before
his mission is accomplished. She consents with great reluctance; and
the marriage feast, with its processions, songs, and ceremonies, is
described in some joyous stanzas. The book ends with these verses:

And now the marriage feast is spread,
And from the finished banquet now
The wedding guests are gone.

Who comes from the bridal chamber?
It is Azrael, the Angel of Death.

The next book opens with Thalaba lying distracted upon her grave,
in the neighbourhood of which he had wandered till 'the sun, and the
wind, and the rain, had rusted his raven locks;' and there he is found
by the father of his bride, and visited by her ghost, and soothed and
encouraged to proceed upon his holy enterprize. He sets out on his
lonely way, and is entertained the first night by a venerable dervise:
As they are sitting at meal, a *bridal procession* passes by, with dance, and
song, and merriment. The old dervise blessed them as they passed; but

Thalaba looked, 'and breathed a low deep groan, and hid his face.'
These incidents are skilfully imagined, and are narrated in a very
impressive manner.

Though the *witchery* scenes are in general but poorly executed, and
possess little novelty to those who have read the Arabian Nights'
Entertainments, there is, occasionally, some fine description, and
striking combination. We do not remember any poem indeed that
presents, throughout, a greater number of lively images, or could
afford so many subjects for the pencil.

The introductory lines have a certain solemn and composed beauty:

> How beautiful is night!
> A dewy freshness fills the silent air;
> No mist obscures, no little cloud
> Breaks the whole serene of heaven:
> In full-orbed glory the majestic moon
> Rolls thro' the dark blue depths.
> Beneath her steady ray
> The desert circle spreads,
> Like the round ocean, girdled with the sky.
> How beautiful is night!

There are many fine sketches of tropical scenery in the description
of Aloadin's Paradise. The following verses breathe the true spirit of
Oriental poetry.

> And oh! what odours the voluptuous vale
> Scatters from jasmine bowers,
> From yon rose wilderness,
> From clustered henna, and from orange groves
> That with such perfumes fill the breeze,
> As Peris to their Sister bear,
> When from the summit of some lofty tree
> She hangs, encaged, the captive of the Dives.
>
> They from their pinions shake
> The sweetness of celestial flowers,
> And as her enemies impure
> From that impervious poison far away
> Fly groaning with the torment, she the while
> Inhales her fragrant food.
> Such odours flowed upon the world,
> When at Mohammed's nuptials, word
> Went forth in heaven to roll

The everlasting gates of Paradise
Back on their living hinges, that its gales
Might visit all below; the general bliss
Thrilled every bosom, and the family
Of man, for once, partook one common joy.

The picture of Maimuna sitting by a fire in a solitary cavern, and singing 'a low, sweet, unintelligible song' as she spun, reminds us of the appearance of Calypso in the *Odyssey*. . . .

Maimuna's figure is very striking, too, when she goes up to read the stars.

Lo! on the terrace of the topmost tower
She stands; her darkening eyes,
Her fine face raised to heaven,
Her white hair flowing like the silver streams
That streak the northern night.

The little episode of Laila is one of the most pleasing passages in the whole poem; though it is quite in the style of a fairy tale, and borders on silliness throughout. In the midst of a desart of snow, Thalaba descries a distant light, and finds, on his approach, that it proceeds from

———a little lowly dwelling place,
Amid a garden, whose delightful air
Felt mild and fragrant, as the evening wind
Passing in Summer o'er the coffee-groves
Of Yemen, and its blessed bowers of balm.
A Fount of Fire that in the centre played,
Rolled all around its wonderous rivulets,
And fed the garden with the heat of life.

He enters, and finds a damsel sleeping, who afterwards informs him that she was placed there by her father, who 'saw a danger in her horoscope,' and hid her in that solitude.

——— he made this dwelling, and the grove,
And yonder fountain-fire; and every morn
He visits me, and takes the snow, and moulds
Women and men, like thee; and breathes into them
Motion, and life, and sense, . . but to the touch
They are chilling cold, and ever when night closes
They melt away again, and leave me here
Alone and sad.

She then tells him, that her father had also constructed a guardian of the garden; which, when he asks to see,

> She took him by the hand,
> And thro' the porch they past.
> Over the garden and the grove
> The fountain streams of fire
> Poured a broad light like noon;
> A broad unnatural light
> That made the Rose's blush of beauty pale,
> And dimmed the rich Geranium's scarlet blaze.
> The various verdure of the grove
> Now wore one undistinguishable grey,
> Chequered with blacker shade.

The guardian was a brazen figure, grasping a thunderbolt. As soon as Thalaba appeared,

> The charmed image knew Hodeirah's son,
> And hurled the lightning at the dreaded foe.

His ring saves him; but the Old Magician comes and tells the Destroyer, that he must either kill that innocent maid, or die himself.

> Around her father's neck
> Still Laila's hands were clasped.
> Her face was turned to Thalaba,
> A broad light floated o'er its marble paleness,
> As the wind waved the fountain fire.
> Her large dilated eye, in horror raised,
> Watched his every movement.

Thalaba refuses to stain his hands in the blood of innocence. The Magician, exulting, draws his dagger.

> All was accomplished. Laila rushed between
> To save the saviour Youth.
> She met the blow, and sunk into his arms,
> And Azrael from the hands of Thalaba
> Received her parting soul.

There is some very fine poetry in the two concluding books, from which we would willingly make some extracts, if we had not already extended this article to an unusual length, and given such a specimen of the merits and defects of this performance, as will probably be sufficient to determine the judgment of our readers.

All the productions of this author, it appears to us, bear very distinctly the impression of an amiable mind, a cultivated fancy, and a perverted taste. His genius seems naturally to delight in the representation of domestic virtues and pleasures, and the brilliant delineation of external nature. In both these departments, he is frequently very successful; but he seems to want vigour for the loftier flights of poetry. He is often puerile, diffuse, and artificial, and seems to have but little acquaintance with those chaster and severer graces, by whom the epic muse would be most suitably attended. His faults are always aggravated, and often created, by his partiality for the peculiar manner of that new school of poetry, of which he is a faithful disciple, and to the glory of which, he has sacrificed greater talents and acquisitions, than can be boasted of by any of his associates.

19. William Taylor, unsigned review, *Critical Review*

December 1803, 2nd series, xxxix, 369-79

From the opening of the review.

Taylor (1765-1836), author, reviewer and central figure in the important literary and intellectual society of Norwich, was a close friend of Southey from 1798 until his death. He contributed several generally favourable reviews of Southey's early poetry to a number of different periodicals. In a letter of 1804 Southey described him as 'one of the three great men of my acquaintance, and the more I know him and the longer I know him, the more do I admire his knowledge and love his moral character' (Curry, i, p. 351).

Southey described this review as 'very characteristic of his style, talents, and good-will for the author' (*Life*, ii, p. 287).

Perhaps no work of art so imperfect ever announced such power in the artist—perhaps no artist so powerful ever rested his fame on so imperfect a production—as *Thalaba*. The author calls it a metrical romance; he might have called it a lyrical one; for the story is told, as in an ode, by implication; not directly, as in an epopœïa. It is a gallery of successive pictures. Each is strikingly descriptive: the circumstances strongly delineated, and well selected; but the personages, like the figures of landscape-painters, are often almost lost in the scene: they appear as the episodical or accessory objects. We observe the sea in storm, beating its waves of foam against a cloud-capt rock; but we scarcely heed the stranded corse of Cëyx, or the wild woe of Alcyone. The painter is as accomplished as Poussin: the vigilance of his mind is exerted in the minutest as in the greatest features: not a tree which the botanist, not a building which the architect, not a drapery which the costume-studier, not an emotion which the actor, would wish away or wish otherwise: everywhere warm fancy, exquisite feeling, busy thought. Yet these are not historical pieces, which is what one expects; but views, prospects, descriptions merely, in which the historical anecdotes occur, as if by accident, in order. It is theatric representation reversed: the places seem the realities; the actors the fictitious existences.

No arguments are prefixed to the books of *Thalaba*; in many places it would be difficult to infer the argument, and to write down, in lucid order, the adventures of the personages. Every being bursts into luminousness, like figures in the phantasmagoria; and, before one can ask, Whence and whither dost thou fly? another springs before us more mysterious and aweful, which, in its turn, becomes distincter as it recedes. The verse itself seems to have the wildness and the power of incantation; to call down at will the moon from heaven, or build a palace in the desert; to bid the gardens of Paradise blossom, or the destroying Samiel commence his blast.

So novel a romance it is difficult to praise or to blame too much; and it is more natural, or at least more in unison with the tone of the poem, to do both rhapsodically than methodically, as the alternate but not evanescent impressions occur, than, according to the prescriptive rules of criticism, by the successive analysis of fable, characters, machinery, and style, and the orderly discussion of its historic, ethic, fantastic, and phraseologic peculiarities.

The first time this poem is perused, if it be allowed to judge of others by ourselves, it leaves a strong, but a confused and confusing impression: the memory has attached to itself many a grand moment, many a terrible picture; but there is a want of concatenation, of mutual dependence, of natural arrangement, which renders it impossible to revert in their order to the several parts of the narrative. The adventures do not enough grow out of one another: the fable somewhat wants cohesion: nor is it wholly consistent. The more abrupt and lyrical the form of narration, the more obvious and connected should be the structure of the story: the more wild and rambling the march of event, the more lucid and historical should be the form of narration.

But, after repeating the perusal, when an outline of the story is mapped in the mind, when the main design is become distinct, when the distractions of surprise have relented, and the impatience of curiosity is benumbed, the poem will be frequently interrupted, to give vent to interjections of applause, and to break loose into thrilling exultations of delight.

The hero, however, is far from being an interesting character. His motives are not of this world. His hopes, his fears, his loves, are alien to human nature. A child of destiny, miraculously reared to destroy, by the seisure of talismans, a subterraneous convent of magicians, has little to recommend him to our warm sympathy. These magicians render themselves odious by their attempts on the life of Thalaba; but, in the first instance, they seem to have a right to their house and home. When, at length, this enchanted dwelling crumbles to pieces, and buries the hero in its ruins, we find an end, but not the end of the story. Moral marvels (and the mind of Thalaba, exalted by some unaccountable faith to an indifference for danger, is one) do not act in the imagination like physical marvels. We attribute inferior powers to the mind, and superior powers to the matter, whose extraordinary operations are the subject of our wonder. When the shepherds come to see Orlando, pulling up trees to trouble the rivulet, they call him insane; but, if they had seen a whirlwind do the same, they would have considered the object as sublime. We know by intuition the laws of mind, and can perceive that the absence of caprice is a perfection. But what we suspect of the laws of nature is mere inference from outside appearance: we think, therefore, most highly of that nature, whose outside appearance is most striking. Hence fanaticism, which generates moral miracles, is one of the worst—and magic, which generates physical miracles, one of the best—topics for a poet. Schiller's *Joan of Arc* is too fanatical to interest; we only wish her in Bedlam. Mr. Southey, in the delineation of that heroine, has kept within prudent limits; but the characters in *Thalaba* have something supernatural in their turn of mind, which surely intercepts very much our fellow-feeling.

Indeed, the supernatural characters are the proper heroes of this poem: it is a war of the gods: the action passes among the machinery; every utensil is a talisman; every speech a spell; every incident a prodigy. The figures that appear human are dæmons in disguise, or genii metamorphosed; and even the most natural appearances are effects, not of nature, but of magic. Conformably to the advice of Petronius, the poet is more among deities than men: but what is gained in grandeur is lost in participation. The marvellous must have its conditions, or it mars the moral agency. Where the most gordian knot of difficulty can be untied with an amulet; where a simoom can paralyse the assassin, who has overcome all other difficulties; where every possible change of situation is equally probable; that anxiety is seldom excited, which human energy struggling with difficulty never fails to inspire. Machinery is most in its place when it decorates, without influencing, the human action of the epopœïa. If Pallas descend from heaven, and command Achilles to sheath his sword, there already existed, in his sense of subordination, a sufficient motive for his conduct. If Jupiter be detained on Ida by his consort, while the party he favoured suffers discomfiture, there is still a sufficient quantity of human effort in motion to account for all the terrestrial events. Iris may assume the form of Laodice, to draw Helen to the Scæan gate; but if Iris had not done it, the real Laodice would. Let the gods be busy, but like the sylphs in *The Rape of the Lock*, so that the whole action could go on as well without as with their interposition; else the epic poet will fall short of the dramatist in exciting the trepidations of sympathy.

The style of *Thalaba* has a plasticity and variety, of which epic poetry offers no other example. The favourite formulas of every school of diction have been acquired, and are employed. Many passages display the genitive substances and conjunctions-copulative of the Hebrew, many the picturesque circumstantiality of the Italian, and many the interjected onomatopœias of the German writers: less predilection is shown for the compound adjectives of the Greeks, for the sentences without particles of the Latins, or the abstract allegoric personifications of the English. In turn, the ballad lends its affecting simplicity, the heroic poem its learned solemnity, the drama its dialogue form, and the ode its versatility of metre. All the fountains of expression are brought together, and gush, with sousing vehemence and drifting rapidity, on the reader; who admires, but not at ease, and feels tossed as in the pool of a cataract, not gliding as on a frequented stream. This stunning impression of the style gives pain, we believe, especially to mere English scholars, and to those whose comparison of art is narrow and confined, but falls within the limits of pleasure, and is even a cause of luxurious stimulation, to readers of a wider range and a more tolerant taste. The epithets are judiciously chosen; they are never trivial, never superfluous; they are accommodated, not merely to the substantive they accompany, but to the point of view in which it then attracts notice; and they are studiously picturesque and striking. The more extended sweeps of description are executed with equal skill: the selection of circumstance is always exquisite; the imagery suggested to the mind is always sensible, vivid, distinct. Thomson and Cowper are among the best of our describers; but they are surely left behind by the descriptions in *Thalaba*: there is here no pedantry, no Latin verbiage incapable of exciting pictures in the mind, no substitutions of personified abstractions to definite sensible action. We think, however, that spirit, neatness, and conciseness, might yet, in many places, be added, by expunging superfluous particles, *ands*, *ofs*, *ors*, and *auxiliaries*: that some lines cannot appear metrical, even on the new principles; for instance (iv. 202)—

> *And his camel than the monstrous elephant—*

and that a more habitual use, in the merely narrative passages, of decasyllabic blank verse would diminish the public prejudice against the language.

[Summarizes plot with lengthy quotations.]

AMADIS OF GAUL

1803

Translated and abridged by Southey from the Spanish. Although he thought that the work, published in four small volumes by Longman, was 'most abominably printed' (*Life*, ii, p. 228), Southey was pleased with the success of *Amadis*, which sold 'as much in one year as *Thalaba* in three'. By July 1804 more than half the edition of 1,000 copies had been sold (*Life*, ii, pp. 298, 301).

---

20. Walter Scott on Southey as translator, *Edinburgh Review*

October 1803, iii, 109–36

From his unsigned review. Scott and Southey did not meet until 1805, after which they remained on friendly terms until Scott's death. In 1813 he was instrumental in securing the Laureateship for Southey (see No. 48).

It remains to make some observations on Mr Southey's mode of executing his translation, which appears to us marked with the hand of a master. The abridgements are judiciously made; and although some readers may think too much has still been retained, yet the objection will only occur to such as read merely for the story, without any attention to Mr Southey's more important object of exhibiting a correct example of those romances, by which our forefathers were so much delighted, and from which we may draw such curious inferences respecting their customs, their morals, and their modes of thinking.

The popular romance always preserves, to a certain degree, the manners of the age in which it was written. The novels of Fielding and Richardson are even already become valuable, as a record of the English manners of the last generation. How much, then, should we prize the volumes which describe those of the era of the victors of Cressy and Poitiers! The style of Mr Southey is, in general, what he proposed, rather antique, from the form of expression, than from the introduction of obsolete phrases. It has something of the scriptural turn, and much resembles the admirable translation of Froissart. Some words have inadvertently been used, which, to us, savour more of vulgarity than beseems the language of chivalry. Such are the phrases, 'devilry,' 'Sir Knave,' 'Don False One,' and some others. But we only mention these, to show that our general praise has not been inconsiderately bestowed.

21. From an unsigned review, *British Critic*

November 1804, xxiv, 471–81

Only the final paragraph of the review, reprinted here, refers to Southey's achievement as a translator.

We can recommend this work with confidence, and without any of those abatements which we have been sometimes compelled to make from the praise we bestowed on the original productions of Mr. Southey. The style has an air of antiquity suitable to the subjects of the narrative; and the occasional instances of rude and savage nakedness, which appear in the original, are with great propriety veiled in the translation. We are, however, surprised, that the translator, who is himself a poet, should have presented the public with the old English version of the Sonnets which occur in this romance, and which, as it is rendered from the French of Herberay, he justly denominates 'the

shadow of a shade'. We are still more surprised, that in his Introduction or Preface, he should have published a Portuguese Sonnet of
1403, without any version; since he must be aware that only a small
proportion of the learned are conversant in that language, and that his
Amadis of Gaul will be read by thousands, who are acquainted with no
language but their mother tongue.

MADOC

1805

Although not published until 1805 most of *Madoc* was written before *Thalaba*. One modern critic has described it as 'the longest, the least successful, the most tedious' of the epics (Simmons, p. 209). Southey himself thought that its merits lay in the execution and not in the subject matter: 'The story wants unity, and has perhaps too Greek—too Stoical a want of passion—but as far as I can see with the same eyes wherewith I read Homer and Spenser and Shakespere and Milton, it is still a good poem, and must live' (Curry, i, p. 388).

Madoc was expensively produced. Since Southey had agreed to divide the profits with Longman he was disturbed: 'By its high price, one half the edition is condemned to be furniture in expensive libraries, and the other to collect cobwebs in the publishers' warehouses. I foresee that I shall get no solid pudding by it' (*Life*, ii, p. 328). His profits were, in fact, very small (see Introduction, p. 24).

22. Wordsworth, from two letters to Sir George Beaumont

3 June, 29 July 1805

Reprinted from *The Letters of William and Dorothy Wordsworth, 1787–1805*, 2nd edn revised by C. L. Shaver (1967), pp. 595, 610.

(a) We have read *Madoc*, and been highly pleased with it; it abounds in beautiful pictures and descriptions happily introduced, and there is an animation diffused through the whole story though it cannot perhaps be said that any of the characters interest you much, except perhaps young Llewellyn whose situation is highly interesting, and he appears to me the best conceived and sustained character in the piece. His speech to his Uncle at their meeting in the Island is particularly interesting. The Poem fails in the highest gifts of the poet's mind Imagination in the true sense of the word, and knowledge of human Nature and the human heart. There is nothing that shows the hand of the great Master: but the beauties in description are innumerable; for instance that of the figure of the Bard towards the beginning of the convention of the bards, receiving the poetic inspiration, that of the wife of Tlalalu the Savage going out to meet her husband; that of Madoc and the Aztecan King with the long name preparing for battle, everywhere, indeed, you have beautiful descriptions, and it is a work which does the Author high credit, I think. I should like to know your opinion of it.

(b) I am glad you like the passage in *Madoc* about Llewellyn. Southey's mind does not seem strong enough to draw the picture of a Hero. The character of Madoc is often very insipid and contemptible, for instance when he is told that the Hoamen have surprized Caer-Madoc and of course (he has reason to believe) butcher'd or carried away all the women and children, what does the author make him Do? Think of Goervyl and Llayan, very tenderly forsooth; but not a word about his people! In short, according to my notion, the char-

acter is throughout languidly conceived and as you observe the contrast between him and Llewellyn makes him look very mean. I made
a mistake when I pointed out a beautiful passage as being in the
beginning of the meeting of the bards: it occurs before and ends thus,

> His eyes were closed;
> His head, as if in reverence to receive
> The inspiration, bent: and as he raised
> His glowing Countenance and brighter eye
> And swept with passionate hands the ringing harp.

23. Dorothy Wordsworth, from a letter to Lady Beaumont

11 June 1805

Reprinted from *The Letters of William and Dorothy Wordsworth,
1787–1805*, 2nd edn revised by C. L. Shaver (1967), pp. 600–1.

We have read *Madoc* with great delight, but I will tell you more of
my own particular sentiments of it when I have read it again to
myself. I had one painful feeling throughout, that I did not care as
much about Madoc as the Author wished me to do, and that the
characters in general are not sufficiently distinct to make them have a
separate after-existence in my affections. We were all exceedingly
interested for young Lewellyn, but the women, except Erillyab, do
not seem to me to differ much from women as represented in our
better modern novels, and I could not discover that the characters of
Emma and Goervyl were discriminated from each other. Yet the
manner of telling the story is exceedingly spirited, and the attention is
always kept awake. As you observe the descriptions are often exceedingly beautiful,—they are like resting-places both for repose and
delight. The language occasionally, nay *frequently* gave me pain, and

mostly in cases where it seemed that a very little trouble might have removed the faults. I have not the Book here or I would take down a few of those expressions which I complain of. They are a sort of barbarisms which appear to belong to Southey himself. But indeed I seem to be talking very conceitedly and almost as if I thought I were a great Critic—so I must end with saying again that we have read the Poem with the greatest delight, and I expect much more from reading it alone, for there is a weakness in my mind which makes it exceedingly difficult for me to remember or even *understand* a story when it is read aloud. I do not think I lost much of the spirit of it in this first reading, I mean of the *manner* &c. but many of the incidents escaped from me.

24. John Ferriar, unsigned review, *Monthly Review*

October 1805, n.s. xlviii, 113–22

Ferriar (1761–1815), a Scottish doctor and physician at the Manchester Royal Infirmary, was a regular contributor to the *Monthly Review*. In 1805 he published hostile reviews of both Southey's *Metrical Tales* and *Madoc*. On the present review Southey commented: 'It is stupid and blunt ill nature. A bluebottle fly wriggling his tail and fancying he has a sting in it' (Curry, i, p. 408).

It has fallen to the lot of this writer to puzzle our critical discernment more than once. In the *Annual Anthology*, we had reason to complain that it was difficult to distinguish his jocular from his serious poetry; and sometimes indeed to know his poetry from prose. He has now contrived to manufacture a large quarto, which he has styled a poem, but of what description it is no easy matter to decide. The title of epic, which he indignantly disclaims, we might have been inclined to refuse his production, had it been claimed; and we suppose that Mr. Southey would not suffer it to be classed under the mock-heroic. The poem of *Madoc* is not didactic, nor elegiac, nor classical, in any respect. Neither is it *Macphersonic*, nor *Klopstockian*, nor *Darwinian,*—we beg pardon, we mean *Brookian*. To conclude, according to a phrase of the last century, which was applied to ladies of ambiguous character, *it is what it is.*—As Mr. Southey has set the rules of Aristotle at defiance in his preface, we hope that he will feel a due degree of gratitude for this appropriate definition of his work. It is an old saying, thoroughly descriptive of such an old song as this before us. . . .

Respecting the manners, Mr. Southey appears to have been more successful than in his choice of the story. He has adhered to history where he could discover any facts adapted to his purpose; and when history failed him, he has had recourse to probability. Yet we own that the nomenclature of his heroes has shocked what Mr. S. would call our prejudices. *Coervyl* and *Ririd* and *Rodri* and *Llaian* may have charms for Cambrian ears, but who can feel an interest in *Tezozomoc*, *Tlalala*, or *Ocelopan*? Or, should

> —— —— Tyneio, Merini,
> Boda and Brenda and Aelgyvarch,
> Gwynon and Celynin and Gwynodyl, (p. 129.)

> Those rugged names to our like mouths grow sleek,
> That would have made Quintilian stare and gasp,[1]

how could we swallow *Yuhidthiton*, *Coanocotzin*, and, above all, the yawning jaw-dislocating *Ayayaca*?—These torturing words, particularly the latter, remind us so strongly of the odious cacophony of the Nurse and Child, that they really are not to be tolerated. Mr. Southey's defence (for he has partially anticipated this objection) is that the names are conformable to history or analogy, which we are not inclined to dispute: but it is not requisite to tread so closely in the traces of barbarity. Truth does not constitute the essence of poetry: but it is indispensably necessary that the lines should be agreeable to the ear, as well as to the sense. Sorry, indeed, we are to complain that Mr. Southey, in attempting a new method of writing,—in professing to set aside the old models, and to promote his own work to a distinguished place in the library,—has failed to interest our feelings, or to excite our admiration. The dull tenor of mediocrity, which characterizes his pages, is totally unsuitable to heroic poetry, regular or irregular. Instead of

[1] Milton, Sonnet xi: 'A Book was writ of late'.

viewing him on a *fiery Pegasus*, and 'snatching a grace beyond the reach of art,' we behold the author mounted on a strange animal, something between a rough Welsh poney and a Peruvian sheep, whose utmost capriole only tends to land him in the mud. We may indeed safely compliment Mr. Southey, by assuring him that there is nothing in Homer, Virgil, or Milton, in any degree resembling the beauties of *Madoc*. . . .

It would only fatigue the patience of the reader, to pursue the course of this ponderous work. A greater waste of exertion we have seldom witnessed, and a more severe trial of our patience we have hardly ever sustained.

25. From an unsigned review, *Imperial Review*

November 1805, v, 465–73

This extract forms the conclusion of the second part of a detailed summary of the plot of *Madoc*. The first part was published in the *Imperial Review*, October 1805, v, 417–26.

Before we conclude our account of this celebrated performance, something should be said of the language. This undoubtedly is not its chief excellence. The style, in many places, is trailing, flat, and uninteresting,—deficient both in strength and animation. The author seldom avails himself of any artificial ornaments. Tropes, figures, and similitudes, which are indispensably necessary to support the interest of the narration in poems of such length, are very sparingly introduced. An apparent, not to say affected, simplicity of diction pervades the whole work. Sometimes the language is uncommonly prosaic, and but rarely aspires to the dignity of the epic style. Of this the author seems to be aware, from the triads prefixed to the work. And what lessens its merits, in our estimation, may possibly, in his, be a recommendation of the poem.

Though we feel ourselves compelled to make these observations, it is hardly necessary to add, that upon the whole we think very highly of this performance. The story may claim the first station among those of the best written poems of the kind, both ancient and modern: the characters, taken altogether, are very well supported; the sentiments are just, pure, and elevated; and were the style adorned by a little artificial colouring, and enriched with all the allowable decorations of poetry, *Madoc* would hardly yield to *Paradise Lost*. As it stands, it is certainly the second heroic production in the English language. Its leading characteristics are not fire and sublimity, but tenderness and humanity. Milton astonishes the head—Southey touches the heart. The first we may admire—the last we can love.— To this amiable author the world is indebted for many other valuable and interesting publications. His name, indeed, gained an enviable eminence among his contemporary English bards, at an early period of his literary career, and we are persuaded that the production before us will contribute, in no small degree, to transmit it with undiminished if not increasing lustre to those who shall come after him. Whatever other faults may be discovered in this poem, to the eternal honour of Southey be it spoken, that his muse is always devoted to the service of benevolence, justice, and humanity.

26. From an unsigned review, *Eclectic Review*

December 1805, i, 899–908

This review makes several important critical points about *Madoc*. The numerous quotations cited in support of the argument are omitted in these extracts.

The leading character of the poem is *horror*. It presents a hyperbolical description of the manners and superstitions of the wildest savages in the wildest parts of America, long before Europe had planted her standard among them. We have piles of skulls—skulls for drinking bowls—beads of human hearts incased with gold, and hung round the necks of chiefs and heroes. One of his heroes, Coanocotzin, hangs up the skeleton of his enemy, a neighbouring prince, and makes it hold a lamp, in the hall where he sups and revels. Others of his heroes strip off the skins of the slain, and dance before us, as they wear them, all dropping with blood. Others make their drums out of them. Of cannibals, and human sacrifices, we are sickened almost in every page. . . .

Almost the first thing, that struck us as a defect in the poem, is the author's unfortunate selection of names. But, Aelgyvarch, Gwynon, Gwynodil, Goervyl, (for a *lady!*), Coanocotzin, and Yuhidthiton, though they may be truly Welsh or American, are hardly more poetical than Brobdignag, or Chrononhotonthologos. We are sorry to observe, in this, as in most of Mr. S.'s performances, expressions which border closely on impiety.

> Thus saith the Lord of Ocean (*Madoc!*) in the name
> Of God Almighty, Universal God, &c.

The author, *in propria persona*,[1] speaks of

> ———————————— the blessed sun,
> In unapproachable *divinity*. p. 129.

---

[1] 'In his own person'.

In p. 385, he makes us shudder at a chorus of Pagans, exclaiming,

> Glory to thee, the Great, the Terrible
> Mexitli, Guardian God, &c.

Before we quit the subject of verbal criticism, we remark an absurd partiality for crowding in technical terms and phrases, especially naval and military terms. . . .

Mr. S. seems to be enamoured of any thing either very old, or very new-fashioned, so that it be only out of the common way. We have marked eccentricity enough; but we have as yet touched on a very small portion. As compound epithets, we have 'the-every-where' and 'the-for-ever-one,' 'dwindling our all-too-few;' and an orator is called a 'mouth-piece.' . . .

We have, in other places, *yeugh*, for yew; to *belate*, for to benight; *wonderment*, for wonder; *attent*, for attention; *desperate*, for despairing (*desperate of their country's weal*): *guidage*, for guidance; and many other things, for—we know not what. Mr. S. at other times, is enamoured of alliterations, with sundry nameless fopperies and singularities. . . .

But let us take a more comprehensive view of the forty and five chapters into which Mr. S. has distributed a myriad of *wild and wonderous* verses. The Fable is grossly improbable; for, of such an important expedition as that of first colonising a new world, would no more traces have reached us, than a few worse than Rabbinical traditions? In *conducting* his fable, Mr. S. has *judiciously*, though not in the most *modest* way, disclaimed the title of epic. The manners, and minor historical facts, are most barbarously romantic. At so much snake-worship; so much human sacrifice; at such diabolical painting of savages; and such deification of a marauder, possibly almost as savage as the Indians themselves; at such eulogia on human nature in one case, and such libels on it in the other, we turn away disgusted,—with an *incredulus odi*![1] The poem closes with an act of the most premeditated suicide by an American chief; a very favourite catastrophe with modern poets: and the hero, Madoc, being thus delivered from his last implacable foe, is left with his followers, in peaceable possession of a domain, which the natives had been miraculously deterred from attempting to recover. . . .

It is now high time that we dismiss the work before us; and we do it with our sincere wishes that Mr. S. would no longer disgrace the talents and genius, which he evidently possesses, by an affectation of

---

[1] 'I discredit and revolt at it.' (Horace, *Ars Poetica*.)

singularity which is so much beneath him. We again recommend to him the 'simplicities' mentioned in his *triads*. If he tells us, that antiquated, obsolete language suits an ancient story, why did he not write in Welsh? His unpardonable *innovations* upon his native language, in giving us words and expressions never heard of before, deserve the severest reprehension. His story is considerably too long, and is too much deficient in incident and character, to be interesting. There are some good things in it: but he would do well to reflect, that a diamond among rubbish does not always repay the search. We cannot, therefore, advise our readers to expend their two guineas on this volume, notwithstanding its ornamental appearance, its wire-wove hot-pressed paper, and its costly and elegant typography.

27. From an unsigned review, *Literary Journal*

1805, v, 621–36

Although much of the review is occupied with a summary of the plot the reviewer offers some interesting comments on the versification and diction of *Madoc*.

In the style and the structure of the verse, there are many things very exceptionable. Mr. Southey seems fond of that very easy way of variegating his verse by introducing bad lines. He has indeed abstained from the ridiculous affectation of writing half lines, because Virgil left some of his unfinished. But he is careful, at no very distant intervals, to give his reader's attention a fillip, by unexpectedly grating his ear with a redundant syllable. A few examples will shew future poets, who may be desirous to assist a reader's attention in the same way, the method which Mr. Southey pursues in introducing the figure of *depraved metre*:

> And I, their leader, am not of the sons
> Of the feeble! As he spake, he reached a mace,

When the bowyers of Deheubarth plied so well

And long with obstinate and harassing war
Provoked us, hoping not for victory,

With those whom we hold holy, with the sons
Of the Temple, they who commune with the Gods;

The joyous thrill
Died away: and, as every limb relaxed,

One of the two following lines must limp most woefully:

Besure, for Amalahta leads them on.

Amalahta, rushing, in blind eagerness.

But there are much greater blemishes in the language than the
versification. Our author seems to have conceived an unusual propensity for unusual and forced expressions. 'To lethargy the Briton
blood,' is certainly an expression at least calculated to keep our surprize
awake. When a woman is overcome with joy, who would expect to
be told that 'she had received the shock of happiness.' To employ
'revengeful hope' to denote the hope of revenge, seems quite the same
as if 'mournful hope' were used to signify the hope of mourning.
We have heard of people *reading* a man's face, but it is something
new to be told of a man's face which Madoc 'had *learnt* in childhood.' People are frequently represented as transported with joy at
pleasures they *foresee*; but the hero of Mr. S. by turning his eyes
on the past, was prevented from viewing the future with '*forefeeling
joy*.' The obsolete *ye* is a great favourite in the accusative case, 'on
ye, viewing ye, hearing ye,' &c. When king Tepollomi took down
his arms from the wall, we are told that he 'took his *death-doers*
down.' Our readers might find it difficult to imagine what is meant
by a *spiral roar*, if we did not inform them that it was the sound
of a spiral shell. To 'win a conquest' seems much the same thing
as to 'win a winning.' 'The *frush* of rocks that meet in battle' appears
to contain nothing so corresponding in the sound to the sense as to
cause such an expression to be adopted. 'Thy soon departure,' is in our
times bad grammar. To 'come *by lake*' in contradistinction to coming
by land, has at least an odd appearance; as well as its kinsman 'to set
foot *aland*.'

We are by no means friends to that style which seems to walk on
stilts, whether we meet with it in prose or verse. Pompous bombast

is far more disagreeable to us, than what those who delight in such a style are pleased to denominate mean and vulgar. But although we are thorough admirers of the plain and simple, we see no reason why the mean and vulgar should be sought after and introduced, where it is not of a piece with the rest of the style, and where a more elegant and equally forcible expression could be found. When the Britons and Aztecas hold a solemn conference, our author uniformly will have it to be 'a solemn *talk*;' and the manner in which this chit-chat expression is introduced, has frequently the most ludicrous effect. If this expression is used from any reference to the term employed by the natives, it might have been equally proper, had the scene of the piece been placed in Africa, to have called the conference 'a solemn *palaver*.' Such a pretty old man's phrase as 'a blessing on you, lady!' does not appear to come in very suitably in the midst of a flaming heroic speech. As far as our skill in cheese-making goes, we should imagine it was no commendation of Llain's fare, that she produced 'cheese like curds so white.' In the following passage, the effect of the word *crash* will give an idea of the manner in which the poem is frequently disfigured by similar vulgarisms:

> A sepulchral voice replied,
> Ye have for other Gods forsaken us,
> And we abandon you! . . and crash with that
> The Image fell.

In the following sentence we have seen *whizz* for the first time in an heroic poem:

> At the rustle of the reeds,
> From whence the blow was aimed, I turned in time,
> And heard it *whizz* beside me.

Donning a man's armour has at least antient usage to excuse it; and when a lady is said to seize her enemy 'with *throttling* grasp,' a term is employed which may be very frequently heard applied to similar feats of heroic ladies in common life.

But although the style of *Madoc* is by no means correct, nor the verse in general melodious, yet there are many highly finished passages to be met with throughout. In these the idea and the language are often equally beautiful.

28. From an unsigned review, *General Review of British and Foreign Literature*

June 1806, i, 505–26

The reviewer is primarily concerned to summarize the plot with lengthy quotations. The following short extract forms the conclusion of the review.

The great feature of this poem may be stated to be originality. The subject, the names, the characters, the incidents, the descriptions, are all original. The important feature is in no part more conspicuous than in the battles, in which Epic poets have most usually been servile copyists of Homer. Those in the *Madoc* are full of novelty, of circumstance, and expression, and more interesting than any but those of Homer. We are much pleased to see the old formal similies with their long tails omitted in the *Madoc*. Those antiquated appendages of Epic poems which have been so sedulously imitated from Homer, may sometimes delight us when they have the originality and force which frequently appear in those of Milton; but they are usually feeble, unnecessary, and unnatural. In the *Madoc*, they are very sparingly introduced. When they occur they are short, rapid, and expressive.

The *Madoc* contains none of the machinery or supernatural agency which usually abounds in Epic poems. On the whole, we are pleased with the omission. The introduction of supernatural agency is certainly a powerful instrument of the sublime, but not such agency as Epic poets have been fond of producing. The highest exertions of genius can alone make it interesting; and in the present state of human opinions, it is scarcely possible to frame it so plausibly as to have any hold on our curiosity or our belief. Therefore we are glad for the credit of the poem that it has not been attempted.

In reviewing the faults of the *Madoc* we might notice some unharmonious lines, and feeble expressions, and a few prosaic passages. But no epopea is without these—not even Milton and Homer. Virgil is the only author whose exquisite polish dares our criticism on this subject, though he is almost defenceless on every other ground. The greatest fault we are disposed to find with the *Madoc* is its termination. We do not like its closing incident. The destruction of Patamba by the Volcano and the earthquake is abruptly and indistinctly told; nor did we at first apprehend what was meant by it. It occurs likewise so awkwardly as to seem unnatural, and to disappoint our curiosity, which the preceding incident had made very anxious. In revising the poem perhaps some of the Welsh sections might be compressed with advantage, and a few passages of minor interest omitted.

On the whole, we recommend the poem as abounding with genius and originality, with pure morality and dignified feeling, with animated poetry, and a melodious elocution:—and if we regard it merely as a tale, we think our female readers will find it more interesting than any romance that they may be in the habit of perusing.

METRICAL TALES AND OTHER POEMS

1805

Most of the *Metrical Tales* were reprinted from the *Morning Post*: 'this volume-full is a selection from a large heap, by which I earned £149 4*s*., and is now published for the very same reason for which it was originally composed' (*Life*, ii, p. 313).

29. From an unsigned review, *Critical Review*

February 1805, 3rd series, iv, 118–21

Possibly by John Higgs Hunt, editor of the *Critical Review* from 1805 to 1807. Extract from the opening of the review.

Such is our dislike to the subject, metre, and in short every thing appertaining to what Mr. Southey denominates *Metrical Tales*, that the very title of the book now before us gave us a prejudice against its contents, and we took it up in the full expectation, we had almost said determination, of handling it roughly. But we had not proceeded far, before we found that, in spite of ourselves, we should be obliged to praise it. The author possesses genius and fancy to a considerable extent; he has no common powers of language and versification, and is master of most of those qualities and qualifications without which there can be no poetical excellence. But however great his claims to the ivy wreath, *doctarum præmia frontium*,[1] he has also many faults which are highly reprehensible, the more so perhaps because they are avoidable and voluntary. The greatest, and indeed that which contains in itself the seeds of all his other defects, is that he is an egregious poetical coxcomb. It seems to be his aim to strike out a new model for

[1] Horace, *Odes*, I, i.

English poetry; to be as it were the founder of a new sect. But to this he has no pretensions; it is for Mr. Southey to follow received opinions. In his 'Songs of the American Indians,' as well as on several other occasions, he treats us with that newfangled and non-descript species of poetry, that prose-like verse or verse-like prose, which it is not possible sufficiently to reprobate. We must also decidedly express our disapprobation of the system of coining new words, which is too common in the present publication; such as, for instance, 'unharming,' 'unfatiguable,' 'unrecallable,' 'disbranches,' 'quintessential,' 'brooklet,' and many others too numerous to mention. . . .

It is not only for making words of his own that he has a partiality: he is equally fond of compounding *ad libitum*. But this also he had better let alone; he is invariably unsuccessful. He gives us 'heart-sincerity,' 'heart-delight,' 'blood-banner,' 'death-day,' &c. &c. It would be difficult to discover any beauty in them. He is also occasionally very careless in the construction of his lines; sometimes very tame: instances of the former are to be found—

> My lips pronounc'd the *unrecallable* vow.

> Oh! had I leapt to meet the *merciful* sword.

> These cold raw mists that chill the *comfortless* day.

Of the latter—

> The bloody purpose, *led by which he came.*

> Sincere herself, *impossible to doubt.*

> Mysterious man, *at last* I know thee *now.*

What a ridiculous line is this!

> When the black *and blood-banner* was spread to the gale.

Having now given our general opinion of Mr. Southey's productions, let us proceed to notice separately the variegated contents of this little volume.

30. William Taylor, unsigned review, *Annual Review*

1806, iv, 579–81

From the opening of the review. For note on Taylor see No. 19.

When the Sibyl asked a specific price for her poems, and was refused, she burnt a portion of them. She then asked the same price for the remainder, and was again refused, but with more hesitation. At length she burnt another third, and obtained her original demand for the residue. Could Mr. Southey imitate the conduct of the Sibyl, it would be attended with equal advantage. The poetic rank to which he aspires, would long ago have been conceded, had he laid before us only the specimens of his excellence: he has half-buried his reputation beneath the quantity of his productions.

His 'Old Woman of Berkley' is the best original English ballad extant. Were he known as a ballad-maker only, by that he would stand at the head of the poets in this line; but having produced many ballads of secondary value, he incurs appreciation at the average, and not at the highest rate of his production.

Mr. Southey is adapted for a writer of ballads. He is unaffected beyond all our poets. He never steps aside to pick up an ornament, nor strains the language for a curious felicity. The cleanly simplicity of the good old time adheres to his thoughts and to his expressions. He is natural even to excess; for artists ought to skip, in their delineations, all the uninteresting features; he usually portrays too much. He paints external nature with the deceptive fidelity of the Flemish school, but with too many touches, and with insufficient selection of object. Nor is it in description only that his copiousness borders on prolixity; in the very wording of his phrases, there is a redundance of expletive and unmeaning particles, of *fors* and *ands* and *theres* and *upons*, which, in any other form of composition than the ballad, where one is accustomed to it, would be insupportably trailing. In the rhetorical figure called repetition, Mr. Southey delights; in short, he has all the resources of amplification at command: what he has to learn is to curtail and condense. Milton and Pope are the writers he should study; he has too much of the Spenser and Dryden exuberance already.

SPECIMENS OF THE LATER ENGLISH POETS

1807

Edited by Southey and Grosvenor Charles Bedford (see No. 54). The editorial collaboration was not happy and the work appeared with many imperfections. Southey described it to C. W. Williams Wynn as 'a dismal book . . . worthy of a groan whenever it is mentioned' (Warter, ii, p. 12). His hope that 'If the first edition can be got off, I will make it a curious and good book' (*Life*, iii, p. 130) was defeated by the low sales.

31. From an unsigned review, *Universal Magazine*

July 1807, 2nd series, viii, 32–6

From the opening of the review.

Mr. Southey has earned a name in literature by various productions of various merit; he has aspired to be the founder of a new school of poetry, and he has succeeded to a certain degree; he has succeeded as all attempts at eccentricity, all perversions of genius, all violations of common sense, ever will succeed; by attracting the notice, the imitation, the applause of weak and giddy minds, and by exciting in men of sound judgment and pure taste, ridicule and contempt. We have read Mr. Southey's productions, nor do we wish to deny that they possess some good passages; we having seen in them enough to entitle their author to a decent reputation while he lives, and perhaps, an obscure corner in some future biographical dictionary after his death;

but we have seen likewise, a forced and turgid style, a silly affectation of pathos which has more frequently been the true *bathos*; pages of prosaic inanity, miscalled poetry; every possible fault against true taste and genius; and a nauseating appearance of simplicity in thought and diction, which often reminded us of the infantile puerilities of the nursery. He is an elaborate manufacturer of epics and quartos, in which we believe he already equals Sir Richard Blackmore* of *epopeean* memory; and whose singular fate as an author we recommend to the reflection of Mr. Southey. If men will mistake the habit of writing pensyllable lines *usque ad infinitum*[1] for the inspirations of true genius, they ought to be reminded that the most exuberant powers of mind may degenerate into perfect emptiness, if suffered to dilate upon every topic of fancy with such alarming diffusion. Homer, Virgil, Tasso, Milton, were content with giving one epic to the world, and that the result of many years' painful labour and frequent revision; but Mr. Southey boldly comes forward with them as fast as they can be written; supposing that while he has power to hold a pen, he has power likewise to exercise the most brilliant faculties of invention and of language. But this is a fallacy which Mr. Southey is yet young enough to learn; and we shall now proceed to offer a few remarks upon the work before us.

'It is intended,' says Mr. S. 'to accompany Mr. Ellis's well-known *Specimens of the Early English Poets*.' We do not think that it will answer this purpose; indeed we cannot help regarding the present work as a useless incumbrance upon literature. The utility, interest, and originality of Mr. Ellis's work, gave it permanent claims to notice; it embraced a period respecting which little was known to the general reader; it afforded many curious specimens of early English poetry, which must be read with pleasure by those who delight to contemplate the progress of mind; it comprehended a definite period of time, easily ascertained; for these reasons, therefore, such a work was calculated to become valuable and popular. But Mr. Southey's compilation can lay claim to none of these advantages. It commences at a period familiar to the most careless reader of English poetry; it consists of injudicious extracts from poets that are in the library of an apprentice-boy; and it pretends to fix an era in English literature, the certainty of

---

* Sir Richard Blackmore is a remarkable instance of the imbecility of genius. He wrote so much absolute nonsense, that what was really good was forgotten and confounded with the surrounding dullness. His *Creation* has many excellent passages full of poetical vigour.　　　　　　　　　　　　[1] 'To infinity'.

which can be known only to posterity. These defects are not to be imputed to Mr. Southey, they are inseparable from the object of the work; and we therefore wish he had never undertaken it. Where is the utility of a book that is filled with a few extracts from Dryden, Pope, Young, Goldsmith, and the most popular poets? But it will perhaps be replied, it presents extracts also from Anthony, Motteaux, Mary Leapor, Walter Harte, Charles Gildon, &c. &c.: it does so; but these are authors of no rarity. Those who wish to read them may find them upon every book-stall in the metropolis; and to the philologist they are of no advantage. The stability of the language was too firmly secured by the productions of the *optimates*[1] of English poetry to be susceptible of deterioration or improvement from the works of forgotten scribblers. Upon the principle which has influenced Mr. Southey in the compilation of these volumes, as many more might have been produced; every poetaster, who has published a song, an ode, an elegy, or a satire, ought to have his share of glory. An ideal epoch too of the declension of our literature has been assumed, by confounding the existence of bad writers with the depravity of public taste; not reflecting, that while these *Grubean* heroes were lavishing forth *their* treasures, men of real genius were also giving to the world their lucubrations, which were received by the distinguishing few in the manner they deserved; and the distinguishing few are all that ever will, in any age or in any country, be the encomiasts of undoubted talents. In our own times we have seen proofs of this: we have seen the transitory popularity of the multitude crowning the most worthless productions of degraded genius; but they have had their day, and are now forgotten; those too that at the present are in the dazzling height of their renown, will soon pass away, and leave behind them the solid structure of 'patient merit.'

But independently of this radical defect of plan, Mr. Southey has shewn neither taste nor judgment in his selections; from celebrated authors he has chosen their very worst productions. Is it thus that he meant to shew 'the progress, decline, and revival' of our poetry? This is, as if a man should go into an honest tradesman's shop, and finding an article of inferior quality, hold it up as a specimen of his wares. It is a disingenuous proceeding, and besides it is subversive of the proposed object of the work. To have shewn accurately the progress of literature, he should have considered with deep attention the general character of an author's productions, taking neither the very best nor

1 'Best',

the very worst; but to have done this demanded united skill, taste, and leisure. In fact, Mr. Southey appears just to have chosen at random from each author, careless whether what he adopted was characteristic of that author, or not. From Pope, for example, he has taken an 'Epistle to Mrs. Martha Blount, with a copy of Voiture's Works'— from Dryden, a spiritless epitaph and prologue—from Young, a couple of 'Odes,' that may be almost termed burlesque, &c.—and these he terms *specimens* of the later English poets. We really cannot conceive a more glaring instance of bad taste and erroneous judgment than this; for, besides, failing in its professed plan, it is thus rendered useless and uninteresting as a selection.

Of the prefatory notices we can say nothing that will please their *authors*; for we are informed, that 'an old and dear friend' of Mr. Southey's supplied some of them. They are trite and superficial, vapid, and often erroneous. They appear to us to answer no purpose whatsoever; to call them criticisms would be absurd; to consider them as biographical sketches would be equally so; as registers of the birth and death of each poet, they are of some advantage, but then they might have been much shorter. There is an affectation of brevity and pompous decision in some of them that is ridiculous. Nor can we account why to some authors no prefatory notice is prefixed. Mr. Southey indeed says, 'of a few great writers it was unnecessary to say any thing;' but here is a marked inconsistency—for example, to Dryden, Collins, Goldsmith, and others, these preliminary notices *are* prefixed; to Addison, Pope, Prior, they are *not* prefixed; consequently the former are not to be included among the 'few great names.'

LETTERS FROM ENGLAND

Published under the pseudonym of Don Manuel Alvarez Espriella. The first edition sold quickly. Before the end of 1807 Southey reported that the publishers were suggesting a reprint (*Life*, iii, p. 120). A second edition was published in 1808. Although sales then declined a third edition appeared in 1814 and the book was also translated into French and German.

32. Francis Jeffrey, unsigned review, *Edinburgh Review*

January 1808, xi, 370–90

From the opening of the review. For note on Jeffrey see No. 18.

This publication appears to us to be pretty evidently the work of some experienced *English* bookmaker; and by no means a despicable specimen of the progress which has been made in that laudable art. The name of Don Manuel Alvarez Espriella, in the title-page, is no doubt placed there, however, for very useful purposes. We have of late been so overrun with travels, tours, walks, and journals, through every nook and corner of the island, and they have been presented to the public in such a variety of forms and styles,—picturesque, sentimental, agricultural and evangelical, that it was hardly possible any longer to attract attention to works of this description, by any effort of native ingenuity. Observations on our own country by a stranger or foreigner, on the other hand, never fail to excite curiosity, and obtain at least a temporary circulation. We are all anxious to know what other people say of us; and are apt to suppose, perhaps not very erroneously, that we gain a new knowledge of familiar objects, by seeing them with the eyes of a stranger. This alone would afford a sufficient temptation to the deception which has here been attempted; but the ingenious person who practises it has many other advantages. He is enabled, in the first place, to fill up his pages with a series of trifling and familiar details, that never could have been tolerated in his own character. He has, besides, much greater latitude and freedom allowed him, if he chooses to discuss the more delicate subjects of politics and religion; and if he brings his hero from a part of the world where we can reasonably suppose him to be ignorant of the arts and refinements and peculiar manners of our country, he can very successfully employ him in exposing the follies and vices that have been introduced with these refinements. This is admirably exemplified in the *Lettres Persannes* of Montesquieu.

The author before us has made ample use of the first of these privileges; and has contrived to fill a large portion of his book with such trifling and minute descriptions of the inns, roads, stages, &c. as would have been quite insufferable and ridiculous in his own person. What Englishman, travelling in his own country, would be allowed to enlighten the minds of his countrymen with such information as the following? 'They burn earth coal every where; it is a black shining stone, very brittle, which kindles slowly, making much smoke and much ashes; but as all the houses are built with chimnies, it is neither unwholesome nor disagreeable.'—'The hearth is furnished with a round bar to move the coals, a sort of forceps to arrange them, and a small shovel for the cinders, all of iron, and so shaped and polished as to be ornamental. Besides these, there is what they call the fender, which is a little moveable barrier, either of brass or polished steel, or sometimes of wire painted green and capt with brass, to prevent the live embers from falling on the floor.' In this manner, every article of household furniture is described; and we have equally full accounts of the different modes of travelling, with a most accurate description of all the varieties of stage-coaches, mail-coaches, long-coaches, &c.

To maintain the character of Spaniard, Don Manuel is of course represented as a most zealous member of the Holy Catholic Church, which naturally affords the author an opportunity of filling many pages with lamentations over the miserable heresy which prevails in our unhappy country; but, except enabling him to spin out his book to the requisite length with the least possible exertion of intellect, it serves no good purpose either to himself or his reader, as it necessarily checks all free discussion on the nature and tendency of the Establishment, and harmonizes very ill with the tone of philosophical liberality and intrepid reasoning which is assumed on most other occasions. The same thing may be said with regard to his political remarks; although, in the variety of miscellaneous discussions which occur in these volumes, enough is said to convince us, that the author possesses such a laudable zeal for freedom and love of peace, that however we may be inclined to differ from him in many speculative points, we are satisfied of his philanthropy and the innocence of his intentions.

From what we have already said, our readers may perceive, that we do not think very highly of the plan of this book: indeed, we are pretty well convinced, that if the author had abstained from all attempt at writing in character, he would have been much more successful. He evidently holds the pen of a practised writer; and though he frequently gives proofs of a bad taste in composition, particularly in his attempts at wit, to which he is unfortunately too much addicted, yet there are many passages which display a command of language and power of description far above the common pitch;—we allude particularly to the account of an excursion to the Lakes, which is extremely well executed, and, in our opinion, by far the best part of the book.

Of his powers of reasoning we cannot speak very highly: he goes to the bottom of nothing; when his subject leads him to discuss any of the nicer points of political economy, or any subject which requires minute investigation, or close reasoning, he is uniformly superficial and declamatory, and, at the same time, delivers his opinions in the most dogmatical and peremptory manner. He belongs indeed, on the whole, rather to the sentimental than to the reasoning class of composers; he is continually inveighing against the present constitution of society, and holds in the greatest abhorrence all those great commercial and manufacturing establishments, which, 'while they enable the rich to revel in all kinds of luxurious enjoyment, infallibly tend to sink the great mass of the community into a state of the most abject slavery and misery.' Accordingly, whenever he approaches any great manufacturing town, instead of any expression of admiration at the wonderful exertions of ingenuity and industry which are there displayed, we are sure to be presented with a highly coloured and most lamentable picture of the misery and vice into which a great portion of the inhabitants are plunged, in consequence of their hateful and pernicious

pursuits; and the certain and total ruin of the country is most emphatically denounced, if we are mad enough to continue this system. But his
discontent is not confined to the remarks on our trade and commerce:
the same querulous tone is kept up in his observations on all our
institutions. All this is the more provoking, as he never once deigns
to give us the least glimpse of the clue by which we may escape from
the labyrinth of error in which we are now involved; and, after
having exerted himself to show the darkness of the dungeon which
we have dug for ourselves, he very humanely leaves us to grope our
way out of it, the best way we can. In short, he seems to have no
very clear views on the subject; and finds it, of course, a much easier
task to point out the evils of our situation, than to suggest any scheme
for its improvement.

33. Christopher Lake Moody, unsigned review, *Monthly Review*

April 1808, n.s. lv, 380–6

Moody (1753–1815) was a clergyman who reviewed regularly for
the *Monthly Review*.

Cucullus non facit Monachum;[1] neither will a Spanish cloak at a masquerade, nor a Spanish name in a title page, make a Spaniard. Ample
internal evidence will be perceived by every discriminating reader, to
convince him that the volumes before us could not have a Lusitanian
origin; and the fact we understand to be that Mr. Southey and Mr.
Duppa are the authors of the observations on England here presented
to the public. This discovery, however, does not diminish any real
merit which the remarks possess, though with some persons it may
operate to abate curiosity. It is very probable that these gentlemen

1 'The hood does not make the monk.'

deemed it necessary to assume a foreign mask, in order to indulge with greater freedom in their reflections, thinking that their strictures and sarcasms would be more readily tolerated, when supposed to proceed from the prejudices of a Spaniard, than they would be if the real source had been avowed; and they no doubt supposed also that sentiments respecting English customs, laws, and manners, by a foreigner educated in a country and in a religion so different from our own, would excite peculiar interest.

Whatever may have been their motive, these pseudo-Spaniards have over-acted their part, and have betrayed such an intimate acquaintance with English literature, arts, politics, and sects, as a stranger just landed on our coasts could never have attained; and though in the character of Don Manuel Espriella they affect a violent antipathy to us as *heretics,* they unfortunately make him display a wider scope of ecclesiastical knowledge than a Spanish education ever evolves. Setting aside, however, all that respects the costume or *dressing* of these letters, and viewing them merely as spirited remarks on England, we must pronounce them to deserve in many respects the notice of English readers. They are not meant to flatter but to instruct; and, by removing the medium of national vanity and partiality, to enable us to see ourselves in a different glass from that which Englishmen professedly writing to Englishmen would venture to hold up. Naturally disposed to consider our country as *the best of all possible countries,* we do not sufficiently criticize our characteristic traits and numerous defects; and while our own travellers amuse us with the absurdities of foreign nations, we are not aware that we ourselves, on many accounts; are open to satirical animadversion. Yet, as already observed, we do not recognize the propriety of putting into the mouth of a Spaniard, and a layman, dissertations on our numerous religious sects; for this is a subject with which he could not possibly have been acquainted, and would not probably be interested. He might have compared our established worship with the *culte* of the Romish church, and, with the prejudices natural to a Catholic, have expressed his disapprobation of the want of splendor and ceremonies in the reformed religion: but he would not have descended to trace the shades of difference between our various dissenters, nor have felt his attention excited by disputes between Calvinists and Socinians; much less would he have hunted after Swedenborgians, Quakers, Methodists, Muggletonians, Universalists, Jumpers, &c. &c.

Though, however, this part of the work is improperly attributed to any *Don Manuel*, it ought not for this reason to be passed in silence. A Spaniard is made to deliver himself with more shrewdness, not only on medical but on sectarian mountebankery and fanaticism, than is usually displayed; and the ludicrous view in which both these topics are placed may serve in some measure to counteract these worse than follies.

THE REMAINS
OF HENRY KIRKE WHITE

1807, 1822

Edited by Southey. Two volumes were published in 1807. A third volume was added in 1822.

After White's early death Southey undertook an edition of his remains with biographical introduction, all profits being given to White's family. The sentimental appeal of White's life resulted in exceptionally good sales: the first edition of 750 copies sold in less than three months and the first two volumes were reprinted ten times in sixteen years.

34. Southey as editor, *Cabinet*

March 1808, iii, 177–82

From the conclusion of the unsigned review.

As the editor, Mr. Southey had little to do, and that little is not done so well as his name would lead us to expect. He has shewn great want of selection, even judging from his own works. But his conduct in his editorial capacity is a proof of his benevolence if not of his taste: of his genius none is required.

THE CHRONICLE OF THE CID

1808

Translated by Southey from the Spanish.

Although he did not anticipate any significant financial rewards, Southey claimed in a letter to Scott: 'I expect much credit from this work' (*Life*, iii, p. 127).

35. Coleridge, from a letter to Humphry Davy

7 December 1808

Reprinted from *Collected Letters of Samuel Taylor Coleridge*, ed. E. L. Griggs (1956–   ), iii, p. 136.

Southey is sending to the Press his *History of Brazil*, and at the same Time (the Indefatigable!) composing a defence of religious Missions to the East &c.—Excepting the Introduction (which however I have heard highly praised, but myself think it shallow, flippant, and *ipse dixitish*) I read few Books with such deep Interest, as the *Chronicle of the Cid*. The whole Scene in the Cortes is superior to any equal Part of any Epic Poem, save the *Paradise Lost—me saltem judice*.[1] The deep, glowing, yet ever self-controlled, Passion of the Cid—his austere Dignity so finely harmonizing with his Pride of loyal Humility—the address to his Swords—and the Burst of contemptuous Rage in his final Charge & Address to the Infantes of Carrion—and his immediate Recall of his Mind—are beyond all ordinary Praise.—It delights me to be able to speak thus of a work of Southey's: I am so often forced to

[1] 'At least in my opinion'.

quarrel with his want of Judgment and his Unthinkingness—which, heaven knows, I never do without pain & the vexation of a disappointed Wish.

36. Mrs Thrale on Southey

11 August 1808

From *Thraliana. The Diary of Mrs. Hester Lynch Thrale (later Mrs. Piozzi) 1776-1809*, ed. K. C. Balderston (1942), ii, p. 1096.

Mrs Thrale (1741-1821), remembered primarily as the friend of Dr Johnson, interestingly groups together Southey and Scott in this depreciatory reference.

The fashionable Poetry of Southey & Scott will fall into Decay—it will never be Classical—It leaves too little behind it—Handel and Milton must be for ever *felt*; Bach's Lessons & Pope's moral Essays must be for ever *recollected*; *Madoc* and *Thalaba*, *Teviot Dale* and *Marmion* depend too much on their *Colouring*: In a hundred Years People will wonder why they were so admired.

37. Byron, satire in *English Bards and Scotch Reviewers*

1809

This is the first of Byron's satiric attacks in verse upon Southey. Unlike Byron's later writings these verses show no personal animosity towards Southey himself.

> The time has been, when yet the muse was young,
> When Homer swept the lyre, and Maro sung,
> An epic scarce ten centuries could claim,
> While awe-struck nations hail'd the magic name:
> The work of each immortal bard appears
> The single wonder of a thousand years.
> Empires have moulder'd from the face of earth,
> Tongues have expired with those who gave them birth,
> Without the glory such a strain can give,
> As even in ruin bids the language live.
> Not so with us, though minor bards, content
> On one great work a life of labour spent:
> With eagle pinion soaring to the skies,
> Behold the ballad-monger Southey rise!
> To him let Camoëns, Milton, Tasso yield,
> Whose annual strains, like armies, take the field.
> First in the ranks see Joan of Arc advance,
> The scourge of England and the boast of France!
> Though burnt by wicked Bedford for a witch,
> Behold her statue placed in glory's niche;
> Her fetters burst, and just released from prison,
> A virgin phœnix from her ashes risen.
> Next see tremendous Thalaba come on,
> Arabia's monstrous, wild, and wondrous son:
> Domdaniel's dread destroyer, who o'erthrew
> More mad magicians than the world e'er knew.

Immortal hero! all thy foes o'ercome,
For ever reign—the rival of Tom Thumb!
Since startled metre fled before thy face,
Well wert thou doom'd the last of all thy race!
Well might triumphant genii bear thee hence,
Illustrious conqueror of common sense!
Now, last and greatest, Madoc spreads his sails,
Cacique in Mexico, and prince in Wales;
Tells us strange tales, as other travellers do,
More old than Mandeville's, and not so true.
Oh! Southey! Southey! cease thy varied song!
A bard may chant too often and too long:
As thou art strong in verse, in mercy, spare!
A fourth, alas! were more than we could bear.
But if, in spite of all the world can say,
Thou still wilt verseward plod thy weary way;
If still in Berkley ballads most uncivil,
Thou wilt devote old women to the devil,
The babe unborn thy dread intent may rue:
'God help thee,' Southey, and thy readers too.

THE CURSE OF KEHAMA

1810

The idea for this poem was originally conceived in 1801. After working on it in earnest in 1805 Southey became disheartened by the slow sale of *Thalaba* and abandoned it. His interest was revived by encouragement from Walter Savage Landor in 1808. Southey predicted to Cottle that 'Every body will stare at this poem, and very few persons will like it. . . . It will I doubt not procure for me much immediate abuse, ridicule and some after reputation' (Curry, i, p. 527). Although he frequently stated that he expected little immediate success from the poem, Southey confidently hoped to receive future fame: 'every generation will afford me some half dozen admirers of it, and the everlasting column of Dante's fame does not stand upon a wider base' (*Life*, iii, p. 268).

38. From an unsigned review, *Monthly Mirror*

February 1811, 2nd series, ix, 122–35

Extracts from the opening and conclusion of the review.

Were we called upon to speak generally of Mr. Southey as an author, we should say, with a view to the times in which we live, that there are many who have as much uncorrupted genius, and more who have a greater share of fine taste; but we know and have heard of no man, who with his ardour of mind has possessed such unwearied industry as to bear any comparison with him in both the quantity and quality of his labours. In former works, he has prepared the reader for an indulgence in '*the wild and wondrous*', but here he has out-run himself, and put the *Tales of the Genii* and the *Thousand-and-one Nights* utterly to the blush. The measures of his verse keep pace with those of his imagination, and all is non-conformity.

[Summarizes plot with quotations.]

In this analysis we have detailed the story fairly and tenderly, but the same justice has certainly not been done to the poetry, in which the reptile is embalmed. The plot is, if we may so describe it, powerfully spirit-stirring, but not interesting, in the best sense of the word, because it is utterly impossible for the feelings to travel with the persons of a drama so constituted as the present. We stare and are all alive at the magic of the poet's powers, but we shut the book, and the impression is gone. The pathetic has no place, for there is no room for pity, nor is it possible to shed a tear for those with whom we have nothing in common, and cannot sympathize. Their predicament we can never stand in, and, although it is good that innocence and fortitude should always triumph, no one can refrain from smiling, to see the sufferers protected by gods, who cannot protect themselves. Homer is by some thought to have laughed at his own deities, and we are certainly, by reason and good taste, privileged to do the same. But what are we to say of Seeva, Caysapa, Indra, and Yamen, and the conjuror Kehama! It seems to us that Mr. Southey labours under a great disadvantage, through the choice of his machinery. Of the Hindoo mythology, we may safely say, 'quod supra nos, nihil ad nos.'[1] Homer's gods in his day, Milton's theology, and even Shakespeare's witchcraft in theirs stood on better ground. Belief, combining fears and hopes, affords an interest and effect, which no other means, by human wit devised, can approach, and the want of it is a perpetual stumbling block to the feelings in their march through this volume. Having given this opinion, we are now free to confess that the poet's art is, in the terrific, prodigiously displayed throughout, and we have no doubt that, if Mr. Southey's love of eccentricity had not overcome his better taste, he would have chosen such a machinery, and so conducted his story, as not only to have agitated the nerves, but to have come home to the heart, and rested there. Being what it is, however, we pronounce it a splendid specimen of a daring poetical imagination, fed and supported by vast sources of knowledge and observation.

We are astounded by the workings of the bard's vivid descriptions of surrounding objects, his fertile fancy and his potent imagery, but for

[1] 'Because it is above us it is nothing to us.'

those who put all this into action, his gods, they never appear but to excite our ridicule and contempt. Such might not be the case in every latitude, and we verily believe that Mr. Southey will never acquire all the fame, which his poem is capable of conferring, until he obtain readers who reverence and adore his deities; and that time can never come until *The Curse of Kehama* be translated into *Hindoostanee*.

For the present, we shall content ourselves with adding, that this burlesque (for such it may very possibly seem to many) is calculated to expose our holy and sublime miracles and mysteries, as written in the Sacred Volume, and poetically used by Milton, to all that sort of contempt, which the idle and profane wit of infidelity can heap upon it.

39. From an unsigned review, *Critical Review*

March 1811, 3rd series, xxii, 225–51

After a lengthy summary of plot the reviewer perceptively enumerates some defects in the style and subject of the poem.

What is said by connoisseurs respecting the most highly coloured of Rubens's pictures, that their brilliancy is such as to extinguish every other painting in the room in which they are placed, may in some degree apply to this extraordinary poem of Mr. Southey's, only that it falls far short of conveying its full effect. Suppose the possibility of a picture in which the most powerful tint that Rubens ever employed, should form only the lowest colour, and imagine the consequences which such a glare must produce upon the senses. It would doubtless excite astonishment and even admiration at the first glance; but though it might contain beauties of the very highest order, they would be confused and lost in the blazing atmosphere which envelopes them; the eye would soon be fatigued and oppressed by the endeavour to explore them; and, our wonder once exhausted, we should seldom, or never, perhaps, be tempted to renew our visit.

The Curse of Kehama is a performance of precisely this violent and imposing description. Like the shield of Atlante, it strikes dead every thing that is opposed to it; one might as well hold a farthing candle to the sun, as think of placing Homer or Shakspeare, or Milton or Dante, by the side of it. But it is the false blaze of enchantment, not the steady radiance of truth and nature; and if you gain courage to look at it a second or a third time, the magic has lost its power, and you only wonder what it was that dazzled you. The most unfavourable circumstance to the author in all this is, that the senses having been once deceived, (whether voluntarily or not, no matter), we are apt to look upon every thing that has contributed to the deception in the light of imposture, and thus not only to withdraw our former ill-judged admiration, but to refuse the tribute of our applause where it is justly due. We hope that this will not appear to be the case with ourselves; and yet we are to a certain degree conscious of the impression which we believe will be very generally felt by the readers of Mr. Southey.

We must take it for granted that every body who aspires to the dignity of a poet, writes for something more honourable and lasting than the wonder of a day. Mr. Southey, therefore, than whom no man breathing has been gifted by nature with higher pretensions to the poetical character, must be supposed to have had this nobler object in view. It is our opinion that he has failed; and we think the causes of his failure sufficiently obvious both in his choice of a subject and his manner of conducting it.

In the first place, he has scorned the limits of ordinary poetry, taking for the theatre of his action no less a field than the entire universe. Milton has done the same; but, without entering upon any inquiry (which, however obnoxious to many admirers of that great poet, is, we conceive, still open to be raised), whether the subject of the *Paradise Lost* itself was well chosen, we may safely say that there is no ground of comparison on this score between Milton and Southey. The former built upon the religious belief of those to whom his writings were addressed. The disobedience and fall of our first parents is a point of the highest and most solemn interest to the whole human species; and that interest is the single and undivided object of the poem. The latter has taken for his foundation a system of mythology to which most of us are utter strangers, and which was unknown to the fathers even of those who are now best acquainted with it; in which, therefore, the sentiments of habitual reverence that accompany even the fictions of classical fable are wanting; and which is moreover condemned by

Southey himself in his preface as intrinsically 'anti-picturesque and unpoetical.' And in one of the notes, he adds, 'throughout the Hindoo fables there is the constant mistake of bulk for sublimity.' The charge is indisputably true; and it applies equally to the fabric which he has undertaken to build upon them. Add to this, first, that there is no leading point of interest in the story, except the establishment of a fundamental truth in morality, which might have been maintained at far less cost; and, secondly, that this only object is frequently lost sight of altogether in the vast confusion of strange and cumbrous machinery with which it is overladen.

The next cause which we shall allege of this supposed failure is in the versification. Consider this in detached passages, and we shall find it often at once energetic and harmonious to a surprising degree; but, taken altogether, it has an effect as surprisingly the contrary of this; an effect, which those who are in the habit of inveighing against the insipidity of regular metre will not easily credit; that of an excessively heavy and tiresome monotony.

[Quotes from the poem.]

The specimens we have already given, together with one or two more that we mean to add presently, will be sufficient to shew the *manner* of versification that Mr. Southey has adopted. But our charge of monotony cannot be borne out by any thing short of a perusal of the whole poem; since it is the general impression made by the whole, and not the particular effect of any detached portion, to which we refer. We have not space left us at present to pursue the subject farther; but we are mistaken if it may not very safely be contended, not only that a poem written in regular metre need not be monotonous, (to deny which would be to throw dirt at Pope, Dryden, and Milton), but that in a poem of any length regularity of metre is the best; nay, we will go still further; the only preservative against monotony. This is a point which we should be very glad to hear fairly and ably discussed on both sides, having at present little doubt as to the result of such a discussion.

To say that the work now before us displays, in a greater degree than any of his former publications, the high poetical genius with which Mr. S. is unquestionably gifted, and to add that that genius now and then bursts forth with a lustre superior to most, perhaps to any, of his contemporaries, we hold to be a very different thing from maintaining (as some very injudicious friend of Mr. S.'s has lately done), that he is the first of modern poets. He appears to us to be entirely deficient in that high corrective quality of the mind, without which it is impossible for the most astonishing talents to produce real greatness in any one department of art or science; we mean a cool, steady, and comprehensive judgment. It is the want of this which must, in our opinion, keep Mr. S. for ever below the level even of many who have not half his powers of imagination or half his copiousness and majesty of expression.

[Quotes from the poem.]

In the preceding selections, we think there is quite enough to discover to us how great a poet Mr. Southey *might be*, were the single gift of judgment to be added to the qualities which he undoubtedly possesses. Till then, we fear that we shall never be able to subscribe to the belief in a Trinity* of living poets, of whom Mr. S. is represented as entitled to the foremost honours. There is indeed some ground of comparison between him and his own Seeva; for he stands forward in the poem before us like a column of fire; and myriads of years must elapse before his partners in the Godhead can reach either the surprizing height of his extravagance, or the terrible profundity of his bathos.

* See the *Edinburgh Annual Register*. The first volume of this work, lately published, contains an article on the present state of literature; in which the pretensions of living candidates for poetical fame are discussed, *and compared*, in a strain of dogmatical self-sufficiency which we have seldom seen equalled. Messrs. Southey, Scott, and Campbell, are there pronounced to be the supreme leaders of the nation; and a sort of implied preference is given to the first, over the two last, of those gentlemen.

40. John Foster, unsigned review, *Eclectic Review*

April 1811, vii, 334–50

Foster's review of *The Curse of Kehama* was published in two parts, the first of which appeared in the *Eclectic Review*, March 1811, vii, 185–205. This extract forms the concluding section of the second part. The earlier portion of the review is devoted to a summary of the plot with extensive quotations.

Foster (1770–1843) was a regular contributor to the *Eclectic Review*. A dissenter with a strong interest in theology, his religious preoccupations are evident in this extract.

We must repeat then, in the first place, our censure of the adoption or creation of so *absurd* a fable. It is little enough, to be sure, that we know of the order of the universe. But yet human reason, after earnest and indefatigable efforts of inquiry through several thousands of years, (during a great part of which period the inquiry has been prosecuted under the advantage of a revelation,) finds itself in possession of a few general principles which may, without presumption, be deemed to inhere in, and regulate the universal system:—insomuch that these principles would be very confidently assigned, by thinking men, as reasons for disbelieving a great many propositions that might be advanced, relative to the moral or the physical order of the creation, or any of its parts,—relative to the economy of any supposed class of intelligent beings. And in proportion as we withdraw from the immensity of this subject, and bring our thoughts near this world of our own, we find ourselves authorised to apply still more principles, and to reject or to affirm still more propositions relative to beings that, if they exist at all, must exist according to an order in many points analogous to our own economy. Let it be assumed, for instance, that there are inhabitants in the moon, and we shall be warranted on the ground of the various circumstances of analogy between their place of abode and

ours, to advance a great deal more in the way of probable conjecture respecting their economy, than we could respecting an
order of beings, our only *datum* concerning which should be, that
whatever and wherever it is, its condition has less resemblance to our
own than that of any other race of intelligent creatures. But when we
come actually to this world, and men are the subjects of our thoughts,
we know our ground completely; and can compare the descriptions
and fictitious representations of the nature and condition of man,
with the plain standard fact. It should be added, that our knowledge of
what are called the laws of matter, reaches far further into the universe than our knowledge of the economy of intelligent existences:
and therefore we may be allowed to make very confident assertions
respecting, for instance, the qualities and powers of fire and water, in
the remotest and most singular world in which those elements exist,
while we might be exceedingly diffident and limited in our guesses
concerning the supposed intelligent inhabitants of that world.

Now this degree of knowledge which we have acquired of the
physical and moral order of the creation, has become a Standard of
Probability for the works of imagination. If those fictions conform to
the arrangements of this order, as far as they are ascertained, or
reasonably inferred from general principles, they are pronounced
probable: but if in contrariety to these arrangements, they must be
pronounced—not improbable merely, but absurd:—except, indeed, when
they are legitimately representing what we call miracles; and as miracles
are the works of God only—the *true* God—they can never be legitimately represented as operations of fictitious and pagan divine
powers. Improbable fictions, we repeat, should be held absurd; for,
surely, the actual economy of the creation, as arranged by its Author,
must be the grand prototype of wise and beautiful design—of all the
adaptation, proportions and congruities constituting, or conducing to
the perfection of the whole system of existence. Indeed there could be
no other model from which to draw our ideas of proportion, adaptation, harmony, and whatever else is meant by the term order, than this
created system, unless the Creator had revealed another model, an
ideal model, existing in his infinite mind, widely different from the
actual creation. We therefore cannot represent material and intellectual
existences of a nature, or in relations and combinations inconsistent
with the known laws of the creation, without violating the only true
principles of order which it is possible for us to conceive. This we are
forced practically to acknowledge in all our judgements on the propriety

or absurdity of the creations of fancy; for it is to these laws that we necessarily advert, in pronouncing the representations made by the imagination in dreaming, delirium, and insanity, to be absurd; and it is only on their authority that we can pronounce any thing absurd, except what involves a metaphysical contradiction. Unless the absolute authority of these laws is acknowledged, it shall be perfectly reasonable for a poet to represent a race of people made of steel, or half steel half flesh—or human heads, as in the illuminations of old MSS., growing on twigs of trees—or one man making himself into eight, like Kehama, and then returning into one again—or fire and water in perfect amity. It is, in short, only in deference to these laws of the creation, that we can be excused for refusing our respect and admiration to the infinite puerility and monstrosity of the Hindoo poets, as they are called. Now a very considerable portion of the fictions, constituting the present poem, is constructed in utter defiance of this standard. The whole affair of the operation of the Curse, the story of Lorrinite, the origination of the Ganges, the fire and water palace of Indra, the adventures of Mount Calasay, the transactions and creatures of Padalon, with much more that has been noticed in the analysis, are things of a nature not only in perfect contrariety to the state and laws of the actual creation, but incompatible with any economy of which we can conceive the *possible* existence. A strong, an irresistible impression of flagrant absurdity will, therefore, be the predominant perception of every reader incapable of a temporary abolition of his reason. The disgust at this absurdity will be so very active a feeling, and will be so seldom suffered by the poet to subside, that it will, at many parts of the work, almost wholly preclude the pleasure that would else be imparted by the splendid scenery and eloquent diction by which even the grossest of the absurdities are attempted to be made imposing. We may wonder, in very serious simplicity, why the poet should choose deliberately to labour to excite at once the two opposite sentiments of pleasure and disgust, with the knowledge, too, that any attempt to prolong them both is infallibly certain to end in the ascendancy of the latter. Or does he really think the beauties of his composition are so transcendent, that they will banish all recollection about probability and improbability, or fairly vanquish the repugnance of cultivated minds to gross absurdity? And if he *could* do this, what would be the value of the achievement? What has been the grand object and utility of observing, of investigating, of philosophizing, through all ages, but to put mankind in possession of TRUTH, and to discipline their minds to love truth, to think according to the just laws of thinking, and to hate all fallacy and absurdity;—in short, to advance the human race at last, if it be possible, to something like the manhood of reason? And would it, then, be a meritorious employment of a genius that really *should* be powerful enough to counteract these exertions, and retard this progress, to reduce the human mind, or any one mind, back to a state in which it could love or tolerate puerile and raving absurdity,—to that very state which the generality of the orientals are in at this day, and for being in which they have, (till lately their paganism has recommended them to our favour,) been the objects of our sovereign contempt? But if all our influential poetry were to be of the same character as that of a large portion of the present work, we might justly regard the poetic tribe as a conspiracy to seduce men into a complacency with what involves a total abjuration of sense, and so to defeat the labours for maturing the human understanding,—labours, verily, of which the toil is great enough, and the success little enough, even unobstructed by such intervention.

There can be no danger, we suppose, of hearing pleaded, in maintenance of the privilege of poetry to be absurd, that the scope of probability is too confined to afford sufficient variety of materials. That scope includes nothing less than all that is known of this whole world,—all that may, in strict analogy with what is known, be conjectured or fancied of it, in times past, present and to come,—and all that can be imagined of all other worlds, without violating what we have reason to believe the principles of the order of the creation, and without contradicting any doctrine of revelation. This scope is therefore, in the popular sense of the word, infinite; and to seek for materials which it does not include, will generally be found an indication of a feeble mind. It is quite needless to say, this remark can have no application to Mr. Southey: but it *is* a remark applicable to him, that such feeble minds will be glad to find and plead a warrant for their folly in the example of a strong one.

After all, it would be foolish to affect any great degree of apprehension for the public taste, from the perverting operation of one, or any number of works, attempting to reconcile it to the kind and excess of absurdity exhibited in this poem, even if all such works had all the poetical excellence so conspicuous in this. There is a point in the improvement both of individuals and communities, after which they cannot be even amused to more than a certain latitude, if we may so express it, from the line of their reason.

The next chief point of censure would be, that this absurdity is also *paganism*; but this has been noticed so pointedly and repeatedly in our analysis, that a very few words here will suffice. There are Marriataly, Pollear, Yama, Indra, Veeshnoo, Seeva, Padalon, the Swerga, &c. &c. celebrated in the most Christianized country of Europe, by a native poet. Now if these had been merely the fictions of his own mind, and not parts of a heathen mythology, even then they would have been, as they are here managed, an unpardonable violation of religious rectitude. For (the truth of the religion of the bible being assumed) the poet has no right to frame, with a view to engage our complacency in, such a fictitious economy of divine and human beings as, if it could be real, would constitute the negation or extinction of that religion. But the present fiction, so far and so long as the force of poetry (which the poet would have augmented indefinitely if he could) can render the illusion prevalent on the mind, is not only the making void of the true religion, and the substitution of another and a vile theology in its place; it is no less than the substitution of a positive and notorious system of paganism. It vacates the eternal throne, not only in order to raise thither an imaginary divinity, but absolutely to elevate Seeva, the adored abomination of the Hindoos. He is as much, and as gravely attempted to be represented as a reality, as he could be by the poets of those heathens themselves. And, as if on purpose to preclude the officiousness of any friend that might wish to palliate or justify this proceeding, by the old pretendedly philosophical allegation, that this is only accommodating so far to another division of the human race, as to apply the name under which *they* worship a supreme being, to the supreme being that *we* somewhat more intelligently worship,—as if expressly to forbid any such apology, and to give proof that what he is endeavouring to gain a place for in our minds is genuine and formal heathenism, he has given an equally grave semblance of reality to a variety of other gods as well as Seeva, and to the pagan heaven and hell. These, at any rate, are disclaimed even by that irreligious philosophy that insults revelation with the pretence that it may be, in truth, the same divine Essence that is worshipped 'by saint, by savage, or by sage' under the varied denominations of 'Jehovah, Jove, Lord,' or Seeva. These systematic appendages and connexions, therefore, verify the paganism of the whole theology of this poem. And to this paganism, the poet has most earnestly laboured, as we have before observed and shewn, to transfer what is peculiar to the true theology. Expressions of awful reverence, and ascriptions of divine attributes to

Seeva, are uttered by the poet in his own person; he studies most
solicitously to give every appearance and every epithet of dignity to the
worship represented as rendered to the gods by Ladurlad, Kailyal, and
Ereenia; and the fidelity to this devotion at length attains an eternal
reward. Now we have only to ask, What was the impression which the
poet wished all these combined and co-operating representations to
make on the reader's mind? He will not say, nor any one for him, that
he was unaware that a certain moral effect necessarily accompanies all
striking representations of moral agents, and that all he reckoned on, in
a work of great and protracted effort, was to present simply a series of
images, chasing one another away, like those in a magic lanthorn, or
like the succession of clouds in the sky, making no impression on the
mind but merely that of their splendour, beauty, or monstrousness.
Aware then of a moral effect, and intending it, did he design that effect
should be hostile in the severest manner to heathenism? Throughout
this exhibition of gods, providences, devotions, heavens, and hells, was
it a leading purpose to make the reader detest the fancies about Indra
and Seeva, and the Swerga and Padalon, and pray that such execrable
delusions might be banished from those millions of minds in which they
are entertained as something more than poetry? For any purpose of
this kind, the means, evidently, would not be at all of the nature of
those he has employed. He most clearly had no intention that his
Seeva, his Indra, his Yama, his Baly, and so forth, should appear to the
reader in the full odiousness, or any degree of the odiousness, of the
character of false gods; and that the reader should recoil with abhorrence at all his devotional sentiments towards these divinities. But is it
then to be believed, that he was content or desirious that his bold
conceptions, his fine painting, his rich language, should lend the whole
of that powerful assistance which he knows such things contribute, by
necessary association, in behalf of whatever they are employed to
exhibit and embellish,—to render false gods and their worship, and so
much more of a most execrable system of paganism as the poem allowed
room for admitting, *agreeable* objects to the reader's imagination, and
as far as possible *interesting* to his affections? We do not see how the poet
is to be acquitted of this, unless, as we observed before, we could
suppose so absurd a thing, as that he should regard his work as a
mere piece of scenery, displaying fine colours and strange shapes,
without any moral tendency at all. It is possible our author may have
in his own mind some mode of explaining and justifying such a
conduct, and that without a rejection of rational theism or revealed

religion; with either of which degrees of disbelief we are very far from thinking he is chargeable. But the very least that a Christian critic can say in such a case is, that no man, *rightly* impressed with the transcendent idea of a Supreme Being, and with the unspeakable folly and danger of trifling with the purity and integrity, and sporting away, in any the smallest degree, the awfulness of that idea, could have written this work, or can read it without displeasure and regret.

It was to be foreseen that, sooner or later, one of the many enterprizes of genius would be a very formal and strenuous attempt to confer English popularity on the Hindoo gods. It was a thing not to be endured, that, while we are as proud as Kehama of possessing India, we should not be able to bring to the augmentation of our national splendour that which India itself deems its highest glory, its mythology. And since the attempt *was* to be made, we should be very glad it has been made by a poet, whose failure will be a permanent proof and monument of the utter desperateness of the undertaking,—if we did not regret that so much genius should have been sacrificed to such a contemptible purpose. The grave part of the regret is of the same kind with that which affects us at seeing Sir Thomas More surrender his life in devout assertion of the infallibility, and universal spiritual dominion, of an impious impostor, called the Pope. But there mingles with this regret the same strong perception of the ludicrous, as we should feel in seeing a fine British fleet, in full equipment and appointment, sent out to India just for the purpose of bringing back, each ship, a basket of the gods of crockery, or some portions of that material with which the Lama of Tibet is reported to enrich the craving hands of his devotees, and at length coming into the channel with flags flying, and their cannon thundering, in celebration of the cargo. Or if the reader has not enough of similes, we would compare the poet to an artist who, if such a thing were possible in any other art than poetry, should make choice of the most offensive substances, to be moulded with the utmost delicacy and beauty of workmanship, into forms which should excite a violent contest between the visual and olfactory senses, in which, however, the latter would be sure to be victorious.

After these observations on what we think the two mortal sins of this performance, absurdity and irreverence, subordinate remarks cannot claim room for an extension of this overgrown article. There is not any thing that can properly be called *characters* in the work. Kehama is a personage so monstrous, that nothing extravagant could be said to be out of character in him. There is much ability evinced in giving Ladurlad more of what we can sympathize with, more of purely *human* dignity, amiableness, and distress, than would have been supposed practicable in a representation of human beings under such strange and impossible circumstances. We need not say one word more of the wonderful power of description, displayed in every part of the poem. It appears with unabated vigour in the concluding canto or section, which exhibits Padalon, the Hindoo hell. This exhibition, however, has a kind of coarse hideousness, which would be very remote from any thing awful or sublime, even if it included much less of the clumsy, uncouth monstrosity of the Hindoo fables; and if the measureless power and terrors of Kehama, and his making himself into eight terrible gods, did not appear so insipidly and irksomely foolish. There is too much sameness of fire, steel, and adamant; and there is in the whole scene a certain flaring *nearness*, which allows no retirement of the imagination into wide, and dubious, and mysterious terrors. This puts it in unfortunate contrast with the infernal world of Milton, and the difference is somewhat like that between walking amidst a burning town, and in a region of volcanoes. We must not bring even into thought, any sort of comparison between the display of mind in Milton's infernal personages and those of Padalon.

The general diction of the work is admirably strong, and various, and free; and, in going through it, we have repeatedly exulted in the capabilities of the English language. The author seems to have in a great measure grown out of that affected simplicity of expression, of which he has generally been accused. The versification, as to measure and rhyme, is a complete defiance of all rule, and all example; the lines are of any length, from four syllables to fourteen; there are sometimes rhymes and sometimes none; and they have no settled order of recurrence. This is objectionable, chiefly, as it allows the poet to riot away in a wild wantonness of amplification, and at the very same time imposes on him the petty care of having the lines so printed, as to put the letter-press in the form of a well-adjusted picture.

The notes comprise a large assortment of curious particulars, relating to the eastern mythology and manners, and to natural history.

41. From an unsigned review, *Literary Panorama*

June 1811, ix, 1044-59

From the conclusion of the review.

We shall not repeat the hackney'd allusions to 'the poet's eye' which 'sees more devils than vast hell can hold:'—nor to the thin partitions which divide great wits from madmen: it is enough to say that Mr. S. was determined to produce something extraordinary, and something extraordinary he has produced. His poetry affords the finest possible scenery and subjects for the pencil of art: in fact it is a series of shifting pictures. But to do them justice demands conceptions of immense magnificence; colours of superlative brilliancy; a canvas of endless extent:—in fact, a PANORAMA. If any ask for a moral,—it is to be found, we suppose, in the immortality of woe which ingulphs Kehama, the vicious tyrant: while to the suffering but virtuous Kailyal, and the tormented but undismayed and indefatigable Ladurlad, are assigned an immortality of bliss.

If we were desired to name a poet whose command of language enables him to express in the most suitable and energetic terms the images which agitate his mind, we should name Mr. Southey: if we were requested to point out a poem which to a freedom of manner in the construction of its stanzas, united a condensation of phrase, with a happy collocation of words, thereby producing force, we should recommend *Kehama*;—it contains lines never excelled for vigour, or surpassed in rhythm. Its descriptions are so charming, or so powerful, so delightful, or so tremendous, that we are engrossed by the incident under our perusal, and willingly endeavour to suspend our recollection of the incongruities by which it was introduced or to which it leads. *They* may be too shocking to our faith, or too abhorrent from our knowledge, to be tolerated, while *this* may repay our rivetted attention with delight.

Appended to this poem is a series of notes, which demonstrate the industry, the perseverance, and the extensive research of the learned author. Mr. Southey's *Thalaba* proved his acquaintance with the manners of Arabia, and the genius of the Arab poets; his *Madoc* brought before us, the feelings, the superstitions, and the natural objects of the new world: having exhausted earth, he has now had recourse to heaven and hell:—where will be his next adventure? we, for our parts, could wish that he would 'homeward bend his weary way,' and treat us with a subject in which the sympathy of the human heart, the interior of man, may afford a scope to the powers of his genius; a triumph worthy of immortality to his art and his talents.

THE HISTORY OF BRAZIL

1810–19

The first volume was published in 1810. Two further volumes appeared in 1817 and 1819.

At first Southey saw *The History of Brazil* as merely part of a much more ambitious historical work. By 1815, however, he was describing it less enthusiastically as 'a most laborious work which will be most inadequately remunerated' (Curry, ii, p. 117). His pessimism about the financial rewards of the work was justified. In 1818 he declared that it had not yet brought him so much as a single article in the *Quarterly Review* (*Life*, iv, p. 312).

42. From an unsigned review, *Eclectic Review*

September 1810, vi, 788–800

This extract from a discussion of the first volume includes passages from the opening and conclusion of the review. The criticism that as a historian Southey was too preoccupied with detail and too little concerned with interpretation was to be repeated frequently by later reviewers.

The exploits of the adventurers, which are here recorded, and the incidents connected with them, by no means merited so accurate and minute a delineation, as Mr. S. has thought proper to furnish. We do not mean to say that he has written a dull or an useless book; but his success would unquestionably have been far more splendid, had the subject been equal to his talents. It is no slight proof, indeed, of his genius, that he has been able so completely to carry his reader's attention through such a train of unimportant and monotonous details, and compel them to afford him so much delight.

As far as the knowledge subservient to research on this subject can be considered of importance, it may be safely affirmed, perhaps, that no one among his countrymen was nearly so well qualified as Mr. Southey, by an acquaintance with the Portuguese language and literature, for writing a *History of Brazil*. The work before us affords abundant evidence that he has not been sparing of his labour in the accumulation of facts. The most authentic sources, at least as far as printed books, and not these alone, extend, were open to his inspection, and have been carefully explored. No fact, we are satisfied, which could greatly interest the inquirer in the history of the formation of the settlements in Brazil, has escaped his research. To say this, is to pronounce no ordinary panegyric; and yet we see no indication, in the present work, that Mr. Southey was endowed with the most important qualities of a great historian. The comprehensive views of the great philosopher do not appear to predominate in his mind. We are far from presuming to say that he is not intitled to rank, and rank highly, among enlightened men. But with his good intentions, with his industry, and his talent for composition, we could wish that his depth and originality of thinking were still more conspicuous.

The subject Mr. Southey has undertaken, did not call, perhaps, for many very important exertions of thought; and for that very reason it might not have been selected by a man of greater powers. But of those occasions which it did present, we do not think that Mr. Southey has made the most advantage. Amidst all the details, for example, respecting tribes of savages with which the work abounds, no assistance is offered to the reader in generalizing the phaenomena of savage life; scarcely any in tracing the causes of the peculiarities among different tribes, of which his narrative makes mention; no attempt is made to illustrate the springs of human nature, as exhibited in those unfavourable circumstances; to trace the points of agreement and diversity between this the most unhappy state of society, and that which is presented at all the different stages of civilization. Had Mr. Southey avoided those lengthened statements and explanations, which a full treatment of the subject would have required (though they would have been more instructive and more interesting, too, than so much repetition of the details respecting the particular tribes), comprehensive reflections drawn from a profound insight into the subject, however shortly expressed, would have thrown a light upon his pages for which the work at present contains nothing to compensate. . . .

To sum up our opinion of this book, we do not think it is either a very splendid or very profound production. The state of knowledge respecting the regions and the history of the American continent, is, it must be confessed, so imperfect, that there is scarcely any man who will not derive instruction from a perusal of the present work. But, after all, the settlements in Brazil were far from deserving so many fine paragraphs. And though a considerable portion of the inferences to which the facts here related give occasion, are no less true with regard to a great part of the Spanish conquests than to the Portuguese, yet the history of Brazil is still an obscure and subordinate portion of the history of America; and when once the history of America, or of the Spanish part of it, shall be well written, little will remain to attract notice or yield instruction in the history of Brazil.

43. Joseph Lowe, unsigned review, *Monthly Review*

December 1812, n.s. lxix, 337–52

From his review of the first volume. Little is known about Lowe, who was a regular contributor to the *Monthly Review* between 1808 and 1815. Originally engaged in business, he abandoned this in favour of authorship after the success of his reply in 1806 to Brougham's pamphlet on the state of the nation. He contributed to the *Edinburgh Review* and the *Athenaeum*.

We regret that the multiplied demands on our time have prevented us from bestowing earlier attention on this historical work by Mr. Southey, of which the continuation has lately been announced to be in forwardness. Whether that gentleman will consider it as a compliment or not, we have no hesitation in saying that we like him much better as an historian than as a poet; and though we do not altogether agree with him respecting the mode of writing history, we are well aware of the value which ought to be attached to his extensive erudition and inde-fatigable spirit of research: qualities which, however unpopular may be the form of a book, enable an author to render a lasting service to the cause of truth, and to lay the basis of at least an eventual reputation. A *History of Brazil* is not, indeed, the subject to which we should have wished the labour of a trust-worthy historian to have been, by prefer-ence, directed, since much that it more nearly concerns us to know remains unexplored: but we were, on second thoughts, reconciled to this application of Mr. Southey's time, by a consideration of the aptitude for the task which he had acquired by a residence in Portugal, and a predilection for the history of that country.

[Outlines the contents of the volume, with quotations.]

Our readers will by this time be enabled to form an idea of Mr. Southey's peculiar manner of writing history. His plan is to be sparing of general reflections, and to relate with scrupulous accuracy and minuteness the occurrence of detached events, observing generally the order of their date. The remarks which he permits himself to make are only those which arise out of the subject of the narrative; a course which is very different from that of the writers who concentrate a body of facts for the illustration of a previously-conceived doctrine. On their plan it may be said that the narrative seems to be written for the reflections; and on that of Mr. Southey, that we have facts with scarcely any reflections interspersed. A similar remark was made by us on the writer, whoever he be, of the *Memoirs of Prince Eugene.* Mr. Southey's plan is confirmed in great measure by the authority of the antients, and among ourselves by the recent example of Mr. Fox. Without entering into any general discussion of the best mode of writing history, we must say that Mr. Southey has gone greatly too far into particular detail for the taste of the present generation: which expects something more than a succession of objects and occurrences, clearly and specifically described, but not brought together so as to produce effect by combination. The reader who turns over Mr. Southey's pages, in quest of dazzling description, will experience nearly such a disappointment as the ardent admirer of war would find on exchanging the flattering picture of a campaign drawn by a writer who lets loose his imagination, for the plain unadorned journal of a professional eye-witness.

We differ, however, from the prevailing taste, and are disposed to look with favourable prepossession on the writer who avoids painting, and brings truth and reality in the plainest garb before the eyes of his readers. Yet, while we admire the plan, and regard its successful execution as the true province of taste and genius, we are not prepared to say that Mr. Southey's performance is in complete correspondence with the dignity of his conception. The magnitude of the volume, and the variety of its details, naturally suggest the charge of prolixity; a charge which appears to be better founded with respect to multiplicity of circumstances than to their lengthened description. Few writers are more remote from danger of trespassing by the use of unmeaning epithets; on this score, therefore, Mr. Southey may be called a concise writer: but, in looking to prolixity in another sense,—we mean an accumulation of circumstances,—a very different conclusion must be drawn. True it is that, from the pen of so diligent an investigator, we may safely rely on the fidelity of the enumerated particulars; and it is equally true that all of them may be considered as conducing, in some degree, to the illustration of the history and manners of the people whom he describes: but the mass is too large: its parts are too multiform. If the extent of the historian's research ought to be such as to know no other limit than the range of authentic materials, the exposition of his stores to the public is to be guided by a very different rule. The majority of readers expect a writer to judge as well as to investigate for them; and they will be satisfied to find collateral details subjoined in the notes, or cited in the margin, while in the text they look only for such a selection of circumstances as may suffice to give them a clear conception of leading facts and characteristics. . . .

We resume our observations on Mr. Southey's style. A warning is given by a *black letter* title-page (𝕳𝖎𝖘𝖙𝖔𝖗𝖞 𝖔𝖋 𝕭𝖗𝖆𝖟𝖎𝖑) that this book is not composed in the fashionable manner of the present day; and truly in diction, as well as in method, Mr. Southey discovers no small predilection for the chronicles of other times. His readers will frequently meet with such words as *spake* for *spoke*; *bare* for *bore*; *lack* for *want*; *alway*; *pavais*; *religioner*;—*to win a town, or to win stores*, &c. &c. Foreign names, likewise, are spelt agreeably to the language of the particular country; as Felipe II. of Spain; Joam IV. of Portugal; and Prince Mauritz of Holland. Without discussing the propriety or the prudence of these deviations from common usage, we proceed to a remark which is apparently of little consequence; we mean, the position of the notes. Aware that it is painful for the reader to interrupt his attention during the thread of a narrative, we are desirous of seeing subordinate illustrations either incorporated in the text, or referred, if more remotely connected with the subject, to the end of the volume. The latter mode we have, on several occasions, wished to have seen adopted in the present book; in which, in fact, the great body of the notes is so placed;—and we are mistaken if the first page does not supply an example in point. We must next advert to the want of a map, which is an almost indispensable requisite to the interest of such long and varied details. It is delayed, says Mr. Southey, for the purpose of rendering it 'as full and as little incorrect as possible:' but, on considering the length of time which has already elapsed before the publication of the second Part, and the miserable maps of South America which we as yet possess, it is to be regretted that a sketch or outline was not made to accompany the present volume.

To conclude; imperfect though this publication may be, we regard it as a highly-valuable record, and shall gladly bestow attention on the promised additional portion of it: which, as it will relate to a period nearer our own time, will probably be put together with more attention to the prevailing taste;—an advantage perfectly attainable without any sacrifice of the sterling merits of its precursor.

44. Shelley on Southey

1811-12

Reprinted from *The Letters of Percy Bysshe Shelley*, ed. F. L. Jones (2 vols, 1964). The nineteen-year-old Shelley arrived in Keswick with his young bride early in November 1811. Although he disliked Southey's political opinions Shelley admired his poetry and was prepared to praise him enthusiastically. As he saw more of Southey, however, his attitude quickly became hostile.

(a) To Elizabeth Hitchener, 26 December 1811

I have also been much engaged in talking with Southey. You may conjecture that a man must possess high and estimable qualities, if with the prejudice of such total difference from my sentiments I can regard him great and worthy—In fact Southey is an advocate of liberty and equality; he looks forward to a state when all shall be perfected, and matter become subjected to the omnipotence of mind; but he is now an advocate for existing establishments; he says he designs his three statues in *Kehama* to be contemplated with republican feelings—but not in this age.—Southey hates the Irish, he speaks against Catholic Emancipation, & Parliamentary reform. In all these things we differ, & our differences were the subject of a long conversation.—Southey calls himself a Christian, but he does not believe that the Evangelists were inspired—he rejects the Trinity, and thinks that Jesus Christ stood precisely in the same relation to God as himself.—Yet he calls himself a Christian—now if ever there was a definition of a Deist I think it could never be clearer than this confession of faith.—But Southey tho' far from being a man of great reasoning powers is a great Man. He has all that characterises the poet—great eloquence tho' obstinacy in opinion which arguments are the last things that can shake. He is a man of virtue, he never will belie what he thinks. His professions are in strict compatibility with his practise. [i, pp. 210-12.]

(b) To Elizabeth Hitchener, 2 January 1812

Southey is no believer in original sin: he thinks that which appears to be
a taint of our nature is in effect the result of unnatural political institutions—there we agree—he thinks the prejudices of education and sinister influence of political institutions adequate to account for all the
Specimens of vice which have fallen within his observation. . . . I am
not sure that Southey is *quite* uninfluenced by venality. He is disinterested so far as respects his family, but I question if he is so as far
as respects the world.—His writings solely support a numerous
family.—His sweet children are such amiable creatures that I almost
forgive what I suspect. His wife is very stupid. Mrs. Coleridge is
worse. Mrs. Lovel who was once an actress is the best of them. [i,
pp. 216–19.]

(c) To Elizabeth Hitchener, 7 January 1812

Southey says Expediency ought to be made the ground of politics
but not of morals. I urged that the most fatal error that ever happened
in the world was the separation of political and ethical science, that
the former ought to be entirely regulated by the latter, as whatever was
a right criterion of action for an individual must be so for a society
which was but an assemblage of individuals, 'that politics were morals
more comprehensively enforced.'—Southey did not think the reasoning conclusive—he has a very happy knack when truth goes against him
of saying, 'Ah! when you are as old as I am you will think with me'—
this talent he employed in the above instance. Nothing can well be
more weak. . . . I do not think so highly of Southey as I did—it is to be
confessed that to see him in his family, to behold him in his domestic
circle he appears in a most amiable light.—I do not mean that he is or
can be the great character which once I linked him to. His mind is
terribly narrow compared to it—*Once* he *was* this character, everything
you can conceive of practised virtue.—Now he is corrupted by the
world, contaminated by Custom; it rends my heart when I think what
he might have been. [i, p. 223.]

(d) To William Godwin, 16 January 1812

Southey the Poet whose principles were pure & elevated once, is now
the servile champion of every abuse and absurdity.—I have had much
conversation with him. He says 'You will think as I do when you are as
old.' I do not feel the least disposition to be Mr. S's proselyte. [i, p. 231.]

(e) To Elizabeth Hitchener, ?16 January 1812

Now of Southey.—he has *lost* my good opinion. No private virtues can compensate for public language like this—The following passage is Southeys writing the Edinburgh Annual Register. 'We are not displeased at the *patriotic* expedient to which *the worthy Sir Francis* has thus recourse, as it serves to shew how contemptible are the Burdettite and Wardleite members whose nature is debased by the vile views of faction, and whose unmanly feelings and ungenerous hearts forbid their sympathy in a case where to the everlasting honor of the country be it related so deeply interests with keen (speaking of Spain) solicitude the fond bosoms of a people' [now mark this disgusting abominable flattery and horrible lie—I cant contain myself] 'who in duly appreciating his transcendent virtues prove themselves deserving the best Monarch that ever adorned a throne.'—Now what think you of this. I can only exclaim with Bolingbroke poor human nature!— We have now serious thoughts of immediately going to Ireland. Southeys conversation has lost its charm, except it be the charm of horror, at so hateful a prostitution of talents. [i, p. 233.]

(f) To Elizabeth Hitchener, 3 February 1812

We felt regret at leaving Keswick. I passed Southeys house without *one* sting.—He is a man who *may* be amiable in his *private* character stained and false as is his public one.—he *may* be amiable, but if he is my feelings are liars, and I have been so long accustomed to trust to them in these cases that the opinion of the world is not the likeliest criminator to impeach their credibility. [i, p. 249.]

45. Byron on Southey

1811–13

Extracts from Byron's *Letters and Journals*, ed. R. E. Prothero (1898–1901).

(a) From a letter to William Harness, 6 December 1811

Do read mathematics.—I should think *X plus Y* at least as amusing as *The Curse of Kehama*, and much more intelligible. Master Southey's poems *are*, in fact, what parallel lines might be—viz. prolonged *ad infinitum* without meeting anything half so absurd as themselves. [ii, pp. 74–5.]

(b) From a letter to Thomas Moore, 27 September 1813

Yesterday, at Holland House, I was introduced to Southey—the best-looking bard I have seen for some time. To have that poet's head and shoulders, I would almost have written his Sapphics. He is certainly a prepossessing person to look on, and a man of talent, and all that, and —*there* is his eulogy. [ii, p. 266.]

(c) From a letter to James Wedderburn Webster, 30 September 1813

I have been passing my time with Rogers and Sir James Mackintosh; and once at Holland House I met Southey; he is a person of very *epic* appearance, and has a fine head—as far as the outside goes, and wants nothing but taste to make the inside equally attractive. [ii, pp. 269–70.]

(d) Entry in *Journal*, 22 November 1813

Southey, I have not seen much of. His appearance is *Epic*; and he is the only existing entire man of letters. All the others have some pursuit annexed to their authorship. His manners are mild, but not those of a man of the world, and his talents of the first order. His prose is perfect. Of his poetry there are various opinions: there is, perhaps, too much of it for the present generation; posterity will probably select. He has *passages* equal to any thing. At present, he has *a party*, but no *public*— except for his prose writings. The life of Nelson is beautiful. [ii, p. 331.]

46. Henry Crabb Robinson on Southey

1811-15

Reprinted from *Henry Crabb Robinson on Books and their Writers,*
ed. E. J. Morley (3 vols, 1938). Robinson (1775–1867), constant
reader, correspondent and friend of contemporary writers, first
met Southey in 1808. E. J. Morley's collection of his opinions is
compiled from the extensive records in his diary, travel journals
and reminiscences.

(a) 2 February 1811
Finished *Kehama*. . . . My opinion of this poem has not changed on the
second perusal. The faults are inherent in the subject. I could wish
only a closer union between the incidents which respect Kailyal and
Ladurlad, and the scheme of universal dominion projected by the
'Almighty Man.' There are two unconnected actions running through
the poem. But the beauties of description almost always and of sentiment occasionally more than compensate for this fault. [i, pp. 22–3.]

(b) 12 March 1811
Tea and chess with Mrs. Barbauld. Read going, eight to fourteen
chapters of *Madoc*; exceedingly pleased with the touching painting of
the poem. It has not the splendid glare of *Kehama*, but there is a
uniform glow of pure and beautiful morality, interesting description,
and easy flowing verse which render the work very pleasing. Surely
none but a pedant can affect or be seduced to think slightingly of the
poem. It is doubtful at all events whether the acuteness which could
suggest severe criticism, or the sensibility which feels such beauties, is
the more desirable portion. [i, p. 25.]

(c) 31 March 1811
At night six cantos of *Madoc*. The conclusion of the first volume has all
the interest of a novel. [i, p. 29.]

(d) 1 April 1811

Finished *Madoc* at night. This poem has great beauties principally in description, both moral and natural, but the incidents are overladen, especially in the second part. There is, besides, a prevailing incongruity between the morals and the incidents of the poem. There is an exquisite purity and delicacy of moral sense which is not in harmony with the wild and romantic occurrences. The hero, Madoc, is like Angelica Kaufmann's heroes. There is a want of virility in him. One would think that a virgin had been the poet as well as the painter. In the *Edinburgh* review of *Kehama*, which is, however, a poem of a higher character than *Madoc*, the reviewer certainly manifests a flagrant disposition to exaggerate the defects and depreciate the beauties of the poet, besides a want of poetic sensibility, but the *intelligible* features of Southey's mind are rightly seized and forcibly portrayed.

Madoc is the very first of military heroes, probably, who has flourished in poetry and been drawn altogether exempt from love. There is not the slightest symptom of any other than brotherly and filial love in him. Goervyl, too, his sister, is left in danger of becoming an old maid. [i, pp. 29–30.]

(e) 5 August 1811

Finished *Thalaba*. The last three books are very beautiful, but the tenth is by far the finest. It really interests. The innocent daughter Laila of the Magician Okba, kept by him in a region of intense cold in an enchanted garden warmed by a fountain of fire, and waited on by attendants of snow, is a very fanciful and beautiful object. But through the whole there is little interest or sympathy. Thalaba resembles rather an allegorical than a real personage. He sustains trials, but we do not see the hidden strength that supports him. At one time he is saved only by having unconsciously on his finger a magic ring—then to show his faith he throws it off and is still saved by faith. Then he has again the ring and it protects him once more, and then he throws it away and again triumphs without it. But it should either be always or never necessary. It still has much of the character of *Kehama*—but *Kehama* has all the beauties in greater number and excellence, and the same faults in a lower degree. [i, p. 43.]

(f) 9 December 1812

Reading Southey's *Omniana*—a very insignificant collection of extracts from books, with observations, and the worst book he has ever made. Some few articles by Coleridge are by far the best in the volume. [i, pp. 114–15.]

(g) 20 December 1812
Also finished Southey's *Omniana*—a collection of queer things. It is, perhaps, useful to be acquainted with the perversities and whims which men of intellect have displayed, and which appear also to have infected all ages and countries. *Las Quatro-cientas* of Fray Luys d'Escobar, 1550, furnishes one of the most strange articles. It consists of metrical answers to all imaginary mad questions, theological chiefly. Yet amid the trash of the book occasional gleams of wisdom burst forth. [i, p. 115.]

(h) 18 September 1815
I finished *Don Roderick* this morning. This is spoken of (even by Lamb, if I mistake not) as the best of Southey's long poems. It is, however, for me far less pleasing than *Kehama*, and has fewer delightful passages than *Madoc*. Its merit lies in the judgment which has wrought so much interesting matter out of unpromising materials. Don Roderick, having escaped from the battle in which his people were vanquished by the Moors, repents in solitude, and the whole of the poem treats of his subsequent life, exhibiting as it were the genuineness of his penitence and self-devotion. He is made a sort of monk by a dying monk, and is roused by a female enthusiastic warrior to undertake the stirring up of his countrymen against the infidels. He goes among the foe, finds Pelayo, and is the first, though unknown, to hail him king. With Pelayo he meets with Florinda, whose beauty had stimulated him to the act of violence which produced the calamities of the country. Her he confesses and receives her confession, an unknown. The war breaks out which ended in the deliverance of a part of Spain (the Asturias) from the Moors.

Roderick meets with his bitter enemy, Julian. They dispute on religion. At last Roderick converts the count. Makes himself known to him and his daughter Florinda just as they are dying. He has also an interview with his mother. He is known by Pelayo, but does not make himself known publicly till in the field of battle he seizes a sword, and bare-headed works wonders of bravery. He retires again from glory, for when the victory is gained no one can find him. After many years his tomb is found. This is the ancient legend concerning Roderick.

The greatest fault of the poem is that it is too uniformly religious.

Even Mrs. William Pattisson was not satisfied with the religion. Probably she thought it not quite sincere in the author; and I do think after all, that Southey belongs rather to the *Philo-Christians than the Christians*. It is, I suspect, the poetic capabilities of Christianity which have charmed him. But this is no reproach to Southey or Christianity, according to the higher and juster ideas of poetry which the German critical school has established. [i, pp. 173–4.]

47. James Smith, parody of Southey

1812

From *Rejected Addresses, or The New Theatrum Poetarum* by the brothers James and Horace Smith, first published in 1812. The text and notes were considerably revised for later editions and are reprinted here from the 18th edition of 1833, the last which the authors supervised. Alterations from the first edition are listed in the reprint edited by Andrew Boyle (1929).

THE REBUILDING.

BY R. S.*

[*Spoken by a Glendoveer.*]

I am a blessed Glendoveer:**
'Tis mine to speak, and yours to hear.†
Midnight, yet not a nose

* Robert Southey.
** For the Glendoveer, and the rest of the *dramatis personæ* of this imitation, the reader is referred to *The Curse of Kehama*.
† '*The Rebuilding* is in the name of Mr. Southey, and is one of the best in the collection. It is in the style of the Kehama of that multifarious author; and is supposed to be spoken in the character of one of his Glendoveers. The imitation of the diction and measure, we think, is nearly almost perfect; and the descriptions as good as the original. It opens with an account of the burning of the old theatre, formed upon the pattern of the Funeral of Arvalan.'—*Edinburgh Review*.

From Tower-hill to Piccadilly snored!
Midnight, yet not a nose
From Indra drew the essence of repose!
See with what crimson fury,
By Indra fann'd, the god of fire ascends the walls of
Drury!

Tops of houses, blue with lead,
Bend beneath the landlord's tread.
Master and 'prentice, serving-man and lord,
Nailor and tailor,
Grazier and brazier,
Through streets and alleys pour'd—
All, all abroad to gaze,
And wonder at the blaze.
Thick calf, fat foot, and slim knee,
Mounted on roof and chimney,*
The mighty roast, the mighty stew
To see;
As if the dismal view
Were but to them a Brentford jubilee.

Vainly, all-radiant Surya, sire of Phaeton
(By Greeks call'd Apollo)†
Hollow
Sounds from thy harp proceed;
Combustible as reed,
The tongue of Vulcan licks thy wooden legs:

---

* This couplet was introduced by the Authors by way of bravado, in answer to one who alleged that the English language contained no rhyme to chimney.

† Apollo. A gigantic wooden figure of this deity was erected on the roof. The writer (*horrescit referens!*) is old enough to recollect the time when it was first placed there. Old Bishop, then one of the masters of Merchant Tailors' School, wrote an epigram upon the occasion, which, referring to the aforesaid figure, concluded thus:

> Above he fills up Shakespeare's place,
> And Shakespeare fills up his below—

Very antithetical: but quaere as to the meaning? The writer, like Pluto, 'long puzzled his brain' to find it out, till he was immersed 'in a lower deep' by hearing Madame de Staël say, at the table of the late Lord Dillon, 'Buonaparte is not a man, but a system.' Inquiry was made in the course of the evening of Sir James Mackintosh as to what the lady meant? He answered, 'Mass! I cannot tell.' Madame de Staël repeats this apophthegm in her work on Germany. It is probably understood *there*.

From Drury's top, dissever'd from thy pegs,
Thou tumblest.
Humblest,
Where late thy bright effulgence shone on high;
While, by thy somerset excited fly
Ten million
Billion
Sparks from the pit, to gem the sable sky.

Now come the men of fire to quench the fires:
To Russell Street see Globe and Atlas run,
Hope gallops first, and second Sun;
On flying heel,
See Hand-in-Hand
O'ertake the band!
View with what glowing wheel
He nicks
Phœnix!

While Albion scampers from Bridge Street, Blackfriars—
Drury Lane! Drury Lane!
Drury Lane! Drury Lane!
They shout and they bellow again and again.
All, all in vain!
Water turns steam;
Each blazing beam
Hisses defiance to the eddying spout:
It seems but too plain that nothing can put it out!
Drury Lane! Drury Lane!
See, Drury Lane expires!

Pent in by smoke-dried beams, twelve moons or more,
Shorn of his ray,
Surya in durance lay:
The workmen heard him shout,
But thought it would not pay,
To dig him out.
When lo! terrific Yamen, lord of hell,
Solemn as lead,
Judge of the dead,
Sworn foe to witticism,
By men call'd criticism,

Came passing by that way:
Rise! cried the fiend, behold a sight of gladness!
Behold the rival theatre!
I've set O. P. at her,*
Who, like a bull-dog bold,
Growls and fastens on his hold.
The many-headed rabble roar in madness;
Thy rival staggers: come and spy her
Deep in the mud as thou art in the mire.
So saying, in his arms he caught the beaming one,
And crossing Russell Street,
He placed him on his feet
'Neath Covent Garden dome. Sudden a sound,
As of the bricklayers of Babel, rose:
Horns, rattles, drums, tin trumpets, sheets of copper,
Punches and slaps, thwacks of all sorts and sizes,
From the knobb'd bludgeon to the taper switch,†

* O.P. This personage, who is alleged to have growled like a bull-dog, requires rather a lengthened note, for the edification of the rising generation. The 'horns, rattles, drums,' with which he is accompanied, are no inventions of the poet. The new Covent Garden Theatre opened on the 18th Sept. 1809, when a cry of 'Old Prices' (afterwards diminished to O. P.) burst out from every part of the house. This continued and increased in violence till the 23d, when rattles, drums, whistles, and cat-calls, having completely drowned the voices of the actors, Mr. Kemble, the stage-manager, came forward and said, that a committee of gentlemen had undertaken to examine the finances of the concern, and that until they were prepared with their report the theatre would continue closed. 'Name them!' was shouted from all sides. The names were declared, viz. Sir Charles Price, the Solicitor-General, the Recorder of London, the Governor of the Bank, and Mr. Angersteen. 'All shareholders!' bawled a wag from the gallery. In a few days the theatre re-opened: the public paid no attention to the report of the referees, and the tumult was renewed for several weeks with even increased violence. The proprietors now sent in hired bruisers, to *mill* the refractory into subjection. This irritated most of their former friends, and, amongst the rest, the annotator, who accordingly wrote the song of 'Heigh-ho, says Kemble,' which was caught up by the ballad-singers, and sung under Mr. Kemble's house-windows in Great Russell-street. A dinner was given at the Crown and Anchor Tavern in the Strand, to celebrate the victory obtained by W. Clifford in his action against Brandon the box-keeper, for assaulting him for wearing the letters O. P. in his hat. At this dinner Mr. Kemble attended, and matters were compromised by allowing the advanced price (seven shillings) to the boxes. The writer remembers a former riot of a similar sort at the same theatre (in the year 1792), when the price to the boxes was raised from five shillings to six. That tumult, however, only lasted three nights.

† 'From the knobb'd bludgeon to the taper switch.' This image is not the creation of the poets: it sprang from reality. The Authors happened to be at the Royal Circus when 'God save the King' was called for, accompanied by a cry of 'stand up!' and 'hats off!' An inebriated naval lieutenant perceiving a gentleman in an adjoining box slow to obey the call, struck his hat off with his stick, exclaiming, 'Take off your hat, sir!' The other thus assaulted proved to be, unluckily for the lieutenant, Lord Camelford, the celebrated

Ran echoing round the walls; paper placards
Blotted the lamps, boots brown with mud the benches;
A sea of heads roll'd roaring in the pit;
On paper wings O. P.'s
Reclin'd in lettered ease;
While shout and scoff,
Ya! ya! off! off!
Like thunderbolt on Surya's ear-drum fell,
And seem'd to paint
The savage oddities of Saint
Bartholomew in hell.

Tears dimm'd the god of light—
'Bear me back, Yamen, from this hideous sight;
Bear me back, Yamen, I grow sick,
Oh! bury me again in brick;
Shall I on New Drury tremble,
To be O. P.'d like Kemble?
No,
Better remain by rubbish guarded,
Than thus hubbubish groan placarded;
Bear me back, Yamen, bear me quick,
And bury me again in brick.'
Obedient Yamen
Answered, 'Amen,'
And did
As he was bid.

---

bruiser and duellist. A set-too in the lobby was the consequence, where his lordship
quickly proved victorious. 'The devil is not so black as he is painted,' said one of the
Authors to the other; 'let us call upon Lord Camelford, and tell him that we were witnesses of his being first assaulted.' The visit was paid on the ensuing morning at Lord
Camelford's lodgings, in Bond-street. Over the fire-place in the drawing-room were
ornaments strongly expressive of the pugnacity of the peer. A long thick bludgeon lay
horizontally supported by two brass hooks. Above this was placed parallel one of lesser
dimensions, until a pyramid of weapons gradually arose, tapering to a horsewhip:

Thus all below was strength, and all above was grace.

Lord Camelford received his visitants with great civility, and thanked them warmly
for the call; adding, that their evidence would be material, it being his intention to indict
the lieutenant for an assault. 'All I can say in return is this,' exclaimed the peer with great
cordiality, 'if ever I see you engaged in a row, upon my soul, I'll stand by you.' The
Authors expressed themselves thankful for so potent an ally, and departed. In about a
fortnight afterwards Lord Camelford was shot in a duel with Mr. Best.

There lay the buried god, and Time
Seemed to decree eternity of lime;
But pity, like a dew-drop, gently prest
Almighty Veeshnoo's* adamantine breast:
He, the preserver, ardent still
To do whate'er he says he will,
From South-hill wing'd his way,
To raise the drooping lord of day.
All earthly spells the busy one o'erpower'd;
He treats with men of all conditions
Poets and players, tradesmen, and musicians;
Nay, even ventures
To attack the renters,
Old and new:
A list he gets
Of claims and debts,
And deems nought done, while aught remains to do.
Yamen beheld, and wither'd at the sight;
Long had he aim'd the sunbeam to control,
For light was hateful to his soul:
'Go on!' cried the hellish one, yellow with spite;
'Go on!' cried the hellish one, yellow with spleen,
'Thy toils of the morning, like Ithaca's queen,
I'll toil to undo every night.'

Ye sons of song, rejoice!
Veeshnoo has still'd the jarring elements,
The spheres hymn music;
Again the god of day
Peeps forth with trembling ray,
Wakes, from their humid caves, the sleeping Nine,
And pours at intervals a strain divine.
'I have an iron yet in the fire,' cried Yamen;
'The vollied flame rides in my breath,
My blast is elemental death;
This hand shall tear your paper bonds to pieces;
Ingross your deeds, assignments, leases,
My breath shall every line erase
Soon as I blow the blaze.'
The lawyers are met at the Crown and Anchor,

* Veeshnoo. The late Mr. Whitbread.

And Yamen's visage grows blanker and blanker;
The lawyers are met at the Anchor and Crown,
And Yamen's cheek is a russety brown:
Veeshnoo, now thy work proceeds;
The solicitor reads,
And, merit of merit!
Red wax and green ferret
Are fixed at the foot of the deeds!
Yamen beheld and shiver'd;
His finger and thumb were cramped;
His ear by the flea in't was bitten,
When he saw by the lawyer's clerk written,
Sealed and delivered, ⎫
Being first duly stamped. ⎭
'Now for my turn!' the demon cries, and blows
A blast of sulphur from his mouth and nose.
Ah! bootless aim! the critic fiend,
Sagacious Yamen, judge of hell,
Is judged in his turn;
Parchment won't burn!
His schemes of vengeance are dissolv'd in air,
Parchment won't tear!!

Is it not written in the Himakoot book,
(That mighty Baly from Kehama took)
'Who blows on pounce
Must the Swerga renounce?'
It is! it is! Yamen, thine hour is nigh:
Like as an eagle claws an asp,
Veeshnoo has caught him in his mighty grasp,
And hurl'd him, in spite of his shrieks and his squalls,
Whizzing aloft, like the Temple fountain,
Three times as high as Meru mountain,
Which is
Ninety-nine times as high as St. Paul's.
Descending, he twisted like Levy the Jew,*

---

* Levy. An insolvent Israelite who threw himself from the top of the Monument a short time before. An inhabitant of Monument-yard informed the writer, that he happened to be standing at his door talking to a neighbour; and looking up at the top of the pillar, exclaimed, 'Why, here's the flag coming down.' 'Flag!' answered the other, 'it's a man.' The words were hardly uttered when the suicide fell within ten feet of the speakers.

Who a durable grave meant
To dig in the pavement
Of Monument-yard:
To earth by the laws of attraction he flew,
And he fell, and he fell
To the regions of hell;
Nine centuries bounced he from cavern to rock,
And his head, as he tumbled, went nickety-nock,
Like a pebble in Carisbrook well.

Now Veeshnoo turn'd round to a capering varlet,
Arrayed in blue and white and scarlet,
And cried, 'Oh! brown of slipper as of hat!
Lend me, Harlequin, thy bat!'
He seized the wooden sword, and smote the earth;
When lo! upstarting into birth
A fabric, gorgeous to behold,
Outshone in elegance the old,
And Veeshnoo saw, and cried, 'Hail, playhouse
mine!'
Then, bending his head, to Surya he said:
'Soon as thy maiden sister Di
Caps with her copper lid the dark blue sky,
And through the fissures of her clouded fan
Peeps at the naughty monster man,
Go mount yon edifice,
And shew thy steady face
In renovated pride,
More bright, more glorious than before!'
But ah! coy Surya still felt a twinge,
Still smarted from his former singe;
And to Veeshnoo replied,
In a tone rather gruff,
'No, thank you! one tumble's enough!'

48. Walter Scott recommends Southey as Poet Laureate

1 September 1813

Reprinted from *The Letters of Sir Walter Scott*, ed. Sir H. J. C. Grierson (12 vols, 1932–7), iii, pp. 335–6. After refusing the Laureateship himself Scott wrote this generous letter to Southey.

My dear Southey,—On my return here I found, to my no small surprise, a letter tendering me the laurel vacant by the death of the poetical Pye. I have declined the appointment, as being incompetent to the task of annual commemoration; but chiefly as being provided for in my professional department, and unwilling to incur the censure of engrossing the emolument attached to one of the new appointments which seems proper to be filled by a man of literature who has no other views in life. Will you forgive me, my dear friend, if I own I had you in my recollection. I have given Croker the hint, and otherwise endeavoured to throw the office into your option. I am uncertain if you will like it, for the laurel has certainly been tarnished by some of its wearers, and as at present managed, its duties are inconvenient and somewhat liable to ridicule. But the latter matter might be amended, and I should think the Regent's good sense would lead him to lay aside these regular commemorations; and as to the former point, it has been worn by Dryden of old, and by Warton in modern days. If you quote my own refusal against me, I reply—first, I have been luckier than you in holding two offices not usually conjoined; secondly, I did not refuse it from any foolish prejudice against the situation—otherwise how durst I mention it to you, my elder brother in the muse?—but from a sort of internal hope that they would give it to you, upon whom it would be so much more worthily conferred. For I am not such an ass as not to know that you are my better in poetry, though I have had, probably but for a time, the tide of popularity in my favour. I have not time to add ten thousand other reasons, but I only wished to tell you how the matter was, and to beg you to think before you reject the offer which I flatter myself will be made to you. If I had not been, like Dogberry, a fellow with two gowns already, I should have jumped at it like a cock at a gooseberry. Ever yours most truly,

Walter Scott

THE LIFE OF NELSON

1813

Southey described this work to Scott as 'a subject not self-chosen—
and out of my way, but executed *con amore*' (*Life*, iv, p. 9). The book
was, in fact, commissioned by Murray for a fee of 100 gns.
Southey was annoyed that a miscalculation by the printer caused
it to be published in two volumes instead of one, thus increasing
its cost and reducing its potential market. *Nelson* had a steady sale
during Southey's lifetime but achieved much greater popularity
only after his death.

49. From an unsigned review, *Critical Review*

July 1813, 4th series, iv, 11–26

From the opening of the review.

In our journal for August 1810, and for September of the same year,
we gave a pretty copious account of the life of Lord Nelson by the
Rev. J. S. Clarke, F.R.S. and J. M'Arthur, Esq. L.L.D., in two volumes
4to. of very stately bulk. A work of that magnitude was but ill calculated for the general reader; but the life of Lord Nelson is certainly
one which a great mass of our countrymen, not only in the navy, but
out of the navy, would wish to read. Mr. Southey has, therefore, we
have no doubt, rendered a very acceptable service to a numerous class
of his majesty's liege subjects, who are either rolling on the ocean, or
idling on *terra-firma*, by the present more compendious and more
portable life of the greatest maritime hero whom England ever produced. In two very neat pocket volumes our present author has compressed a sufficiently full and detailed account of the gallant achievements

of Lord Nelson; and his narrative is so stripped of all extraneous matter and superfluous circumstances, and the hero himself is so uniformly made the prominent object of the picture, that the present appears to us a very interesting piece of biography; and we believe that there are few persons who peruse the first page of the first volume, who will not have the edge of their intellectual appetite whetted to proceed to the last page of the second.

As we have already enumerated the principal particulars in the life of Lord Nelson, in our review of the performance of Messrs. Clarke and M'Arthur mentioned above, we shall not accompany Mr. Southey with much regularity or minuteness in his present narrative, but shall select such parts of it as are more peculiarly interesting, or such traits as place the character of the British hero in a light somewhat different from that of his former biographers. As far as we can judge, one very honourable characteristic of the present life is impartiality. The author is not so far dazzled by the glory of Lord Nelson as to be blind to his defects. Mr. Southey has an eagle's, or rather perhaps he would wish us to say, a poet's eye: and he has ventured to look full and fixedly upon the sunny radiance of Nelson's fame; and has both seen and marked the blots of infirmity, by which it was partially obscured. If Mr. Southey had not noted the occasional or partial defects of Nelson, he would have been wanting in biographical probity, which, though often violated, is always to be praised where it is found, while the want of it ought never to pass without rigid animadversion or severe reproof.

50. From an unsigned review, *British Critic*

October 1813, xlii, 360–6

Extracts from the opening and conclusion of the review.

Mr. Southey's idea of a life of Nelson so exactly corresponds with our own, that we subjoin his concise but satisfactory description of the impression under which he compiled it, adding as our opinion that all that was undertaken has been successfully accomplished.

Many lives of Nelson have been written: one is yet wanting, clear and concise enough to become a manual for the young sailor, which he may carry about with him, till he has treasured up the example in his memory and in his heart. In attempting such a work, I shall write the eulogy of our great naval Hero; for the best eulogy of NELSON is the faithful history of his actions: the best history, that which shall relate them most perspicuously.

The reader therefore is here presented with a plain narrative of events and actions which, though familiar to us all, we are all delighted to peruse again. The history is, beyond all question, faithful. The great and splendid achievements of the Hero are detailed with vigour, accompanied with a circumstantial attention to the incidents and anecdotes which they involve. His defects and follies, for alas the greatest, the wisest, and the best, have their proportion of these, are neither overlooked nor descanted upon with unbecoming severity. The great error of all, the unfortunate and unjustifiable infatuation in favour of Lady Hamilton, to the prejudice of the natural and legitimate claim on his affection and his honour, is introduced with much feeling and delicacy. That other momentous deviation also from the path of rectitude which took place in the Bay of Naples, equally discreditable to Nelson's prudence, honour, and humanity, is introduced with some, though not quite its due share of animadversion. . . .

If we have not protracted this article by animadverting upon many of the compiler's private and political opinions, Mr. Southey must not think that they were either unobserved, or approved. In the first place, they do not often obtrude themselves, and whether the part which the English government took at the commencement of the French revolution, was as this writer thinks, 'a miserable error,' or whether, as many politicians, as sound and as wise as Mr. Southey, believe it to have been, not only judicious, but unavoidable, it can hardly, at this period, be worth while to argue. We are, on the whole, exceedingly well pleased with the performance, and think it admirably adapted to answer the purpose for which it was intended.

51. From an unsigned review, *Eclectic Review*

June 1814, 2nd series, i, 606–22

Possibly by James Montgomery, poet and regular contributor to the *Eclectic Review*. Most of the review is concerned with an assessment of Nelson's character and achievement. This short extract, however, discusses Southey's success as a historian.

In the spring of 1801, [Nelson] was appointed second in command to Admiral Sir Hyde Parker, over a fleet sent to the Baltic, to chastise Denmark, Sweden, and Russia, for a coalition with France, against the maritime rights of Britain. Mr. Southey's narrative of this expedition, though minute in detail, is admirable in execution, and more picturesque and impressive than any thing that we have met with in these volumes. The talents of the historian, and the powers of his hero, are here displayed to the utmost advantage. We shall quote the description of the passage of the Sound by the British fleet, which ushers in the awful tragedy of the battle of Copenhagen, and presents to the mind a scene of beauty and solemnity, of magnificence and terror, that makes the heart throb with expectation and fear, while it is dilated with sublime and ineffable emotion, as the pictures, drawn by the poetical writer, by land and water, of living and inanimate nature, are perfectly realized in the reader's imagination.

RODERICK, THE LAST OF THE GOTHS

1814

Southey began work on *Roderick* in December 1809, within a week of completing *The Curse of Kehama*. Shortly before the poem's publication he wrote to Cottle: 'I am neither sanguine about its early, nor doubtful about its ultimate, acceptation in the world' (*Life*, iv, p. 82). Financially, however, *Roderick* was the most successful of his epics. Two further editions appeared in 1815 and a fourth edition in 1816. By 1818 the poem had brought Southey £700.

52. From an unsigned review, *Theatrical Inquisitor*

December 1814, v, 389–93

From the opening of the review.

It is scarcely possible to view the errors of exalted genius without breathing a sigh of compassion and regret. The generous mind feels humiliated at the contemplation; it grieves that the highest intellect should be thus partially overshadowed, and shorn of the beams of its brightness; while the feeble, and the envious, smile in derision, and glory in its aberrations.

Such are the feelings that must be excited by the reader of Southey's poems; in all his effusions there is enough to testify the vigour of his mind, and enough to teach us to lament the illusion of so powerful an intellect. His genius runs to waste in its luxuriance; it bursts forth with the impetuosity of a stream, and instead of rolling in one deep majestic channel, it is frittered into a thousand little rills, that are at length lost in the weeds and briars that surround it.

The story of the present poem is interesting, and would probably have made an excellent romance. It has, however, several capital defects, that make it altogether unfit for an heroic poem; it has no principal character, no conspicuous personage on whom the attention may rest; there is in the catastrophe an imperfect hastiness that seems borrowed from the drama of the Germans: the intended hero of the tale vanishes, and the curtain drops, leaving all unfinished and in doubt.

53. John Herman Merivale, unsigned review, *Monthly Review*

March 1815, n.s. lxxvi, 225–40

Merivale (1779–1844), lawyer, scholar and minor poet, was a regular reviewer for the *Monthly Review* and also contributed to the *Critical Review*.

We have no scruple in declaring our opinion that this production will contribute to the advancement of the author's legitimate fame more largely than any of his former poems. Its principal faults are that it is too long by half, too declamatory, and consequently often cold and spiritless where it ought to be most impassioned, and that it is incumbered by a pervading affectation of scriptural phraseology:—but these defects are counterbalanced by a well chosen subject, happily suited to the prevailing enthusiasm of the author's mind in favour of Spanish liberty, by a deep tone of moral and religious feeling, by an exalted spirit of patriotism, by fine touches of character, by animated descriptions of natural scenery, (the effect of which is often injured, however, by a too great minuteness of detail,) and by an *occasional* excellence of versification worthy of the best and purest age of English poetry. We are sorry to be obliged to qualify this praise by repeating that it applies to the work before us only in part, the remainder being mere prose, divided off into feet, and not unfrequently by a very blundering measure.

[Summarizes plot with extensive quotations.]

We have now noticed the principal characters and incidents of the poem, as far as we have found it practicable consistently with the design of not anticipating the reader's curiosity, and of stimulating rather than satiating his interest. Still, we have by no means done complete justice either to the poet or to our own feelings; since, in our anxiety to discover as much of the plan and dramatic tendency of the poem as our purpose required, we have passed over innumerable beauties of sentiment and description with which we were charmed in the perusal. The night-journey of the travellers from Cordoba over the mountains, the picture of Cordoba itself, the moonlight-scene at the opening of the fifteenth book, and the laboured and highly wrought landscape of the vale of Coradonga, are all fine specimens of the picturesque in poetry; and that strain of moral tenderness, in which Mr. Southey has often before shewn himself pre-eminently successful, he has again indulged with all its usual harmony of tone and colouring in the description of Pelayo in the bosom of his family. . . .

To the prevailing defects of the work, having once pointed them out, we gladly refrain from recurring; and the quotations which we have made will afford but few specimens of them. We had much rather leave it to our readers, by a personal inspection, to confirm or reject our opinion on this part of the subject. To the plan of the poem, however, we have still something to object. The minor personages are too frequently introduced, and made too prominent, considering the very little diversity that is thrown into their characters and circumstances. Alphonso, for instance, is an ardent young soldier, with nothing to distinguish him from that very numerous tribe, and he conduces no more to the interest of the drama than any one individual patriot in the whole host of Pelayo's adherents; yet he is brought almost as much forward on the canvas as Pelayo himself. Roderick's mother also acts a very poor though a long part, considering the importance attached to her by the leading incident to which we have already alluded;—it would have been much better to have killed her before the period of Roderick's emigration from his cell. The nature of Roderick's crime renders the subject peculiarly difficult to manage, with a view to the interest which it is necessary to attach to his character; and yet almost any deviation from the generally received historical fact is certain of being attended with a greater or less degree of incongruity. We do not think that Mr. Southey's plan of representing it as the effect of a vehement (though in its origin a virtuous) passion, returned with the most devoted affection by the unfortunate object of it, but wrought to a temporary delirium by the force of conflicting circumstances, is by any means exempt from this charge; and, whatever effect may in some respects be thus obtained, it is at least attended with this faulty consequence, that the despair and penitence of Roderick, almost unexampled in severity and duration, are thus made to bear no proportion to an offence in which, extenuated as it now appears, the will can scarcely be said to have had any part. It also makes the vengeance of Julian for a fault not only in great measure reparable, but which the perpetrator had the most ardent wish to repair as far as it was possible, little less than diabolical, and the conduct of the lady, by her outrageous virtue actuating that vengeance, much more than mischievously perverse. In short, according to our way of contemplating it, Mr. Southey has sacrificed all the moral as well as the actual, probability of the story to the design of extenuating the fault of his hero, when in fact the strength of the subject consists in the very enormity of the crime.

54. Grosvenor Charles Bedford, unsigned review, *Quarterly Review*

April 1815, xiii, 83–113

From the conclusion of his review.

Bedford (1773–1839), a civil servant, was a close friend of Southey from their schooldays at Westminster School. He collaborated with Southey in editing *Specimens of the Later English Poets*. A friend of William Gifford, he secured Southey's services as a contributor to the *Quarterly Review*. With Walter Scott, Bedford reviewed *The Curse of Kehama* in the *Quarterly* in 1811.

The critic who undertakes to give an epitome of a poem of so high a rank as *Roderick*, has little to do but to point out in the mass of admirable matter those things which strike him as most worthy of admiration. Original in its plan, true in its fundamental elements, and consistent in its parts, it rouses the feelings, and stimulates those powers of the imagination, which rejoice in the consciousness of exertion. When we rise from the contemplation of a work, which has so involuntarily called forth the vigilance of attention by its development of character, its display of the capabilities of human nature, and by the interest which it creates, we are made to feel that our intellectual and moral existence is enlarged. This effect is produced, in the first instance, by the character of Roderick. His remorse, which awakens us to a horror of his crime, and holds out, even to 'the full-fraught man, the best endued,' a profitable example of the evils into which inordinate passions may betray him in an unguarded moment, proves the ingenuousness of his mind, and, while he is lowest in his own esteem, gives the first and surest earnest of his future energy and virtue. When, by an effort consistent with his character, he rises above the despair in which he feels it disgraceful to be involved, we recognize the salutary workings of repentance in the self-devotedness with which he seeks to retrieve the consequences of his faults. From this point he springs into a new state of moral existence, and his progress, though rapid, is regular and consistent. In solitude and in contemplation he has obtained a knowledge of his own heart, and acquired self-controul; the powers with which nature has originally endowed him, enable him to controul others, and strengthen the influence of his enthusiasm over all within the sphere of his example. The priestly form in which he appears may be considered as necessary for all that passes with Florinda and Julian. His sacred character secures attention, while the remoteness of the era in which the action of the poem is placed, and the obscurity of its history, preclude the necessity for tying him down to the observance of any particular order. Every incident in the poem is brought about by his direction, the energies of all the actors are kindled by his influence, and the victory, which effects the consummation of his wishes, is ensured by his example.

The person next in importance is Adosinda. The story of her injuries first gives a form to the sentiment with which Roderick's mind is occupied. The evidence of her sufferings operates as a powerful call upon him to revenge them, and suggests to his imagination the universal distress of his country. It required no small management to derive from her services all that was necessary to the author's plan, without suffering her to trespass upon it; and to drop or suspend her office without appearing to have neglected or forgotten her. We think that Mr. Southey has steered clear of these difficulties. We recognise her exertions, without seeing her, in the eleventh book; she makes her appearance again in the fourteenth, where she is enabled to fulfil the prophecy she made when parting with Roderick at Auria; and in the twenty-third a part is allotted to her worthy of herself, and of the expectations entertained on her behalf.

The character of Count Julian, and the situation in which he is placed, are of material importance in furthering the object of the poem. The consciousness of shame which he tries to conceal by obstinacy; the self-justification which he vainly endeavours to establish by sophistry; the suspected light in which he is viewed by his adopted friends; the injuries which he and his followers are made to endure at their hands; —all these hold forth a lesson, if one were wanting, to shew that he who forgets the natural obligations of duty, and forsakes his country and its cause, must never hope for refuge in the approbation of his own heart, nor in the confidence or esteem of others. The better part of his character serves to illustrate and exemplify the principles whose operation is developed throughout the poem; and which, as we have observed, furnish its most efficient agency—the retrieving power of virtue, the force of enthusiasm and will. Julian, at his death, rewards the filial piety of his daughter; and in his reconversion to his country and his God, the triumph of her constancy and goodness is acknowledged.

Of the *manners* of the poem, or at least of their authenticity, we can say but little—as little of what may be called its costume. We believe that there are no Gothic buildings existing in Europe from even the ruins of which the author could have collected materials for embellishment; still less can we look for any record of the habits of life of a people who have so long since disappeared, and of whom so few literary monuments remain. Where, however, any notice of them could be gleaned, they have not escaped the observation of Mr. Southey. With regard to the Moors, history has afforded more ample materials, and we have, therefore, portraits of them which we can recognise, because, as their habits are less liable to change, tradition and continued customs have brought them more nearly within our view. Great praise is due to the poet for the introduction of that difference in the manners of the two parties, which he has made to result from the difference of their creeds. On the side of the Spaniards, we find a spirit unbroken by adversity, hope enlivened by the justice of their cause, the courage of action as well as of sufferance, enthusiasm in the leaders, and confidence in the people. The Mussulmen are actuated by more sensual motives—the desire of worldly possessions, a spirit of conquest, and the hope of success in this life, as an earnest of reward hereafter. The christian clings to his faith, with full trust in its support and assistance, and lights up all his other passions from the altar of his adoration. The Mussulman, in his reliance on the decrees of Providence, loses his concern for results, without feeling his ardour for exertion paralysed. Each has something of that vanity universal among mankind, which ascribes to the special favour of heaven the natural effects of ordinary causes; but it is most apparent on the side of the Spaniards, where it is sanctioned by superstition and strengthened by credulity.

These are the materials out of which Mr. Southey has constructed his poem. We trace in it the same hand that produced his former works, but improved in skill, and power of application to the topics introduced. It has not the variety of *Madoc*, nor are there in it those examples of tenderness, and the more humane feelings, with which that work abounds. The object of the poet seems to have been to display the intensity of passion, and the action of the severer virtues.

Those milder affections, in the description of which he has sometimes indulged himself to an extent that has weakened the effect of their beauty, have found a place here only in the retirement of Gaudiosa and her children, where the solitude, and the stillness of the scene has prepared the mind of the reader to receive them. The high and tumultuous tide of feeling which flows through the whole poem, would admit of no interruption or distraction, even by allusion to sentiments of a softer nature. The very love, which Florinda confesses for Roderick, partakes of the same lofty character; it is founded upon admiration and sympathy, and, though concealed by female pride and a sense of duty, it rises to the utmost pitch of passion, and reigns predominant in her breast.

Of the versification which Mr. Southey has employed we have given our readers sufficient specimens to enable them to judge for themselves. The variety of its cadences gives a spirit which relieves its grandeur, and the redundant syllable at the end of many of the lines prevents the majesty of its tone from oppressing the ear. The language is such as the best authors of the best era of our literature would acknowledge, nor can we give it higher praise than to say that its standard worth would be admitted in the mint of Queen Elizabeth's age. Many words corrupted by familiarity are here restored to their original meaning, and rescued from the perversion to which they have been subjected by fashion or negligence. For the mode in which Mr. Southey has treated his subject he alone is answerable; it is built upon no model, there is nothing which even the rage for classification can class with it, nor has it any thing which partakes of the character of a 'school,' except it be that school in which the moralist and the philosopher pursue their studies of the human heart, and learn to record their observation and experience.

We must now take our leave of Mr. Southey, congratulating him upon the success of his labours, which will form an epoch in the literary history of his country, convey to himself 'a name perdurable on earth,' and to the age in which he lives a character that need not fear comparison with that of any by which it has been preceded.

55. John Taylor Coleridge, unsigned review, *British Critic*

April 1815, 2nd series, ii, 353–89

From the opening of his review.

Coleridge (1790–1876), nephew of Samuel Taylor Coleridge, was a barrister. In 1825 Southey was successful in his efforts to secure his appointment as editor of the *Quarterly Review* in succession to Gifford. He described Coleridge to Scott as 'a man of sound judgement, great discretion, excellent opinions, and high principle' (Curry, ii, p. 268). Coleridge's period as editor of the *Quarterly* was brief. His career was distinguished and he subsequently became a judge and was knighted.

This is the first time that we have had an opportunity of paying Mr. Southey the attention which he deserves; and we avail ourselves of it gladly. His name is one, which, we confess, we dwell on with peculiar pleasure; in all the ranks of contemporary literature, there is none more honourably, or more enviably distinguished. Whether considered as a biographer, historian, or poet, it will be found that his writings breathe uniformly the same excellent spirit, and are calculated to produce the same good effect. Whatever be their fate or popularity now, (and this depends so much on whim and fashion, that we venture on no predictions,) from them all he will hereafter derive a higher praise than that which is due to the mere exhibition of talent; for they display a pure singleness of heart, actively disposed to benevolence and justice; and their tendency is to encourage in each sex of our fellow-citizens their appropriate virtues—to make our men bold, honest, and affectionate, and our women meek, tender, and true.

We are quite of opinion with a celebrated lady, with whom it is not always our good fortune to agree, that there is somewhat too little of enthusiasm in the character of the present age. Chivalry, perhaps, is not so *necessary* now as formerly, yet we should not be sorry to see the *chivalrous spirit* revived amongst us. It would be too much to expect that the majority of general society should feel it, but it is indeed melancholy to see finer natures taming themselves down to the littleness of daily life, and souls of a more heavenly frame awkwardly assuming the garb of common men. How many a youthful heart struggles with its better feelings, and laughs in public at what has moved it to tears in private. And why? does coldness imply prudence; or is it necessary to the interests of society?—Surely there is nothing to be feared from excess of feeling in the world; enough selfishness will always remain without making generosity ridiculous. *His* writings, then, acquire additional value, who in politics, in common life, or in poetry, equally sustains the triumphant merits of the milder virtues; who adds to splendid heroism domestic charities, to lion-hearted courage the gentleness and truth of tender affections; and who, feeling himself, would make others feel, that these ornaments are even of superior value to those great qualities which they adorn. Therefore, in coming days, if England remain a nation, and our language pass not away, we are sure that the philosophic critic will place the memory of Southey, though not within the same high shrine where Milton sits for ever in undivided majesty, yet with no mean or perishable glory, first at his feet, his reverent, and his worthy son.

Mr. Southey is eminently a moral writer; to the high purpose implied in this title, the melody of his numbers, the clear rapidity of his style, the pathetic power which he exercises over our feelings, and the interesting manner of telling his story, whether in verse or prose, are all merely contributive. It would therefore be no less useful than pleasant, if we had time, or opportunity, or if we could do the subject justice, to contemplate him rising independently and virtuously from small beginnings; in many temptations, and under many difficulties, still cherishing the pure light that was within him; always fearless and full of cheerful hope; never pausing for a moment to decide between faulty indulgence and self-denying sacrifice; sometimes ridiculed and despised, sometimes condemned or forgotten, yet ever self-justified, and in the end rewarded. He now stands extorting respect from the scorner, and honourable acquittal from the judge;—from the world he receives fame, and is blessed with more intense affection from those who watched his progress with anxiety, but never doubted of his final success.

Let us not be mistaken; of him, whom we praise, we personally know nothing, and we can have no interest in flattering him; our remarks are made in the spirit of justice, and are founded on facts, which all the literary world know as well as ourselves. We proceed, however, without further preface to the examination of the poem before us; of which we propose to give a faithful analysis, interweaving such remarks as may occur to us, and making such extracts as may be necessary to give a full idea of it to our readers. The subject is the foundation of the Spanish monarchy in the mountainous province of Asturia on the overthrow of the Moorish invaders; its hero is Roderick, the last of the Gothic dynasty. The name of this personage is already familiar to our readers, from the spirited poem of Walter Scott, which bears it for its title, but they are not to expect the same character. Nothing can be more different; though both, we believe, are founded on sufficient authority for all the purposes of poetry; in the one case, without any palliation for his fault, we are presented with a semi-barbarian chief, struggling with remorse, and bent by circumstances, rather than by conviction, to an unwilling and ineffectual repentance—in the very act of confession proudly shrinking from shame, and in submission still imperious; one, in short, of those very faulty characters whom it has been too much the fashion of modern poets to render somewhat dangerous by investing them with military gallantry, or cheap generosity. Mr. Southey's Don Roderick, on the other hand, is a man, who with some excuse to plead for a guilty act, is yet so overpowered by its fatal consequences, and so properly sensible of its own foulness, that all the energies of a powerful mind become directed to a sincere effectual penitence, and to compensation for the evils of which he has been the author. In this light we look upon him as new among the heroes of poetry; had Spenser written the poem, he would have been the hero of the Legend of Penitence; in the course of it, without forgetting the frailty of human nature, is displayed one constant triumph of principle over the most besetting temptations; and before it ends, there is not a turbulent, unruly feeling of an ill regulated mind, that is not subdued into 'the perfect peace, the peace of Heaven.'

There are some of our readers, whom such a declaration will alarm; they are so accustomed to divest poetry of its moral, that when they hear of a hero with grey locks in a friar's gown, they will apprehend that the poem is but a sermon in blank verse. Courage, however, *chers enfans*;[1] here is plenty of sword and dagger, war-horse and chariot, a bugle or two, some little love, several beauties, and even a marriage

1 'Dear children'.

in *prospectu*, with all other ingredients of a 'charming poem.' If any one doat so desperately on 'love and glory,' that this does not content him, we are very sorry, but we cannot honestly recommend Don Roderick to his attention.

56. Lamb, from a letter to Southey

6 May 1815

Reprinted from *The Letters of Charles and Mary Lamb*, ed. E. V. Lucas (1935), ii, pp. 163–5.

I have received from Longman a copy of *Roderick*, with the author's compliments, for which I much thank you. I don't know where I shall put all the noble presents I have lately received in that way; the *Excursion*, Wordsworth's two last vols., and now *Roderick*, have come pouring in upon me like some irruption from Helicon. The story of the brave Maccabee was already, you may be sure, familiar to me in all its parts. I have, since the receipt of your present, read it quite through again, and with no diminished pleasure. I don't know whether I ought to say that it has given me more pleasure than any of your long poems. *Kehama* is doubtless more powerful, but I don't feel that firm footing in it that I do in *Roderick*; my imagination goes sinking and floundering in the vast spaces of unopened-before systems and faiths; I am put out of the pale of my old sympathies; my moral sense is almost outraged; I can't believe, or with horror am made to believe, such desperate chances against omnipotences, such disturbances of faith to the centre. The more potent the more painful the spell. Jove and his brotherhood of gods, tottering with the giant assailings, I can bear, for the soul's hopes are not struck at in such contests; but your Oriental almighties are too much types of the intangible prototype to be meddled with without shuddering. One never connects what are called the attributes with Jupiter. I mention only what diminishes my delight at the wonder-workings of *Kehama*, not what impeaches its power, which I confess with trembling.

But *Roderick* is a comfortable poem. It reminds me of the delight I took in the first reading of the *Joan of Arc*. It is maturer and better than *that*, though not better to me now than that was then. It suits me better than *Madoc*. I am at home in Spain and Christendom. I have a timid imagination, I am afraid. I do not willingly admit of strange beliefs or out-of-the-way creeds or places. I never read books of travel, at least not farther than Paris or Rome. I can just endure Moors, because of their connection as foes with Christians; but Abyssinians, Ethiops, Esquimaux, Dervises, and all that tribe, I hate. I believe I fear them in some manner. A Mahometan turban on the stage, though enveloping some well known face (Mr. Cook or Mr. Maddox, whom I see another day good Christian and English waiters, innkeepers, &c.), does not give me pleasure unalloyed. I am a Christian, Englishman, Londoner, *Templar*. God help me when I come to put off these snug relations, and to get abroad into the world to come! I shall be like *the crow on the sand*, as Wordsworth has it; but I won't think on it—no need, I hope, yet.

The parts I have been most pleased with, both on 1st and 2nd readings, perhaps, are Florinda's palliation of Roderick's crime, confessed to him in his disguise—the retreat of Palayo's family first discovered,—his being made king—'For acclamation one form must serve, *more solemn for* the *breach of old observances.*' Roderick's vow is extremely fine, and his blessing on the vow of Alphonso:

> Towards the troop he spread his arms,
> As if the expanded soul diffused itself,
> And carried to all spirits *with the act*
> Its affluent inspiration.

It struck me forcibly that the feeling of these last lines might have been suggested to you by the Cartoon of Paul at Athens. Certain it is that a better motto or guide to that famous attitude can no where be found. I shall adopt it as explanatory of that violent, but dignified motion.

I must read again Landor's *Julian*. I have not read it some time. I think he must have failed in Roderick, for I remember nothing of him, nor of any distinct character as a character—only fine-sounding passages. I remember thinking also he had chosen a point of time after the event, as it were, for Roderick survives to no use; but my memory is weak, and I will not wrong a fine Poem by trusting to it.

The notes to your poem I have not read again; but it will be a take-downable book on my shelf, and they will serve sometimes at breakfast, or times too light for the text to be duly appreciated. Though some of 'em, one of the serpent Penance, is serious enough, now I think on't.

57. From an unsigned review, *Christian Observer*

September 1815, xiv, 592–616

From the conclusion of the review. This criticism of Southey's notes to his epics was frequently made by reviewers.

To the poem of *Roderick*, Mr. Southey has annexed a voluminous collection of notes. The taste of our elder authors in this respect is now entirely obsolete. Our Shakespeares and Miltons never thought it necessary to ballast their poetry with a mass of prose, and perhaps felt secure that, if they found the text, posterity would not fail to find the commentary. If this was laying too heavy a tax on posterity, at least our modern poets seem resolved not to augment the burden. It may undoubtedly be expedient that a few explanatory notes should be given by the author of a work, who must best know his own meaning; but all fair limits are transgressed, when he environs every sentence with as much commentary as would explain an equal portion of Lycophron. Mr. Southey has, however, adopted the modern and convenient rule of arrangement, by which the notes are swept to the end of the volume, instead of clustering together, like barnacles, at the bottom of each page, and perpetually retarding the reader's progress.

It is not the only objection to the notes on *Roderick*, that they are

long. They are crowded with histories of various and degrading superstitions; sometimes related in the author's own words; sometimes
quoted, but with remarks,—and the compound does not appear very
attractive. In their general effect, they differ materially from the text,
not merely as prose might be expected to differ from poetry, and the
fictions of the chronicle of king don Rodrigo form the fictions of
Mr. Southey, but in the different style of thinking and feeling which
they appear to shew in the poet and the commentator. A casual
reader of the present volume would certainly conceive very differently
of the author, according as he judged from his poetry or his prose:
and we rather believe that the same remark is applicable to some of
his former works. In his poetry there seems to be traceable a remarkable seriousness and simplicity of mind—a pure and lofty enthusiasm,
a childlike genuineness of feelings and affections, a sort of character
nursed up amidst study and retirement, amidst the purifying charities
of domestic life, and the ennobling beauties of wild nature; a character,
singularly unhackneyed in worldly ways, and unspoiled by a familiarity
with the use of ridicule. His notes have less interesting and individual
peculiarities. There is considerable information in them undoubtedly,
and, in what is original, there is talent, and spirit, and ease; but, taking
their whole effect, there is something hard, something sarcastic, something scoffing. And there is too much of an approximation to that
free, all-assured, sneering species of writing which has grown up in the
present day, and which, for want of a better term, may perhaps be
called, 'the *knowing* style.' It might almost seem as if the poet were
eager to unplume in his notes the 'eagle-genius' which soars in his
text, and were affecting to be exempt from any real or permanent
subjection to those fine fancies and feelings with which his poetic composition overflows. It is not, however, intended really to impute to
him this inverted vanity, although there may be a semblance of it.
Habit and haste may unconsciously have led him to adopt a style of
annotation not altogether correspondent with his higher and more
deliberate productions. Those productions, in the mean time, have a
far more than compensating merit. On the present occasion, if the
commentator of *Roderick* appears scarcely worthy of the poet, yet
he must be a very fastidious, or a very dull reader, who does not find
the evil of possessing the commentary, infinitely overpaid by the
gratification of reading the poem.

58. From an unsigned review, *British Review*

November 1815, vi, 287–306

After a lengthy summary of the plot of the poem the reviewer analyses Southey's achievement.

The plot naturally claims our first notice, and we think that in this Mr. Southey has been very successful. It is highly dramatic, and affords scope for much play both of passion and feeling, though the latter predominates. Its materials are of heroic caliber, sufficiently dignified for the epic tone, yet blended with those topics to which a chord vibrates in every heart, and to relish which the common feelings of our nature are the only requisite qualification. Its incidents too are inter-woven with much ingenuity, and considerable skill is displayed in bringing about meetings with apparent ease which seemed very un-likely to take place; such, for instance, as that between Roderick, Florinda, and Julian. One fault, however, the poem has in this depart-ment, and that one of no small importance. It is a bold infringement of Horace's veto,

Ne, quodcunque volet, poscat sibi fabula credi.[1]

The poet, no doubt, has, by ancient right and charter, a wider range of assertion than any other man, excepting the sailor; nor has the privilege ever been forfeited by disuse. But yet there are certain limits which he must not transgress, if he would maintain that illusion so favourable, or rather so necessary to his empire over the feelings. And more especially where, as in the present instance, he has of his own accord straitened those limits in some degree by grounding his fiction on a portion of real history, and disdaining the aid of the machinery employed by other poets, and by himself indeed in other cases, as a convenient resort, where the trifling hinderance of an impossibility was to be surmounted. Homer, who cannot be accused of timidity in fiction . . . did not trust for the concealment of that hero

1 'Your story must not ask for belief in whatever it chooses.' (Horace, *Ars Poetica*.)

[Odysseus] to *twenty years* of absence, and nearly incessant hardships. When he returns to his native country, the powerful wand of Minerva is employed to disguise him effectually, and screen him from discovery. Mr. Southey, with a bolder daring, supposes Roderick so metamorphosed by grief in considerably less than half that time, as to escape the penetrating glance of the fondest and most deeply-rooted attachment. His victory over Witiza had taken place but ten years before his foster-father details to him, as to a stranger, the subsequent triumph; and some years must have elapsed between that victory and his defeat by the Moors. We confess therefore that, in spite of our wish to give the imagination its fullest scope, and to go to the utmost verge of poetic credence, this gross improbability has met us at every turn in this poem with a broad glare of fiction, which has considerably lessened its hold upon the fancy.

But if we turn from the plot to the manners and sentiments of the poem, with much to praise, we have to lament one striking inconsistency in its tone, to which we have already alluded; it is the totally unqualified expression of a deeply vindictive spirit. It must be admitted, that the circumstances of the plot made it necessary to exhibit the workings of such a spirit to a certain degree, in order to be true to nature: but the fault lies in the apparent zest and relish with which this is done. Instead of being cast into the shade, as a necessary but unwelcome blemish in the picture, it is forced upon the eye both by prominence of situation and strength of colouring.

> And pray'd the while for patience for himself
> And him, and prayed for vengeance too, and *found*
> *Best comfort in her curses.*

> —————————————Go, join Witiza now,
> *Where he lies howling,* the avenger cried,
> And tell him, Roderick sent thee.

No one could have objected to these and similar expressions, had they been attributed to appropriate characters, had Witiza and Orpas been represented as nourishing these remorseless feelings, instead of exciting them in the breasts of Rusilla and Roderick. But as it is, and especially in the latter case, they are grating to the ear, from their evident inconsistency with those high principles, the operation of which on the mind of the penitent King forms the characteristic feature, and leading interest of the poem. With this exception, Mr. Southey has succeeded in giving a beautiful and useful display of the powerful efficacy of those principles. We have heard some of his readers carp at the frequent reference that is made to them; but this, we think, is owing partly to their overlooking this intention in the author, and partly to the same baneful squeamishness, and extravagant fear of being deemed puritanical, which has unnerved and impoverished the style of our theology, and weeded our colloquial vocabulary at the expense of some of its fairest flowers. There is a medium between the adoption of a cant phraseology, and the studied rejection of all reference to what ought to be always uppermost in our minds. If, as we have the best reason to suppose, the prevailing tone of our conversation is to be regarded as a fair sample of 'the abundance of our hearts,' the inference to be drawn from the general tone of our social intercourse is by no means a favourable one. Did Mr. Southey's poem afford any instances of a levity of association in this respect, we should be amongst the first to reprobate such an abuse; but, as it is, we think that so far from deserving censure, his introduction of the rich vein of pure and golden ore, which may be traced from the beginning to the end of his work, is worthy of praise and imitation.

The extracts which we have made from the poem will convey a pretty clear notion of its language and versification, the flow of which might with advantage have been more varied, but is as easy as was consistent with a due degree of sonorous dignity, which is successfully maintained throughout. We should not think it worth while to pick out the scattered passages which lie open to criticism, but for the hope that, should our observations chance to meet the author's eye, they may help, in however trifling a degree, to give a higher polish to future editions of his work. There is something rather Della-cruscan in these lines:

> Nay, quoth Pelayo; what hast thou to do
> With oaths? *Bright emanation* as thou art.

The fourth sentence in the tenth Canto, beginning with 'eagerly at every foot-fall,' is imperfect in its construction, a repetition of the nominative case being necessary before the verb 'obeyed.'

There is rather too strong a family likeness between the closing lines of the twelfth Canto, and these lines in the eighteenth.

> ———————————— The passing air
> Bore with it from the woodland undisturb'd
> The ringdove's wooing, and the quiet voice
> Of waters warbling near.

The following lines and expressions occur to us as open to criticism:

> Each strengthening each, and all confirming all.

> With the venerable primate took his part.

> —— only thought *of* how to make.

> The armour which in Wamba's wars I wore.

'Cold accoil;' 'commeasurable strength;' 'mouldering fires;' 'remote from frequentage;' 'an auriphrygiate mitre.'

We cannot conclude without entering a strong protest against the modern fashion of encumbering a poem with a body of notes, swelled by quotations, which nobody reads, and every body must pay for. It is a heavy tax on the reading part of the community, and we doubt whether it is one which answers in the end even to those who impose it, since it must raise the price of the article so encumbered above the limit, by which a large class of purchasers think it right to bound their literary indulgences.

CARMEN TRIUMPHALE FOR THE COMMENCEMENT OF THE YEAR *1814*

1814

This topical poem was considerably altered before publication. Both John Rickman and John Wilson Croker, to whom Southey submitted the manuscript, advised him to omit his violent denunciations of France and Bonaparte. Although Southey accepted the advice he complained: 'I spoilt my poem . . . by cutting out all that related to Bonaparte, and which gave strength, purport, and coherence to the whole' (*Life*, iv, p. 54). The five rejected stanzas were extended to form an 'Ode, written during the negociations with Buonaparte, in January, 1814', published anonymously in the *Courier* and reprinted in the third volume of Southey's *Poetical Works*.

59. From an unsigned review, *Critical Review*

February 1814, 4th series, v, 203–8

From the opening of the review.

When Mr. Southey, 'in happy hour,' was appointed to the laurel, all the world was astonished. Critics of twenty years standing, with much gravity, expatiated on the operations of time, the mutability of man, and the poetry of the *Antijacobin*; while the vast body of people, who read birth day odes, waited with extraordinary impatience for the first courtly effusions of a converted muse. Fortunately for the bard, all Europe conspired to furnish him with a subject; and in consequence, *Carmen Triumphale, for the commencement of the year 1814*, by Robert

Southey, Esq. Poet Laureat, with more than poetical punctuality, appeared on New Year's Day.

With great respect for the talents of Mr. Southey, he is exactly the last poet of the day, whom we would have selected to sound the lyre upon public event. In our opinion, there is not one among them, who would not be more likely to catch the spirit of popular enthusiasm, and excite interest upon broad and obvious associations. Mr. Southey commenced his bardship with the social virtues; the gentler affections, when not his theme, were always his distinction;—his poetical soul. Cowper struck into the same path, and has been universally appreciated. Mr. Southey is not so fortunate. Even in his appeal to the primitive feelings, he is so abstracted, so peculiar, so removed from common apprehension, that, however he may affect a few, he seldom awakens sympathy in the great mass of mankind. Contrary to the usual progression of mind, his more advanced career has been distinguished by an increased attachment to the marvellous:—but his marvellous is not that of the many,—it lacks *terra firma*. There is a wildness of imagination as purely metaphysical, and as difficult to follow, as the abstruse speculations which are especially termed so. We can suggest no guide to Mr. Southey, but a course of reading, as capricious and desultory as his own. Few can be expected to surmount the difficulty by this means; and thus the beauties with which his most eccentric flights never fail to abound, obtain a very limited portion of the admiration they so pre-eminently deserve. While passages from Scott, Campbell, Byron, Moore, and many others, are continually ringing in our ears, we seldom remark a quotation from Southey. We hear him uniformly spoken of as a man of genius; the prejudices against him which might once exist, are unquestionably done away; if not then to the causes we have assigned, or something like them,—to what is it owing, that he never appears to hit the prevalent sense of his contemporaries,— that he is always 'Caviare to the multitude'?

With these prepossessions, we took up the *Carmen Triumphale*, and as far as regards the public tase, we think it will be found what we were led to anticipate. The shout exultant of a martial and high spirited people it certainly is not. If, without resorting to another language, it had been called, 'a thanksgiving hymn,' we think the title would have conveyed a tolerably clear impression of what it most resembles. We must not be supposed to speak of the devotional flow of it, in disparagement; we merely allude to the fact, as being new to the laurel. It may also serve to account for the sobriety of pulse, with which the production may be perused from one end to the other. At the same time, we confess, that as the 'crowned in the capitol,' have hitherto been more solicitous to remind us of Pindar, than David, some time will be necessary to do away the effect of early impressions. We observe this, with the less hesitation, from a conviction that no small proportion of the readers of *Carmen Triumphale*, will require similar indulgence.

60. From an unsigned review, *Scourge*

February 1814, vii, 122–30

From the opening of the review.

At the commencement of his poetical career, Mr. Southey was one of the most enthusiastic advocates for reform; a zealot in the cause of universal freedom; the determined enemy to princes and 'courts tyrannic;' and a proud supporter of the dignity and independence of the poetical office. His early productions breathe the most pure and manly sentiments of liberty, intermixed occasionally with the disgusting affectation of the school of Wordsworth, on the distresses of the lower, and the vices of the higher circles of society; and in the lines on a portrait by himself, he characterizes the friends who had predestined him to tread the primrose path of preferment as ill-judging ones. Within the last few years his tone and sentiments have undergone an extraordinary revolution. He is now the champion of social order, the eulogist of kings, the servant of the Prince Regent, a decided opponent of the most popular advocates of independence, and the eulogist of war! He ridicules the mistakes and inconsistencies of the *Edinburgh Review*, while he has himself been an example of the most enthusiastic ardor in a cause which he now acknowledges to be bad. On both sides of the question he has displayed more valor than discretion, more energy than talent. He is himself ashamed of his contributions to the *Anthology*: and the production before us presents un-equivocal evidence that talent does not always correspond with enthusiasm, and that it is possible to be at the same time vehement and dull, elated and feeble, agitated yet monotonous. . . .

If any proof were wanting that Mr. Southey mistakes rapidity for elegance, and regards deliberation or correction as unworthy of a man of genius, the poem before us would at once elucidate his opinion and his practice. Incorrect beyond example, abounding with common-place imagery and hackneyed diction; high sounding without magnificence, and quaint without originality; the merest dunce that ever wore the laurel that now encircles the brow of Mr. Southey, would have derived no honor from his claims to its composition.

Did the excellence of Mr. Southey's stanza atone for its singularity, we might forgive the ambition that deviates from the standard models of poetical excellence, and congratulate the author on the successful execution of a dangerous enterprize. But who can read without a smile the eighth line of the second stanza, 'single and undismayed;' or con-template without disgust the continued repetition of the exclamation 'O!' and the prominence of the common-place sentiment, expressed with little felicity of numbers, or of diction, 'Glory to God! Deliver-ance to mankind!' We should not have vehemently objected, however, to the employment of a novel stanza, had its construction been uni-form; but the author of *Carmen Triumphale* indulges in all his former caprices, and concatenates his verse, and arranges the sequence of his lines with unaccountable irregularity. The third stanza consists of eleven lines, and the eighth of sixteen. Amidst the variety of metre, the irregularity of stanzas, and the repetition of the same rhymes, symmetry, beauty, and propriety, are lost: and the chastened eloquence, the refined regular construction of our legitimate poets, and all the graces that genius has in other ages combined with the most exalted senti-ments, and the most brilliant imagery, are substituted by pomp of epithet, and frequency of exclamation; by the affectation of unwonted energy; by the perpetual obtrusion of unmeaning and ostentatious vehemence; and by the monotony of a style successfully conceived, but involving in its fluency little that the memory retains, by which the judgment is satisfied, or the fancy enraptured.

61. Unsigned review, *Eclectic Review*

April 1814, 2nd series, i, 431–6

If it be necessary, for the glory of the British Court, to have a Poet Laureat, we presume it is equally so, that he should be a man of genius, and that the emoluments of the office should be worthy of the munificence of the Sovereign. We recollect no living bard, who has more ability to confer honour on the bays, or less occasion to seek honour from princes, than Mr. Southey. But, we think some objections lie against the place itself, considered in its present degraded state, as being beneath the dignity of the court to offer to a man of transcendent intellect,—not to say whether it be not beneath the dignity of such a man to accept it. From the manner in which its duties have hitherto been performed, the office can confer on him who holds it but a small portion of credit, inferior even to its scanty emolument. To furnish laudatory odes, at certain seasons, appears to be a servile duty; yet surely the annals of this country, in an age so fruitful of great events as the present, might, twice a-year, supply themes, on which the noblest talents might be happily employed in the small compass of an ode. A hundred pounds and a butt of sack, were, we confess, monstrous overpayment for such annual strains of stupefying praise as Cibber, Whitehead, and Pye, were wont to pour into the ear of royalty, being after the rate of twenty shillings a line for pigmy lyrics. Brevity, indeed, was their principal merit; a merit of no ordinary *size* in dull poetry, which, like a humming-top, spins the longest when it sleeps; for, when the quality of poetry is indifferent, the quantity cannot be too small. Mr. Southey's booksellers might not perhaps venture to purchase the copyright of his best verses at the royal price; yet, considered as being the bounty of a great monarch, which ought to reflect lustre on himself, and for such services as might be rendered by a poet of high order, the remuneration is mean. In the reign of James I, a hundred pounds a year were adequate to the support of one of his Majesty's servants in ease and affluence, according to the style of those days; and a butt of sack, even in the present day, is quite as much wine, as any poet, accustomed to purer and more delightfully exhilarating draughts from Helicon, could well drink, yet probably far too little for 'rare Ben Jonson,' to whom this inspiring perquisite was first awarded. To continue the same stipend, from generation to generation, while the modes and expences of living are progressively changing and increasing, is to sink the office lower and lower in poverty, and consequently into disrepute, the inevitable attendant on splendid poverty. On a recent occasion, the Court has done only half a good deed,—it has conferred the laurel on a man unquestionably worthy to wear it; but to have done the whole, and to have done it well, it ought to have made the emolument equivalent to a hundred pounds in the days of Old Ben; and also, to have given the poet a *carte blanche*, to be filled up in respect both to time and subject, according to his own judgement. That no degrading conditions have been imposed on Mr. Southey, we have the evidence of his first Ode now before us, in which there is not a line of flattery to the great personage who at present exercises the sovereign authority, and to whom an expression of gratitude for the appointment, could neither have been unseasonable nor reprehensible. The poem is wholly national; and Mr. Southey has conferred, both on his Royal Patron and on himself, the highest honour, by coming out as the Poet Laureat of the British Isles rather than of Carlton House.

But ought a man of integrity and independence of mind to accept such a post? Upon this point we do not think ourselves competent to say any thing decisive. Yet there does not appear, at least, to us, any sufficient reason that should influence a highly gifted and truly honest man to reject it, if proffered to him. The discussion of this question, may, however, well be suspended, till there be another vacancy;—a vacancy which, we sincerely hope, will not take place in our day. A man, of whose integrity and independence of mind we have always entertained an exalted opinion, notwithstanding some change in the tone of his politics, has accepted the post, and long may he live to celebrate the glories of his country,—once, and *but* once more in war, and ever after in peace and prosperity. Since the time of Dryden, the Court has not bestowed the bays on any poet comparable to Mr. Southey. Warton alone deserved the name; and yet we have never felt that he was a poet of Nature's making, but such an one as any man of mind and study can make of himself by patient brooding within the walls of a college. A king is always a king, a poet always a poet. The actor who assumes the dignity of a monarch, however excellently he may sustain it, is a monarch only while he is performing the part: as soon as that is finished, he returns into himself, or transmigrates into another character. But he who inherits a throne is, at all times, and under all circumstances, like poor mad Lear, 'every inch a king.' He, too, who is born a poet, is a poet in all things, in prose as well as in verse, in his greatest failures as well as in his most glorious performances. In every production of his mind there is the peculiar form of thought, habit of feeling, and tone of expression, which belong to him exclusively, and distinguish him unequivocally from the man who merely loves poetry, and practises it as an art,—who *is* a poet only when he *acts* a poet's part. Mr. Southey is eminently a poet, in the first sense of the term as we have used it: Mr. Warton was one in the second sense. In his *History of English Poetry*, Warton is thoroughly the critic and the antiquary; he understands, admires, and loves his subject; but if he had never written a line of metre, we doubt whether he would have written a line of those three heavy quartos otherwise than as it is written. Southey, who busies himself with literature in every shape, whether he writes history, biography, criticism, romance, or 'Omniana,' inevitably shews himself to be a poet; for though he may occasionally be prosaic in his poetry, he is always poetical in his prose; we do not mean ostentatiously, or even meritoriously so, but that he treats all these subjects as no one but a poet would treat them. We therefore augur well of the laureatship during his reign; for though his periodical lyrics should be deemed tame in comparison with the choice themes of his heart, into which he has breathed his whole soul, they will still be of a character far superior to the feeble, cold, and insipid effusions of ordinary laureats, and possess more natural interest than the gorgeous pageants exhibited by Warton's Gothic Muse.

It was a perilous experiment to take so long a first flight as the new Laureat has done in his *Carmen Triumphale*. We remember no precedent, except the late Mr. Pye's *Carmen Seculare*, on the commencement of the present century, of which we now recollect nothing but the first two lines, and that there were several hundreds equally energetic and sublime.

> Incessant down the stream of Time,
> *And* days, *and* years, *and* ages roll.

In his attempt to give a poetical bird's eye view of the progress of 'the deliverance of Europe,' from the time that Spain, aided by Britain, unexpectedly made a stand against the usurpation of Bonaparte, and turned the tide of fortune against him, from the straits of Gibraltar to the shores of the Baltic, Mr. Southey has succeeded as well as poetical talent could be expected to succeed. A good political poem, we think, does not exist. Even in Lucan's *Pharsalia*, (which, however, is rather an *historical* romance,) the patriotism overpowers the poetry: and what can be made of a chronicle in verse of modern warfare, of which the scene alternately lies in Spain, Germany, Holland, and Russia, and remains in neither long enough to make the reader feel at home in it? The sentiments, personages, and events, the hopes and fears, specula- tions and realities, contemplated or described in this multifarious com- position, are so immediately connected with politics,—the politics of to-day, or rather the politics of yesterday, for to-day every interest in the war centres in the heart of France itself—that all the fine 'ideal,' the quickening, invisible, undefinable spirit of poetry, is lost, or so mingled with grosser matter, as to be rarely felt, and perceived with difficulty, amidst the tumult of ordinary sensations excited by the public details of these events;—from which details we have received our first and strongest impressions of them. We do not intend the whole weight of our objections to bear against Mr. Southey. We entertain an opinion of his Song of Victory far more favourable than has yet been publicly expressed; but we regret that he should spend his strength in beating the air from Lisbon to Moscow, and from Moscow to Amsterdam, instead of displaying his admirable powers to the highest advantage in a narrower compass. When we see a poem, equally long and excursive, accomplishing all that has been unreason- ably expected of Mr. Southey, we will judge him by *that* as a stan- dard. Filicaja's two Odes, on the siege of Vienna, and that addressed to Sobiesky, King of Poland, rank among the noblest lyrics of any age or country; but there is an undistracted interest, a perfect unity in the subject of the former two, while the latter is a crown of glory to both. Had Filicaja himself attempted to sketch in rhyme the history of Europe for only twelve months, he would not have succeeded better than our countryman has done in his poetical retrospect of five years.

Of all the forms of verse which Mr. Southey has attempted, we think he shines least in the Ode. His measures are frequently slow, interrupted, or inharmonious. In the work before us, abounding with vigorous, manly, and patriotic sentiments, the diction, the pauses, the turns, and the whole strain of argument, are rather those of eloquence than of poetry. The following lines will illustrate our meaning, and also discover the politics of the piece: the latter, however, we shall not presume to criticise.

O virtue, which above all former fame,
Exalts her venerable name!
O joy of joys for every British breast!
That with that mighty peril full in view,
The Queen of Ocean to herself was true!
That no weak heart, no abject mind possess'd
Her counsels, to abase her lofty crest,—
Then had she sunk in everlasting shame,—
But ready still to succour the oppress'd,
Her Red-Cross floated on the waves unfurl'd,
Offering redemption to the groaning world.

First from his trance the heroic Spaniard woke;
His chains he broke,
And casting off his neck the treacherous yoke,
He call'd on England, on his generous foe:
For well he knew that wheresoe'er
Wise policy prevailed, or brave despair,
Thither would Britain's succours flow,
Her arm be present there.
Then too regenerate Portugal display'd
Her ancient virtue, dormant all-too-long.
Rising against intolerable wrong,
On England, on her old ally for aid
The faithful nation call'd in her distress:
And well that old ally the call obey'd,
Well was her faithful friendship then repaid.

The following is incomparably the grandest stanza in the poem.

From Spain the living spark went forth;
The flame hath caught, the flame is spread!
It warms,—it fires the farthest North.
Behold! the awaken'd Moscovite
Meets the Tyrant in his might;
The Brandenberg, at Freedom's call,
Rises more glorious from his fall;
And Frederic, best and greatest of the name,
Treads in the path of duty and of fame.
See Austria from her painful trance awake!
The breath of God goes forth,—the dry bones shake!
Up Germany!—with all thy nations rise!
Land of the virtuous and the wise,
No longer let that free, that mighty mind,
Endure its shame! She rose as from the dead,

She broke her chains upon the oppressor's head—
Glory to God! Deliverance for Mankind!

Though the march of the numbers in this magnificent stanza is at first heavy, there is a rising gradation of thought, language, harmony, interest, and emotion, amidst the changes of scene, subject, and imagery, to the very last line, when

Glory to God! Deliverance for Mankind!

is sounded forth with a voice of music and of power, that might 'create a soul under the ribs of death.'[1] Three such stanzas would have constituted a finer New Year's Ode than we have ever met with from a Poet Laureat's pen. Further criticism and quotation are equally unnecessary, the Poem itself having been made universally public by the periodical press.

[1] Milton, *Comus.*

ODES TO HIS ROYAL HIGHNESS THE PRINCE REGENT, HIS IMPERIAL MAJESTY THE EMPEROR OF RUSSIA, AND HIS MAJESTY THE KING OF PRUSSIA

1814

62. From an unsigned review, *British Critic*

July 1814, 2nd series, ii, 95–8

Extracts from the opening and conclusion of the review.

Whatever proceeds from the pen of Mr. Southey on so triumphant an occasion, is delivered as it were *ex cathedrâ*, and commands attention and respect. We are not disposed with many of our contemporaries to hold dulness as an essential prerogative of the laurelled head, nor to believe that the genius of Southey, like the breath of Clarence, will be overwhelmed in a butt of Sack. Whatever he has sent forth into the world since the *Royal bays* have been conferred upon him, has partaken of the same genius, and the same faults, which are so eminently conspicuous in all his former poems.

[Quotes from the *Odes*.]

These *Odes* the reader will have observed to be monostrophic, in the strict sense of the word. Mr. Southey has disdained the shackles of rhyme, in some passages with much success, but in others, where the spirit flags, and the poet falls into his accustomed error of approaching too nearly to prose, we regret its absence. We approve highly of the strain of piety which pervades these songs of triumph, it adds a grandeur and dignity to the whole. Mr. Southey's style, as a laureat, is decidedly new; it appears to have been formed upon the prophetic poetry of scripture, as arranged by Bishop Lowth; we can scarcely give an opinion on the judgment of our bard in his selection of this model for secular poetry, as our ears are not sufficiently accustomed to the flow. We have no hesitation, however, in asserting that these *Odes* far exceed his *Carmen Triumphale* at the commencement of the year, and if his future improvement is in the same proportion, he will do honour to the laurels which adorn his brow.

THE POET'S PILGRIMAGE TO WATERLOO

1816

This poem, written after a visit to the field of Waterloo in October 1815, was unique among Southey's Laureate poems since he made a profit by it. The first edition of 2,000 copies sold within two months, yielding him a profit of £215.

63. From an unsigned review, *Critical Review*

May 1816, 5th series, iii, 470–82

From the opening of the review.

> Me, most of all men, it behoved to raise
> The strain of triumph for this foe subdued;
> To give a voice to joy, and in my lays
> Exalt a nation's hymn of gratitude,
> And blazon forth in song that day's renown,
> For I was grac'd with England's laurel crown.

Such is stated by Mr. Southey to be his principal motive for writing the small work before us, and it bears evident symptoms of being the production of a sense of duty—'For I was graced with England's laurel crown.' It is undoubtedly true, that the contemplation of such a stupendous achievement seems to set at defiance all individual eulogium, and to be well applauded only by the general gratitude of united nations. All the tributes hitherto poured forth, have appeared comparatively mean and contemptible, and they will be held unworthy of their subject until the present generation, which may be said to have contemplated the very scene, shall have passed away, and until its remote posterity shall have partially neglected the immediate source of their happiness in the tranquil and habitual enjoyment of the blessings that have flowed from the victory. Under present impressions, no man is competent to form an opinion upon these effusions; and even Mr. Walter Scott (whose descriptions of battles have by some of his admirers been raised to a level with the mighty efforts of the father of poetry, and whose talent and spirit we are far from denying) is acknowledged by his friends to have failed in his attempt. It will be asked if the inspiration of the poet does not rise with the worthiness of his subject? Yes—but there are some exalted themes in the contemplation of which all men are in a degree poets, at least as far as feeling is concerned, and this is one of them: nearly the utmost the best poet could accomplish in treating it, would be the employment of appropriate expressions for those delightful sensations which he enjoyed only in common with the rest of mankind.

64. From an unsigned review, *Monthly Review*

June 1816, n.s. lxxx, 189–99

From the opening of the review.

The *Pilgrimage to Waterloo* appears to us to be not only the best of the numerous effusions on that victory, but, on the whole, the most pleasing, the most classical, and the least prosaic of all Mr. Southey's compositions. This last epithet is, in truth, indicative of the sin which most easily and most uniformly besets the author. A want of figurative and poetical expression is the prevailing defect of his writings *in verse*; while a great clearness, simplicity, and freedom from bombast, form their prevailing excellence.

65. From an unsigned review, *Augustan Review*

July 1816, iii, 45–54

From the opening of the review.

Few authors have been more the subject of criticism than Mr. Southey, and none, perhaps, regards it less. We know too much of authors, to suppose that their prejudices can ever be entirely removed by the opinions of others: and we only observe, that it is not decorous or usual in a writer to preface his work with an open declaration of his perfect indifference to the judgment of the public.

> This was the morning-light vouchsaf'd, which led
> My favour'd footsteps to the Muses' hill,
> Whose arduous paths I have not ceas'd to tread,
> From good to better, persevering still;
> And, if but self-approv'd, to praise or blame
> Indifferent, while I toil for lasting fame.

We do not expect from Mr. Southey—a veteran in literature, the shrinking sensibility, or timid solicitude, of a young traveller to Parnassus; but we do think that he ought to assume a less lofty tone, and pay some deference to the opinion of mankind, who can punish him sufficiently merely by neglecting him. This deference will appear the more reasonable, when it is considered, that this performance is not merely not the best that has appeared on the subject of the field of Waterloo, but by much the worst of the poet's own performances.

Mr. Southey is gifted with powers of mind superior to those of most of his contemporaries; but these powers have often been greatly misapplied. This was the case also with the eminent talents of Warburton. His deviations, however, always displayed the astonishing force of his intellect; and his extravagances were uniformly stamped with a character of magnificence. Mr. Southey's aberrations, which are numerous, are not the aberrations of an ordinary man; yet justice to him and the public requires that we should affirm, that they exhibit, in the present work at least, more of silliness than of that simplicity which he affects; and quite as much of bad taste as of true genius.

Waterloo is not a subject like the exploits of some of the heroes of the fabulous ages. . . . Various travellers, on foot and in vehicles of every imaginable description—together with a multitude of prosaic poets, and an host of poetic prose-writers, have combined to celebrate that famous scene, and to familiarise with it the minds of the people of England. And we are, both in conscience and in duty, bound to state, that its horrors were just as much felt, and its glories as fully displayed, before *The Poet's Pilgrimage* was penned, as they are now. It does not, indeed, seem to have been to these that the poet directed his chief attention; but to himself and his own adventures (for he is a prodigious egotist)—to his family—his fellow-travellers, and all who hate Buonaparte with a hearty hatred. We by no means approve of his performance, convinced that it is not at all calculated to impress the minds of foreigners with favorable sentiments of the taste and genius of the nation—especially as he is foolish enough to call upon the world to view him as the bard of Britain, acting *ex officio, et pro bono publico*.[1]

1 'From his official position and for the public good'.

66. Josiah Conder, unsigned review, *Eclectic Review*

August 1816, 2nd series, vi, 1–18

From the opening of the review which discusses Southey's poem and Wordsworth's *Thanksgiving Ode, January 18, 1816*.

Conder (1789–1855), a bookseller and nonconformist, was proprietor and editor of the *Eclectic Review* from 1814 to 1836, during which period he was a regular reviewer. In 1814 Southey wrote of him: 'I wish my coadjutors in the *Quarterly* had thought half so much upon poetry, and understood it half so well' (*Life*, iv, p. 73).

It ought to occasion no surprise, that modern poets have rarely succeeded in the attempt to please or to interest, when subjects of present political concern have been their theme. Seldom, very seldom are the feelings awakened by public events, of a nature to blend with the emotions of taste, or to admit of that pleasing exaggeration which it is the business of the poet to produce. The poet himself, in venturing upon a political theme, finds it difficult to exercise the power of abstraction sufficiently to enable him to select and combine the appropriate materials for poetry, and still more difficult to carry the enthusiasm of a cultivated mind into subjects, the familiar details of which are often mean, painful, or disgusting.

The time was, when the wreath of the victor was entwined by the hand of the bard; and when the poet alternately wielded the sword, and recited in rude melody the songs of heroes. But those times are gone by, we trust for ever. We do not believe that the poet exists, who could succeed in making war, as a *present event*, interesting to the imagination. As to deeds of other times,—battles fought before the invention of gunpowder,—wars which have left us no legacy of taxes, —the burthens and the griefs of which we have never had to feel; —these it is very possible to render poetical enough; and by that sympathy with which genuine poetry inspires us, we may be so far transported in imagination to those times, as to adopt for the moment the characteristic feelings of its heroes and warriors. But stronger sympathies than those awakened by the poet, connect us with the present events, and they are such as preclude the indulgence of the fancy in scenes of modern war.

Poetry is the expression of passionate sentiment. At the earlier periods of civilization, when the imagination is the actuating principle of the multitude, and the objects of passion are those which relate wholly to the imagination, poetry and eloquence will be found to have the most power as the means of exciting popular feeling with respect to contemporaneous events. The orations of Demosthenes were addressed to a nation less advanced in civilization than that which Cicero harangued; but the actual effect of the Grecian's eloquence was probably not greater than that produced by a North American Indian's address to his tribe. At a more advanced period of civilization, when knowledge becomes more generally diffused, the stronger feelings are less easily excited. Men have learned to define their wants, to suppress from necessity or policy their emotions, to calculate, to fear, and to balance present interest against the indefinite objects which lead on the warrior to death and glory. The poet must then change his method with his object. Instead of seeking to move the feelings by exciting the imagination, he will more generally succeed in addressing the imagination through the feelings. It will be upon cultivated minds only that eloquence or poetry will then be adapted to operate, and by other and more refined art than sufficed to set in motion the ideas of the vulgar. Yet, how, with respect to events of present interest, shall the poet avail himself of considerations more impressive than those which the reality has already suggested, or succeed in placing the subject in a light more interesting to the fancy? He must strike in with the feeling of the moment, and if possible carry on this feeling to a degree of passion beyond what the event itself seemed to demand; and he must appear to be himself actuated by the enthusiasm which he seeks to impart;—an enthusiasm, which, if not obviously justified by the occasion, will infallibly appear ridiculous. But how seldom do events occur in the concerns of nations, the causes, the attendant circumstances, or the issue of which, are sufficiently dignified in a moral respect, or sufficiently creditable to human nature, to allow of their being expatiated on with honest enthusiasm!

Events, indeed, in the sense of mere occurrences, of a most momentous nature, have rapidly succeeded one another of late, too vast for imagination to comprehend the details. But it must be remembered, that poetry interests never as the simple record of events, but as it exhibits human feelings and develops human passions, and holds up the living portrait of our nature, as an object of complacent sympathy.

The writers of most of the poems which appear on public occasions, —ode, elegy, or sonnet,—betray an utter ignorance of the nature and purpose of poetry. The occasion on which they write, has evidently set their ideas in motion without directing them into any particular channel; and their verses are insipid because they are wholly artificial, warmed by no glow of passion, and prompted by no definite impulse. Loyalty devoid of affection, patriotism destitute of virtue, triumph without joy, and hope without confidence;—what can be expected from the inspiration of such feelings, but cold adulation, unmeaning boasts, empty predictions, and common place sentiment? A man may be a true poet, and yet, if, on the particular subject which he undertakes, he does not feel as a poet,—if this characteristic does not predominate over the spirit of a partizan or of a censor, he may write high sounding blank verse, with the author of *Liberty*, or compose spirited and energetic odes, like Akenside, but he will not give birth to productions of permanent interest as poetry.

No living author, we believe, is more competent to appreciate, or has shewn himself more able to surmount these disadvantages in treating of contemporary events, than the Poet Laureate. Upon him it properly devolves to redeem, if possible, the character of poems written on national occasions. No man appears so habitually to regard every subject that presents itself to his mind, with the eye and the heart of a poet,—the imaginative eye that discriminates and appropriates in all things the fair and the good, and the heart warmly alive to the best interests of human kind,—as Mr. Southey. No writer impresses us more strongly with the conviction that the opinions he avows, are his genuine sentiments, and the warmth he discovers is unaffected earnestness; and this conviction, even where we do not think and feel in unison with him, strengthens in a considerable degree the impression of what he writes.

We will confess than when Mr. Southey's poem was first announced, we were not without apprehensions that it would partake of too martial a character. We feared, lest identifying too closely the downfall of Bonaparte with the triumph of the general cause of Europe, he should have been led to adopt a strain of exultation in reference to the

'Glorious Victory,' at variance with those better feelings of horror and indignation with which he would regard war in the abstract. Mr. Southey indeed never descends to *common-place*, and we might, therefore, have safely presumed that he would not be betrayed into any heroical descriptions of the battle itself, in the death and glory style; and that he would not even attempt to tell in poetry what must always be far more affecting in simple narrative. Mr. Southey has judged wisely with respect to such details.

> This were the historian's, not the poet's part;
>   Such task would ill the gentle muse beseem,
> Who to the thoughtful mind and pious heart
>   Comes with her offering from this awful theme;
> Content if what she saw and gathered there,
>   She may in unambitious song declare.

Still, we did not distinctly anticipate how the field of Waterloo was to be made the subject of an interesting poem, without throwing a false glory on the circumstances of that horrible conflict. But Mr. Southey merits high praise for what he has not done, no less than for what he has done, in *The Poet's Pilgrimage*.

It is not with any view of bringing our two greatest living poets into direct comparison with each other, that we have coupled a publication of Mr. Wordsworth's with that of his friend. It is interesting, however, to observe the characteristic difference between the two authors. Mr. Wordsworth, always metaphysical, loses himself perpetually in the depths of abstraction on the simplest subject; and frequently employing words as the arbitrary signs of recondite and mystical meanings, exhibits a singular inequality of style, varying from Miltonic majesty of thought and diction, to apparent poverty and meanness. It is only at intervals that he comes within reach of the sympathy of ordinary readers. We never think of claiming kindred with Mr. Wordsworth as a man of the same nerve and texture and heart's blood with ourselves. He looks on nature with other than human senses. He appears to regard God and man through the medium of a philosophy taught in no secular and in no sacred schools. Mr. Southey, on the contrary, is never to be mistaken for any other than a husband, a father, a friend;—a man whose sympathies all link him to his country and his fellow-men; whose errors whether poetical or political, proceed from the warmth of feeling or the force of prejudice, and are never the deliberate sins of a perverse intellect, or the indications of dubious principles. Moral objects seem in his mind to hold the place of meta-physical ones, and he takes too much interest in the passing scenes of the real world, to cultivate the habit of severe abstraction. Whatever he writes, is at least interesting. It bears the stamp of character,—of the man and of the poet. Wordsworth *can* interest. He has written some whole poems, and there are passages in all his poems, that are fitted with exquisite skill to find their way to the heart. But in much of his loftiest poetry he is any thing but interesting. When he aims to teach, he fails to please. He aspires to sit in Milton's chair; but the spirit whose nightly visitation Milton enjoyed, was not the spirit of mere poetry. The spirit of Milton has not rested upon Mr. Wordsworth, unless it be in some of his noble sonnets, in which he more than rivals the great puritan champion of liberty. Southey and Wordsworth have some obvious peculiarities of diction in common, but the resemblance is very superficial. Wordsworth's affectation lies more in the thoughts than in the manner. If Southey be at any time chargeable with a fault of this kind, it will be found confined to the expression; his thoughts are always natural. The poems of the one are altogether so different from those of the other, that it is not conceivable that Wordsworth could have written *Madoc* or *Roderick*, or Southey, the *Excursion*. Wordsworth displays at times an intellectual grandeur and a depth of pathos, peculiarly his own. Southey excels in force of dramatic con-ception, in the development of character, and in the expression of the tender affections. Wordsworth's poetry, if we may be allowed so trite a comparison, reminds us of a mountain torrent issuing from some unknown solitude, and rolling its rarely navigable waters through barren and uninhabited regions, over rocks and shallows, now linger-ing round some green and sunny islet, now thundering in precipitous grandeur, now tamely diffusing its waters over a wide spread channel. Southey's is the mighty stream, eccentric, but clear, rapid, and beautiful, that loves the imaged heavens on its surface, and the racy verdure of the earth, and flows and murmurs for man.

THE LAY OF THE LAUREATE.
CARMEN NUPTIALE

1816

67. Francis Jeffrey, unsigned review, *Edinburgh Review*

June 1816, xxvi, 441–9

The opening of the review offers an interesting, if partisan, discussion of the functions and prestige attached to the office of Poet Laureate. The final paragraph in the extract forms the conclusion of the review.

A Poet-laureate, we take it, is naturally a ridiculous person; and has scarcely any safe course to follow, in times like the present, but to bear his faculties with exceeding meekness, and to keep as much as possible in the shade. A stipendiary officer of the Royal household, bound to produce two lyrical compositions every year, in praise of his Majesty's person and government, is undoubtedly an object which it is difficult to contemplate with gravity; and which can only have been retained in existence, from that love of antique pomp and establishment which has embellished our Court with so many gold-sticks and white rods, and such trains of beef-eaters and grooms of the stole—though it has submitted to the suppression of the more sprightly appendages of a king's fool, or a court jester. That the household poet should have survived the other wits of the establishment, can only be explained by the circumstance of his office being more easily converted into one of mere pomp and ceremony, and coming thus to afford an antient and well-sounding name for a moderate sinecure. For more than a century, accordingly, it has existed on this footing: and its duties, like those of the other personages to whom we have just alluded, have been discharged with a decorous gravity and unobtrusive quietness, which has provoked no derision, merely because it has attracted no notice.

The present possessor, however, appears to have other notions on the subject; and has very distinctly manifested his resolution not to rest satisfied with the salary, sherry, and safe obscurity of his predecessors, but to claim a real power and prerogative in the world of letters, in virtue of his title and appointment. Now, in this, we conceive, with all due humility, that there is a little mistake of fact, and a little error of judgment. The laurel which the King gives, we are credibly informed, has nothing at all in common with that which is bestowed by the Muses; and the Prince Regent's warrant is absolutely of no authority in the court of Apollo. If this be the case, however, it follows, that a poet-laureate has no sort of precedency among poets,—whatever may be his place among pages and clerks of the kitchen;—and that he has no more pretensions as an author, than if his appointment had been to the mastership of the stag-hounds. When he takes state upon him with the public, therefore, in consequence of his office, he really is guilty of as ludicrous a blunder as the worthy American *Consul,* in one of the Hanse towns, who painted the Roman *fasces* on the pannel of his buggy, and insisted upon calling his footboy and clerk his *lictors.* Except when he is in his official duty, therefore, the King's house-poet would do well to keep the nature of his office out of sight; and, when he is compelled to appear in it in public, should try to get through with the business as quickly and quietly as possible. The brawney drayman who enacts the Champion of England in the Lord Mayor's show, is in some danger of being sneered at by the spectators, even when he paces along with the timidity and sobriety that becomes his condition; but if he were to take it into his head to make serious boast of his prowess, and to call upon the city bards to celebrate his heroic acts, the very apprentices could not restrain their laughter,—and 'the humorous man' would have but small chance of finishing his part in peace.

Mr Southey could not be ignorant of all this; and yet it appears that he could not have known it all. He must have been conscious, we think, of the ridicule attached to his office, and might have known that there were only two ways of counteracting it,—either by sinking the office altogether in his public appearances, or by writing such very good verses in the discharge of it, as might defy ridicule, and render neglect impossible. Instead of this, however, he has allowed himself to write rather worse than any Laureate before him, and has betaken himself to the luckless and vulgar expedient of endeavouring to face out the thing by an air of prodigious confidence and assumption:—and has had the usual fortune of such undertakers, by becoming only more conspicuously ridiculous. The badness of his official productions indeed is something really wonderful,—though not more so than the amazing self-complacency and self-praise with which they are given to the world. With the finest themes in the world for that sort of writing, they are the dullest, tamest, and most tedious things ever poor critic was condemned, or other people vainly invited, to read. They are a great deal more wearisome, and rather more unmeaning and unnatural, than the effusions of his predecessors Messrs Pye and Whitehead; and are moreover disfigured with the most abominable egotism, conceit and dogmatism, that we ever met with in any thing intended for the public eye. They are filled, indeed, with praises of the author himself, and his works, and his laurel, and his dispositions; notices of his various virtues and studies; puffs of the productions he is preparing for the press, and anticipations of the fame which he is to reap by their means, from a less ungrateful age; and all this delivered with such an oracular seriousness and assurance, that it is easy to see the worthy Laureate thinks himself entitled to share in the prerogatives of that royalty which he is bound to extol, and has resolved to make it

—his great example as it is his theme.

For, as sovereign Princes are permitted, in their manifestoes and pro-clamations, to speak of their own gracious pleasure and royal wisdom, without imputation of arrogance, so, our Laureate has persuaded him-self that he may address the subject world in the same lofty strains, and that they will listen with as dutiful an awe to the authoritative exposition of his own genius and glory. What might have been the success of the experiment, if the execution had been as masterly as the design is bold, we shall not trouble ourselves to conjecture; but the contrast between the greatness of the praise and the badness of the poetry in which it is conveyed, and to which it is partly applied, is abundantly decisive of its result in the present instance, as well as in all the others in which the ingenious author has adopted the same style. We took some notice of the *Carmen Triumphale*, which stood at the head of the series. But of the *Odes* which afterwards followed to the Prince Regent, and the Sovereigns and Generals who came to visit him, we had the charity to say nothing; and were willing indeed to hope, that the lamentable failure of that attempt might admonish the author, at least as effectually as any intimations of ours. Here, however, we have him again, with a *Lay of the Laureate*, and a *Carmen Nuptiale*, if possible still more boastful and more dull than any of his other celebrations. It is necessary, therefore, to bring the case once more before the Public, for the sake both of correction and example; and as the work is not likely to find many readers, and is of a tenor which would not be readily believed upon any general representation, we must now beg leave to give a faithful analysis of its different parts, with a few specimens of the taste and manner of its execution.

[Outlines plan of the poem with quotations.]

It is impossible to feel any serious or general contempt for a person of Mr Southey's genius;—and, in reviewing his other works, we hope we have shown a proper sense of his many merits and accomplishments. But his Laureate odes are utterly and intolerably bad; and, if he had never written any thing else, must have ranked him below Colley Cibber in genius, and above him in conceit and presumption. We have no toleration for this sort of perversity, or prostitution of great gifts; and do not think it necessary to qualify the expression of opinions which we have formed with as much positiveness as deliberation.—We earnestly wish he would resign his livery laurel to Lord Thurlow, and write no more odes on Court galas. We can assure him too, most sincerely, that this wish is not dictated in any degree by envy, or any other hostile or selfish feeling. We are ourselves, it is but too well known, altogether without pretensions to that high office—and really see no great charms either in the salary or the connexion—and, for the glory of writing such verses as we have now been reviewing, we do not believe that there is a scribbler in the kingdom so vile as to think it a thing to be coveted.

68. William Hazlitt, unsigned review, *Examiner*

7 July 1816, 426–8

This violently hostile review by Hazlitt was continued in the *Examiner*, 14 July 1816, 441–3.

The poetry of the *Lay* is beneath criticism; it has all sorts of obvious common-place defects, without any beauties either obvious or recondite. It is the Namby-Pamby of the Tabernacle; a Methodist sermon turned into doggrel verse. It is a gossipping confession of Mr. Southey's political faith—the *Practice of Piety* or the *Whole Duty of Man*, mixed up with the discordant slang of the metaphysical poets of the nineteenth century. Not only do his sentiments every where betray the old jacobinical leaven, the same unimpaired desperate unprincipled spirit of abstraction, regardless of time, place, and circumstance, and of every thing but its own headstrong will, there is a gipsey jargon in the expression of his sentiments which is equally indecorous. Does our Laureate think it according to court-etiquette that he should be as old-fashioned in his language as in the cut of his clothes?—On the present occasion, when one might expect a truce with impertinence, he addresses the Princess neither with the fancy of the poet, the courtier's grace, nor the manners of a gentleman, but with the air of an Inquisitor or Father Confessor. Geo. Fox, the Quaker, did not wag his tongue more saucily against the Lord's anointed in the person of Charles II., than our Laureate here assures the daughter of his Prince, that so shall she prosper in this world and the next, as she minds what he says to her. Would it be believed (yet so it is) that, in the excess of his unauthorised zeal, Mr. Southey in one place advises the Princess conditionally to rebel against her Father? Here is the passage. The Angel of the English Church thus addresses the Royal Bride:—

> Bear thou that great Eliza in thy mind,
> Who from a wreck this fabric edified;
> And HER who to a nation's voice resigned,

> When Rome in hope its wiliest engines plied,
> *By her own heart and righteous Heaven approved,*
> *Stood up against the Father whom she loved.*

This is going a good way. Is it meant, that if the Prince Regent, 'to a nation's voice resigned,' should grant Catholic Emancipation in defiance of the *Quarterly Review*, Mr. Southey would stand by the Princess in standing up against her Father, in imitation of the pious and patriotic daughter of James II.?

This quaint effusion of poetical fanaticism is divided into four parts, the Proem, the Dream, the Epilogue, and the L'Envoy. The Proem opens thus:—

> There was a time when all my youthful thought
> Was of the Muse; and of the Poet's fame,
> How fair it flourisheth and fadeth not, . . .
> Alone enduring, when the Monarch's name
> Is but an empty sound, the Conqueror's bust
> Moulders and is forgotten in the dust.

This may be very true, but not so proper to be spoken in this place. Mr. Southey may think himself a greater man than the Prince Regent, but he need not go to Carlton-house to tell him so. He endeavours to prove that the Prince Regent and the Duke of Wellington (put together) are greater than Bonaparte, but then he is by his own rule greater than all three of them. We have here perhaps the true secret of Mr. Southey's excessive anger at the late Usurper. If all his youthful thought was of his own inborn superiority to conquerors and kings, we can conceive that Bonaparte's fame must have appeared a very great injustice done to his pretensions: it is not impossible that the uneasiness with which he formerly heard the names of Marengo, of Austerlitz, of Jena, of Wagram, of Friedland, and of Borodino, may account for the industrious self-complacency with which he harps upon those of Busaco, Vimiera, Salamanca, Vittoria, Thoulouse, and Waterloo; and that the Iron Crown of Italy must have pressed upon his (Mr. Southey's) brows, with a weight most happily relieved by the light laureat-wreath! We are justified in supposing Mr. Southey capable of envying others, for he supposes others capable of envying him. Thus he sings of himself and his office:—

> Yea in this now, while malice frets her hour,
> Is foretaste given me of that meed divine;
> Here undisturbed in this sequestered bower,

> The friendship of the good and wise is mine;
> And that green wreath which decks the Bard when dead,
> That laureate garland crowns my living head.
> That wreath which in Eliza's golden days
> My master dear, divinest Spenser, wore,
> That which rewarded Drayton's learned lays,
> Which thoughtful Ben and gentle Daniel bore . . .
> Grin envy through thy ragged mask of scorn!
> In honour it was given, with honour it is worn!

Now we do assure Mr. Southey, that we do not envy him this honour. Many people laugh at him, some may blush for him, but nobody envies him. As to Spenser, whom he puts in the list of great men who have preceded him in his office, his laureatship has been bestowed on him by Mr. Southey; it did not 'crown his living head.' We all remember his being refused the hundred pounds for his *Fairy Queen*. Poets were not wanted in those days to celebrate the triumphs of Princes over the People. But why does he not bring his list down nearer to his own time—to Pye and Whitehead and Colley Cibber? Does Mr. Southey disdain to be considered as the successor even of Dryden? That green wreath which decks our author's living head, is so far from being, as he would insinuate, an anticipation of immortality, that it is no credit to any body, and least of all to Mr. Southey. He might well have declined the reward of exertions in a cause which throws a stigma of folly or something worse on the best part of his life. Mr. Southey ought not to have received what would not have been offered to the author of *Joan of Arc*.

Mr. Southey himself maintains that his song has still been, 'to Truth and Freedom true;' that he has never changed his opinions; that it is the cause of French liberty that has left him, not he the cause. That may be so. But there is one person in the kingdom who has, we take it, been at least as consistent in his conduct and sentiments as Mr. Southey, and that is the King. Thus the Laureate emphatically advises the Princess—

> Look to thy Sire, and in *his steady way*,
> *As in his Father's he*, learn thou to tread.

Now the question is, whether Mr. Southey agreed with his Majesty on the subject of the French Revolution when he published *Joan of Arc*. Though Mr. Southey 'as beseems him well' congratulates the successes of the Son, we do not recollect that he condoled with the disappointments of the Father in the same cause. The King has not changed, therefore Mr. Southey has. The sun does not turn to the sun-flower; but the sun-flower follows the sun. Our poet has thoughtlessly committed himself in the above lines. He may be right in applauding that one sole purpose of his Majesty's reign which he formerly con-demned: that he can be consistent in applauding what he formerly condemned is impossible That his Majesty King George III. should make a convert of Mr. Southey rather than Mr. Southey of George III. is probable for many reasons. The King by siding with the cause of the people could not, like King William, have gained a crown: Mr. Southey by deserting it has got a hundred pounds a-year.

69. From an unsigned review, *Augustan Review*

August 1816, iii, 151–5

From the conclusion of the review.

Even in *Lycidas*, the fault of mixing real, immaterial, and allegorical persons is very prominent—what, then, must the same folly be in this poem? We do not see that it was absolutely necessary to place Faith on the steps of the throne, in the attitude of a maid of honour—or to make the other ideal being a kind of chamberlain. Why huddle together into one room Lord Castlereagh and the Angel of the English Church, Lord Liverpool and Experience, and Lord Wellington and the lecturer on education? or why class together the fine ladies in gaudy court-dresses and the simple figures of Hope and Charity? They remind us of the contrast between Pleasure and Virtue, in Guido's picture. If an ode must be written, why not have recourse to the established congratulatory phrases, without encumbering us with all this superfluous absurdity?

We have many such elegant phrases as eschew—jostling—re-risen
—aye-enduring—lethal—eftsoon—distraught, &c. &c. The verses, too,
sometimes hobble in this manner:

> In perilous times provided female means,
> Blessing it beneath the rule of pious queens.

The titles of thief, and usurper, and 'recreant tyrant, bearing the
curse of God and man upon his head,' and similar elegant epithets, are
bestowed upon Buonaparte with no sparing hand; and Mr. S. treats the
cause of Catholic emancipation with equal liberality—styling Popery
'that harlot old,' and charitably giving the scarlet strumpet all the
deadly attributes which the most fanatic independent of the days of
Cromwell would have conferred upon her. Now all this, though it may
supply the place of argument in a furious newspaper, seems to us to
be 'no necessary adjunct to true poetry,'—and really makes some
people doubt the sincerity of Mr. Southey's political conversion, just
as, for a similar reason, they doubt of the pious conversions recorded
in the *Methodist Magazine*. But it is with Mr. Southey's *poetry*, and not
with his *politics*, that we have to do—and we sincerely regret to say,
that it requires not much of prophetic power to discover, that, if he
goes on in his present course, he will soon outdo most of his predecessors in *dullness*, as he has already outdone them in *childishness and
fanaticism*, and that he will very soon convince the public of what
they already begin to suspect—that although the pernicious influences
of the wreath were not unfelt even by Dryden and Warton, yet that
the laurel never bestowed on them such powers of sinking as it has
given to Mr. Southey—for we see that he finds 'even in the lowest
deep, a lower still,'[1] towards which he hastens, impelled by a principle
as irresistible and as unaccountable as that of gravitation.

---

[1] Milton, *Paradise Lost*.

70. Unsigned notice, *New Monthly Magazine*

August 1816, vi, 55

The pen of the Laureate is that of a ready writer, and none of his pre-decessors ever equalled him in the number of his poetical progeny. He comes upon us on every public occasion, with a new performance, so that at all events he cannot be said to have grown languid by his connexion with the court. Levity apart, however, we must in justice say that he has been peculiarly happy in his offering to the royal pair in this instance. He has caught the spirit of Spenser with great effect, and by adopting a dream as the vehicle through which to communicate his congratulations and advice, he has been enabled to speak more freely than he could in his own person. Various shadowy forms, the representatives of Honour, Faith, Experience, and other virtues, are described as addressing the illustrious bride, each in turn, in good poetry and better morality. We should have been glad to have selected the solemn and seasonable monition of the Angel of the English Church, but it is too long for an extract, and a part could not be given without injury to the whole.

71. James Hogg, parody in
The Poetic Mirror

1816

James Hogg (1770–1835), the 'Ettrick Shepherd', friend of Scott,
Wordsworth and Southey, included two parodies of Southey in
The Poetic Mirror, or The Living Bards of Britain. 'The Curse of the
Laureate', a parody of *Carmen Nuptiale*, is reprinted here from the
edition by T. E. Welby (1929). In 1814 Southey described Hogg
as 'a man of very extraordinary powers' (*Life*, iv, p. 93).

THE
CURSE OF THE LAUREATE

CARMEN JUDICIALE

I

In vale of Thirlmere, once on a time,
　When birds sung sweet and flowers were in the spring,
While youth and fancy wanton'd in their prime,
　I laid me down in happy slumbering;
The heavens in balmy breezes breathed deep,
My senses all were lull'd in grateful, joyous sleep.

2

Sleep had its visions—fancy all unsway'd,
　Revell'd in fulness of creative power:
I ween'd that round me countless beings strayed,
　Things of delight, illusions of an hour;
So great the number of these things divine,
Scarce could my heart believe that all the imps were mine.

3

Yet mine they were, all motley as they moved;
　Careless I viewed them, yet I loved to view;

225

The world beheld them, and the world approved,
  And blest the train with smiles and plaudits due;
Proud of approval, to myself I said,
From out the group I'll chuse, and breed one favourite maid.

4

Joan I chose, a maid of happy mien;
  Her form and mind I polished with care;
A docile girl she proved, of moping vein,
  Slow in her motions, haughty in her air;
Some mention'd trivial blame, or slightly frown'd;
Forth to the world she went, her heavenly birth it own'd.

5

The next, a son, I bred a Mussulman;
  With creeds and dogmas I was hard bested,
For which was right or wrong I could not tell,
  So I resolved my offspring should be bred
As various as their lives—the lad I loved,
A boy of wild unearthly mien he proved.

6

Then first I noted in my mazy dream
  A being scarcely of the human frame,
A tiny thing that from the north did seem,
  With swaggering, fuming impotence he came;
I fled not, but I shudder'd at his look;
Into his tutelage my boy he took.

7

Each principle of truth and purity,
  And all that merited the world's acclaim,
This fiend misled—nor could I ever free
  From his destroying grasp my darling's fame;
But yet I could not ween that heart of gall
Could be a foe to one, whose heart beat kind to all.

8

My third, a Christian and a warrior true,
  A bold adventurer on foreign soil,
And next, his brother, a supreme Hindu,
  I rear'd with hope, with joy, and painful toil.

Alas! my hopes were vain! I saw them both
Reft by an emmet!—crush'd before a moth!

9

Still could I not believe his vengeful spite,
  For in his guise a speciousness appear'd;
My bitterness of heart I feigned light;
  But wholly as he urged my next I rear'd;
He said of all the gang he was the best,
And wrung his neck before mine eyes in jest.

10

From that time forth, an independent look,
  A bold effrontery I did essay;
But of my progeny no pains I took,
  Like lambs I rear'd them for the lion's prey;
And still as playful forth they pass'd from me,
I saw them mock'd and butcher'd wantonly.

11

'Just Heaven!' said I, 'to thy awards I bow,
  For truth and vengeance are thine own alone;
Are these the wreaths thou deignest to bestow
  On bard, whose life and lays to virtue prone,
Have never turn'd aside on devious way?
Is this the high reward, to be of fools the prey?'

12

A laugh of scorn the welkin seem'd to rend,
  And by my side I saw a form serene;
'Thou bard of honour, virtue's firmest friend,'
  He said, 'can'st thou thus fret? or dost thou ween
That such a thing can work thy fame's decay?
Thou art no fading bloom—no flow'ret of a day!

13

'When his o'erflowings of envenom'd spleen
  An undistinguish'd dunghill mass shall lie,
The name of SOUTHEY, like an ever-green,
  Shall spread, shall blow, and flourish to the sky;
To Milton and to Spencer next in fame,
O'er all the world shall spread thy laurell'd name.'

227

14

'Friend of the bard,' I said, 'behold thou hast
   The tears of one I love o'er blushes shed;
Has he not wrung the throb from parent's heart,
   And stretch'd his hand to reave my children's bread?
For every tear that on their cheeks hath shone,
O may that Aristarch with tears of blood atone!'

15

'If cursing thou delight'st in,' he replied,
   'If rage and execration is thy meed,
Mount the tribunal—Justice be thy guide,
   Before thee shall he come his rights to plead;
To thy awards his fate forthwith is given,
Only, be justice thine, the attribute of heaven.'

16

Gladly I mounted, for before that time
   Merit had crown'd me with unfading bays.
Before me was brought in that man of crime,
   Who with unblushing front his face did raise;
But when my royal laurel met his sight,
He pointed with his thumb, and laughed with all his might.

17

Maddening at impudence so thoroughbred,
   I rose from off my seat with frown severe,
I shook my regal sceptre o'er his head—
   'Hear, culprit, of thy crimes, and sentence hear!
Thou void of principle! of rule! of ruth!
Thou renegade from nature and from truth!

18

'Thou bane of genius!—party's sordid slave!
   Mistaken, perverse, crooked is thy mind!
No humble son of merit thou wilt save,
   Truth, virtue, ne'er from thee did friendship find;
And while of freedom thou can'st fume and rave,
Of titles, party, wealth, thou art the cringing slave!

19

'Thou hast renounced Nature for thy guide,
   A thousand times hast given thyself the lie,

And raised thy party-curs to wealth and pride,
  The very scavengers of poetry.
Thy quibbles are from ray of sense exempt,
Presumptuous, pitiful, below contempt!

20

'Answer me, viper! here do I arraign
  Thy arrogant, self-crowned majesty!
Hast thou not prophesied of dole and pain,
  Weakening the arms of nations and of me?
Thou foe of order!—Mercy lingers sick—
False prophet! Canker! Damned heretick!'

21

Then pointing with my sceptre to the sky,
  With vehemence that might not be restrain'd,
I gave the awful curse of destiny!
  I was asleep, but sore with passion pain'd.
It was a dreadful curse; and to this day,
Even from my waking dreams it is not worn away.

THE CURSE

May heaven and earth,
And hell underneath,
Unite to unsting thee
In horrible wrath.
May scorning surround thee,
And conscience astound thee,
High genius o'erpower,
And the devil confound thee.
The curse be upon thee
In pen and in pocket,
Thy ink turn to puddle,
And gorge in the socket;
Thy study let rats destroy,
Vermin and cats annoy,
Thy base lucubrations
To tear and to gnaw,
Thy false calculations
In Empire and Law.

The printers shall harass,
The devils shall dun thee,
The trade shall despise thee,
And C—t—e shun thee.
The judge shall not hear thee,
But frown and pass by thee,
And clients shall fear thee,
And know thee, and fly thee!
I'll hunt thee, I'll chase thee,
To scorn and deride thee,
The clouds shall not cover,
The cave shall not hide thee;
The scorching of wrath
And of shame shall abide thee,
Till the herbs of the desert
Shall wither beside thee.
Thou shalt thirst for revenge
And misrule, as for wine,
But genius shall flourish!
And royalty shine!
And thou shalt remain
While the Laureate doth reign,
With a fire in thy heart,
And a fire in thy brain,
And Fame shall disown thee
And visit thee never,
And the curse shall be on thee
For ever and ever!

WAT TYLER

1817

Wat Tyler. A Dramatic Poem was written by Southey in three mornings during 1794 when he was an enthusiastic republican. It was accepted by a London publisher, Ridgeway, but was not published. In February 1817 it was discovered and published by Southey's enemies as proof of his political apostasy. Its enormous sale and the wide notice it attracted in newspapers and magazines did much to influence public opinion against him. Southey wrote to John Murray: 'I am very little concerned at this dirty transaction. My heart as well as my mind has been well disciplined, and I have not profited so ill by real and severe affliction, as to suffer any thing from trifles' (Curry, ii, p. 151). Nevertheless, he could not fail to be affected by the publicity afforded to *Wat Tyler.* His attempt to reclaim his property by a legal injunction against the publishers failed when Lord Eldon determined that 'a person cannot recover in damages for a work which is in its nature calculated to do an injury to the public' (*Life*, iv, p. 251n.).

72. William Hone, *Reformists' Register*

22 February 1817, i, 157–8

Hone (1780–1842), bookseller, publisher and writer, issued his *Reformists' Register and Weekly Commentary* between February and October 1817 at the price of two pence.

Wat Tyler is attributed by the *Morning Chronicle*, to no less a person than the Poet Laureate, one Mr. Robert Southey, a gentleman of credit and renown, and, until he became Poet Laureate, a Poet. The present poem appears to have been written many years ago, when Mr. Southey had not merely reforming opinions, but very wild notions indeed. In consideration of a Court pension, he now regularly inflames his muse, in praise of official persons and business, at certain periods throughout the year, as precisely stated and rehearsed in verse, as the days whereon his pension is made payable and receivable. His present muse, however, is no more like to that which he formerly courted, than the black doll at an old rag shop is like Petrarch's Laura. Poor Southey! a pensioned Laureate! compelled to sing like a blind linnet by a sly pinch, with every now and then a volume of his old verses flying into his face, and putting him out! I have no doubt, he would at this moment exchange his situation, fleshpots and all, for that of the Negro, who earns his 'daily,' by sweeping the crossing at Mr. Waithman's corner!

73. William Hazlitt, unsigned review, *Examiner*

9 March 1817, 157–9

In this review Hazlitt cleverly contrasts *Wat Tyler* with Southey's reactionary article 'On Parliamentary Reform', published in the *Quarterly Review* for October 1816.

> So was it when my life began,
> So is it now I am a man;
> So shall it be when I grow old and die.
> The child's the father of the man;
> Our years flow on
> Link'd each to each by natural piety.
>
> Wordsworth[1]

According to this theory of personal continuity, the author of the Dramatic Poem, to be here noticed, is the father of Parliamentary Reform in the *Quarterly Review*. It is said to be a wise child that knows its own father; and we understand Mr. Southey (who is in this case reputed father and son) utterly disclaims the hypostatical union between the Quarterly Reviewer and the Dramatic Poet, and means to enter an injunction against the latter as a bastard and impostor. Appearances are somewhat staggering against the legitimacy of the descent, yet we perceive a strong family likeness remaining in spite of the lapse of years and alteration of circumstances. We should not indeed be able to predict that the author of *Wat Tyler* would ever write the article on Parliamentary Reform, nor should we, either at first or second sight, perceive that the Quarterly Reviewer had ever written a poem like that which is before us: but if we were told that both performances were literally and *bona fide* by the same person, we should have little hesitation in saying to Mr. Southey, 'Thou art the man.' We know no other person in whom fierce extremes meet with

---

[1] 'My heart leaps up when I behold.'

233

such mutual self-complacency; whose opinions change so much with-out any change in the author's mind; who lives so entirely in the 'present ignorant thought,' without the smallest 'discourse of reason looking before or after.' Mr. Southey is a man incapable of reasoning connectedly on any subject. He has not strength of mind to see the whole of any question; he has not modesty to suspend his judgment till he has examined the grounds of it. He can comprehend but one idea at a time, and that is always an extreme one, because he will neither listen to nor tolerate any thing that can disturb or moderate the petulance of his self-opinion. *The woman that deliberates is lost.* So it is with the effeminate soul of Mr. Southey. Any concession is fatal to his consistency; and he can only keep out of one absurdity by the tenaciousness with which he stickles for another. He calls to the aid of his disjointed opinions a proportionable quantity of spleen; and regularly makes up for the weakness of his own *reasons*, by charging others with *bad motives*. The terms *knave and fool, wise and good,* have undergone a total change in the last twenty years: the former he applies to all those who agreed with him formerly,—the latter to all those who agree with him now. His public spirit was a prude and a scold; and 'his poor virtue,' turned into a literary prostitute, is grown more abusive than ever. *Wat Tyler* and the *Quarterly Review* are an illustration of these remarks. The author of *Wat Tyler* was an Ultra-jacobin; the author of Parliamentary Reform is an Ultra-royalist; the one was a frantic demagogue; the other is a servile court-fool: the one maintained second-hand paradoxes; the other repeats second-hand common-places: the one vented those opinions which gratified the vanity of youth; the other adopts those prejudices which are most conducive to the convenience of age: the one saw nothing but the abuses of power; the other sees nothing but the horrors of resistance to those abuses: the one did not stop short of general anarchy; the other goes the whole length of despotism: the one vilified kings, priests, and nobles; the other vilifies the people: the one was for universal suffrage and perfect equality: the other is for seat-selling and the increasing influence of the Crown: the one admired the preaching of John Ball; the other recommends the Suspension of the Habeas Corpus, and the putting down of the *Examiner* by the sword, the dagger, or the thumb-screw,—for the pen, Mr. Southey tells us, is not sufficient. We wonder that in all this contempt which our prose-poet has felt at different times for different persons and things, he has never felt any dissatisfaction with himself, or distrust of his own infallibility. Our differing from others sometimes staggers our confidence in our own conclusions: if we had been chargeable with as many contradictions as Mr. Southey, we suppose we should have had the same senseless self-sufficiency. A changeling is your only oracle. Those who have undergone a total change of sentiment on important questions ought certainly to learn modesty in themselves and moderation towards others: on the contrary, they are generally the most violent in their own opinions, and the most intolerant towards others; the reason of which we have shewn elsewhere, to the satisfaction of the proprietor of the *Old Times*. Before we have done, we shall perhaps do the same thing to the satisfaction of the publisher of the *Quarterly Review*; for these sort of persons, the patrons and paymasters of the band of gentlemen pensioners and servile authors, have 'a sort of squint' in their understanding, and look less to the dirty sacrifices of their drudges or the dirtier they are ready to make, than to their standing well with that great keeper, the public, for purity and innocence. The band of gentlemen pensioners and servile authors do not know what to make of this, and hardly believe it: we shall in time convince them.

[Quotes specimens from *Wat Tyler*.]

74. From a debate in the House of Commons

14 March 1817

Extracts from *Hansard's Parliamentary Debates* January—April 1817, xxv, pp. 1090-4. During a debate on the Seditious Meetings Bill on 14 March 1817 Southey was attacked by William Smith, an Opposition member for Norwich, and defended by Charles Watkin Williams Wynn, a friend of Southey from his schooldays.

(a) From the speech by Smith:

The hon. member then adverted to that tergiversation of principle which the career of political individuals so often presented. He was far from supposing, that a man who set out in life with the profession of certain sentiments, was bound to conclude life with them. He thought there might be many occasions in which a change of opinion, when that change was unattended by any personal advantages, when it appeared entirely disinterested, might be the result of sincere conviction. But what he most detested, what most filled him with disgust, was the settled, determined malignity of a renegado. He had read in a publication (the *Quarterly Review*), certainly entitled to much respect from its general literary excellences, though he differed from it in its principles, a passage alluding to the recent disturbances, which passage was as follows:

When the man of free opinions commences professor of moral and political philosophy for the benefit of the public—the fables of old credulity are then verified—his very breath becomes venomous, and every page which he sends abroad carries with it poison to the unsuspicious reader. We have shown, on a former occasion, how men of this description are acting upon the public, and have explained in what manner a large part of the people have been prepared for the virus with which they inoculate them. The dangers arising from such a state of things are now fully apparent, and the designs of the incendiaries, which have for some years been proclaimed so plainly, that they ought, long ere this, to have been prevented, are now manifested by overt acts.

With the permission of the House, he would read an extract from a poem recently published, to which, he supposed the above writer

alluded (or at least to productions of a similar kind), as constituting a
part of the virus with which the public mind had been infected:

> My brethren, these are truths and weighty ones:
> Ye are all equal; nature made ye so.
> Equality is your birthright;—when I gaze
> On the proud palace, and behold one man,
> In the blood-purpled robes of royalty,
> Feasting at ease, and lording over millions;
> Then turn me to the hut of poverty,
> And see the wretched labourer, worn with toil,
> Divide his scanty morsel with his infants,
> I sicken, and indignant at the sight,
> 'Blush for the patience of humanity.'

He could read many other passages from these works equally strong
on both sides; but, if they were written by the same person, he should like
to know from the hon. and learned gentleman opposite, why no pro-
ceedings had been instituted against the author. The poem *Wat Tyler*,
appeared to him to be the most seditious book that was ever written;
its author did not stop short of exhorting to general anarchy; he vilified
kings, priests, and nobles, and was for universal suffrage and perfect
equality. The Spencean plan could not be compared with it; that miserable and ridiculous performance did not attempt to employ any arguments; but the author of *Wat Tyler* constantly appealed to the passions,
and in a style which the author, at that time, he supposed, conceived to
be eloquence. Why, then, had not those who thought it necessary to
suspend the Habeas Corpus act taken notice of this poem? Why had not
they discovered the author of that seditious publication, and visited him
with the penalties of the law? The work was not published secretly, it
was not handed about in the darkness of night, but openly and publicly
sold in the face of day. It was at this time to be purchased at almost every
bookseller's shop in London: it was now exposed for sale in a bookseller's shop in Pall-mall, who styled himself bookseller to one or two
of the royal family. He borrowed the copy, from which he had
just read the extract, from an hon. friend of his, who bought it in the
usual way; and, therefore he supposed there could be no difficulty in
finding out the party that wrote it. He had heard, that when a man
of the name of Winterbottom was some years ago confined in Newgate, the manuscript had been sent to him, with liberty to print it for
his own advantage, if he thought proper; but that man, it appeared
did not like to risk the publication; and, therefore, it was now first

issued into the world. It must remain with the government, and their legal advisers, to take what steps they might deem most advisable to repress this seditious work, and punish its author. In bringing it under the notice of the House, he had merely spoken in defence of his constituents, who had been most grossly calumniated; and he thought that what he had said would go very far to exculpate them. But he wished to take this bull by the horns.

(b) From the reply by Wynn:

Mr. *Wynn* said, he had already expressed his assent to the measure now before the House, and he had heard nothing, during the present debate, that could induce him to alter his opinion. Indeed much of what had been offered, did not bear at all on the question. The hon. member who spoke last, had thought fit—in order to divert the attention of the House from the serious consideration of an important subject—to amuse them with a criticism on two anonymous works—two works which, though they did not bear the name of any author, were, he believed, as the hon. member had insinuated, the productions of the same hand. But, was it liberal—was it fair—was it manly—on an occasion like the present, to introduce an extract from the *Quarterly Review*, and a trifling poem, to the notice of the House? What had they to do with the question before the House, or with the hon. member's constituents at Norwich? He (Mr. Wynn) had been for many years, intimate with the gentleman (Mr. Southey) who had thus been attacked; and from that intimacy he had derived, and did still derive, the utmost pleasure.—The hon. gentleman, in his opinion, had acted with some degree of irregularity in dragging him before the House, without his knowledge, and, consequently, without his consent. True it was, that the poem alluded to was written by him at the early age of nineteen. It was intended for publication; but the author had listened to the better advice of his friends, and it did not appear. What became of the manuscript he was perfectly unconscious of, until he saw the work printed. Was it fair, then, he asked, was it manly, to arraign this gentleman with such severity? What was put into the mouth of the person introduced in the poem was, in point of historical accuracy, very correct. But, was it just that these sentiments should be quoted as the opinion of him who produced the work? Was it fit—was it just—to say, that because at the age of nineteen—at an era when the heat of politics affected most men—he was betrayed into the composition of a poem which he afterwards disapproved, that, therefore he was to be reproached all the rest of his life, as a man without principle? Was he, because he had altered certain opinions, to be condemned for ever?—Neither to his former opinions, nor to all his opinions now, did he subscribe. But this should be observed, that he maintained his opinions by argument—and by argument they ought to be answered. He thought there were public methods by which controversy might be carried on with more justice, and with more advantage, than by personal reflections on an individual, in a place where that individual could not be present to make his defence [Hear, hear!].

Mr. *W. Smith*, in explanation, said, that the hon. gentleman must have totally forgotten his observation, or he would not have made the remarks he had offered. He had distinctly said, in effect—'God forbid I should say that any man ought to be blamed for a fair change of opinion; but I censure those who, having changed their opinions, conceive that no severity of language is too strong to be made use of against those who still adhered to their former sentiments.'

Mr. *Wynn* did not understand the hon. member to have used any such language. He conceived him to have thrown out severe and unjust censure on those who had receded from a particular set of opinions.

75. From an unsigned review, *Black Dwarf*

26 March 1817, 139–44

From the conclusion of the review.

The publication teems with this political blasphemy from beginning to end. And, but for the reason we shall assign in our important discovery, there is no question, but the poet laureate ere this had been in custody. It has been pretty generally thought that the ministers were at the bottom of the late plot; and Mr. Southey seems to have been employed as the agent and the instigator of the whole conspiracy. Of course, on such a business he could not do better than consult his own book, for he had exhausted all his faculties in the composition. There are to be met with all the incidents that *did take place*; and all the reasoning that has been employed. It was not *reform*, but *revolution* that he advocated; but unluckily for him, the minor agents had not read *his book;* they only followed the garbled comments of Mr. Hunt and Mr. Cobbett. They only wanted to reform parliament and to instruct the king; while the poet-laureate boldly exclaims all would be better though 'neither king nor parliament existed.' Poor, wretched man! What must he have felt, when obliged to solicit the law to prohibit the publication of opinions, written with so much enthusiasm, and supported with so much zeal? Forced to disclaim the favorite of his most careful nurture; a child of fancy, to which he once fondly hoped that a republican posterity would do ample justice; and in reading *Wat Tyler* forget the apostacy that brought him bread in his declining years. How is he degraded. He has confessed himself guilty of throwing opinions like fire-brands amongst the people, which he now says would lead them to destruction, and to cure which he has dared to mark his own disciples as fit objects of ministerial vengeance, and deserving of a halter as traitors to the state. In what does such a man differ from the received opinion of the character of the Devil? The agency of hell can do no more, than first seduce to sin, and then betray to punishment.

76. Unsigned notice, *Literary Gazette*

29 March 1817, 147–8

This notice is unusual for its defence of Southey.

Sarah, Duchess of Marlborough, having an electioneering object to carry against Lord Grimstone, got into her possession the manuscript of a foolish play, called *Love in a Hollow Tree,* written by that noble man when a boy at school. This comedy she published and circulated with great industry, and at a considerable expense, for the purpose of covering her opponent with ridicule; but all that her Grace gained by the vindictive manœuvre was the raising a laugh against his Lordship and herself. The artifice of the Duchess, however, was a harmless piece of pleasantry, compared with the rancorous malevolence or wicked cupidity of those persons who have, contrary to all honour and honesty, sent the poem of *Wat Tyler* into the world, without the consent of the author. Whether their intention has been to hold him up to public ridicule, or to put money into their own pockets, at his expense, the inference drawn by every liberal mind will be equally decisive in reprobating the nefarious transaction. But if this conduct be so reprehensible, what apology can be made for those legislators (we speak without the slightest reference to party, with which we have nothing to do, and for which we feel only contempt,) who, forgetful of their intimate connexion with the laws and constitution of the country, have dragged this surreptitious piece into their political debates, with the view of wounding the feelings of the author still more severely, and of aggravating an injury which was already sufficiently enormous. The poem, it seems, was composed at the early age of nineteen, and at a period, too, when older heads than that of the author were heated to a degree of enthusiastic transport by revolutionary doctrines, then rendered dazzling through the deceitful medium of the French declaration of equal rights. That a youth of lively imagination, under such circumstances, should take a popular story out of the English annals, and turn it into a scenic representation, corresponding in sentiment with what was actually passing on the great stage of the world, ought neither to excite surprize, nor to provoke severity. But the poem, though it does in fact make the insurgents of the fourteenth century speak the language of modern zealots on the subjects of liberty and equality, is so far in character, that the truth of the history is by no means violated, unless it be in the hypocrisy ascribed to the Archbishop, and the charge of treachery cast upon the King. Our object here, however, is not to review the drama, which does not fairly come before us as an article for investigation, because, being stolen property, it of course ought to be restored to the real owner, who, if he should chuse to acknowledge and publish it, must in that case submit to the ordeal of criticism, as well as the adjudication of other courts.

77. Byron, from a letter to John Murray

9 May 1817

From Byron's *Letters and Journals*, ed. R. E. Prothero (1898–1901), iv, pp. 117–18.

Southey's *Wat Tyler* is rather awkward; but the Goddess Nemesis has done well. He is—I will not say what, but I wish he was something else. I hate all intolerance, but most the intolerance of Apostacy, and the wretched vehemence with which a miserable creature, who has contradicted himself, lies to his own heart, and endeavours to establish his sincerity by proving himself a rascal—*not* for changing his opinions, but for persecuting those who are of less malleable matter. It is no disgrace to Mr. Southey to have written *Wat Tyler*, and afterwards to have written his birthday or Victory odes (I speak only of their *politics*), but it is something, for which I have no words, for this man to have endeavoured to bring to the stake (for such would he do) men who think as he thought, and for no reason but because they think so still, when he has found it convenient to think otherwise. Opinions are made to be changed, or how is truth to be got at? We don't arrive at it by standing on one leg, or on the first day of our setting out, but, though we may jostle one another on the way, that is no reason why we should strike or trample. *Elbowing*'s enough. I am all for moderation, which profession of faith I beg leave to conclude by wishing Mr. Southey damned—not as a poet but as a politician. There is a place in Michael Angelo's last judgment in the Sistine Chapel which would just suit him, and may the like await him in that of our Lord and (*not his*) Saviour Jesus Christ—Amen!

78. Southey satirized: *The Changeling*

1817

The Changeling: A Poem in Two Cantos, Addressed to a Laureat was published anonymously in London in 1817. The first canto is reprinted here. These inept verses are interesting as an example of the virulent attacks launched against Southey. Quotations from *Wat Tyler* are inserted at intervals throughout the poem.

CANTO I

Oh! Bard immortal, of a well-known Isle,
And close allied to Tyler vile,
To thee I sing; who from thy youth
Wert wont to wander from the paths of Truth.
    The aid of Poverty ran in thy strains,
And blood of *Liberty* throbb'd thro' thy veins,
Who in the fervor of Wat Tyler's cause,
Denounced his country and her sacred laws:
Who sought Society's bonds to free,
And 'stablish mistaken Liberty:
Who sought to equal both the low and great,
And banish hence the Regal state.
Of Royalty he the avenging god,
Who raised Wat Tyler as a scourging rod,
Not he of moderate Reform the Friend,
But at one stroke all Form to end;
To harrow up the poor to discontent,
Were his firm endeavours relentless bent;
To entail the miseries of Rebellion's self,
Plunder, ravages, and daring pelf.
    Thus want of principle mark'd his early age,
And time this want could not assuage,
For now he holds a Laureat's place,
In gilded charms to seek disgrace,

And cares not 'Who should pay for
The luxuries and riots of the Court;
Or who should support the flaunting Courtier's pride;
Pay for their midnight revels, their rich garments.'
And yet so strenuously does pretend,
That he was e'er his Country's Friend:
'And I was once like this   *   *
*   *   *   *   * twenty years
Have wrought strange alteration.'
Oh! vile Changeling; Oh! disgraceful man;
How canst thou thy former conduct scan,
And talk of principle. Of that bereft,
When you Republicanism for Royalty left.
Avarice, indeed, thy sordid soul's delight,
Sees no difference 'twixt wrong and right.
But thou, alas! *Art too fair a flower*
To bear the wintry wind of Poverty.'
And *'Yet I have often heard you speak of Riches*
Even with contempt: they cannot purchase Peace,
OR INNOCENCE, OR VIRTUE. Sounder sleep
Waits on the weary Plowman's lowly head
Than on the downy Couch of Luxury
Lulls the *rich Slave of Pride* and Indolence;
I NEVER WISH FOR WEALTH.'
Who can without horror and execration read,
Hypocrisy cover'd with fair Virtue's meed;
Thus in the people Sedition to excite,
To banish Justice, crush all Right,
And in its stead Rebellion raise,
To plunge in misery their future days.
Is't not 'Rank Sedition,
High Treason every syllable, my child,'
'Mongst industrious Poverty to sow the seeds
Of Discontent and Hatred, these rank weeds;
To set their souls on fire, and persuade
The Mob, Prerogative to invade:
To tear the diadem from heads of Kings,
And place instead the Rights of Men and Things;
And Anarchy, all good men's hate,
To succeed the blessings of a happy State?

His motives were, but happily in vain,
To raise the standard of the mad Tom Paine.
  Look in his later age, you'll see
A Changeling of the worst degree,
That flies to bondage from the Free.
Who can but in detestation hold,
Him who prostitutes for gold
Every liberal feeling of the heart,
And scruples not with *Liberty* to part;
The proudest child of England's claim,
The Briton's love, the Briton's aim.
Such is the Man whose tale I tell,
Whose former principles but mark too well,
The degradation that hangs o'er his head,
A blasted reputation and for ever dead.
Yet he flies not to Seclusion's arms,
But brasses infamy in golden charms;
Thus forsaking that to decency belongs
By adding insult to his country's wrongs.
Virtue, the comforter of all our sorrows,
Makes man stedfast to the cause he follows:
But void of Virtue is the Man I sing,
The Laureat he of a redoubted king;
A Changeling—to no man's cause a friend,
Where aggrandizement marks his only end,
And who hereafter, in evolution of the times,
Will expiate his guilt by other crimes.
What then can he expect, who strives
To make a licentious man appear the best alive?
But what other than servility will you find,
In him who thinks with bonded mind,
And writes to libel all his better kind.
Gracious Heaven! true or false, he sings
The *glorious* praises of *illustrious* Kings!
The Father of Rebellion once was he,
Tho' now the holder of a Laureatry.

A LETTER TO WILLIAM SMITH, ESQ., M.P.

1817

After William Smith's public attack upon *Wat Tyler* in the House of Commons (No. 74) Southey attempted to defend himself in a letter to the *Courier* (17 March). Coleridge also supported him in the *Courier*. In April Southey justified himself at greater length in his open *Letter to William Smith*. Although this offered a reasoned defence of his position it did little to improve his cause.

79. Leigh Hunt, 'Extraordinary Case of the Late Mr. Southey', *Examiner*

11 May 1817

This satirical essay succeeds Hunt's previous article in the *Examiner*, 13 April 1817, entitled 'Death and Funeral of the Late Mr. Southey'. Before Southey became Poet Laureate in 1813 Hunt had praised his poetry. Thereafter he attacked him for his political volte-face.

. . . It is with great grief and concern then (to use the expressive climax customary on occasions of mourning) that we have to record a singular proceeding on the part of the dead body of Mr. Southey. It shews how unquietly he is disposed to lie in his tomb; and what care the mason should take when cutting his epitaph, lest the deceased should frighten him out of his wits by knocking on the other side of the stone, and telling him to beware how he omitted a syllable of his perfections.

Our readers remember the account of his death and funeral a week or two back. We had not then been apprised of a remarkable circumstance which took place in the interval, and which was published Saturday fortnight—a day selected, it is said, by Murrain his bookseller, from certain unaccountable apprehensions lest the Sunday papers should be profane on the subject. We appeal to our readers whether we afford any ground for the man's alarm.

But to the point. Murrain's back parlour was lighted up, it seems, with some large tapers from the chapel of the Escurial, and hung with black coats curiously turned inside out and painted with escutcheons of the different legitimate sovereigns. In the middle of it, the corpse was lying in state; and Murrain, with the exception of one or two private friends, was left alone with it. Mr. Canning had departed to pay his respects to Lord Castlereagh. Mr. Croker had gone home to write an account for the *Courier* of the 'admirable' behaviour of the body—how tastefully it had disposed its limbs, and what vigour there was in its very impotence. Dr. Stothard, in a lamentably weak condition, had exclaimed he was 'sick of the Times,' and been taken home to bed. Nobody knew what had taken Mr. Gifford away; only he was heard muttering as he went along something about 'no patience,' and was seen to lame a few applewomen with some passing kicks. As to Mr. Coleridge, he was gone to bed, having been sitting up all night consoling himself with brandy and water, proving at the same time that it was the only temperate drink, and that the undertakers (some of whom drank with him) were the only men besides himself and particular friends, who knew anything about religion and politics. He begged pardon, we understand, for using a pun on an occasion so reverent and solemn, and said that he hoped the company would not think the less of his moral honesty (though punning, in fact, had greater authority than some might be aware), 'but, Gentlemen,' added he, 'the undertakers are your only grave expounders.' To all these observations, as well as to those of the other mourners, Murrain invariably said, with all the pithy and quick indifference yet submission of a coffee-house waiter, 'Yes, Sir'; and then addressing him with more familiarity, attempted to shew how sincerely he lamented the loss of the deceased, having nobody left who could toss off a sheet with such regularity—upon which Mr. Coleridge always grinned with great suavity, and resumed.

Well—the public mourners having thus departed, and Murrain, during the silence of the others, having retired to a corner to do a bit of his ledger, all of a sudden there came through the street door a furious shower of pebbles at the room window, followed by a shout of the word 'Renegado.' The voices seemed young—like those of a school for instance. Murrain said, 'Yes, Sir,' as usual, and then turned pale. But he turned paler in a moment; for the dead body rose with great gravity, and coming majestically towards him, commenced a speech in these words:—

'*Mister William Smith*, I know very well who it was, among others, that set the whole world hooting at me in this irreverent manner. It was you, Mister William Smith; and let me tell you, Mister William Smith, that it is no longer to be borne. You accuse me of scandalous inconsistencies, and of having been a Renegado. I shall condescend to shew you that I, Robert Southey, Esq., Poet-Laureat and Ex-Jacobin, am nothing but consistency, and that you, *Mister* William Smith, are nothing but revilement and insult. In shewing your inconsistencies, I shall prove the reverse in myself.' (Here Murrain being somewhat recovered, though still much agitated, said, 'Yes, Sir,' as usual—of which the eminent corpse took no notice, but proceeded:)

'And first, for consistency the first. Not only, Sir, did you make this accusation in Parliament, but it was "a premeditated thing"; for you "*stowed*" (it can't be a vulgar word, since I use it) you "stowed," Sir, "the *Quarterly Review* in one pocket, and *Wat Tyler* in the other";—a very atrocious thing in a Member of Parliament! What, Sir, a Member of Parliament put books in his pocket! You may think, Mister William Smith, that I have been accustomed to put books in my pocket? I have, Sir; but not for the purpose, certainly not for the avowed purpose, of cutting them up. They used to be sent me down by the coach.' ('Yes, Sir.')

'Consistency 2. You say, in the second place, that I wrote the article in question in the *Quarterly Review.* How do you know that? "You may happen to be as much mistaken" in trusting to report for that matter, as I was when I took you for a man of candour. "You have no right to take for granted what you cannot possibly know." It is *I* only who have a right to that sort of gratuitousness, and accordingly (though it is "not necessary" to do so) I denounce "Mr. Brougham" by name as a writer in the *Edinburgh Review,* and as "carrying the quarrels as well as practices of it into the House of Commons." "*I* am as little answerable" for the review I may write in, as the review is for me; but it is evidently the reverse with him. "I hope here be truths." ' ('Yes, Sir.')

'Consistency 3. The *Quarterly Review*, Mister William Smith, has no such "practises." The *Edinburgh* names a man now and then, (which makes it very bitter) and never notices the *Quarterly*: the *Quarterly*, on the other hand, is repeatedly noticing the *Edinburgh*, and names almost everybody it dislikes, from Bonaparte down to Mister Bristol Hunt—which, of course, does away the bitterness.' (Here Murrain ventured to look a little sceptical.)

'Consistency 4. The question, as respects the *Quarterly Review*, is not who wrote the paper which happens to have excited Mr. William Smith's displeasure, but whether the facts which are there stated are true, the quotations accurate, and the inferences just. This is clearly not the case with *your* statements, Mister William Smith, *your* quotations, and *your* inferences; for you come forward in your own name, which is very atrocious; whereas what I write in the *Quarterly Review* is anonymous, which of course ought to be as great a shield *against*, as it is a weapon *for*, personalities. "I hope *here* be truths." ' ('Yes, Sir.')

'Consistency 5. Now, Sir, as to *Wat Tyler*. You knew that that book was published without my consent—that it must have been obtained from me by infamous means—that I had long abjured its opinions— "that the transaction bore upon its face every character of baseness and malignity." And yet you quoted it, and yet you contrasted it with the opinions I hold at present! Why, Sir, have you not lived long enough to know that these sort of quotations and contrasts are never allowable but against such persons as Cobbett and Bonaparte? The *Quarterly Review* may contrast Cobbett's past and present opinions, as much as it pleases; and we are all at liberty to taunt Bonaparte with his old name of Brutus; but *us*! *us*!—I shudder to think of the unfairness.' (Here Murrain shrugged his shoulders.)

'Consistency 6. Sir, I am ashamed for you. You may smile, but I repeat it; I am ashamed for *you*, and really wish—I mean to say, think— that you would recall your charges if possible. As to myself, "I never felt either shame or contrition" for my opinions. It is for those who have adopted them, to feel it—not for me, who have abandoned. Mark that. It is particularly incumbent on them too to feel so ashamed, if my writings had any influence in assisting the adoption; for I have now changed, and warned them off. Mark *that* also.' (Murrain almost jumped.)

'Consistency 7. That book, Mister William Smith, was written when I was a boy, and a very excellent boy too. (I was also—see my Poems—a very pretty boy; but let that rest.) The book is full of errors,

I allow; but in *me*, such errors "bear no indication of an ungenerous spirit or of a malevolent heart." It was written when such opinions exposed people "to personal danger"—which in *me* was true boldness. It was written "in disregard of all worldly considerations"—which in *me* was amiable and noble, not riotous desperation. It was written "when republicanism was confined to a very small number of the educated classes"—which, together with my subsequent conduct, shewed *my* selectness of taste and eternal freedom from vulgarity. Finally, Mister William, it was written "when a spirit of antijaco-binism was predominant, which I cannot characterize more truly than by saying, that it was as unjust and intolerant, though not quite as ferocious as the jacobinism of the *present* day." This is manifest upon the bare mention of a few names. At that time, jacobinism, besides myself and friends, was confined to Danton, Marat, Robespierre, and a few other over-zealous people: it denounced kings in the lump, particularly certain kings (see my friend Landor's poem)—it preached open sedition, rebellion, and total changes—wished to decapitate whole assemblies here, and actually did it in France—all which shews that it acted from real zeal, though misguided; but in the present day, there are scarcely any but contemptible half-jacobins, fellows, forsooth, who tattle about their legal rights, mere anarchists in secret, skulking knaves from whom it is difficult to muster up a single desperado, and then only among the naked and the hungry. Are we, the old, well-educated, daring jacobins, who followed the opinions of the French Revolution "with ardour, wherever they led," to be compared with constitutional dastards like these!' (Here Murrain, as the phrase is, was dumb-founded.)

'Consistency 8. And yet, Sir, you accuse me of attributing "bad motives to men merely for holding now the same doctrines which I myself formerly professed"; and you add that I exhibit "the malignity and baseness of a renegade." (Here the departed orator became very red.) Sir, I never attributed those motives to men merely for what you say; I have attributed them also to men who never professed *half* of what I did, and I have called the Reformers, in a lump, "no better than house-breakers."

'Consistency 9. So, Sir, if you call me Renegado, I refute the charge by saying that it is "false"; and I teach you how to be "coarse and insulting" another time, by letting you know that you are a "reviler," a premeditated stower of books in your pocket, an accuser of the absent, an assaulter of the unprotected, "a gross and wanton insulter," "disgraceful speaker," a "sober opponent of your country's cause," "foul asperser," a "slanderer," a "retail" dealer to the "panders of malice and pioneers of rebellion," a forgetter of "your Parliamentary character and of the decencies between man and man," a "calumniator, a—what shall I say—" a certain Mister William Smith!'

(Here Murrain began to feel a sort of lethargy, and put his hand to his head; upon which the didactic dust and ashes proceeded:)

'Nay, Sir, salve the mark as you will, it is ineffaceable—you must bear it with you to your grave.' (At this part of his speech the departed Christian, who as Mr. Coleridge says knows his duty too well to retaliate, looked quite delighted; and gradually becoming more so, exclaimed at last, 'And now, Sir, let me speak a little of *myself*!')

At this announcement, by which it appears that the short memories of the witty accompany them to the grave, Murrain fairly dropped his head on the back of the chair, and began snoring; but the deceased Member of the Royal Spanish Academy took it only for a fainting fit accompanied with groans, and smilingly continued.

In consequence however of Murrain's lethargy, and of a similar attack which seized the other mourners in spite of repeated pinches of snuff, this part of his speech has not properly transpired. But it can be gathered with certainty that he talked a long while about his being right on every possible point in morals, politics, and religion—that he made a sudden transition from his 'retirement' to the 'mail-coach,' and from his 'books' to 'spinning engines' (at which latter, by the bye, one of the mourners laughed in his sleep); and that, after insisting it was the People and not the Government, the Reformers and not Croker and Castlereagh, who stood in need of reformation, he said, somewhat mysteriously (Consistency 9) that the said Government should not neglect its 'duties,' especially 'its first duty' of enlightening the 'worse than heathen ignorance' of the poor, nor leave the brave defenders of their country unprovided for, nor suffer whole districts to lie waste while multitudes were famishing. These were certainly odd evidences of a Government in no need of reform; but a *caput mortuum*[1] may be allowed to wander a little. He also, in expressing his agreement in many things with that excellent person, Mr. Owen of Lanark, confessed notwithstanding, in a happy Latin phrase, that he differed '*toto coelo*'[2] from him in one main point, which was (Consistency 10) that building the justice and happiness of society upon any other foundation than that of believing in the indispensability of faith and

---

[1] Pun: 'A corpse; a worthless person'.   [2] 'Completely'.

the flames of eternal punishment, was building upon sand. As to the press, he said, with great agitation, that it 'must be curbed, and kept curbed'—that 'if the laws were not at present effectual, they should be made so'; and that he mentioned all this out of pure regard to liberty and equal dealing, though he knew 'how grossly and impudently his meaning would be *misrepresented*'—a fancy in which we may venture to assure him he will find himself mistaken. It must not be omitted also that the ingenious body politic, who is not a jot more malicious now he is dead than when alive, took particular pains to impress on the perverted understanding of the imaginary Unitarian before him, the necessity of restoring the whole power of the Church Establishment; nor, what is very curious, that he ended one of his instructive paragraphs to Government (for he never quits his claim to be didactic to all about him) with a recommendation to remedy 'the *worst grievance which exists*'—namely, 'the enormous expenses, the chicanery, and the ruinous delays of the law.' We trust the *Chancellor* will take the hint from a quarter so solemn, and manage his re-considerations and injunctions better in future.

The conclusion of the speech luckily was heard by all present, for just as the deceased came to it, he hemmed two or three times with prodigious loudness, and thus wound up his peroration:

'How far the name of Southey will be immortal, time will decide; and I have no doubt, decide as he has done himself. I shall not perish, that's certain; I shall have lives of me "always prefixed to my works," and "transferred to literary histories, and to the biographical dictionaries, not only of this, but of other countries." It strikes me also that I shall be in all accounts of eminent men, in indexes, catalogues, lists, references, quotations, extracts, choice flowers, and other reminiscences of infinite sorts, both here, herafter, and everywhere. There it will be related, among other excellent traits, that I lived in the bosom of my family (which of course nobody else does), and "in absolute retirement" (which is a merit in me, though not in others). There it will be related also that in all my writings I "breathed the same abhorrence of oppression and immorality" (see my odes for and against despots), "the same spirit of devotion" (see my song, joking about Death on the White Horse), and the same ardent wishes for the amelioration of mankind (see *Wat Tyler* and the *Quarterly Review*). There, furthermore, it will be said that the "only charge which malice could bring against him was"—not that I charged others with bad motives for thinking half of what I did myself, nor that I wrote all sorts of personal,

THE CRITICAL HERITAGE

intolerant, and arbitrary things under cover of the *Quarterly Review*—but that I grew older as most people do, and altered my opinions as many (silly) people do not. Finally, there it will be said that "in an age of personality, I abstained from satire," with the small exception of the instances just mentioned; and that the "only occasion on which I condescended to *reply*" instead of attack anonymously, was when a certain Mister in Parliament—namely you, *Mister* William Smith—was base, mean, odious, foolish, peevish, egotistical, and atrocious enough to attack me openly.'

So saying, to the great apparent satisfaction of himself and relief of poor Murrain, the posthumous orator returned majestically to his bier, and adjusting his repose with a greater and more Caesarean dignity than ever Liston did on a like occasion, gave one look around him of mixed triumph and contempt, and relapsed into his proper mortality.

Peace be to his shade.

80. Unsigned notice, *Monthly Review*

June 1817, n.s. lxxxiii, 223–4

Mr. William Smith, the Member for Norwich, whose liberal principles are well known, and acknowledged even by his opponents, is reported to have lately read in the House a passage from Mr. Southey's poem of *Wat Tyler*, in which the rights of equality are strongly enforced; and then to have contrasted it with another quotation attributed to the same author, selected from a recent number of a periodical work, of a tendency directly opposite, and vehemently abusing those who still hold any of Mr. S.'s former opinions. At the end of six weeks from the commission of this offence, Mr. Southey issued forth a letter of vindication; in which, as he terms it, he purposes to treat 'his calumniator with just and *memorable* severity.' With regard to the passage from the periodical work, he endeavours to shelter himself from responsibility because that publication is anonymous, and report, which may be mistaken, is the only authority by which any particular paper can be attributed to one person or to another. This defence we should be inclined to allow in its full force, were not the antient and established rule of secrecy in periodical criticism now so much disregarded, and the names of the contributors to the publication in question circulated with every degree of notoriety. Mr. Southey must therefore be contented to take the consequences of the exposure which has been courted.—He enters into a laboured defence of his gradual change from 'the political opinions which the French revolution scattered throughout Europe,' to those which he now holds; and, in a strain of alternate defence and abuse, he remarks on the production which has created so much notice. This is surely unnecessary. Mr. Smith does not find fault with the work, nor with Mr. Southey for changing his political creed: but it is the virulence with which Mr. Southey visits those who differ from his present sentiments, and who avow opinions if not entirely, at least nearly, the same with those which he formerly professed, that has called forth the observation and excited the disgust not only of Mr. William Smith, but of every other moderate man.

It is ludicrous, while Mr. S. disclaims 'the habit of egotism,' to observe the numberless instances of inordinate vanity with which these forty-five pages are filled. We lately had occasion to notice this vice in one of his *laurelled* poems; and, from its reappearance in prose, we fear that it is a rooted habit. The concluding passage, in which he writes a page in his own history, and proclaims the imperishable nature of his productions and his name,—in which, in short, he is 'his own glass, his own trumpet, his own chronicle,'—forms a climax of self-conceit that has no parallel.

81. Unsigned notice, *New Monthly Magazine*

June 1817, vii, 444

One of the few defences of Southey.

The *argumentum ad hominem*[1] was never more successfully applied than in this admirable epistle, and upon the whole the public may be grateful to the Member for Norwich in having been the occasion of so spirited an exposition. The poet-laureat has satisfactorily vindicated himself from the illiberal charges of apostacy; and he has done it with candour, in acknowledging the youthful errors which he held in common with numbers who have since seen reason to change their opinions on political subjects. We should gladly have made extracts from Mr. Southey, particularly of those parts which illustrate his own biography, did not the length of the passages lay a restraint upon our inclination in this respect: and we could not with propriety attempt any thing like an abridgment.

[1] 'Argument directed at the character of the man'.

82. George Ticknor meets Southey

18 May 1817

Ticknor (1791–1871), Professor of *Belles-Lettres* and French and Spanish at Harvard University from 1819 to 1835, travelled extensively in Europe. This extract from his *Life, Letters, and Journals* (2 vols, 1876), i, pp. 135–6, records his first meeting with Southey.

This evening, by a lucky accident, I went earlier than usual to Miss Williams's, and found there, by another mere accident, Southey. . . . There was little company present, and soon after I went in I found myself in a corner with him, from which neither of us moved until nearly midnight. He is, I presume, about forty-five, tall and thin, with a figure resembling the statues of Pitt, and a face by no means unlike his. His manners are a little awkward, but the openness of his character is so great that this does not embarrass him. He immediately began to talk about America, and particularly the early history of New England, with which he showed that sort of familiarity which I suppose characterizes his knowledge wherever he has displayed it. Of Roger Williams and John Eliot I was ashamed to find that he knew more than I did. Roger Williams, he thought, deserved the reputation which Penn has obtained, and Eliot he pronounced one of the most extraordinary men of any country. Once, he said, he had determined to write a poem on the war and character of King Philip, and at that time studied the Indian history and manners which he thinks highly poetical. So near has the Plymouth Colony come to being classical ground! While engaged in these researches, and as he was once travelling in a post-chaise to London, he bought at a stall in Nottingham, Mather's *Magnalia*, which he read all the way to town, and found it one of the most amusing books he had ever seen. Accident and other occupations interrupted these studies, he said, and he has never taken them up again. He had read most of our American poetry, and estimated it more highly than we are accustomed to, though still he did not praise it foolishly.

Barlow's *Columbiad*, Dwight's *Conquest of Canaan*, *McFingal*, etc., were all familiar to him, and he not only spoke of them with discrimination, but even repeated some lines from them in support of his opinion of their merits. By accident we came upon the review of *Inchiquin*, which, he said, was written in a bad spirit; and he added that he had seldom been so chagrined or mortified by any event of his literary life, as by being thought its author, though he should rather have written the review than the New York answer to it. . . . He talked with me about the Germans and their literature a good deal, and said if he were ten years younger he would gladly give a year to learn German, for he considered it now the most important language, after English, for a man of letters; and added with a kind of decision which showed he had thought of the subject, and received a good deal of information about it, that there is more intellectual activity in Germany now than in any other country in the world. In conversation such as this three hours passed very quickly away, and when we separated, I left him in the persuasion that his character is such as his books would represent it,—simple and enthusiastic, and his knowledge very various and minute.

83. Coleridge on Southey

1817

From *Biographia Literaria*, ed. J. Shawcross (2 vols, 1907), i, pp. 45–9. In this third chapter of the *Biographia* Coleridge recalls the attacks by reviewers upon Southey's early poems and expresses the hope that these will be remembered by future critics. He offers an eloquent tribute not only to Southey's literary achievement but also to his personal character.

I have in imagination transferred to the future biographer the duty of contrasting Southey's fixed and well-earned fame, with the abuse and indefatigable hostility of his anonymous critics from his early youth to his ripest manhood. But I cannot think so ill of human nature as not to believe, that these critics have already taken shame to themselves, whether they consider the object of their abuse in his moral or his literary character. For reflect but on the variety and extent of his acquirements! He stands second to no man, either as an historian or as a bibliographer; and when I regard him as a popular essayist, (for the articles of his compositions in the reviews are for the greater part essays on subjects of deep or curious interest rather than criticisms on particular works*) I look in vain for any writer, who has conveyed so much information, from so many and such recondite sources, with so many just and original reflections, in a style so lively and poignant, yet so uniformly classical and perspicuous; no one in short who has combined so much wisdom with so much wit; so much truth and knowledge with so much life and fancy. His prose is always intelligible and always entertaining. In poetry he has attempted almost every species of composition known before, and he has added new ones; and if we except the highest lyric, (in which how few, how very few even of the greatest minds have been fortunate) he has attempted every species successfully: from the political song of the day, thrown off in the

---

* See the articles on Methodism, in the *Quarterly Review*: the small volume on the New System of Education, &c.

playful overflow of honest joy and patriotic exultation, to the wild ballad*, from epistolary ease and graceful narrative, to the austere and impetuous moral declamation; from the pastoral claims and wild streaming lights of the *Thalaba*, in which sentiment and imagery have given permanence even to the excitement of curiosity; and from the full blaze of the *Kehama*, (a gallery of finished pictures in one splendid fancy piece, in which, notwithstanding, the moral grandeur rises gradually above the brilliance of the colouring and the boldness and novelty of the machinery) to the more sober beauties of the *Madoc*; and lastly, from the *Madoc* to his *Roderic*, in which, retaining all his former excellencies of a poet eminently inventive and picturesque, he has surpassed himself in language and metre, in the construction of the whole, and in the splendour of particular passages.

Here then shall I conclude? No! The characters of the deceased, like the encomia on tombstones, as they are described with religious tenderness, so are they read, with allowing sympathy indeed, but yet with rational deduction. There are men, who deserve a higher record; men with whose characters it is the interest of their contemporaries, no less than that of posterity, to be made acquainted; while it is yet possible for impartial censure, and even for quick-sighted envy, to cross-examine the tale without offence to the courtesies of humanity; and while the eulogist detected in exaggeration or falsehood must pay the full penalty of his baseness in the contempt which brands the convicted flatterer. Publicly has Mr. Southey been reviled by men, who, (as I would fain hope for the honor of human nature) hurled fire-brands against a figure of their own imagination, publicly have his talents been depreciated, his principles denounced; as publicly do I therefore, who have known him intimately, deem it my duty to leave recorded, that it is SOUTHEY's almost unexampled felicity, to possess the best gifts of talent and genius free from all their characteristic defects. To those who remember the state of our public schools and universities some twenty years past, it will appear no ordinary praise in any man to have passed from innocence into virtue, not only free from all vicious habit, but unstained by one act of intemperance, or the degradations akin to intemperance. That scheme of head, heart, and habitual demeanour, which in his early manhood, and first controversial writings, Milton, claiming the privilege of self-defence, asserts of himself, and challenges his calumniators to disprove; this will his school-mates, his fellow-collegians, and his maturer friends, with a

---

* See the incomparable 'Return to Moscow' and the 'Old Woman of Berkeley'.

confidence proportioned to the intimacy of their knowledge, bear witness to, as again realized in the life of Robert Southey. But still more striking to those, who by biography or by their own experience are familiar with the general habits of genius, will appear the poet's matchless industry and perseverance in his pursuits; the worthiness and dignity of those pursuits; his generous submission to tasks of transitory interest, or such as *his* genius alone could make otherwise; and that having thus more than satisfied the claims of affection or prudence, he should yet have made for himself time and power, to achieve more, and in more various departments than almost any other writer has done, though employed wholly on subjects of his own choice and ambition. But as Southey possesses, and is not possessed by, his genius, even so is he master even of his virtues. The regular and methodical tenor of his daily labours, which would be deemed rare in the most mechanical pursuits, and might be envied by the mere man of business, loses all semblance of formality in the dignified simplicity of his manners, in the spring and healthful cheerfulness of his spirits. Always employed, his friends find him always at leisure. No less punctual in trifles, than stedfast in the performance of highest duties, he inflicts none of those small pains and discomforts which irregular men scatter about them, and which in the aggregate so often become formidable obstacles both to happiness and utility; while on the contrary he bestows all the pleasures, and inspires all that ease of mind on those around him or connected with him, which perfect consistency, and (if such a word might be framed) absolute *reliability*, equally in small as in great concerns, cannot but inspire and bestow: when this too is softened without being weakened by kindness and gentleness. I know few men who so well deserve the character which an antient attributes to Marcus Cato, namely, that he was likest virtue, in as much as he seemed to act aright, not in obedience to any law or outward motive, but by the necessity of a happy nature, which could not act otherwise. As son, brother, husband, father, master, friend, he moves with firm yet light steps, alike unostentatious, and alike exemplary. As a writer, he has uniformly made his talents subservient to the best interests of humanity, of public virtue, and domestic piety; his cause has ever been the cause of pure religion and of liberty, of national independence and of national illumination. When future critics shall weigh out his guerdon of praise and censure, it will be Southey the poet only, that will supply them with the scanty materials for the latter. They will likewise not fail to record, that as no man was ever a more constant friend, never had poet more friends and honorers among the good of all parties; and that quacks in education, quacks in politics, and quacks in criticism were his only enemies.

84. Byron, dedication of *Don Juan*

1818

I

Bob Southey! You're a poet—Poet-laureate,
    And representative of all the race;
Although 'tis true that you turn'd out a Tory at
    Last,—yours has lately been a common case;
And now, my Epic Renegade! what are ye at?
    With all the Lakers, in and out of place?
A nest of tuneful persons, to my eye
Like 'four and twenty Blackbirds in a pye;

II

'Which pye being open'd they began to sing'
    ('This old song and new simile holds good),
'A dainty dish to set before the King,'
    Or Regent, who admires such kind of food;—
And Coleridge, too, has lately taken wing,
    But like a hawk encumber'd with his hood,—
Explaining metaphysics to the nation—
I wish he would explain his Explanation.

III

You, Bob! are rather insolent, you know,
    At being disappointed in your wish
To supersede all warblers here below,
    And be the only Blackbird in the dish;
And then you overstrain yourself, or so,
    And tumble downward like the flying fish

261

Gasping on deck, because you soar too high, Bob,
And fall, for lack of moisture quite a-dry, Bob!

IV

And Wordsworth, in a rather long 'Excursion'
    (I think the quarto holds five hundred pages),
Has given a sample from the vasty version
    Of his new system to perplex the sages;
'Tis poetry—at least by his assertion,
    And may appear so when the dog-star rages—
And he who understands it would be able
To add a story to the Tower of Babel.

V

You—Gentlemen! by dint of long seclusion
    From better company, have kept your own
At Keswick, and, through still continued fusion
    Of one another's minds, at last have grown
To deem as a most logical conclusion,
    That Poesy has wreaths for you alone:
There is a narrowness in such a notion,
Which makes me wish you'd change your lakes for ocean.

VI

I would not imitate the petty thought,
    Nor coin my self-love to so base a vice,
For all the glory your conversion brought,
    Since gold alone should not have been its price.
You have your salary: was't for that you wrought?
    And Wordsworth has his place in the Excise.
You're shabby fellows—true—but poets still,
And duly seated on the immortal hill.

VII

Your bays may hide the baldness of your brows—
    Perhaps some virtuous blushes;—let them go—
To you I envy neither fruit nor boughs—
    And for the fame you would engross, below,
The field is universal, and allows
    Scope to all such as feel the inherent glow:
Scott, Rogers, Campbell, Moore, and Crabbe, will try
'Gainst you the question with posterity.

VIII

For me, who, wandering with pedestrian Muses,
  Contend not with you on the winged steed,
I wish your fate may yield ye, when she chooses,
  The fame you envy, and the skill you need;
And recollect a poet nothing loses
  In giving to his brethren their full meed
Of merit, and complaint of present days
Is not the certain path to future praise.

IX

He that reserves his laurels for posterity
  (Who does not often claim the bright reversion)
Has generally no great crop to spare it, he
  Being only injured by his own assertion;
And although here and there some glorious rarity
  Arise like Titan from the sea's immersion,
The major part of such appellants go
To—God knows where—for no one else can know.

X

If, fallen in evil days on evil tongues,
  Milton appealed to the Avenger, Time,
If Time, the Avenger, execrates his wrongs,
  And makes the word 'Miltonic' mean 'sublime,'
He deign'd not to belie his soul in songs,
  Nor turn his very talent to a crime;
He did not loathe the Sire to laud the Son,
But closed the tyrant-hater he begun.

XI

Think'st thou, could he—the blind Old Man—arise,
  Like Samuel from the grave, to freeze once more
The blood of monarchs with his prophecies,
  Or be alive again—again all hoar
With time and trials, and those helpless eyes,
  And heartless daughters—worn—and pale—and poor;
Would he adore a sultan? he obey
·The intellectual eunuch Castlereagh?

XII

Cold-blooded, smooth-faced, placid miscreant!
  Dabbling its sleek young hands in Erin's gore,

And thus for wider carnage taught to pant,
    Transferr'd to gorge upon a sister shore,
The vulgarest tool that Tyranny could want,
    With just enough of talent, and no more,
To lengthen fetters by another fix'd,
And offer poison long already mix'd.

XIII

An orator of such set trash of phrase
    Ineffably—legitimately vile.
That even its grossest flatterer dare not praise,
    Nor foes—all nations—condescend to smile;
Not even a sprightly blunder's spark can blaze
    From that Ixion grindstone's ceaseless toil,
That turns and turns to give the world a notion
Of endless torments and perpetual motion.

XIV

A bungler even in its disgusting trade,
    And botching, patching, leaving still behind
Something of which its masters are afraid,
    States to be curb'd, and thoughts to be confined,
Conspiracy or Congress to be made—
    Cobbling at manacles for all mankind—
A tinkering slave-maker, who mends old chains,
With God and man's abhorrence for its gains.

XV

If we may judge of matter by the mind,
    Emasculated to the marrow *It*
Hath but two objects, how to serve, and bind,
    Deeming the chain it wears even men may fit,
Eutropius of its many masters,—blind
    To worth as freedom, wisdom as to wit,
Fearless—because *no* feeling dwells in ice,
Its very courage stagnates to a vice.

XVI

Where shall I turn me not to *view* its bonds,
    For I will never *feel* them;—Italy!
Thy late reviving Roman soul desponds
    Beneath the lie this State-thing breathed o'er thee—
Thy clanking chain, and Erin's yet green wounds,

Have voices—tongues to cry aloud for me.
Europe has slaves, allies, kings, armies still,
And Southey lives to sing them very ill.

XVII

Meantime, Sir Laureate, I proceed to dedicate,
  In honest simple verse, this song to you.
And, if in flattering strains I do not predicate,
  'Tis that I still retain my 'buff and blue;'
My politics as yet are all to educate:
  Apostasy's so fashionable, too,
To keep *one* creed's a task grown quite Herculean:
Is it not so, my Tory, ultra-Julian?

85. Thomas Love Peacock on Southey

1818

From a footnote to *Nightmare Abbey*, ch. 10. Having attacked Burke for political apostasy Peacock brings the same charge against Southey. Although Peacock had referred to Southey as 'the incomparable' in 1809, he felt that Southey's motives for accepting the Laureateship were hypocritical and selfish. Much of the satire of *Sir Proteus* is directed against Southey and he is frequently ridiculed in Peacock's novels.

Our immaculate laureate (who gives us to understand that, if he had not been purified by holy matrimony into a mystical type, he would have died a virgin,) is another sublime gentleman of the same genus: he very much astonished some persons when he sold his birthright for a pot of sack; but not even his *Sosia*[1] has a grain of respect for him,

[1] 'Peacock uses Sosia here to mean Southey's other self, the author of his early republican poems.' (David Garnett, note to *The Novels of Peacock*.)

though, doubtless, he thinks his name very terrible to the enemy, when he flourishes his criticopoeticopolitical tomahawk, and sets up his Indian yell for the blood of his old friends: but, at best, he is a mere political scarecrow, a man of straw, ridiculous to all who know of what materials he is made; and to none more so, than to those who have stuffed him, and set him up, as the Priapus of the garden of the golden apples of corruption.

86. 'The nine-pin of reviews,' Byron on Southey

1819

From 'Some observations upon an article in *Blackwood's Magazine*, no. xxix, August, 1819'. This was Byron's reply to an article entitled 'Remarks upon *Don Juan*'. Reprinted from *Letters and Journals*, ed. R. E. Prothero (1898–1901), iv, pp. 482–6.

One of '*these lofty-minded and virtuous men,*' in the words of the *Edinburgh Magazine*, made, I understand, about this time, or soon after, a tour in Switzerland. On his return to England, he circulated—and for any thing I know, invented—a report, that the gentleman to whom I have alluded and myself were living in promiscuous intercourse with two sisters, 'having formed a league of incest' (I quote the words as they were stated to me), and indulged himself on the natural comments upon such a conjunction, which are said to have been repeated publicly, with great complacency, by *another* of that poetical fraternity, of whom I shall say only, that even had the story been true, *he* should not have repeated it, as far as it regarded myself, except in sorrow. The tale itself requires but a word in answer—the ladies were *not* sisters, nor in any degree connected, except by the second marriage of their respective parents, a widower with a widow, both being the offspring of former marriages; neither of them were, in 1816, nineteen years old. 'Promis-cuous intercourse' could hardly have disgusted the great patron of pantisocracy, (does Mr. Southey remember such a scheme?) but there was none.

How far this man, who, as author of *Wat Tyler*, has been maintained by the Lord Chancellor guilty of a treasonable and blasphemous libel, and denounced in the House of Commons, by the upright and able member for Norwich, as a 'rancorous renegado,' be fit for sitting as a judge upon others, let others judge. He has said that for this expression 'he brands William Smith on the forehead as a calumniator,' and that 'the mark will outlast his epitaph.' How long William Smith's epitaph will last, and in what words it will be written, I know not, but William Smith's words form the epitaph itself of Robert Southey. He has written *Wat Tyler*, and taken the office of poet laureate—he has, in the *Life of Henry Kirke White*, denominated reviewing 'the ungentle craft,' and has become a reviewer—he was one of the projectors of a scheme, called 'pantisocracy,' for having all things, including women, in common, (*query*, common women?) and he sets up as a moralist—he denounced the battle of Blenheim, and he praised the battle of Waterloo —he loved Mary Wollstoncraft, and he tried to blast the character of her daughter (one of the young females mentioned)—he wrote treason, and serves the king—he was the butt of the *Anti-jacobin*, and he is the prop of the *Quarterly Review*; licking the hands that smote him, eating the bread of his enemies, and internally writhing beneath his own contempt,—he would fain conceal, under anonymous bluster, and a vain endeavour to obtain the esteem of others, after having for ever lost his own, his leprous sense of his own degradation. What is there in such a man to 'envy?' Who ever envied the envious? Is it his birth, his name, his fame, or his virtues, that I am to 'envy?' I was born of the aristocracy, which he abhorred; and am sprung, by my mother, from the kings who preceded those whom he has hired himself to sing. It cannot, then, be his birth. As a poet, I have, for the past eight years, had nothing to apprehend from a competition; and for the future, 'that life to come in every poet's creed,' it is open to all. I will only remind Mr. Southey, in the words of a critic, who, if still living, would have annihilated Southey's literary existence now and hereafter, as the sworn foe of charlatans and impostors, from Macpherson downwards, that 'those dreams were Settle's once and Ogilby's;'[1] and for my own part, I assure him, that whenever he and his sect are remembered, I

[1] Samuel Johnson, 'The Young Author'.

shall be proud to be 'forgot.' That he is not content with his success as a poet may reasonably be believed—he has been the nine-pin of reviews; the *Edinburgh* knocked him down, and the *Quarterly* set him up; the government found him useful in the periodical line, and made a point of recommending his works to purchasers, so that he is occasionally bought, (I mean his books, as well as the author,) and may be found on the same shelf, if not upon the table, of most of the gentlemen employed in the different offices. With regard to his private virtues, I know nothing—of his principles, I have heard enough. As far as having been, to the best of my power, benevolent to others, I do not fear the comparison; and for the errors of the passions, was Mr. Southey *always* so tranquil and stainless? Did he *never* covet his neighbour's wife? Did he never calumniate his neighbour's wife's daughter, the offspring of her he coveted? So much for the apostle of pantisocracy.

Of the 'lofty-minded, virtuous' Wordsworth, one anecdote will suffice to speak his sincerity. In a conversation with Mr. — upon poetry, he concluded with, 'After all, I would not give five shillings for all that Southey has ever written.' Perhaps this calculation might rather show his esteem for five shillings than his low estimate of Dr. Southey; but considering that when he was in his need, and Southey had a shilling, Wordsworth is said to have had generally a sixpence out of it, it has an awkward sound in the way of valuation. This anecdote was told me by persons who, if quoted by name, would prove that its genealogy is poetical as well as true. I can give my authority for this; and am ready to adduce it also for Mr. Southey's circulation of the falsehood before mentioned.

Of Coleridge, I shall say nothing—*why*, he may divine.

I have said more of these people than I intended in this place, being somewhat stirred by the remarks which induced me to commence upon the topic. I see nothing in these men as poets, or as individuals— little in their talents, and less in their characters, to prevent honest men from expressing for them considerable contempt, in prose or rhyme, as it may happen. Mr. Southey has the *Quarterly* for his field of rejoinder, and Mr. Wordsworth his postscripts to *Lyrical Ballads*, where the two great instances of the sublime are taken from himself and Milton. 'Over her own sweet voice the stock-dove broods;' that is to say, she has the pleasure of listening to herself, in common with Mr. Wordsworth upon most of his public appearances. 'What divinity doth hedge' these persons, that we should respect them? Is it Apollo? Are they not of those who called Dryden's *Ode* 'a drunken song?' who have discovered that Gray's *Elegy* is full of faults, (see Coleridge's *Life*, vol. i. *note*, for Wordsworth's kindness in pointing this out to him,) and have published what is allowed to be the very worst prose that ever was written, to prove that Pope was no poet, and that William Wordsworth is?

In other points, are they respectable, or respected? Is it on the open avowal of apostasy, on the patronage of government, that their claim is founded? Who is there who esteems those parricides of their own principles? They are, in fact, well aware that the reward of their change has been any thing but honour. The times have preserved a respect for political consistency, and, even though changeable, honour the unchanged. Look at Moore: it will be long ere Southey meets with such a triumph in London as Moore met with in Dublin, even if the government subscribe for it, and set the money down to secret service. It was not less to the man than to the poet, to the tempted but unshaken patriot, to the not opulent but incorruptible fellow citizen, that the warm-hearted Irish paid the proudest of tributes. Mr. Southey may applaud himself to the world, but he has his own heartiest contempt; and the fury with which he foams against all who stand in the phalanx which he forsook, is, as William Smith described it, 'the rancour of the renegado,' the bad language of the prostitute who stands at the corner of the street, and showers her slang upon all, except those who may have bestowed upon her her 'little shilling.'

Hence his quarterly overflowings, political and literary, in what he has himself termed 'the ungentle craft,' and his especial wrath against Mr. Leigh Hunt, notwithstanding that Hunt has done more for Wordsworth's reputation as a poet (such as it is), than all the Lakers could in their interchange of self-praises for the last twenty-five years.

And here I wish to say a few words on the present state of English poetry. That this is the age of the decline of English poetry will be doubted by few who have calmly considered the subject. That there are men of genius among the present poets makes little against the fact, because it has been well said, that 'next to him who forms the taste of his country, the greatest genius is he who corrupts it.' No one has ever denied genius to Marino, who corrupted not merely the taste of Italy, but that of all Europe for nearly a century. The great cause of the present deplorable state of English poetry is to be attributed to that absurd and systematic depreciation of Pope, in which, for the last few years, there has been a kind of epidemical concurrence. Men of the most opposite opinions have united upon this topic. Warton and Churchill began it, having borrowed the hint probably from the heroes of the *Dunciad*, and their own internal conviction that their proper reputation can be as nothing till the most perfect and harmonious of poets—he who, having no fault, has had REASON made his reproach—was reduced to what they conceived to be his level; but even *they* dared not degrade him below Dryden. Goldsmith, and Rogers, and Campbell, his most successful disciples; and Hayley, who, however feeble, has left one poem 'that will not be willingly let die' (the *Triumphs of Temper*), kept up the reputation of that pure and perfect style; and Crabbe, the first of living poets, has almost equalled the master. Then came Darwin, who was put down by a single poem in the *Antijacobin*; and the Cruscans, from Merry to Jerningham, who were annihilated (if *Nothing* can be said to be annihilated) by Gifford, the last of the wholesome satirists.

At the same time Mr. Southey was favouring the public with *Wat Tyler* and *Joan of Arc*, to the great glory of the Drama and Epos. I beg pardon, *Wat Tyler*, with *Peter Bell*, was still in MS., and it was not till after Mr. Southey had received his Malmsey butt, and Mr. Wordsworth became qualified to gauge it, that the great revolutionary tragedy came before the public and the Court of Chancery. Wordsworth was peddling his lyrical ballads, and brooding a preface, to be succeeded in due course by a postscript, both couched in such prose as must give peculiar delight to those who have read the prefaces of Pope and Dryden; scarcely less celebrated for the beauty of their prose, than for the charms of their verse. Wordsworth is the reverse of Molière's gentleman who had been 'talking prose all his life, without knowing it;'[1] for he thinks that he has been all his life writing both prose and verse, and neither of what he conceives to be such can be properly said to be either one or the other. Mr. Coleridge, the future *vates*, poet and seer of the *Morning Post*, (an honour also claimed by Mr. Fitzgerald, of the *Rejected Addresses*,) who ultimately prophesied the downfall of Buonaparte, to which he himself mainly contributed, by giving him the nickname of '*the Corsican*,' was then employed in predicating the damnation of Mr. Pitt, and the desolation of England, in the two very best copies of verses he ever wrote: to wit, the infernal eclogue of *Fire, Famine, and Slaughter*, and the *Ode to the departing Year*.

These three personages, Southey, Wordsworth, and Coleridge, had all of them a very natural antipathy to Pope; and I respect them for it, as the only original feeling or principle which they have contrived to

[1] *Le Bourgeois gentilhomme.*

preserve. But they have been joined in it by those who have joined them in nothing else: by the Edinburgh Reviewers, by the whole heterogeneous mass of living English poets, excepting Crabbe, Rogers, Gifford, and Campbell, who, both by precept and practice, have proved their adherence; and by me, who have shamefully deviated in practice, but have ever loved and honoured Pope's poetry with my whole soul, and hope to do so till my dying day. I would rather see all I have ever written lining the same trunk in which I actually read the eleventh book of a modern epic poem at Malta, in 1811, (I opened it to take out a change after the paroxysm of a tertian, in the absence of my servant, and found it lined with the name of the maker, Eyre, Cockspur Street, and with the epic poetry alluded to,) than sacrifice what I firmly believe in as the Christianity of English poetry, the poetry of Pope.

But the Edinburgh Reviewers, and the Lakers, and Hunt and his school, and every body else with their school, and even Moore without a school, and dilettanti lecturers at institutions, and elderly gentlemen who translate and imitate, and young ladies who listen and repeat, baronets who draw indifferent frontispieces for bad poets, and noblemen who let them dine with them in the country, the small body of the wits and the great body of the blues, have latterly united in a depreciation, of which their fathers would have been as much ashamed as their children will be. In the mean time, what have we got instead? The Lake school, which begun with an epic poem, 'written in six weeks,' (so *Joan of Arc* proclaimed herself,) and finished with a ballad composed in twenty years, as *Peter Bell's* creator takes care to inform the few who will enquire. What have we got instead? A deluge of flimsy and unintelligible romances, imitated from Scott and myself, who have both made the best of our bad materials and erroneous system. What have we got instead? *Madoc*, which is neither an epic nor any thing else; *Thalaba*, *Kehama*, *Gebir*, and such gibberish, written in all metres and in no language.

THE LIFE OF WESLEY AND THE RISE AND PROGRESS OF METHODISM

1820

In February 1819, while working on the book, Southey wrote to Cottle: 'I have taken a wide view of the subject: the existing lives of Wesley are scandalously imperfect, either observing a total silence upon what they did not like to acknowledge, or slurring it over. My work will be perfectly faithful as far as extreme diligence—and the scrupulous desire of fidelity can make it so' (Curry, ii, pp. 195–6). In March 1820 he wrote to Bedford: 'In parts I think some of my own best writing will be found. It is written with too fair a spirit to satisfy any particular set of men. . . . Some will complain of it as being heavy and dull; others will not think it serious enough. I shall be abused on all sides, and you well know how little I shall care for it' (*Life*, v, pp. 34–5).

87. Unsigned notice, *Monthly Magazine*

June 1820, xlix, 448–9

The Life of Wesley and the Rise and Progress of Methodism, by Robert Southey, esq. Poet Laureate (and author of *Wat Tyler*), is one of those numerous attempts at reconciling a love of popularity and lucre with the propagation of secret, and insidious and poisonous doctrines, for which this proteus of political, religious, and even *poetical tergiversation* is so notoriously distinguished. Through the thin veil of candour and impartiality with which he pretends to clothe the subject, the cloven hoof however unwillingly is too frequently protruded, and the organ by which he conveys opinions favorable to the cause of tyranny and superstition, is artfully concealed under the ground of due subordination, and religious principle. With these exceptions (which we do not think quite so lightly of as our author) we are of opinion, that the work is composed in a style of language well adapted to biographical research, and exhibits views of the peculiar character and sect to which it relates, which are both curious and interesting to those who study the history of religious enthusiasm.

88. A Methodist view

1820

From the opening of Richard Watson, *Observations on Southey's 'Life of Wesley'. Being a defence of the character, labours, and opinions, of Mr. Wesley, against the misrepresentations of that publication* (1820).

Watson (1781–1833) was a Wesleyan minister, notable for his active support of foreign missions and his opposition to the slave trade. His *Observations* were written at the request of the Wesleyan Conference. In its 228 pages the book offers a detailed and able criticism of the defects of Southey's theological knowledge and understanding of Wesley.

Methodism has been usually assailed by a violence so blind and illiberal, that those writers who have attempted to confute its principles, or to exhibit it alternately as an object of ridicule and alarm, have, in most cases, sufficiently answered themselves, and controversy has been rendered unnecessary. A few, and only a few, defences of Mr. Wesley, and his opinions, have therefore been published. The time of those best qualified for such a task has been better employed in works of active piety and benevolence. They have held on their way '*through good report and evil report*,' thinking it enough, that, by the writings of their Founder, and other subsequent publications, the candid might acquaint themselves with their views of Christianity; and that a people spread throughout the land presented points of observation, sufficiently

numerous, to enable unprejudiced persons to form an accurate estimate
of their character and influence.

Mr. Southey's *Life* of the venerable Founder of Methodism, presents itself under another aspect. It is not a hasty production, and it
betrays no want of temper. The facts and incidents which make up
the life and history of the remarkable man, of whom he has somewhat
strangely become the Biographer, have been collected with diligence;
and the narrative is creditable to the literary character of the writer.
He has the higher praise of considerable candour—candour, exercised
on a subject on which there was some temptation to more frequent
sarcasm and censure, had he aimed at gratifying the prejudices and
feelings of a great number of his readers; and he has ventured to say
more in praise of the character and public usefulness of Mr. Wesley,
than will be found in most publications of the kind, not emanating
from persons connected with the Wesleyan Society. Notwithstanding
this candour, and, as I believe, intended impartiality, there are still
great and serious objections to the Book. The Wesley of Mr. Southey
is not in several of its most important characteristics, Mr. Wesley
himself; and the picture of Methodism which he has drawn is not
exact, either in tone or composition. The impression made by the
whole is indeed equally as unfavourable to Christianity itself, as to the
views of that particular society, through whom some of its vital principles are assaulted; and it is quite as much as Christians, as a religious
body, that the Methodists will be dissatisfied with it. Panegyric was not
wished for, and there is more of justice and fairness than was hoped,
considering the quarter from which the work was to proceed. What
is defective and perverted may be charitably imputed, less to the intention of the writer, than to his total want of qualifications for the
undertaking. *The Life of Wesley* was not a subject for the pen of
Southey.

Had the Biographer been either less or more acquainted with theological subjects, his work would have borne a character more decided.
It would have been better or worse; and, in either form, been more
acceptable to all parties. It would have done more good or less mischief. As it is, it has a singularly hybridous character. It is distorted
with inconsistencies, and abounds in propositions which neutralize
each other as to any good effect, and yet retain activity enough to do
injury. Religion itself, if, not only Mr. Wesley was right in his views
of its nature and influence, but if the Church of England has rightly
exhibited it in her formularies, and in the writings of her greatest

divines, is very incautiously and generally resolved into enthusiasm, and other natural causes; and every stirring of religious feeling which may appear new and irregular to a cold and torpid formality, has a ready designation in the equally undefined term fanaticism. There are, it is true, occasional admissions on these subjects, which indicate respect and veneration for what is sacred; but they often prove no more than a convenient medium through which to convey impressions of a contrary kind with greater force. It is with no reluctance that I admit, that this was not always intended; but if any thing more than experience has already furnished were necessary to show the mischievousness of writing on subjects of religion, without steady and digested principles, it would be supplied by this publication. On all such topics Mr. Southey is extremely flippant and assuming, without any qualification to support the pretension. Educated, as it is reported, in the Socinian school; afterwards allured farther from the truth by the glare of a false philosophy, he has corrected many of his former errors, and is now a professed orthodox member of the Church of England. I am happy to see him in that fold; it would be illiberal to remember the aberrations of his youth, and not to allow him the praise of having for several years employed his talents well and usefully.—His, is evidently, an amiable and elevated, as well as a highly cultivated mind; but his views are yet too dim, and his theological attainments far too scanty, to give him a right to all that authority which he claims on many of those vital and solemn subjects which he decides with so censurable a confidence.

It is much to be regretted, that no general principles appear to have been laid down by Mr. Southey, to guide him in his estimate of Mr. Wesley's conduct and character. He is constantly vacillating between the philosopher and the Christian; but unhappily the tendency to philosophize most frequently predominates. The *cause* of every movement of the soul, and of every singularity in the conduct of Mr. Wesley and his followers, is eagerly sought, and abundantly laboured out, and it is sure to be one purely *natural*. Devotional feelings are resolved into constitutional habits; joys and depressions into buoyancy of the spirits, and the influence of disease; Mr. Wesley's selection of the means of usefulness into the impression of surrounding circumstances; his active zeal into ambition; the great effects of his preaching into his eloquence, and the opportune occurrence of a new contagious disease; his enterprize into a consciousness of his own powers; and his want of clerical regularity into his natural unsubmissiveness of mind. Some of these points shall be examined in the sequel; but this mode of determining such questions savours too much of the school from which we trust Mr. Southey is on many great points happily rescued; and it is too great a concession to the infidel and superficial philosophy of the day, of the evil tendency of which, when otherwise applied, he has a deep conviction. This is a weapon which he knows, or ought to know, may as easily be wielded against Christianity as against Methodism; and against every distinguished character in the annals of the Church of Christ as against Mr. Wesley.

Is Mr. Southey a believer in Christianity? If so, waiving for the present a minuter consideration of the following points, he must believe in the providential designation of distinguished characters to produce great and beneficial effects upon society;—he must believe in the influence of the Holy Spirit upon the minds of men, exciting them to their duty, and assisting them in it; he must believe that the work of renewing a corrupt heart, and giving real effect to the Christian Ministry, is the work of God, though carried on by human agents— he is not a Christian if he admits not these doctrines, he is not a Churchman; his Christianity is a name, a pretence: and if, in reality he admits them, they were unhappily, too often absent from his mind, and too often confused by the lingering traces of former erring sentiments, when he applied himself to determine the questions which presented themselves in the course of his late researches into Methodism.

Another cause of the wavering and unsteady judgment which he forms of Mr. Wesley, though far less blameable, is, that when he assumes something of the character of a Christian in the view of a case, it is not so much of a Christian generally, as of a zealous advocate of the order and discipline of the Church of England. I do not blame this rule in subordinate cases, but it is objectionable as a primary one. The religious character and motives of Mr. Wesley are in question, but surely the order and rule of any Church, however excellent, are not the standard by which either can be determined. That standard is to be found in the principles of our common Christianity. The order of a Church may have been violated by an irregularity which it does not allow. The fault may have been in the breadth of the zeal of the individual, or in the narrowness of the rule which his zeal has violated; these are other considerations, and are not surely to influence the judgment as to general character and motive. His Christianity must be tried by other laws, and can only be determined by the Bible itself. Modern times cannot exhibit a character in which all the great, and all the graceful virtues of Christianity were more fully embodied, and, through a long life, more amply realized, than in the Founder of Methodism. They have not presented a more laborious, a more successful minister of Christ. On what principle then is he ceaselessly charged with ambition, and the love of power, as the leading, though sometimes the unconscious motives of his actions? Why does Mr. Southey delight to rake into the corruption of our general nature, to stain the lustre and dissipate the fragrance of the eminent virtues of this distinguished man, as though those virtues must necessarily have struck root into that corruption as their soil, and have drawn from them a sickly exuberance, and a deleterious and earthly odour? Where virtues so eminent were exhibited by evidence so lofty, why has Mr. Southey, in so many instances, suffered himself to be seduced by a paltry philosophy which resolves all virtue into selfishness, or more properly into vice itself; and in others determined motives by a rule drawn from party predilections, to the neglect of those more favourable decisions which the general Christian rule would have supplied? Mr. Southey may say, these were Mr. Wesley's infirmities, and the best of men are not without them. But ambition, taken in the generally-received sense, as Mr. Southey uses the term, is not an infirmity. It is a vice, and is utterly incompatible with the spirit and temper of a real Christian; and, if he did not intend very greatly to lower Mr. Wesley's character by the charge, as indeed it seems but fair to acknowledge, this only proves that Mr. Southey has very low, and inadequate notions of practical Christianity itself.—He either trifles with Mr. Wesley's character, or with religion.

Southey's *Life of Wesley* is not a mere narrative of the incidents which occurred in the career of the individual, and of the rise, progress, and opinions of the religious body of which he was the Founder. The author passes judgment on every thing as it occurs, and, not unfrequently, so marshals his facts as to give the greater plausibility to his censures. We acknowledge that the opinions of Biographers and Historians, who are supposed to be calm and unprejudiced observers of persons and things, respecting which sufficient time has elapsed to allow a judgment to be formed, unbiassed by partial impressions, often form the most instructive part both of Biography and History. We read works of this kind not merely for the facts they contain, but for the sake of the opinions of those who profess to have studied their subject; and willingly put ourselves under the direction of a guiding mind for the discovery of those lessons which Providence designed to teach mankind, by the occasional introduction of great and singular characters, and important actions, upon the stage of our world. Unless, however, we have taken the resolution to submit our judgments implicitly to every writer who kindly undertakes to think for the public, it is natural for us to enquire into the competency of an author for so high an office. To this enquiry Mr. Southey must be subjected.

The question, however, is not whether he had habits sufficiently diligent to collect the facts necessary for fairly exhibiting the character of Mr. Wesley and of Methodism; nor whether he had the ability to work them into clear and spirited narrative. Neither will be denied; but these are minor considerations. He has not contented himself with narrative; he has added 'reflections to his tale,' and both as a theologist, and an advocate of the National Church, he has assumed the critic and the censor. His qualifications under these characters are, therefore, proper subjects of enquiry.

The leading points on which Mr. Southey, as the Biographer of Mr. Wesley, was called to express a judgment were, his religious character; his doctrines; his labours as a minister; and their results. All these evidently involve theological principles, and with them Mr. Southey's mind is but slenderly furnished. Of this, the account he has given of Mr. Wesley's conversion is a pregnant example.

89. John Gibson Lockhart, *Blackwood's Edinburgh Magazine*

February 1824, xv, 208–19

From the opening of his unsigned review.

Lockhart (1794–1854) was a major contributor to *Blackwood's* from 1817 until his appointment as editor of the *Quarterly Review* in 1825. This review, which appeared four years after the publication of the *Life of Wesley*, opens with an introductory survey of Southey's achievement. Although Lockhart ridicules Southey, greater malice is reserved for his depiction of Wesley in the later part of the review.

The worthy Laureate is one of those men of distinguished talents and industry, who have not attained to the praise or the influence of intellectual greatness, only because they have been so unfortunate as to come too late into the world. Had Southey flourished forty or fifty years ago, and written half as well as he has written in our time, he might have ranked *nem. con.*[1] with the first of modern critics, of modern historians, perhaps even of modern poets. The warmth of his feelings and the flow of his style would have enabled him to throw all the prosers of that day into the shade—His extensive erudition would have won him the veneration of an age in which erudition was venerable—His imaginative power would have lifted him like an eagle over the versifiers who then amused the public with their feeble echoes of the wit, the sense, and the numbers of Pope. He could not have been the Man of the Age; but, taking all his manifold excellencies and qualifications into account, he must have been most assuredly *Somebody*, and a great deal more than somebody.

How different is his actual case! As a poet, as an author of imaginative works in general, how small is the space he covers, how little is he talked or thought of! The Established Church of Poetry will hear of

[1] *Nemine contradicente:* 'no one contradicting'.

nobody but Scott, Byron, Campbell: and the Lake Methodists themselves will scarcely permit him to be called a burning and a shining
light in the same day with their Wordsworth—even their Coleridge.
In point of fact, he himself is now the only man who ever alludes to
Southey's poems. We can suppose youngish readers starting when they
come upon some note of his in the *Quarterly*, or in these new books of
history, referring to '*the Madoc*,' or '*the Joan*,' as to something universally known and familiar. As to criticism and politics of the day, he
is but one of the *Quarterly* reviewers, and scarcely one of the most
influential of them. He puts forth essays half antiquarianism, half
prosing, with now and then a dash of a sweet enough sort of literary
mysticism in them—and more frequently a display of pompous self-
complacent simplicity, enough to call a smile into the most iron
physiognomy that ever grinned. But these lucubrations produce no
effect upon the spirit of the time. A man would as soon take his
opinions from his grandmother as from the Doctor. The whole
thing looks as if it were made on purpose to be read to some
antediluvian village club—The fat parson—the solemn leech—the
gaping schoolmaster, and three or four simpering Tabbies. There is
nothing in common to him and the people of this world. We love
him—we respect him—we admire his diligence, his acquisitions, his
excellent manner of keeping his note-books—If he were in orders, and
one had an advowson to dispose of, one could not but think of him.
But good, honest, worthy man, only to hear him telling us his opinion
of Napoleon Buonaparte!—and then the quotations from Coleridge,
Wordsworth, Lamb, Landor, Withers, old Fuller, and all the rest of
his favourites—and the little wise-looking maxims, every one of them
as old as the back of Skiddaw—and the delicate little gleams of pathos
—and the little family-stories and allusions—and all the little paren-
theses of exultation—well, we really wonder after all, that the Laureate
is not more popular.

The first time Mr Southey attempted regular historical composition
he succeeded admirably. His *Life of Nelson* is truly a masterpiece;—a
brief—animated—glowing—straightforward—manly English work,
in two volumes duodecimo. That book will be read three hundred
years hence by every boy that is nursed on English ground.—All his
bulky historical works are, comparatively speaking, failures. His
History of Brazil is the most unreadable production of our time. Two
or three elephant quartos about a single Portugueze colony! Every
little colonel, captain, bishop, friar, discussed at as much length as if they

were so many Cromwells or Loyolas—and why?—just for this one simple reason, that Dr Southey is an excellent Portugueze scholar, and has an excellent Portugueze library. The whole affair breathes of one sentiment, and but one—Behold, O British Public! what a fine thing it is to understand this tongue—fall down and worship me! I am a member of the Lisbon Academy, and yet I was born in Bristol, and am now living at Keswick.

This inordinate vanity is an admirable condiment in a small work, and when the subject is really possessed of a strong interest. It makes one read with more earnestness of attention and sympathy. But carried to this height, and exhibited in such a book as this, it is utter nonsense. It is carrying the joke a great deal too far.—People do at last, however good-natured, get weary of seeing a respectable man *walking* his hobby-horse.

Melancholy to say, the *History of the Peninsular War* is, in spite of an intensely interesting theme, and copious materials of real value, little better than another Caucasus of lumber, after all. If the campaigns of Buonaparte were written in the same style, they would make a book in thirty or forty quarto volumes, of 700 pages each. He is overlaying the thing completely—he is smothering the Duke of Wellington. The underwood has increased, is increasing, and ought without delay to be smashed. Do we want to hear the legendary history of every Catholic saint, who happens to have been buried or worshipped near the scene of some of General Hill's skirmishes? What in the devil's name, have we to do with all these old twelfth century miracles and visions, in the midst of a history of Arthur Duke of Wellington, and his British army? Does the Doctor mean to write his Grace's Indian campaigns in the same style, and to make them the pin whereon to hang all the wreck and rubbish of his commonplace book for *Kehama*, as he has here done with the odds and ends that he could not get stuffed into the notes on *Roderick* and *My Cid*? Southey should have lived in the days of 2000 page folios, triple columns, and double indexes—He would then have been set to a *corpus* of something at once, and been happy for life. Never surely was such a mistake as for him to make his appearance in an age of restlessly vigorous thought, disdainful originality of opinion, intolerance for long-windedness, and scorn of mountains in labour—Glaramara and Penmanmaur among the rest.

In all these greater histories, the Laureate has been much the worse for some unhappy notion he has got into his head, of writing *à la* Clarendon. Clarendon is one of the first English classics, and one of the first historical authors the world can boast; but nobody can deny that he is, nevertheless, a most prolix penman. The things that carry him through, in spite of all his prolixity, are, first, the amazing abstract interest of his subject matter; secondly, his own prodigious knowledge of human nature; and, thirdly, the admirable opportunities he had for applying this knowledge to the individual characters he has to treat of, in the course of a long life spent in the most important offices of the state, and during the most important series of changes that the state has ever witnessed. Now, the Doctor, to balance a caricature of the Chancellor's tediousness, brings really but a slender image of the Chancellor's qualifications. He writes not about things and persons that he has seen, and if he did, he has extremely little insight into human character, and a turn of mind altogether different from that which is necessary for either transacting or comprehending the affairs of active life. He has the prolixity—without the graphic touches, the intense knowledge, the profound individual feeling, of a writer of memoirs. He reads five or six piles of old books, and picks up a hazy enough view of some odd character there, and then he thinks he is entitled to favour us with this view of his, at the same length which we could only have pardoned from some chosen friend, and life-long familiar associate of the hero himself.

Perhaps Southey's *Life of Wesley* is the most remarkable instance extant, of the ridiculous extremities to which vanity of this kind can carry a man of great talents and acquirements. Who but Southey would ever have dreamt that it was possible for a man that was not a Methodist, and that had never seen John Wesley's face, nor even conversed with any one of his disciples, to write two thumping volumes under the name of a *Life of Wesley*, without turning the stomach of the Public? For whom did he really suppose he was writing this book? Men of calm sense and rational religion, were certainly not at all likely to take their notion of the Founder of the Methodists, from any man who could really suppose that Founder's life to be worthy of occupying one thousand pages of close print. The Methodists them-selves would, of course, be horrified with the very name of such a book, on such a subject, by one of the uninitiated. Probably, few of them have looked into it at all; and, most certainly, those that have done so, must have done so with continual pain, loathing, and disgust. But our friend, from the moment *he* takes up any subject, no matter what it is, seems to be quite certain, first, that that subject is the only one in the world worth writing about; and, secondly, that he is the only man who has any right to meddle with it. On he drives—ream after ream is covered with his beautiful, distinct, and print-like autograph. We have sometimes thought it possible that the very beauty of this hand-writing of his, may have been one of his chief curses. One would think, now, that writing out, in any hand, dull and long-winded quotations from Wesley's Sermons, Whitefield's Sermons, their Journals, their Magazines, &c. &c. &c., would be but poor amusement in the eyes of such a man as Southey—more especially as it must be quite obvious, that they who really think these people worthy of being studied like so many Julius Cæsars, will, of course, study them in their own works, and in the works of their own ardent admirers; and that, as to mankind in general, they will still say, after reading all that the Laureate has heaped together, 'Did this man never read Hume's *one* chapter on the Puritan Sects?'

The truth is, that a real historian, either a Hume, or a Clarendon, or a Du Retz, or a Tacitus, would have found no difficulty in concentrating all that really can be said, to any purpose, about Wesley, Zinzendorf, Whitefield, and all the rest of these people, in, at the most, fifty pages. And then the world would have read the thing and been the better for it. At present, the Methodists stick to their own absurd Lives of Wesley, and there exists no Life of him adapted for the purposes of the general reader, or composed with any reference to the ideas of any extensive body of educated men whatever.

A VISION OF JUDGEMENT

1821

90. From an unsigned review, *Literary Gazette*

17 March 1821, 161–3

From the opening of the review.

Notwithstanding the names of Messrs. Longman and Company, on the title page of this work, we can with difficulty be persuaded that it is not a hoax on the Poet Laureate. That Mr. Southey should have written, and, still more, that he should have consented to publish such a mass of absurdity, are hardly within the bounds of human belief. Yet the evidence of the fact is so irresistible, that we fear we must admit this volume to be certainly the production of his hand, and an extraordinary instance of the extent of delusion to which genius may be betrayed by self-love. Mr. Southey has indeed indulged in a *Vision*, but in the *Judgment* part of the matter he has been lamentably deficient; as the public judgment on his performance must inevitably and painfully convince him. The sin of *Wat Tyler* was nothing to this.

We do not so much complain of the phantasy of endeavouring to torture hexameters into the form of English versification, and trying to persuade the world that such a line as—

Otherwhere else, be sure, his doom had now been appointed—

is as sweet poetry as the dulcet lyrick,[1]

> When all shall praise, and every lay
> Devote a wreath to thee—
> That day, for come it will, that day
> Shall I lament to see.

David Lewis, 'Where none shall rail'.

But what we do dislike exceedingly is the trash which, even granting him his own medium, Mr. Southey has got together in this *Vision*. Were his name not high, (and few more deservedly high in poetry,) we should spare ourselves the unpleasant task of expressing our opinions upon the subject; but precedent in such a quarter is dangerous; and in the hope of crushing it in the bud, we must plainly say, that we have no words to describe the mixture of pity, contempt, and disapprobation, with which the perusal of this piece has filled us.

[Summarizes the argument of the poem with quotations.]

91. From an unsigned review, *Literary Chronicle and Weekly Review*

24 March 1821, 180–3

From the opening of the review.

How are the mighty fallen? how is the fine gold changed? must be the exclamation of every admirer of Mr. Southey, when he reads this abortion of his genius, the *Vision of Judgment*. Is this the man who sung the *Maid of Orleans*, *Wat Tyler*, and 'of *Thalaba* the wild and wondrous song?' To what extent the debasement of talents, and the prostitution of principle may be carried, Mr. Southey furnishes a memorable instance. We know not which to condemn most, the prosing absurdity of this poem, its wanton political profligacy, or its blasphemy. Let us no longer be told of the licentiousness of the press, of the irreligious tenets of Carlile, or of the parodies of Hone; the poet laureate—yes, the poet laureate himself, outstrips them all, in a poem which he has the hardihood to inscribe, in a fulsome dedication, to his sovereign, not without the hope, we suppose, that this production, wretched as it is, will be afterwards considered as one of 'the achievements of the Georgian age.'

Mr. Southey, it appears, has long been of opinion, that an English metre might be constructed in imitation of the ancient hexameter, which would be perfectly consistent with the character of our language, and capable of great richness, variety, and strength; and although Sir Philip Sidney failed in the 'attempt to naturalize this fine measure,' yet Mr. Southey, by making the experiment, has 'fulfilled one of the hopes and intentions of his early life,' and has the vanity to think that it 'may be considered hereafter as of some importance in English poetry.' Of what importance, we think we can enable our readers to decide, without entering at all into the inquiry, how far the English metre is suited to hexameters.

92. Dorothy Wordsworth, from a letter to Mrs Clarkson

27 March 1821

Reprinted from *The Letters of William and Dorothy Wordsworth, 1821–30*, ed. E. de Selincourt (1939), pp. 30–1.

Have you seen Southey's *Vision of Judgment*? I like both the metre, and most part of the Poem, very much. It is composed with great animation, and some passages are very beautiful; but the intermixture of familiar names pushes you down a frightful descent at times, and I wish he had avoided the very words of Scripture. The king has sent him a message that he had read the poem twice over, and thanks him for the Dedication.

93. From an unsigned review, *Monthly Review*

June 1821, n.s. xcv, 170–8

After attacking the ideas expressed in the poem the reviewer considers Southey's versification.

No sophistry, and least of all such lame and impotent sophistry as that which pervades the Preface to the *Vision*, can reconcile an Englishman of any sense or fancy (unperverted by silly theories of variety) to *English hexameters*. Mr. Southey may be right, or wrong, as to the bibliographical question about their real authors:—we leave him to decide it with any of the knights of Roxburghe:—but the question, of any general interest, is this; Is the English language adapted to such a metre? Mr. Southey, we think, has fully answered this question by the best of all replies, a practical reply; and well may we ask in our turn,

> Southey, what can you *mean*? &c. &c.

laying a strong emphasis on '*mean*;' and on all corresponding syllables in this extraordinary measure, which consists in fact, rather of two verses than one.

If it be expected of us to exhibit this celebrated Preface (the happy counterpart to Wordsworth's equally famous Lyrical Pro-emium, or Self-panegyrical Overture,) in its own colours, we shall favour the reader with a choice specimen: but of its delightful strain of egotistical composure, no adequate idea can be formed except by the patience of a thorough perusal. It would place any body but so gifted a being as Mr. Southey at the very zenith of the poetico-prosaic '*Duncery*,' or '*Dunderheadery*,' as it perhaps may better be called.

The feet must too frequently be made up of monosyllables, and of distinct words, whereby the verse is resolved and decomposed into its component feet, and the feet into their component syllables, instead of being articulated and inosculated throughout, as in the German, still more in the Greek, and most in the Latin measure. This is certainly a great defect. From the same cause the

287

cæsura generally coincides with a pause in the sentence; but, though this breaks the continuity of the verse, it ought perhaps rather to be considered as an advantage; for the measure, like blank verse, thus acquires greater variety. It may possibly be objected, that the four first feet are not metrical enough in their effect, and the two last too much so.

In our opinion, the author has here completely cut the throat of his own preposterous attempt, in the very act of *most strenuously* defending it: for he adds that 'he does not *feel*' the last 'objection,' although 'one whose opinion would make him distrust his own' has advanced it. In this *most strenuous defence*, we descry the following *acknowledgements* and *contradictions*:—first, the absolute necessity of *reading* this verse, to a certain degree, as if we were *scanning* it, which follows from the '*decomposition*' acknowledged; and, secondly, the dead stop in the *middle*, producing the effect of a horse first refusing a leap, and then taking it by a violent effort from the place where he stands:

> Reach'd the remotest East, or invading the kingdom of Winter,

and so throughout, where the verse is legitimately constructed. Even a slight deviation from this construction produces some proportionable awkwardness.

> While of the *Georgian age* they thought, and the glory of England.

Here the horse stops,—a fearful space indeed,—and then takes a short jump at last, most threatening to his rider. In some lines, however, the rhythm is wholly or partially lost, by the very want of this *bear-and-fiddle* fault, of stopping in the middle. For example:

> Or in foreign earth they have moulder'd, hastily cover'd;

> Not without ingenuous shame, and a sense of compunction;

in a passage already quoted.

Will it do no harm to literary taste and classical nurture, to teach our ingenuous students that such things as these are *English verses*? Is not the tone of our compatriot poetry lowered enough, without these new relaxations? . . .

If any of our readers have not discovered the '*contradictions*' in the foregoing prose-quotation from Mr. Southey, we beg that they will be pleased to observe that, when Mr. Southey *confesses* that 'the cæsura *generally* coincides with a pause in the sentence,' and then adds that 'the measure thus acquires *greater variety*,' he forgets that what *generally* occurs cannot well contribute to *variety*; especially when the occurrence, in almost ninety-nine cases out of a hundred of the said break in the rhythm, takes place as precisely in the centre of the verse as the *cæsura* in the French Alexandrine. Mr. S. has either not weighed with his usual diligence (for we believe he is diligence personified) the whole of this particular subject of metre, or he has some *perverted theory* about it; or, finally, he labours under that deficiency which many wise and worthy men betray, of a full and perfect knowledge in the curious craft or mystery of antient and modern quantity and accentuation. He does not, in a word, possess his *Arsis* and *Thesis* as he ought.

We have deemed it incumbent on us to endeavour to set to its right pitch the tone of lofty exultation, with which these new discoverers of wonders in the world of poetry announce their own inventions. We are too old, we confess, to expect any fresh '*mare's nests*' of this nature; and we recollect the time when the most ardent enthusiast for the composition of English hexameters would have *blushed*, and not *gloried*, to make his metrical aberrations public: '*mais nous avons changé tout cela*,'[1] in 'the *Georgian age!*'

We now take leave of Mr. Southey, whatever he may think, with unfeigned depression at the sight of such ample powers so uselessly diffused in poetry; and so sadly 'giving up to party what was meant for mankind,' in the sacred offices of reason.

[1] 'But we have changed all that'.

94. Byron, *The Two Foscari*

1821

From Byron's *Letters and Journals*, ed. R. E. Prothero (1898–1901), vi, pp. 387–9. In this note in the appendix to *The Two Foscari* Byron countered the attacks made in Southey's *Vision of Judgement*. Southey replied with a letter to the *Courier*. Writing to Grosvenor Bedford in January 1822, Southey stated: 'His affectation of contempt comes to my hands curiously, just after I have received from Murray an account of the manner in which he extolled *Roderick* upon its first appearance. But this inconsistency, which must be known to all his friends, is beneath my notice' (Curry, ii, p. 233).

Mr. Southey, too, in his pious preface to a poem whose blasphemy is as harmless as the sedition of *Wat Tyler*, because it is equally absurd with that sincere production, calls upon the 'legislature to look to it,' as the toleration of such writings led to the French Revolution: *not* such writings as *Wat Tyler*, but as those of the 'Satanic School.' This is not true, and Mr. Southey knows it to be not true. Every French writer of any freedom was persecuted; Voltaire and Rousseau were exiles, Marmontel and Diderot were sent to the Bastille, and a perpetual war was waged with the whole class by the existing despotism. In the next place, the French Revolution was *not* occasioned by any writings whatsoever, but must have occurred had no such writers ever existed. It is the fashion to attribute every thing to the French revolution, and the French revolution to every thing but its real cause. That cause is obvious—the government exacted too much, and the people could neither *give* nor *bear more*. Without this, the Encyclopedists might have written their fingers off without the occurrence of a single alteration. And the *English* revolution—(the first, I mean)—what was it occasioned by? The *puritans* were surely as pious and moral as Wesley or his biographer? Acts—acts on the part of government, and *not* writings against them, have caused the past convulsions, and are tending to the future.

I look upon such as inevitable, though no revolutionist: I wish to see the English constitution restored and not destroyed. Born an aristocrat, and naturally one by temper, with the greater part of my present property in the funds, what have *I* to gain by a revolution? Perhaps I have more to lose in every way than Mr. Southey, with all his places and presents for panegyrics and abuse into the bargain. But that a revolution is inevitable, I repeat. The government may exult over the repression of petty tumults; these are but the receding waves repulsed and broken for a moment on the shore, while the great tide is still rolling on and gaining ground with every breaker. Mr. Southey accuses us of attacking the religion of the country; and is he abetting it by writing lives of *Wesley*? One mode of worship is merely destroyed by another. There never was, nor ever will be, a country without a religion. We shall be told of *France* again: but it was only Paris and a frantic party, which for a moment upheld their dogmatic nonsense of theo-philanthropy. The church of England, if overthrown, will be swept away by the sectarians and not by the sceptics. People are too wise, too well informed, too certain of their own immense importance in the realms of space, ever to submit to the impiety of doubt. There may be a few such diffident speculators, like water in the pale sunbeam of human reason, but they are very few; and their opinions, without enthusiasm or appeal to the passions, can never gain proselytes —unless, indeed, they are persecuted—*that*, to be sure, will increase any thing.

Mr. S., with a cowardly ferocity, exults over the anticipated 'death-bed repentance' of the objects of his dislike; and indulges himself in a pleasant *Vision of Judgement*, in prose as well as verse, full of impious impudence. What Mr. S.'s sensations or ours may be in the awful moment of leaving this state of existence neither he nor we can pretend to decide. In common, I presume, with most men of any reflection, *I* have not waited for a 'death-bed' to repent of many of my actions, notwithstanding the 'diabolical pride' which this pitiful renegado in his rancour would impute to those who scorn *him*. Whether upon the whole the good or evil of my deeds may preponderate is not for me to ascertain; but, as my means and opportunities have been greater, I shall limit my present defence to an assertion (easily proved, if necessary,) that I, 'in my degree,' have done more real good in any one given year, since I was twenty, than Mr. Southey in the whole course of his shifting and turncoat existence. There are several actions to which I can look back with an honest pride, not to be damped by the calumnies of a hireling. There are others to which I recur with sorrow and repentance; but the only *act* of *my* life of which Mr. Southey can have any real knowledge, as it was one which brought me in contact with a near connexion of his own, did no dishonour to that connexion nor to me.

I am not ignorant of Mr. Southey's calumnies on a different occasion, knowing them to be such, which he scattered abroad on his return from Switzerland against me and others: they have done him no good in this world; and, if his creed be the right one, they will do him less in the next. What *his* 'death-bed' may be, it is not my province to predicate: let him settle it with his Maker, as I must do with mine. There is something at once ludicrous and blasphemous in this arrogant scribbler of all work sitting down to deal damnation and destruction upon his fellow creatures, with *Wat Tyler*, the Apotheosis of George the Third, and the Elegy on Martin the regicide, all shuffled together in his writing desk. One of his consolations appears to be a Latin note from a work of a Mr. Landor, the author of *Gebir*, whose friendship for Robert Southey will, it seems, 'be an honour to him when the ephemeral disputes and ephemeral reputations of the day are forgotten.' I for one neither envy him 'the friendship,' nor the glory in reversion which is to accrue from it, like Mr. Thelusson's fortune in the third and fourth generation. This friendship will probably be as memorable as his own epics, which (as I quoted to him ten or twelve years ago in *English Bards*) Porson said 'would be remembered when Homer and Virgil are forgotten, and not till then.' For the present I leave him.

95. Southey satirized: *Peter Pindar's Ghost*

1821

Peter Pindar's Ghost!! or, Poetic Epistles from the Other World was published in pamphlet form in London in 1821. The first poem in the volume attacks Southey's political apostasy. The British Museum tentatively attributes the volume to C. F. Lawler.

FROM

PETER TO S——Y,

FROM PARNASSUS

Ah! master S——y, I expected
When I was gone you'd be elected
   To play the pipes of state.
Pr'ythee then, brother poet, say,
What *kind of compliment* you pay
   To flatter *Hum the great.*

Doubtless *his virtues* are as bright
As any claiming *divine right,*
   That peace and plenty brings;
Tho' honour you may lay aside,
Thy verse may gratify the pride
   Of this same league of K——gs.

Perhaps the laureat pen doth trace
The *chastity* and *modest* grace
   Of thy *esteem'd* employer.
For what has history to do
With men like G——e the —— or you,
   Except to call thee *liar.*

I've heard it whisper'd here about,
And of the fact I scarce can doubt,
   That thou hast turn'd thy coat,

And from a democrat wheel'd round
To take up *ministerial* ground,
    And *swallow* all you wrote.

And that, O poet! as thou'rt styl'd,
Thy *former* creed thou hast revil'd,
    And turn'd a *whig* compiler;
Adopting maxims not thine own,
Servile thou bow'd before the throne,
    Disowning *poor Wat Tyler.*

What hast thou got for all thy pains,
Beating for compliments thy brains,
    A ministerial hack.
S——y, sit down, enjoy thy cheer,
Thy paltry hundred pounds a year,
    And pipe of royal sack.

Thank heav'n, none yet could Peter blame,
Or say he sacrificed his fame,
    By ratting or a bribe;
And tho' he *loyal* couplets sung,
He never basely got among
    The rotten-borough tribe.

Now mark me, Bob, I know thy song
Cannot at court support thee long;
    Thy friends, as I have heard,
Are on the point of turning out,
And from the rats, I'm much in doubt,
    You'll gain but small reward.

96. Byron's *Vision of Judgment*

1822

The Vision of Judgment, written as a counterblast to Southey's poem, contains the most effective of all Byron's satiric attacks upon Southey. Extracts from (a) the prose preface, and (b) the concluding stanzas of the poem.

(a)

It hath been wisely said, that 'One fool makes many;' and it hath been poetically observed—

> 'That fools rush in where angels fear to tread.'—Pope.[1]

If Mr. Southey had not rushed in where he had no business, and where he never was before, and never will be again, the following poem would not have been written. It is not impossible that it may be as good as his own, seeing that it cannot, by any species of stupidity, natural or acquired, be *worse*. The gross flattery, the dull impudence, the renegado intolerance, and impious cant, of the poem by the author of *Wat Tyler*, are something so stupendous as to form the sublime of himself—containing the quintessence of his own attributes.

So much for his poem—a word on his preface. In this preface it has pleased the magnanimous Laureate to draw the picture of a supposed 'Satanic School,' the which he doth recommend to the notice of the legislature; thereby adding to his other laurels the ambition of those of an informer. If there exists anywhere, except in his imagination, such a School, is he not sufficiently armed against it by his own intense vanity? The truth is, that there are certain writers whom Mr. S. imagines, like Scrub, to have 'talked of *him*; for they laughed consumedly.'

I think I know enough of most of the writers to whom he is supposed to allude, to assert, that they, in their individual capacities, have

[1] *An Essay on Criticism.*

done more good, in the charities of life, to their fellow-creatures, in any one year, than Mr. Southey has done harm to himself by his absurdities in his whole life; and this is saying a great deal. But I have a few questions to ask.

1stly, Is Mr. Southey the author of *Wat Tyler*?

2ndly, Was he not refused a remedy at law by the highest judge of his beloved England, because it was a blasphemous and seditious publication?

3rdly, Was he not entitled by William Smith in full parliament, 'a rancorous renegado'?

4thly, Is he not poet laureate, with his own lines on Martin the regicide staring him in the face?

And, 5thly, Putting the four preceding items together, with what conscience dare *he* call the attention of the laws to the publications of others, be they what they may?

I say nothing of the cowardice of such a proceeding, its meanness speaks for itself; but I wish to touch upon the *motive*, which is neither more nor less than that Mr. S. has been laughed at a little in some recent publications, as he was of yore in the *Anti-jacobin* by his present patrons. Hence all this 'skimble-scamble stuff' about 'Satanic', and so forth. However, it is worthy of him—'*qualis ab incepto.*'[1]

If there is anything obnoxious to the political opinions of a portion of the public in the following poem, they may thank Mr. Southey. He might have written hexameters, as he has written everything else, for aught that the writer cared—had they been upon another subject. But to attempt to canonise a monarch, who, whatever were his household virtues, was neither a successful nor a patriot king,—inasmuch as several years of his reign passed in war with America and Ireland, to say nothing of the aggression upon France,—like all other exaggeration, necessarily begets opposition. In whatever manner he may be spoken of in this new 'Vision,' his *public* career will not be more favourably transmitted by history. Of his private virtues (although a little expensive to the nation) there can be no doubt.

With regard to the supernatural personages treated of, I can only say that I know as much about them, and (as an honest man) have a better right to talk of them than Robert Southey. I have also treated them more tolerantly. The way in which that poor insane creature, the Laureate, deals about his judgments in the next world, is like his own judgment in this. If it was not completely ludicrous, it would be

[1] 'Such he was from the beginning'.

something worse, I don't think that there is much more to say at present.

(b)

LXXXV

At length with jostling, elbowing, and the aid
   Of cherubim appointed to that post,
The devil Asmodeus to the circle made
   His way, and look'd as if his journey cost
Some trouble. When his burden down he laid,
   'What's this?' cried Michael; 'why, 'tis not a ghost?'
'I know it,' quoth the incubus; 'but he
Shall be one, if you leave the affair to me.

LXXXVI

'Confound the renegado! I have sprain'd
   My left wing, he's so heavy; one would think
Some of his works about his neck were chain'd.
   But to the point; while hovering o'er the brink
Of Skiddaw (where as usual it still rain'd),
   I saw a taper, far below me, wink,
And stooping, caught this fellow at a libel—
No less on history than the Holy Bible.

LXXXVII

'The former is the devil's scripture, and
   The latter yours, good Michael: so the affair
Belongs to all of us, you understand.
   I snatch'd him up just as you see him there,
And brought him off for sentence out of hand:
   I've scarcely been ten minutes in the air—
At least a quarter it can hardly be:
I dare say that his wife is still at tea.'

LXXXVIII

Here Satan said, 'I know this man of old,
   And have expected him for some time here;
A sillier fellow you will scarce behold,
   Or more conceited in his petty sphere:
But surely it was not worth while to fold
   Such trash below your wing, Asmodeus dear:

We had the poor wretch safe (without being bored
With carriage) coming of his own accord.

LXXXIX

'But since he's here, let's see what he has done.'
  'Done!' cried Asmodeus, 'he anticipates
The very business you are now upon,
  And scribbles as if head clerk to the Fates.
Who knows to what his ribaldry may run,
  When such an ass as this, like Balaam's, prates?'
'Let's hear,' quoth Michael, 'what he has to say:
You know we're bound to that in every way.'

XC

Now the bard, glad to get an audience, which
  By no means often was his case below,
Began to cough, and hawk, and hem, and pitch
  His voice into that awful note of woe
To all unhappy hearers within reach
  Of poets when the tide of rhyme's in flow;
But stuck fast with his first hexameter,
Not one of all whose gouty feet would stir.

XCI

But ere the spavin'd dactyls could be spurr'd
  Into recitative, in great dismay
Both cherubim and seraphim were heard
  To murmur loudly through their long array;
And Michael rose ere he could get a word
  Of all his founder'd verses under way,
And cried, 'For God's sake stop, my friend! 'twere best—
Non Di, non homines—you know the rest.'

XCII

A general bustle spread throughout the throng,
  Which seem'd to hold all verse in detestation;
The angels had of course enough of song
  When upon service; and the generation
Of ghosts had heard too much in life, not long
  Before, to profit by a new occasion:
The monarch, mute till then, exclaim'd, 'What! what!
Pye come again? No more—no more of that!'

XCIII

The tumult grew; an universal cough
  Convulsed the skies, as during a debate,
When Castlereagh has been up long enough
  (Before he was first minister of state,
I mean—the *slaves hear now*); some cried 'Off, off!'
  As at a farce; till, grown quite desperate,
The bard Saint Peter pray'd to interpose
(Himself an author) only for his prose.

XCIV

The varlet was not an ill-favour'd knave;
  A good deal like a vulture in the face,
With a hook nose and a hawk's eye, which gave
  A smart and sharper-looking sort of grace
To his whole aspect, which, though rather grave,
  Was by no means so ugly as his case;
But that, indeed, was hopeless as can be,
Quite a poetic felony '*de se.*'

XCV

Then Michael blew his trump, and still'd the noise
  With one still greater, as is yet the mode
On earth besides; except some grumbling voice,
  Which now and then will make a slight inroad
Upon decorous silence, few will twice
  Lift up their lungs when fairly overcrow'd;
And now the bard could plead his own bad cause,
With all the attitudes of self-applause.

XCVI

He said—(I only give the heads)—he said,
  He meant no harm in scribbling; 'twas his way
Upon all topics; 'twas, besides, his bread,
  Of which he butter'd both sides; 'twould delay
Too long the assembly (he was pleased to dread),
  And take up rather more time than a day,
To name his works—he would but cite a few—
'Wat Tyler'—'Rhymes on Blenheim'—'Waterloo.'

XCVII

He had written praises of a regicide;
  He had written praises of all kings whatever;

He had written for republics far and wide,
    And then against them bitterer than ever;
For pantisocracy he once had cried
    Aloud, a scheme less moral than 'twas clever;
Then grew a hearty anti-jacobin—
Had turn'd his coat—and would have turn'd his skin.

XCVIII

He had sung against all battles, and again
    In their high praise and glory; he had call'd
Reviewing 'the ungentle craft,' and then
    Become as base a critic as e'er crawl'd—
Fed, paid, and pamper'd by the very men
    By whom his muse and morals had been maul'd:
He had written much blank verse, and blanker prose,
And more of both than anybody knows.

XCIX

He had written Wesley's life:—here turning round
    To Satan, 'Sir, I'm ready to write yours,
In two octavo volumes, nicely bound,
    With notes and preface, all that most allures
The pious purchaser; and there's no ground
    For fear, for I can choose my own reviewers:
So let me have the proper documents,
That I may add you to my other saints.'

C

Satan bow'd, and was silent. 'Well, if you,
    With amiable modesty, decline
My offer, what says Michael? There are few
    Whose memoirs could be render'd more divine.
Mine is a pen of all work; not so new
    As it was once, but I would make you shine
Like your own trumpet. By the way, my own
Has more of brass in it, and is as well blown.

CI

'But talking about trumpets, here's my Vision!
    Now you shall judge, all people; yes, you shall
Judge with my judgment, and by my decision
    Be guided who shall enter heaven or fall.

I settle all these things by intuition,
   Times present, past, to come, heaven, hell, and all
Like King Alfonso. When I thus see double,
I save the Deity some worlds of trouble.'

CII

He ceased, and drew forth an MS.; and no
   Persuasion on the part of devils, saints,
Or angels, now could stop the torrent; so
   He read the first three lines of the contents;
But at the fourth, the whole spiritual show
   Had vanish'd, with variety of scents,
Ambrosial and sulphureous, as they sprang,
Like lightning, off from his 'melodious twang.'

CIII

Those grand heroics acted as a spell:
   The angels stopp'd their ears and plied their pinions;
The devils ran howling, deafen'd, down to hell;
   The ghosts fled, gibbering, for their own dominions—
(For 'tis not yet decided where they dwell,
   And I leave every man to his opinions);
Michael took refuge in his trump—but, lo!
His teeth were set on edge, he could not blow!

CIV

Saint Peter, who has hitherto been known
   For an impetuous saint, upraised his keys,
And at the fifth line knock'd the poet down;
   Who fell like Phaeton, but more at ease,
Into his lake, for there he did not drown;
   A different web being by the Destinies
Woven for the Laureate's final wreath, whene'er
Reform shall happen either here or there.

CV

He first sank to the bottom—like his works,
   But soon rose to the surface—like himself;
For all corrupted things are buoy'd like corks,
   By their own rottenness, light as an elf,
Or wisp that flits o'er a morass: he lurks,
   It may be, still, like dull books on a shelf,

In his own den, to scrawl some 'Life' or 'Vision,'
As Welborn says—'the devil turn'd precisian.'

CVI

As for the rest, to come to the conclusion
  Of this true dream, the telescope is gone
Which kept my optics free from all delusion,
  And show'd me what I in my turn have shown;
All I saw farther, in the last confusion,
  Was, that King George slipp'd into heaven for one;
And when the tumult dwindled to a calm,
I left him practising the hundredth psalm.

HISTORY OF THE PENINSULAR WAR

1823-32

The three volumes were published in 1823, 1827 and 1832.

---

97. From an unsigned review, *Literary Gazette*

14 December 1822, 783-4

From the opening of the review of the first volume. The review was continued in *Literary Gazette*, 21 December 1822, 802–4.

In last week describing a French picture styled a great work, we pointed out that it could only justly be so designated with reference to its immense size; and now, we find ourselves most agreeably called upon to reverse our mode of expression, and say, if this book be termed, in the common phrase, a heavy quarto, it can only justly be with reference to its bulk. For it is a noble History; and if the name of its author had not already stood so eminently high, this production alone would have engraved it on that splendid roll where the names of Gibbon, of Hume, and of Robertson, are inscribed in immortal characters.

We confess that we opened these pages with apprehensions of fatigue; we thought that at best the narrative must come upon us like a twice told tale, for the events seemed to be recent, and too important to admit of forgetfulness, and too well known to allow of any novelty in disposition and colouring. We were entirely mistaken. The deep interest of the story grew upon us from page to page, till our whole mind was engrossed; and we now as truly state our opinion, that Mr. Southey has begun the consummation and consolidation of his literary fame in this admirable Volume. Ours indeed is but a lowly voice of praise, but we persuade ourselves it will be felt by the author as a grateful offering, because he can well appreciate its honest sincerity; and it will probably be the first to hail him through a public organ on his masterly achievement.

We can hardly communicate to our readers an idea of the impression made by the devotion of a few hours to this History. Any extracts, by detaching the continued interest, must injure it. There are, no doubt, links of the chain more perfectly wrought than others; but it is the whole chain, unbroken, and binding the senses, which compels from us the strong acknowledgment of the writer's powers. The matters recorded are worthy of the ablest pen; the style is peculiar, and peculiarly vivid; sometimes highly elevated, always clear and forcible, and generally subdivided (as will appear from our selections) in a new manner, which relieves us from the rounding of long periods without being abrupt, but on the contrary giving full development to the author's meaning.

One prominent consideration attached to every historical work is that of its political bias. Upon this view we have (trying to have as little bias as possible ourselves) maturely weighed Mr. Southey's production. The result of our examination leads us to say that the evident leaning of his mind to what for want of a better understood appellation we must call Tory principles, does not in any material degree affect the impartiality and integrity of his Work. It is true that he speaks of Buonaparte, of his Generals on the Peninsula, and of the Revolution, in indignant terms, but his facts bear out his language; and when errors or crimes are committed by those towards whom greater leniency might be anticipated, we do not perceive that he spares to reprove or stigmatize them as they deserve.

98. From an unsigned review,
Monthly Censor

March 1823, ii, 278–92

From the opening of the review of the first volume.

Mr. Southey has at length given to the world the first portion of the work on which his most substantial pretensions to literary eminence will be honourably planted. It is impossible that an historical writer of our age should desire a more magnificent and invigorating occasion for the strenuous exercise of talent, and the unwearied devotion of labour, than has here, happily for his reputation, been assigned to his lot. And he is fortunate above all his contemporaries, that the direction of his studies, and the bent of his tastes, expressly prepared him for an undertaking, to which the original powers of his mind, and his literary ability and experience, would, of themselves, have rendered him fully adequate. In almost all the former productions of his pen, various and important and skilfully wrought as they were, it was manifest that the cultivation of Spanish history and literature was his darling passion; and equally observable, that whenever he drew from the stores with which these pursuits had enriched his mind, the attributes of his genius were displayed in their most imposing and captivating form. In poetry, he had unquestionably many superiors among his contemporaries, and there were not wanting those who denied to him altogether the 'mens divinior'[1] of the art; in the discussion of the ordinary political questions of the times, his warmest admirers were reduced to admit that he was too often carried away by the intensity and vehemence of his feelings, and always rather the zealous partizan than the impartial judge of the cause; but, in critical and historical literature, his excellence was universally acknowledged and warmly appreciated. A deeply read and an accomplished scholar, an enthusiastic lover of letters, and a writer of extraordinary fluency and elegance, there were

[1] 'Inspired soul'.

few subjects of general information which did not derive embellishment from his touch; but it was above all in illustrating the learning, the romantic poesy, the drama, and the authentic chronicles of the nations of the Spanish Peninsula, that he occupied the vantage ground of his strength. As a miscellaneous prose author he had few living equals; here he was confessedly unrivalled.

When, therefore, after the termination of the Peninsular War, Mr. Southey stood forth the promised historian of its glories, he was invited to the task no less by his inclination and leisure, than by the national confidence that he would produce a record commensurate, in brilliant and careful execution, with the transcendant splendour and magnitude of the subject. He had chosen for his theme the most memorable epoch in the annals of our modern wars; he was known to be deeply interested in the history and fate of the gallant and suffering people for whose liberation the conflict was supported; he was familiar with the scenes of the achievements by which it was distinguished; and no other author of the age could unite in his person so many qualifications for the particular design in which he embarked. Even they who differed from him in their public opinions, and would, under other circumstances, have doubted to commit to his judgment and candour the delineation of the political events of the age, could here feel little such hesitation. For, however the public mind may be divided upon other practical and speculative questions of politics, the voice of the world has been unanimous in stigmatizing the iniquitous project of Buonaparte, for the subjugation of the Peninsula, with every epithet of detestation and infamy.

99. From an unsigned review, *Eclectic Review*

July 1823, 2nd series, xx, 1–22

From the opening of the review of the first volume.

Dr. Southey is certainly happy in his choice of subjects. In his dramatic, epic, romantic, biographical, and historical compositions, we never find him taking up an insignificant name, an obscure theatre, or an uninteresting story. Nor has he, in the present instance, been unmindful of his former discretion. He has chosen a part of history, not only in the highest degree important, but for the illustration of which he is excellently furnished by local knowledge, ample materials, skill in the requisite languages, and indefatigable industry. With all these advantages on his side, we must nevertheless confess that he has somewhat disappointed us. There is altogether a want of effect about the narrative. We seldom find that dexterity in detecting the secret motives and springs of action, which is so indispensable a faculty in the historian. There is but little profound or vigorous political discussion. The characters concerned in the respective transactions, do not appear to us very happily discriminated; nor is the composition distinguished by vivacity. In one of the most important features of his undertaking, the distinct description of military movements and manœuvres, he has, in our apprehension, entirely failed. We entertain, however, sanguine expectations, that he will gain strength as he proceeds. The details of the Guerilla system will call forth his peculiar powers; and the heroic perseverance of the Spanish nation against the most fearful disparity of means and numbers, will rouse him into more vigorous narrative.

100. Wordsworth, from a letter to Southey

February–March 1827

This letter was written on receipt of the second volume of the *Peninsular War*. Reprinted from *The Letters of William and Dorothy Wordsworth, 1821–30*, ed. E. de Selincourt (1939), p. 264.

Edith thanked you, in my name, for your valuable present of the *Peninsular War*. I have read it with great delight: it is beautifully written, and a most interesting story. I did not notice a single sentiment or opinion that I could have wished away but one—where you support the notion that, if the Duke of Wellington had not lived and commanded, Buonaparte must have continued the master of Europe. I do not object to this from any dislike I have to the Duke, but from a conviction—I trust, a philosophic one—that Providence would not allow the upsetting of so diabolical a system as Buonaparte's to depend upon the existence of any individual. Justly was it observed by Lord Wellesley, that Buonaparte was of an order of minds that created for themselves great reverses. He might have gone further, and said that it is of the nature of tyranny to work to its own destruction.

The sentence of yours which occasioned these loose remarks is, as I said, the only one I objected to, while I met with a thousand things to admire. Your sympathy with the great cause is every where energetically and feelingly expressed. What fine fellows were Alvarez and Albuquerque; and how deeply interesting the siege of Gerona!

In 1821 Southey noted that 'while I have been employed upon the *Book of the Church*, [Wordsworth] has been writing a series of historical sonnets upon the same subjects, of the very highest species of excellence. My book will serve as a running commentary to his series, and the one will very materially help the other' (*Life*, v, p. 65). In 1822 he predicted that 'my *Book of the Church*, which I am writing *con amore* and with great diligence, will strike both the Catholics and the Puritans harder blows than they have been of late years accustomed to receive' (*Life*, v, p. 112). One Roman Catholic, Charles Butler, replied to Southey in *The Book of the Roman Catholic Church*. Southey decided to 'open a battery upon the walls of Babylon' (*Life*, v, p. 201). His answer, *Vindiciae Ecclesiae Anglicanae*, was published in 1825. Both Southey's works had disappointing sales.

101. From an unsigned review, *Universal Review*

March 1824, i, 81–91

From the opening of the review.

'There is a time for all things,' said Solomon; but we are satisfied, that he never contemplated a time for meagre motive and paltry performance—a time for a *Book of the Church*. If he did, he was not the Solomon we took him for.

This is a Laureate of all trades—war and divinity, navy and army, church and state, Waterloo and Wat Tyler, Wellington and Roderic the Goth, Admiral Nelson and the Abipones, John Wesley and Joan the Pucelle. Such are among the *omniana* that *Keswick* showers down with unmitigated ferocity on an unoffending world.

To 'watch for the wind that blows,' says an older writer than Mr. Southey, and to be ready for every wind, that is the thing which gives 'the sailor fair weather wherever he goes.' What spirit of a weathercock has transmigrated into our favourite bard, politician, royalist, republican, and reviewer, we may not tell. But no man alive knows the turns of the wind half so sensitively. Nelson dies—a midshipman's duodecimo! the quartos are anticipated. Portugal is at odds with Brazil—a *History of Brazil*, ready to go off with the first gun, two quartos! Wellington is in Spain—*Don Espriella*! The great Captain is reposing upon his laurels—the *Peninsular War*! The Laureateship is vacant—a Poem and a Dedication exquisitely *timed*, and fired point blank into the proper quarter! The Methodists are an ungleaned field— a *Life* of their apostle! Some old women have thought that the kibe of the Church has been trodden on—the *Book of the Church*, by way of embrocation. Thus all times and tastes are provided for with a commercial keenness equally dexterous, practised, and profitable.

102. From an unsigned review, *British Critic*

May 1824, 2nd series, xxi, 449–63

After an introductory statement of the need for such a work, the reviewer comments generally on Southey's success before describing the contents in detail.

The plan of the work is decidedly good; and the execution of it, with a few inconsiderable exceptions, is worthy of the biographer of Nelson. Desirous of stimulating curiosity, rather than satiating it, Mr. Southey avoids that prolix narrative, and lengthed detail, which are so delightful to the student of antiquity, and so insupportable to the general reader. The learning of Collier, the wit of Fuller, and the pathos of Fox, have not sufficed to fix the public attention upon their massy volumes. And it would be difficult to bring their works within a moderate compass, except by squeezing out the flesh and blood, and retaining no more than a lifeless skeleton. Mr. Southey therefore has laboured rather to catch the spirit, and pourtray the general air and semblance, than to give a minutely finished picture. He sketches manners, courts, and systems, with a bold and rapid pencil. He teaches us a valuable lesson—of which not the least valuable part is that there remains much more to learn. And if readers do not rise from the perusal of his book with a profound or professional knowledge of its subject, at least they will have obtained a distinct view of the Church, of its services, and its merits; and they will be enabled to prosecute their enquiries in any particular direction, with diminished trouble, and greater probability of success.

103. From an unsigned review, *Examiner*

17 October 1824, 660–1

Mr. Southey is certainly a man of letters. He has read much and written a great deal more. If singularity may confer distinction, he is entitled to no ordinary share of praise. With a versatility of talent which nothing can subdue, he has run through every stage of litera-ture, and reconciled apparent contradictions. Poetry, Politics, and Religion, have alternately hailed him as their champion; and with a felicity peculiar to himself, he has contrived to please all parties, while he adheres to none. He has flattered the Whigs, and followed the Tories—he has eulogized Wat Tyler, and canonized George the Third —he has commended the piety of the Methodists, and is now the staunch advocate of the Established Church. In this last character we must take leave to address him. His *Book of the Church* is assuredly a most singular production. In hardihood of assertion, dogmatical arrogance, and bold contempt of historical truth, it stands almost

without a rival. There is a tone of dignified assurance and lofty pretension which we cannot but admire. His sentences are so many oracles
delivered with all the solemnity of an inspired demigod. You are
presented with a sacred text-book without note or comment; and
when you call for proof, you are reminded of the 'good old John Fox,'
or referred to an article in the *Quarterly Review*. . . . Mr. Southey has
not forgotten the privilege of his profession. His pictures are all fancy-
scenes 'goodly to look to' and highly wrought, but without a prototype in nature, or a shadow of foundation in truth. Like those dramatic
daubs, which attract the eye by their gaudy colouring and distant
perspective, his canvass presents a series of broad artificial sketches
calculated solely for effect; and when held up to the light of day,
exhibit a motley group of incongruous images, distorted shapes, and
monstrous inconsistencies.—To be plain, Mr. Southey's work is a
tissue of misrepresentation and falsehood. It is somewhat singular that,
in an historical outline comprising a period of sixteen hundred years,
he should scarcely have been betrayed into one faithful and accurate
statement. From the story of Edwin and Elgiva, to the tragical tale of
Chancellor Gardiner's death, we trace the same spirit of unworthy
bias, disingenuous artifice, and pitiful perversion of truth. Fie! Mr.
Southey, this is too bad. With all the heroic sacrifice of personal
character which such a task must have required, there is still a portion
of respect due to the public; and your own good sense might have
pointed out the propriety of adhering to the semblance, while you
violated the substance, of truth. If the scheme of your work precluded
all reference to authority (and what a miserable subterfuge is this!) you
might at least have spared us the insult of quoting the tales of visionary
fanatics, or appealing to the legends of John Fox. If you must needs
chaunt the goodly martyrs of the Reformation, and revel in all the
barbarous horrors of bloody Mary, you ought in fairness to have
hinted at the counterpart in the reign of her virgin sister. The more
enlightened of your readers, who hate the subject most, know well
which scale will preponderate in the balance of accounts. But there
is a portion of the community whose diseased appetite can only feed
on the follies of their forefathers; and there are 'Ministering Spirits'
too, who deem it no disgrace to flatter the foul propensity and pander
to the worst passions of the mob.

I have viewed Mr. Southey's work as a narrative of events. Such,
I presume, it purports to be. Its real object is to vilify and degrade the
Church of Rome. . . .

But I have done.—How far *The Book of the Church* is calculated to promote one good or useful purpose, I willingly leave the public to determine. To Mr. Southey I would address two words, and conclude. I put the matter fairly to issue. I charge him, first, with having knowingly and designedly falsified many historical facts, and, secondly, with having deliberately slandered a numerous portion of his fellow-subjects. I say knowingly and deliberately, for ignorance is here out of the question.—These are heavy charges. Should Mr. Southey call for proofs, I pledge myself in the face of the public to substantiate the first charge; and if the objects of his calumny are silent in their own cause, to enforce and make good the second. Should he shrink from the contest and be silent, the conclusion is inevitable, and he will learn to be more circumspect in future. In tenderness to himself, let him retire to the haunts of fiction, and labour in the business of his calling. Beneath the shade of his variegated laurels he may repose in happy security, indite birth-day odes without number, and revel in all the loyal luxury of his butt of sherry. His leisure hours may be devoted to a Book of Retractions. Or, if that subject be repugnant to his feelings, he may write a Panegyric on Popery, which will rank by the side of *Espriella's Letters*, and complete his character as a man of all parties and a friend of none.

104. William Hazlitt, *The Spirit of the Age*

1824

Although dated 1825 the first edition of *The Spirit of the Age* appeared in 1824. The text is reprinted here from the annotated edition by E. D. Mackerness (1969). The tone of this essay is notably temperate when compared with Hazlitt's earlier tirades against Southey. Hazlitt's perceptive evaluation of Southey's prose style should be supplemented by his further comments in *The Plain Speaker* (No. 109).

Mr. Southey, as we formerly remember to have seen him, had a hectic flush upon his cheek, a roving fire in his eye, a falcon glance, a look at once aspiring and dejected—it was the look that had been impressed upon his face by the events that marked the outset of his life, it was the dawn of Liberty that still tinged his cheek, a smile betwixt hope and sadness that still played upon his quivering lip. Mr. Southey's mind is essentially sanguine, even to over-weeningness. It is prophetic of good; it cordially embraces it; it casts a longing, lingering look after it, even when it is gone for ever. He cannot bear to give up the thought of happiness, his confidence in his fellow-man, when all else despair. It is the very element, 'where he must live or have no life at all.' While he supposed it possible that a better form of society could be introduced than any that had hitherto existed, while the light of the French Revolution beamed into his soul (and long after, it was seen reflected on his brow, like the light of setting suns on the peak of some high mountain, or lonely range of clouds, floating in purer ether!) while he had this hope, this faith in man left, he cherished it with child-like simplicity, he clung to it with the fondness of a lover, he was an enthusiast, a fanatic, a leveller; he stuck at nothing that he thought would banish all pain and misery from the world—in his impatience of the smallest error or injustice, he would have sacrificed himself and the existing generation (a holocaust) to his devotion to the right cause. But when he once believed after many staggering doubts and painful struggles, that this was no longer possible, when his chimeras and golden dreams of human perfectibility vanished from him, he turned suddenly round, and maintained that 'whatever *is*, is right.' Mr. Southey has not fortitude of mind, has not patience to think that evil is inseparable from the nature of things. His irritable sense rejects the alternative altogether, as a weak stomach rejects the food that is distasteful to it. He hopes on against hope, he believes in all unbelief. He must either repose on actual or on imaginary good. He missed his way in *Utopia*, he has found it at Old Sarum—

His generous *ardour* no cold medium knows:[1]

his eagerness admits of no doubt or delay. He is ever in extremes, and ever in the wrong!

The reason is, that not truth, but self-opinion is the ruling principle of Mr. Southey's mind. The charm of novelty, the applause of the multitude, the sanction of power, the venerableness of antiquity, pique, resentment, the spirit of contradiction have a good deal to do with his preferences. His inquiries are partial and hasty: his conclusions raw and unconcocted, and with a considerable infusion of whim and humour and a monkish spleen. His opinions are like certain wines, warm and generous when new; but they will not keep, and soon turn flat or sour, for want of a stronger spirit of the understanding to give a body to them. He wooed Liberty as a youthful lover, but it was perhaps more as a mistress than a bride; and he has since wedded with an elderly and not very reputable lady, called Legitimacy. *A wilful man, according to the Scotch proverb, must have his way.* If it were the cause to which he was sincerely attached, he would adhere to it through good report and evil report; but it is himself to whom he does homage, and would have others do so; and he therefore changes sides, rather than submit to apparent defeat or temporary mortification. Abstract principle has no rule but the understood distinction between right and wrong; the indulgence of vanity, of caprice, or prejudice is regulated by the convenience or bias of the moment. The temperament of our politician's mind is poetical, not philosophical. He is more the creature of impulse, than he is of reflection. He invents the unreal, he embellishes the false with the glosses of fancy, but pays little attention to 'the words of truth and soberness.' His impressions are accidental, immediate, personal, instead of being permanent and

---

[1] Cf. Pope's translation of Homer's *Iliad*, ix, 725: 'A generous friendship no cold medium knows'. (Note by E. D. Mackerness to his edition of *The Spirit of the Age*.)

universal. Of all mortals he is surely the most impatient of contradiction, even when he has completely turned the tables on himself. Is not this very inconsistency the reason? Is he not tenacious of his opinions, in proportion as they are brittle and hastily formed? Is he not jealous of the grounds of his belief, because he fears they will not bear inspection, or is conscious he has shifted them? Does he not confine others to the strict line of orthodoxy, because he has himself taken every liberty? Is he not afraid to look to the right or the left, lest he should see the ghosts of his former extravagances staring him in the face? Does he not refuse to tolerate the smallest shade of difference in others, because he feels that he wants the utmost latitude of construction for differing so widely from himself? Is he not captious, dogmatical, petulant in delivering his sentiments, according as he has been inconsistent, rash, and fanciful in adopting them? He maintains that there can be no possible ground for differing from him, because he looks only at his own side of the question! He sets up his own favourite notions as the standard of reason and honesty, because he has changed from one extreme to another! He treats his opponents with contempt, because he is himself afraid of meeting with disrespect! He says that 'a Reformer is a worse character than a house-breaker,' in order to stifle the recollection that he himself once was one!

We must say that 'we relish Mr. Southey more in the Reformer' than in his lately acquired, but by no means natural or becoming character of poet-laureat and courtier. He may rest assured that a garland of wild flowers suits him better than the laureat-wreath: that his pastoral odes and popular inscriptions were far more adapted to his genius than his presentation-poems. He is nothing akin to birth-day suits and drawing-room fopperies. 'He is nothing, if not fantastical.' In his figure, in his movements, in his sentiments, he is sharp and angular, quaint and eccentric. Mr. Southey is not of the court, courtly. Every thing of him and about him is from the people. He is not classical, he is not legitimate. He is not a man cast in the mould of other men's opinions: he is not shaped on any model: he bows to no authority: he yields only to his own wayward peculiarities. He is wild, irregular, singular, extreme. He is no formalist, not he! All is crude and chaotic, self-opinionated, vain. He wants proportion, keeping, system, standard rules. He is not *teres et rotundus*.[1] Mr. Southey walks with his chin erect through the streets of London, and with an umbrella sticking out under his arm, in the finest weather. He has not sacrificed to the

---

1 'Polished and smooth'.

Graces, nor studied decorum. With him every thing is projecting, starting from its place, an episode, a digression, a poetic license. He does not move in any given orbit, but like a falling star, shoots from his sphere. He is pragmatical, restless, unfixed, full of experiments, beginning every thing a-new, wiser than his betters, judging for himself, dictating to others. He is decidedly *revolutionary*. He may have given up the reform of the State: but depend upon it, he has some other *hobby* of the same kind. Does he not dedicate to his present Majesty that extraordinary poem on the death of his father, called *A Vision of Judgement*, as a specimen of what might be done in English hexameters? In a court-poem all should be trite and on an approved model. He might as well have presented himself at the levee in a fancy or masquerade dress. Mr. Southey was not *to try conclusions* with Majesty—still less on such an occasion. The extreme freedoms with departed greatness, the party-petulance carried to the Throne of Grace, the unchecked indulgence of private humour, the assumption of infallibility and even of the voice of Heaven in this poem, are pointed instances of what we have said. They show the singular state of over-excitement of Mr. Southey's mind, and the force of old habits of independent and unbridled thinking, which cannot be kept down even in addressing his Sovereign! Look at Mr. Southey's larger poems, his *Kehama*, his *Thalaba*, his *Madoc*, his *Roderic*. Who will deny the spirit, the scope, the splendid imagery, the hurried and startling interest that pervades them? Who will say that they are not sustained on fictions wilder than his own Glendoveer, that they are not the daring creations of a mind curbed by no law, tamed by no fear, that they are not rather like the trances than the waking dreams of genius, that they are not the very paradoxes of poetry? All this is very well, very intelligible, and very harmless, if we regard the rank excrescences of Mr. Southey's poetry, like the red and blue flowers in corn, as the unweeded growth of a luxuriant and wandering fancy; or if we allow the yeasty workings of an ardent spirit to ferment and boil over—the variety, the boldness, the lively stimulus given to the mind may then atone for the violation of rules and the offences to bed-rid authority; but not if our poetic libertine sets up for a law-giver and judge, or an apprehender of vagrants in the regions either of taste or opinion. Our motley gentleman deserves the strait-waistcoat, if he is for setting others in the stocks of servility, or condemning them to the pillory for a new mode of rhyme or reason. Or if a composer of sacred Dramas on classic models, or a translator of an old Latin author (that will hardly bear translation)

or a vamper-up of vapid cantos and Odes set to music, were to turn
pander to prescription and palliater of every dull, incorrigible abuse,
it would not be much to be wondered at or even regretted. But in
Mr. Southey it was a lamentable falling-off. It is indeed to be deplored,
it is a stain on genius, a blow to humanity, that the author of *Joan of
Arc*—that work in which the love of Liberty is exhaled like the breath
of spring, mild, balmy, heaven-born, that is full of tears and virgin-
sighs, and yearnings of affection after truth and good, gushing warm
and crimsoned from the heart—should ever after turn to folly, or
become the advocate of a rotten cause. After giving up his heart to that
subject, he ought not (whatever others might do) ever to have set his
foot within the threshold of a court. He might be sure that he would
not gain forgiveness or favour by it, nor obtain a single cordial smile
from greatness. All that Mr. Southey is or that he does best, is independent, spontaneous, free as the vital air he draws—when he affects
the courtier or the sophist, he is obliged to put a constraint upon
himself, to hold in his breath, he loses his genius, and offers a violence
to his nature. His characteristic faults are the excess of a lively, unguarded temperament:—oh! let them not degenerate into cold-
blooded, heartless vices! If we speak or have ever spoken of Mr.
Southey with severity, it is with 'the malice of old friends,' for we
count ourselves among his sincerest and heartiest well-wishers. But
while he himself is anomalous, incalculable, eccentric, from youth to
age (the *Wat Tyler* and the *Vision of Judgement* are the Alpha and
Omega of his disjointed career) full of sallies of humour, of ebullitions
of spleen, making *jets-d'eaux*, cascades, fountains, and water-works of
his idle opinions, he would shut up the wits of others in leaden cisterns,
to stagnate and corrupt, or bury them under ground—

Far from the sun and summer gale![1]

He would suppress the freedom of wit and humour, of which he has
set the example, and claim a privilege for playing antics. He would
introduce an uniformity of intellectual weights and measures, of irregular metres and settled opinions, and enforce it with a high hand. This
has been judged hard by some, and has brought down a severity of
recrimination, perhaps disproportioned to the injury done. 'Because
he is virtuous,' (it has been asked,) 'are there to be no more cakes and
ale?' Because he is loyal, are we to take all our notions from the
Quarterly Review? Because he is orthodox, are we to do nothing but

[1] Not traced.

read the *Book of the Church*? We declare we think his former poetical scepticism was not only more amiable, but had more of the spirit of religion in it, implied a more heartfelt trust in nature and providence than his present bigotry. We are at the same time free to declare that we think his articles in the *Quarterly Review*, notwithstanding their virulence and the talent they display, have a tendency to qualify its most pernicious effects. They have redeeming traits in them. 'A little leaven leaveneth the whole lump'; and the spirit of humanity (thanks to Mr. Southey) is not quite expelled from the *Quarterly Review*. At the corner of his pen, 'there hangs a vapourous drop profound' of independence and liberality, which falls upon its pages, and oozes out through the pores of the public mind. There is a fortunate difference between writers whose hearts are naturally callous to truth, and whose understandings are hermetically sealed against all impressions but those of self-interest, and a man like Mr. Southey. *Once a philanthropist and always a philanthropist.* No man can entirely baulk his nature: it breaks out in spite of him. In all those questions, where the spirit of contradiction does not interfere, on which he is not sore from old bruises, or sick from the extravagance of youthful intoxication, as from a last night's debauch, our 'laureate' is still bold, free, candid, open to conviction, a reformist without knowing it. He does not advocate the slave-trade, he does not arm Mr. Malthus's revolting ratios with his authority, he does not strain hard to deluge Ireland with blood. On such points, where humanity has not become obnoxious, where liberty has not passed into a by-word, Mr. Southey is still liberal and humane. The elasticity of his spirit is unbroken: the bow recoils to its old position. He still stands convicted of his early passion for inquiry and improvement. He was not regularly articled as a Government-tool!— Perhaps the most pleasing and striking of all Mr. Southey's poems are not his triumphant taunts hurled against oppression, are not his glowing effusions to Liberty, but those in which, with a mild melancholy, he seems conscious of his own infirmities of temper, and to feel a wish to correct by thought and time the precocity and sharpness of his disposition. May the quaint but affecting aspiration expressed in one of these be fulfilled, that as he mellows into maturer age, all such asperities may wear off, and he himself become

Like the high leaves upon the holly-tree![1]

Mr. Southey's prose-style can scarcely be too much praised. It is

[1] Southey, 'The Holly Tree'.

plain, clear, pointed, familiar, perfectly modern in its texture, but with a grave and sparkling admixture of *archaisms* in its ornaments and occasional phraseology. He is the best and most natural prose-writer of any poet of the day; we mean that he is far better than Lord Byron, Mr. Wordsworth, or Mr. Coleridge, for instance. The manner is perhaps superior to the matter, that is, in his Essays and Reviews. There is rather a want of originality and even of *impetus*: but there is no want of playful or biting satire, of ingenuity, of casuistry, of learning and of information. He is 'full of wise saws and modern' (as well as ancient) 'instances.' Mr. Southey may not always convince his opponents; but he seldom fails to stagger, never to gall them. In a word, we may describe his style by saying that it has not the body or thickness of port wine, but is like clear sherry with kernels of old authors thrown into it!—He also excels as an historian and prose-translator. His histories abound in information, and exhibit proofs of the most indefatigable patience and industry. By no uncommon process of the mind, Mr. Southey seems willing to steady the extreme levity of his opinions and feelings by an appeal to facts. His translations of the Spanish and French romances are also executed *con amore*, and with the literal fidelity and care of a mere linguist. That of the *Cid*, in particular, is a masterpiece. Not a word could be altered for the better, in the old scriptural style which it adopts in conformity to the original. It is no less interesting in itself, or as a record of high and chivalrous feelings and manners, than it is worthy of perusal as a literary curiosity.

Mr. Southey's conversation has a little resemblance to a commonplace book; his habitual deportment to a piece of clock-work. He is not remarkable either as a reasoner or an observer: but he is quick, unaffected, replete with anecdote, various and retentive in his reading, and exceedingly happy in his play upon words, as most scholars are who give their minds this sportive turn. We have chiefly seen Mr. Southey in company where few people appear to advantage, we mean in that of Mr. Coleridge. He has not certainly the same range of speculation, nor the same flow of sounding words, but he makes up by the details of knowledge, and by a scrupulous correctness of statement for what he wants in originality of thought, or impetuous declamation. The tones of Mr. Coleridge's voice are eloquence: those of Mr. Southey are meagre, shrill, and dry. Mr. Coleridge's *forte* is conversation, and he is conscious of this: Mr. Southey evidently considers writing as his stronghold, and if gravelled in an argument, or at a loss for an explanation, refers to something he has written on the subject, or brings out his port-folio, doubled down in dog-ears, in confirmation of some fact. He is scholastic and professional in his ideas. He sets more value on what he writes than on what he says: he is perhaps prouder of his library than of his own productions—themselves a library! He is more simple in his manners than his friend Mr. Coleridge; but at the same time less cordial or conciliating. He is less vain, or has less hope of pleasing, and therefore lays himself less out to please. There is an air of condescension in his civility. With a tall, loose figure, a peaked austerity of countenance, and no inclination to *embonpoint*, you would say he has something puritanical, something ascetic in his appearance. He answers to Mandeville's description of Addison, 'a parson in a tye-wig.' He is not a boon companion, nor does he indulge in the pleasures of the table, nor in any other vice; nor are we aware that Mr. Southey is chargeable with any human frailty but— *want of charity*! Having fewer errors to plead guilty to, he is less lenient to those of others. He was born an age too late. Had he lived a century or two ago, he would have been a happy as well as blameless character. But the distraction of the time has unsettled him, and the multiplicity of his pretensions have jostled with each other. No man in our day (at least no man of genius) has led so uniformly and entirely the life of a scholar from boyhood to the present hour, devoting himself to learning with the enthusiasm of an early love, with the severity and constancy of a religious vow—and well would it have been for him if he had confined himself to this, and not undertaken to pull down or to patch up the State! However irregular in his opinions, Mr. Southey is constant, unremitting, mechanical in his studies, and the performance of his duties. There is nothing Pindaric or Shandean here. In all the relations and charities of private life, he is correct, exemplary, generous, just. We never heard a single impropriety laid to his charge; and if he has many enemies, few men can boast more numerous or stauncher friends.—The variety and piquancy of his writings form a striking contrast to the mode in which they are produced. He rises early, and writes or reads till breakfast-time. He writes or reads after breakfast till dinner, after dinner till tea, and from tea till bed-time—

> And follows so the ever-running year
> With profitable labour to his grave—[1]

on Derwent's banks, beneath the foot of Skiddaw. Study serves him for business, exercise, recreation. He passes from verse to prose, from

[1] Shakespeare, *Henry V.*

history to poetry, from reading to writing, by a stop-watch. He writes a fair hand, without blots, sitting upright in his chair, leaves off when he comes to the bottom of the page, and changes the subject for another, as opposite as the Antipodes. His mind is after all rather the recipient and transmitter of knowledge, than the originator of it. He has hardly grasp of thought enough to arrive at any great leading truth. His passions do not amount to more than irritability. With some gall in his pen, and coldness in his manner, he has a great deal of kindness in his heart. Rash in his opinions, he is steady in his attachments—and is a man, in many particulars admirable, in all respectable —his political inconsistency alone excepted!

A TALE OF PARAGUAY

1825

The last of Southey's longer poems had a disappointingly small sale. At the end of the first twelve months following publication Southey reported that his profits fell short of £80 (*Life*, v, p. 296).

105. From an unsigned review, *Blackwood's Edinburgh Magazine*

September 1825, xviii, 370–7

From the opening of the review.

We fear that Mr Southey has greatly over-rated the merits of this poem, and that it is unworthy of his high genius and reputation. He takes his motto from Wordsworth—[1]

> Go forth, my little book,
> Go forth, and please the gentle and the good.

Now, perhaps Mr Southey will not acknowledge those readers to be among 'the gentle and the good,' who are not pleased with his little book. For our own parts we have been pleased—considerably pleased with it—but our admiration of Mr Southey's powers cannot blind us to that which the whole world, himself excepted, will speedily pronounce to be a somewhat melancholy truth—namely, that the *Tale of Paraguay* is, with many paltry, and a few fine passages, an exceedingly poor poem, feeble alike in design and execution.

[1] Wordsworth, *Memorials of a Tour on the Continent*, xxxviii.

106. From an unsigned review, *Eclectic Review*

1825, xlii, 328–37

Extracts from the opening and conclusion of the review.

In our review of Mr. Campbell's *Theodric*, we ventured to remark, that the Author could no more write a long poem, than Southey can a short one, who, of all our living poets, is the least lyrical and the best story-teller. The present volume will, we imagine, be admitted as ample confirmation of our critical sentence. To contrast it with *Theodric*, would indeed be as unfair and invidious as to bring the *Vision of Judgement* or the *Carmen Triumphale* into comparison with any one of the thrilling lyrics of the Poet of Hope and Freedom. But with *Gertrude of Wyoming*, we may fairly compare the *Tale of Paraguay*, in which Dr. Southey, 'ceasing from desultory flight,' and renouncing the lawless freedom of versification in which he has so long expatiated, has clothed his verse with the golden shackles and sweet constraint of the Spenserian stanza. The scene too, as in the rival poem, is transatlantic, the personages Indians. Thus, whether designedly or not, we have the two poets fairly placed in comparison; and the general result, may, we think, be summed up in a few words. No single stanza in the poem before us can be compared with some in the *Gertrude*; but the interest that the story excites, is far more intense, the scene presents itself to the imagination in much more vivid colours, and the impression which it makes as a whole, though less pleasing, is more powerful. There is a certain breadth and freedom in Southey's style, an apparent facility, and a complete mastery of his subject, which give a peculiar charm to his narrative poems. Notwithstanding the slow, measured march of the stanza he has adopted, there is a rapidity of movement in his verse, by which we are constantly borne along, and the interest is seldom suffered to languish. On the other hand, the melody of Campbell's less flowing and copious verse atones for its occasional restraint and inequalities, its rapids and its shallows, —like a wild rivulet, exquisite in parts, but not navigable. *Theodric*, if we may be allowed to pursue the comparison, was an attempt to turn this wild stream into a canal, for which it was never designed, and it became despoiled of all its native character. But, in his lyrical pieces, we seem to see it near its source, where, pure, deep, and strong, it foams and sparkles along its narrow channel, all life, and spirit, and beauty.

Our object in drawing this comparison, it will be seen, is to do justice to both. We have in some circles heard the admirers of Campbell speak in terms of ignorant depreciation, of Southey and the Lakers; to whom, however, as the disciples of Cowper, literature is chiefly indebted for the completion of the reform, begun by the Author of *The Task*, in the character of our national poetry, and its emancipation from the French school of Pope and his imitators. On the other hand, we have known the votaries of the Poet-laureate speak most haughtily and contemptuously, and a little bitterly of Campbell, —(as perhaps the admirers of Thomson might, in his day, have spoken of Collins,) measuring his merit by the quantity of his productions, and mistaking short poems for little ones. The transcendent beauty of Campbell's odes, such persons have not ventured to deny; but these, it has been said, are 'few and far between.' Can he shew his ten octavo volumes of poetry like Scott, or his fourteen foolscaps like the Author of *Madoc*? Such comparisons as these, it must be admitted, shew neither good sense, nor taste, nor candour. The quality of lyric poetry of the higher order, is such as forbids its being produced with the facility with which canto after canto and volume after volume may be furnished by a writer endowed with a talent for narrative and descriptive poetry. The grass is always growing; the violet has its season: how ridiculous would be a comparison between them! Handel is reported to have said, that he would forego the credit of any whole oratorio that he had composed, to have been the author of a certain simple, but matchless air. Southey might, with less sacrifice, make a similar declaration with regard to one of his five epics, set against *Hohenlinden* or the *Soldier's Dream*. But we all love our own; and such transfers, even were they practicable, would be inadmissible. Posterity, careless of the disputes between contemporary authors about precedence, will cherish alike the fame of both Southey and Campbell, as each in his peculiar walk unrivalled. As to the political animosities which sometimes give edge and bitterness to poetical rivalries, prompting the angry names of servile and liberal, radical and renegade, we wish they were for ever banished from the peaceful regions of literature. We however, who are well known, though we say it of ourselves, to be as loyal as we are liberal, and as orthodox as we are tolerant, have honestly endeavoured to give to each claimant of poetical honours his due, without any reference to his creed or his party. But now to business.

[Summarizes plot with lengthy quotations.]

Why, why has the Author ever deserted his proper path? It is on works like this, which the public will not willingly let die, that his fame must stand, when his politics and his polemics shall be forgiven and forgotten. Born to delight as the poet, and to interest as the friend, exemplary in all the charities of life, in an evil hour he assumed the livery of party and the cap and bells of the laureate, which, if we might, we would thus tear from him, and crown him with the never-dying bay.

107. William Benbow, *A Scourge for the Laureate*

1825(?)

From *A Scourge for the Laureate, in reply to his infamous letter of the 13th of December, 1824, meanly abusive of the deceased Lord Byron.*

Benbow was a London publisher noted for his radical activities. His tract attacks Southey for his letter to the *Courier* which was hostile to Byron. This extract indicates the tone of the attack.

The charge the Doctor makes against me of sending forth *Obscenity*, I presume, alludes to my publishing *Don Juan*. I am no print, caricature, or novel publisher, so he can hint at nothing else. God help us! there is more obscenity in his *Curse of Kehama* and *Thalaba* than in all the *Don Juans* ever written or acted on the stage. Is it not *obscenity*, *Doctor Southey*, to describe a man intriguing with his *own Sister*, and then place him as a punishment to live for eternity on a burning candlestick, in a place worse than Hell? the very description of which is so horribly obscene, that I would not let it into the hands of my children, for treble the pension the hireling writer now enjoys.

And now for the charge of vending *Sedition*. To that I plead Guilty, —for I published *WAT TYLER, a Poem, by Doctor SOUTHEY*. This is 'the head and front of my offending.' I *published* the Sedition which His Majesty's Poet Laureate *wrote*; but my motives were different from the writer's—mine were to do *good*; his to accomplish *evil*. He first sent that work into the world when all England was agitated by the fever of Revolution, it was well calculated to add fuel to fire, and bring forth the blaze of anarchy and rebellion. No one doubted the intentions for which it was written, and if the bolt fell harmless, it was not from want of strength in the arm that hurled it, but the honest virtue which parried the blow, and made it, twenty years after, fall on his head who aimed it. Yes, after *Wat Tyler* had slumbered twenty years, I was one of the first that roused him to bring disgrace on the author of his being. Look into *Wat Tyler*, and then into the *Vision of Judgement*,—mark the vile apostate's principles at the poor and miserable part of his existence, and at the rich and court-fed period, when he stands covered with forced laurels from a political hot-house—and then say, where got Doctor Southey the effrontery to charge Lord Byron with *want of principle and not acting up to the high honor of his family name.*

108. Thomas Love Peacock, 'Fly-by-Night'

1825-6

One of Peacock's *Paper Money Lyrics*, written during the financial crisis of 1825/6 but not published until 1837. This poem made an earlier appearance in the *Guide*, a threepenny weekly by Henry Cole, 21 May 1837. The subjects of *Paper Money Lyrics* are the evils of paper currency and the growth and collapse of country banks founded on insufficient capital. In style and diction the *Lyrics* loosely parody a variety of contemporary poets. Reference to Southey is immediately established in this poem by the repetition of 'How troublesome is day', recalling the opening of *Thalaba*: 'How beautiful is night.' For Peacock's attitude to Southey see No. 85.

PROŒMIUM OF AN EPIC

WHICH WILL SHORTLY APPEAR IN QUARTO, UNDER THE TITLE OF

FLY-BY-NIGHT,

By R— S—, Esq., Poet Laureate.

His promises were, as he once was, mighty;
And his performance, as he is now, nothing.
Hen. VIII.

How troublesome is day!
It calls us from our sleep away;
It bids us from our pleasant dreams awake,
And sends us forth to keep or break
Our promises to pay.
How troublesome is day!

Now listen to my lay;
Much have I said,
Which few have heard or read,

328

And much have I to say,
Which hear ye while ye may.
Come listen to my lay,
  Come, for ye know me, as a man
  Who always praises, as he can,
All promisers to pay.

So they and I on terms agree,
And they but keep their faith with me,
Whate'er their deeds to others be,
They may to the minutest particle
Command my fingers for an ode or article.

Come listen while I strike the Epic string,
And, as a changeful song I sing,
  Before my eyes
  Bid changeful Proteus rise,
Turning his coat and skin in countless forms and dyes.

Come listen to my lay,
While I the wild and wondrous tale array,
How Fly-by-Night went down,
And set a bank up in a country town;
How like a king his head he reared;
And how the Coast of Cash he cleared;
And how one night he disappeared,
When many a scoffer jibed and jeered;
And many an old man rent his beard;
And many a young man cursed and railed;
And many a woman wept and wailed;
And many a mighty heart was quailed;
And many a wretch was caged and gaoled:
Because great Fly-by-Night had failed.
And many a miserable sinner
Went without his Sunday dinner,
Because he had not metal bright,
And waved in vain before the butcher's sight,
The promises of Fly-by-Night.

And little Jackey Horner
Sate sulking in the corner,
And in default of Christmas pie

Whereon his little thumb to try,
He put his finger in his eye,
And blubbered long and lustily.

Come listen to my lay,
And ye shall say,
That never tale of errant knight,
Or captive damsel bright,
Demon, or elf, or goblin sprite,
Fierce crusade, or feudal fight,
Or cloistral phantom all in white,
Or castle on accessless height,
Upreared by necromantic might,
Was half so full of rare delight,
As this whereof I now prolong,
The memory in immortal song—
The wild and wondrous tale of Fly-by-Night.

109. William Hazlitt on Southey's prose style

1826

In *The Spirit of the Age* (see No. 104) Hazlitt declared: 'Mr. Southey's prose-style can scarcely be too much praised.' This favourable estimate is confirmed and supplemented in the following paragraph on Southey from the essay 'On the Prose Style of Poets' in *The Plain Speaker* (1826).

I think the poet-laureat is a much better prose-writer [than Coleridge]. His style has an antique quaintness, with a modern familiarity. He has just a sufficient sprinkling of *archaisms*, of allusions to old Fuller, and Burton, and Latimer, to set off or qualify the smart flippant tone of his apologies for existing abuses, or the ready, galling virulence of his personal invectives. Mr. Southey is a faithful historian, and no in-efficient partisan. In the former character, his mind is tenacious of facts; and in the latter, his spleen and jealousy prevent the 'extravagant and erring spirit' of the poet from losing itself in Fancy's endless maze. He 'stoops to *earth*,' at least, and prostitutes his pen to some purpose (not at the same time losing his own soul, and gaining nothing by it) —and he vilifies Reform, and praises the reign of George III. in good set terms, in a straightforward, intelligible, practical, pointed way. He is not buoyed up by conscious power out of the reach of common apprehensions, but makes the most of the obvious advantages he possesses. You may complain of a pettiness and petulance of manner, but certainly there is no want of spirit or facility of execution. He does not waste powder and shot in the air, but loads his piece, takes a level aim, and hits his mark. One would say (though his Muse is ambidexter) that he wrote prose with his right hand; there is nothing awkward, circuitous, or feeble in it. 'The words of Mercury are harsh after the songs of Apollo:' but this would not apply to him. His prose-lucubrations are pleasanter reading than his poetry. Indeed, he is equally practised and voluminous in both; and it is no improbable conjecture,

331

that Mr. Southey may have had some idea of rivalling the reputation of Voltaire in the extent, the spirit, and the versatility of his productions in prose and verse, except that he has written no tragedies but *Wat Tyler*!

110. John Henry Newman on Southey's epics

1829

From 'Poetry, with reference to Aristotle's *Poetics*', published in the first number of the *London Review*, 1829, and reprinted in *Essays Critical and Historical* (2 vols, 1871).

It is scarcely possible for a poet satisfactorily to connect innocence with ultimate unhappiness, when the notion of a future life is excluded. Honours paid to the memory of the dead are some alleviation of the harshness. In his use of the doctrine of a future life, Southey is admirable. Other writers are content to conduct their heroes to temporal happiness;—Southey refuses present comfort to his Ladurlad, Thalaba, and Roderick, but carries them on through suffering to another world. The death of his hero is the termination of the action; yet so little in two of them, at least, does this catastrophe excite sorrowful feelings, that some readers may be startled to be reminded of the fact. If a melancholy is thrown over the conclusion of the *Roderick*, it is from the peculiarities of the hero's previous history.

SIR THOMAS MORE, OR, COLLOQUIES ON THE PROGRESS AND PROSPECTS OF SOCIETY

1829

Colloquies was written during a period of about twelve years. Southey's own estimate was expressed in a letter to Grosvenor Bedford immediately on its publication: 'Unless I greatly deceive myself it is a work which will be deemed worthy of preservation' (Curry, ii, p. 334). He predicted to his brother Thomas that the book was 'very far too good to have much sale. Murray says that if religion and politics had been excluded, it would have sold ten times as much. To be sure these are matters of little importance in the Progress and Prospects of Society!! But such are booksellers—and what is worse—such is the Public!' (Curry, ii, p. 340).

Despite the brilliance of Macaulay's attack (No. 113) *Colloquies* has attracted considerable serious and sympathetic attention from modern readers (see Introduction, p. 29).

111. Wordsworth, from a letter to George Huntly Gordon

14 May 1829

Reprinted from *The Letters of William and Dorothy Wordsworth, 1821–30*, ed. E. de Selincourt (1939), p. 380.

Mr Southey means to present me (as usual) his *Colloquies*, etc. There is, perhaps, not a page of them that he did not read me in MS.; and several of the Dialogues are upon subjects which we have often discussed. I am greatly interested with much of the book, but upon its effect as a whole I can yet form no opinion as it was read to me as it happened to be written. I need scarcely say that Mr Southey ranks very highly, in my opinion, as a prose writer. His style is eminently clear, lively, and unencumbered, and his information unbounded; and there is a moral ardour about his compositions which nobly distinguishes them from the trading and factious authorship of the present day.

112. From an unsigned review,
Monthly Review

1829, n.s. cxix, 382–95

The public are already persuaded that Dr. Southey's pen is too quick
for his thoughts. He goes on year after year, labouring at the production
of new books, apparently without caring much about the fate of his
past works, or perhaps trusting with overweening confidence to their
superlative merit for their final triumph over criticism and time. By
thus incessantly wielding the weapon of language, sometimes in sport,
but oftener in obstinate conflict, he has acquired a skill and readiness
in the management of it, which frequently conceal his constitutional
deficiency of vigour. With one or two exceptions, no living writer
is so thoroughly possessed with confidence in his own powers, or in the
patience of mankind. He conceives every possible topic to be accessible
to his genius, and has no doubt whatever but that men will stop the
wheel of public business, or of pleasure, to listen to the music of his
periods, which are not, however, the most musical that could be
constructed.

The subject at least of the present work must be allowed to be
important. It is no less a theme than the history and destiny of mankind. The idea, also, of throwing the discussion into the form of
dialogue was felicitous, as this form of composition enables an author
to bring forward, without becoming tiresome, all that has been, or, in
his opinion, can be advanced against his hypothesis; and at the same
time, if he be at all inclined to play the sophist, so to state the objections
that they shall either appear absurd in themselves, or weak in comparison with his replies. But Dr. Southey has merely adopted the
appearance of dialogue. The interlocutors, viz. himself, and the Ghost
of Sir Thomas More, fall almost immediately into the same strain;
and rather relieve each other as they happen alternately to be out of
breath, (if this may be said of a ghost), than conduct a polemical
discussion. It may perhaps be thought that it was scarcely worth while
to bring back from the dead the spirit of one of the wisest men that
England has ever produced, merely to make him a kind of stalking-

horse, behind which the author might stand to shoot his arrows at the peculiar game which he delights to pursue. These dialogues, therefore, are not dialogues, but monologues, and monologues, too, of a very heavy and wearisome nature. No doubt Southey was betrayed into this species of writing, for which he is utterly unfit, by his friend Landor, who, in his turn, was led to adopt it by the examples of Plato and Cicero. But Mr. Landor's '*Imaginary*' *Conversations*, as they are very properly termed, want altogether that verisimilitude which constitutes one of the greatest charms of Plato's *Dialogues*. We are sure that the author had no means, which we have not, of knowing what *Aristotle*, and Callisthenes, or Cicero and his brother Quintus, thought or said upon any particular occasion; and therefore, while we admire the historical truth, or the dramatic propriety, with which his characters are sometimes represented, we at the same time feel that the vision before us is the mere creation of the writer's brain. Not so in Plato's *Dialogues*. There the characters are real, and the conversations not only possible but probable. Socrates did not complain that Plato had put him into positions in which he never stood, or made him take part in conversations at which he was not present. He merely remarked that the *young man* attributed to him *more* than he had said. In Dr. Southey's *Dialogues*, since we must call them so, the Ghost does not preserve the slightest identity with the man called Sir Thomas More. On the contrary, it utters opinions and sentiments which that great man, when living, spurned and detested; and therefore, instead of appearing to us as he ought, in the light of a great man's beatified spirit, he is only a duplicate of the author himself.

Upon the propriety or wisdom of interrogating the dead, respecting the prospects of the living, our opinions are probably not very different from those of Dr. Southey. The human race are like plants, which, though they may be ameliorated or rendered worse, by being planted in a favourable or an untoward soil, are yet always essentially the same, and must be benefited or injured by the same circumstances. By choosing a ghost, however, for his companion, when he wished to wrestle with profound and difficult questions, the Doctor seems to insinuate, that he is acquainted with no living man worthy to sift his cogitations, and perhaps he may never be convinced of the contrary. But unless we are much deceived, the public will find that, previous to the revelations from Keswick, men were not wholly in the dark respecting the nature and destiny of society; and that, even had Sir Thomas More been permitted to slumber undisturbed in his shroud, the conviction that irreligion, and famine, and pestilence, are fearful evils, to which society, in all its stages, is liable, would have been no less strong than it will be, when these *dialogues* shall have been perused by *all the world.*

If the reader supposes that, by what we have said above, we desire it should be inferred, that the work before us is a feeble or contemptible production, he will have deceived himself. It has great and obvious faults, among which, a spirit of intolerance is not the least; but it has also, in spite of these drawbacks to the author's powers, great merits, and considerable beauties to recommend it. The writer, himself, is a phenomenon, peculiarly worthy of contemplation. Owing to certain circumstances, he appears to be subject to the sway of two species of influences, which alternately, urge him towards moderation, benevolence, and charity, and towards the reverse of these. We believe, however, that the former are the original gift of nature, the latter the fruit of circumstances.

To convey to the reader a proper idea of the nature and character of the work, it should be observed, that it commences with an account of the state of the author's mind, at the time when he describes himself as entering seriously and systematically upon the contemplation of the progress and prospects of society. It is important, that in all momentous concerns the initiative movement should be discovered, and, if possible, all the circumstances in which it originated, or by which its first operations were accompanied. It is, therefore, with much satisfaction, that we learn that it was in the November of the year in which the Princess Charlotte died, when the whole kingdom was stricken with grief, that Dr. Southey had his first interview with the ghost. The particulars are related with the utmost solemnity and minuteness. Step by step we are carried on from the simple and common-place occurrences of life, to the startling, preternatural colloquy which forthwith takes place, and is carried on, if not with the brevity and conciseness of the interrogations and responses of oracles, at least, with a considerable portion of the obscurity and magisterial dignity with which the Gods conveyed their decisions to mortals. . . .

The changes which have taken place in Dr. Southey's opinions, are matters of public notoriety, and have been spoken of with bitterness or indulgence, according as the speakers were actuated by their particular and private sentiments. For our own part, we do not so much blame him for his mutability (as we are all mutable creatures), as for his uncharitableness towards those who profess the opinions he once thought well-founded, and in the profession of which we doubt not he was, as Mr. Coleridge says of himself, 'most sincere, most disinterested.' Cannot he imagine, that the same sincerity, the same disinterestedness may actuate those who still worship before the altars which he has deserted! His reasons for deserting them are more than once hinted at in the volumes before us, and, among other examples, in the following passage. Striving to place his own conduct in the same light with that of Sir Thomas More, who is supposed to have lost much of his liberal enthusiasm towards the end of his life, he makes the Ghost observe:

We have both speculated in the joy and freedom of our youth upon the possible improvement of society; and both in like manner have lived to dread with reason the effects of that restless spirit, which, like the Titaness Mutability described by your immortal Master, insults Heaven and disturbs the earth.

And again, alluding to the same subject, he says,—

Montesinos.—If it be your aim to prove that the savage state is preferable to the social, I am perhaps the very last person upon whom any arguments to that end could produce the slightest effect. The notion never for a moment deluded me: not even in the ignorance and presumptuousness of youth, when first I perused Rousseau, and was unwilling to believe that a writer whose passionate eloquence I felt and admired so truly, could be erroneous in any of his opinions. But now, in the evening of life, when I know upon what foundation my principles rest, and when the direction of one peculiar course of study has made it necessary for me to learn every thing which books could teach concerning savage life, the proposition appears to me one of the most untenable that ever was advanced by a perverse or a paradoxical intellect.

The logic by which the author endeavours to establish the persuasion that his interview with Sir Thomas More was not a dream, is a striking example of his system of reasoning.

It was no dream, of this I was well assured: realities are never mistaken for dreams, though dreams may be mistaken for realities; and therefore this being a dream, might be mistaken for reality. Moreover I had long been accustomed in sleep to question my perceptions with a wakeful faculty of reason, and to detect their fallacy. But, as well may be supposed, my thoughts that night sleeping as well as waking, were filled with this extraordinary interview; and when I arose the next morning, it was not till I had called to mind every circumstance of time and place, that I was convinced the apparition was real, and that I might again expect it.

From all which an ordinary reasoner would infer, that this interview, being a dream, had been mistaken for a reality. The Doctor proceeds in another way. He informs us that he was *well assured* it was not a dream, *because realities* are never mistaken for dreams: that is, he first assumes that it was a reality, and then argues most cogently, that, this being the case, it could not possibly be a dream. To make the matter still more clear, and to convince us invincibly that it could not have been a dream mistaken for a reality, he adds *that dreams are sometimes mistaken for realities*: that is, that what we suspect to have taken place in this instance, does sometimes take place. A peculiar and extraordinary mode of arguing!

Dr. Southey would not, we imagine, be very ready to acknowledge that he had borrowed any portion of his philosophical creed from the Buddhists; but let the Oriental reader compare the opinions contained in the following singular passage, with the doctrines upon the destruction and renovation of the world, which are held by the followers of Gautama, and he will be convinced that they are derived, not from the Bible, but from the cosmogony of the Singalese and Burmans.

Montesinos.—When I have followed such speculations as may allowably be indulged, respecting what is hidden in the darkness of time and of eternity, I have sometimes thought that the moral and physical order of the world may be so appointed as to coincide; and that the revolutions of this planet may correspond with the condition of its inhabitants; so that the convulsions and changes whereto it is destined should occur, when the existing race of men had either become so corrupt, as to be unworthy of the place which they hold in the universe, or were so truly regenerate by the will and word of God, as to be qualified for a higher station in it. Our globe may have gone through many such revolutions. We know the history of the last; the measure of its wickedness was then filled up. For the future we are taught to expect a happier consummation.

One of the principal charms of Dr. Southey's writings arises from the evidence they every where present of the vast reading and research of the writer. We are always sure that if he should be wrong, it is not from ignorance or want of reflection. He has ever at hand apt quotations to illustrate his meaning or enforce his arguments; and we every where discover traces of his acquaintance with the great authors of ancient and modern times, but more particularly with travellers. Occasionally this exuberance of reading, or, at least, the displaying it, is injurious to him. He loads his pages with references to other writers, and the quotations detached from the work they are meant to illustrate, would frequently form a volume themselves. . . .

There is a truth and delicacy of touch in the following picture of a

November day, which remind us strongly of the Dutch painters, in their most happy productions.

It is no wonder that foreigners, who form their notions of England from what they see in its metropolis, should give such dismal descriptions of an English November; a month when, according to the received opinion of continental writers, suicide comes as regularly in season with us as geese at Michaelmas, and green pease in June. Nothing indeed can be more cheerless and comfortless than a common November day in that huge overgrown city; the streets covered with that sort of thick greasy dirt, on which you are in danger of slipping at every step, and the sky concealed from sight by a dense, damp, oppressive, dusky atmosphere, composed of Essex fog and London smoke. But in the country November presents a very different aspect: there its soft, calm weather has a charm of its own; a stillness and serenity unlike any other season, and scarcely less delightful than the most genial days of Spring. The pleasure which it imparts is rather different in kind than inferior in degree: it accords as finely with the feelings of declining life as the bursting foliage and opening flowers of May with the elastic spirits of youth and hope.

But a fine day affects children alike at all seasons as it does the barometer. They live in the present, seldom saddened with any retrospective thoughts, and troubled with no foresight. Three or four days of dull sunless weather had been succeeded by a delicious morning. My young ones were clamorous for a morning's excursion. The glass had risen to a little above change, but their spirits had mounted to the point of settled fair. All things, indeed, animate and inanimate, seemed to partake of the exhilirating influence. The blackbirds, who lose so little of their shyness even where they are most secure, made their appearance on the green, where the worms had thrown up little circles of mould during the night. The smaller birds were twittering, hopping from spray to spray, and pluming themselves; and as the temperature had given them a vernal sense of joy, there was something of a vernal cheerfulness in their song. The very flies had come out from their winter quarters where, to their own danger and my annoyance, they establish themselves behind the books, in the folds of the curtains, and the crevices of these loose window-frames. They were crawling up the sunny panes, bearing in their altered appearance the marks of uncomfortable age; their bodies enlarged, and of a greyer brown; their wings no longer open, clean, and transparent, but closed upon the back, and as it were encrusted with neglect. Some few were beginning to brush themselves, but their motions were slow and feeble: the greater number had fallen upon their backs, and lay unable to recover themselves. Not a breath of air was stirring; the smoke ascended straight into the sky, till it diffused itself equally on all sides and was lost. The lake lay like a mirror, smooth and dark. The tops of the mountains, which had not been visible for many days, were clear and free from snow: a few light clouds, which hovered upon their sides, were slowly rising and melting in the sunshine.

Notwithstanding the sedentary habits of Dr. Southey, which appear to deprive him of half the pleasures of the country, he seems occasionally to be liable to the inroad of sudden bursts of enjoyment which confound his habits of calculation and penetration, and cause him to associate the delight with which his breast is at such moments overflowing, with the simple or indifferent objects which happen to surround him.

113. Thomas Babington Macaulay, unsigned review, *Edinburgh Review*

January 1830, l, 528–65

This long essay constitutes the most extensive attack ever made upon Southey's social and economic ideas. Macaulay later referred in his journal to 'the nonsense which Southey talked about political economy' and his arrogance 'beyond any man in literary history' (cf. G. O. Trevelyan, *The Life and Letters of Lord Macaulay*, World's Classics edition, ii, pp. 380–2).

It would be scarcely possible for a man of Mr Southey's talents and acquirements to write two volumes so large as those before us, which should be wholly destitute of information and amusement. Yet we do not remember to have read with so little satisfaction any equal quantity of matter, written by any man of real abilities. We have, for some time past, observed with great regret the strange infatuation which leads the Poet-laureate to abandon those departments of literature in which he might excel, and to lecture the public on sciences of which he has still the very alphabet to learn. He has now, we think, done his worst. The subject which he has at last undertaken to treat is one which demands all the highest intellectual and moral qualities of a philosophical statesman,—an understanding at once comprehensive and acute,—a heart at once upright and charitable. Mr Southey brings to the task two faculties which were never, we believe, vouchsafed in measure so copious to any human being,—the faculty of believing without a reason, and the faculty of hating without a provocation.

It is, indeed, most extraordinary that a mind like Mr Southey's,— a mind richly endowed in many respects by nature, and highly cultivated by study,—a mind which has exercised considerable influence on the most enlightened generation of the most enlightened people that ever existed—should be utterly destitute of the power of discerning truth from falsehood. Yet such is the fact. Government is to Mr Southey one of the fine arts. He judges of a theory or a public measure, of a religion, a political party, a peace or a war, as men judge of a picture or a statue, by the effect produced on his imagination. A chain of associations is to him what a chain of reasoning is to other men; and what he calls his opinions, are in fact merely his tastes.

Part of this description might, perhaps, apply to a much greater man, Mr Burke. But Mr Burke, assuredly, possessed an understanding admirably fitted for the investigation of truth,—an understanding stronger than that of any statesman, active or speculative, of the eighteenth century,—stronger than every thing, except his own fierce and ungovernable sensibility. Hence, he generally chose his side like a fanatic, and defended it like a philosopher. His conduct, in the most important events of his life,—at the time of the impeachment of Hastings, for example, and at the time of the French Revolution,— seems to have been prompted by those feelings and motives, which Mr Coleridge has so happily described:

> Stormy pity, and the cherish'd lure
> Of pomp, and proud precipitance of soul.[1]

Hindostan, with its vast cities, its gorgeous pagodas, its infinite swarms of dusky population, its long-descended dynasties, its stately etiquette, excited in a mind so capacious, so imaginative, and so susceptible, the most intense interest. The peculiarities of the costume, of the manners, and of the laws, the very mystery which hung over the language and origin of the people, seized his imagination. To plead in Westminster Hall, in the name of the English people, at the bar of the English nobles, for great nations and kings separated from him by half the world, seemed to him the height of human glory. Again, it is not difficult to perceive, that his hostility to the French Revolution

[1] *Sonnets on Eminent Characters: Burke.*

342

principally arose from the vexation which he felt, at having all his old political associations disturbed, at seeing the well-known boundary-marks of states obliterated, and the names and distinctions with which the history of Europe had been filled for ages, swept away. He felt like an antiquarian whose shield had been scoured, or a connoisseur, who found his Titian retouched. But however he came by an opinion, he had no sooner got it, than he did his best to make out a legitimate title to it. His reason, like a spirit in the service of an enchanter, though spell-bound, was still mighty. It did whatever work his passions and his imagination might impose. But it did that work, however arduous, with marvellous dexterity and vigour. His course was not determined by argument; but he could defend the wildest course by arguments more plausible, than those by which common men support opinions which they have adopted, after the fullest deliberation. Reason has scarcely ever displayed, even in those well-constituted minds of which she occupies the throne, so much power and energy as in the lowest offices of that imperial servitude.

Now, in the mind of Mr Southey, reason has no place at all, as either leader or follower, as either sovereign or slave. He does not seem to know what an argument is. He never uses arguments himself. He never troubles himself to answer the arguments of his opponents. It has never occurred to him, that a man ought to be able to give some better account of the way in which he has arrived at his opinions than merely that it is his will and pleasure to hold them,—that there is a difference between assertion and demonstration,—that a rumour does not always prove a fact,—that a fact does not always prove a theory,—that two contradictory propositions cannot be undeniable truths,—that to beg the question, is not the way to settle it,—or that when an objection is raised, it ought to be met with something more convincing, than 'scoundrel' and 'blockhead.'

It would be absurd to read the works of such a writer for political instruction. The utmost that can be expected from any system promulgated by him is that it may be splendid and affecting,—that it may suggest sublime and pleasing images. His scheme of philosophy is a mere day-dream, a poetical creation, like the Domdaniel caverns, the Swerga, or Padalon; and indeed, it bears no inconsiderable resemblance to those gorgeous visions. Like them, it has something of invention, grandeur, and brilliancy. But like them, it is grotesque and extravagant, and perpetually violates that conventional probability which is essential to the effect even of works of art.

The warmest admirers of Mr Southey will scarcely, we think, deny that his success has almost always borne an inverse proportion to the degree in which his undertakings have required a logical head. His poems, taken in the mass, stand far higher than his prose works. The Laureate *Odes*, indeed, among which the *Vision of Judgement* must be classed, are, for the most part, worse than Pye's, and as bad as Cibber's; nor do we think him generally happy in short pieces. But his longer poems, though full of faults, are nevertheless very extraordinary productions. We doubt greatly whether they will be read fifty years hence,—but that if they are read, they will be admired, we have no doubt whatever.

But though in general we prefer Mr Southey's poetry to his prose, we must make one exception. *The Life of Nelson* is, beyond all doubt, the most perfect and the most delightful of his works. The fact is, as his poems most abundantly prove, that he is by no means so skilful in designing, as in filling up. It was therefore an advantage to him to be furnished with an outline of characters and events, and to have no other task to perform than that of touching the cold sketch into life. No writer, perhaps, ever lived, whose talents so precisely qualified him to write the history of the great naval warrior. There were no fine riddles of the human heart to read—no theories to found—no hidden causes to develope—no remote consequences to predict. The character of the hero lay on the surface. The exploits were brilliant and picturesque. The necessity of adhering to the real course of events saved Mr Southey from those faults which deform the original plan of almost every one of his poems, and which even his innumerable beauties of detail scarcely redeem. The subject did not require the exercise of those reasoning powers the want of which is the blemish of his prose. It would not be easy to find in all literary history, an instance of a more exact hit between wind and water. John Wesley, and the Peninsular War, were subjects of a very different kind,—subjects which required all the qualities of a philosophic historian. In Mr Southey's works on these subjects, he has, on the whole, failed. Yet there are charming specimens of the art of narration in both of them. *The Life of Wesley* will probably live. Defective as it is, it contains the only popular account of a most remarkable moral revolution, and of a man whose eloquence and logical acuteness might have rendered him eminent in literature, whose genius for government was not inferior to that of Richelieu, and who, whatever his errors may have been, devoted all his powers, in defiance of obloquy and derision, to what he sincerely considered as the highest good of his species. The *History of the Peninsular War* is already dead:—indeed, the second volume was dead-born. The glory of producing an imperishable record of that great conflict seems to be reserved for Colonel Napier.

The Book of the Church contains some stories very prettily told. The rest is mere rubbish. The adventure was manifestly one which could be achieved only by a profound thinker, and in which even a profound thinker might have failed, unless his passions had been kept under strict control. In all those works in which Mr Southey has completely abandoned narration, and undertaken to argue moral and political questions, his failure has been complete and ignominious. On such occasions, his writings are rescued from utter contempt and derision solely by the beauty and purity of the English. We find, we confess, so great a charm in Mr Southey's style, that, even when he writes nonsense, we generally read it with pleasure, except indeed when he tries to be droll. A more insufferable jester never existed. He very often attempts to be humorous, and yet we do not remember a single occasion on which he has succeeded farther than to be quaintly and flippantly dull. In one of his works, he tells us that Bishop Sprat was very properly so called, inasmuch as he was a very small poet. And in the book now before us, he cannot quote Francis Bugg without a remark on his unsavoury name. A man might talk folly like this by his own fireside; but that any human being, after having made such a joke, should write it down, and copy it out, and transmit it to the printer, and correct the proof-sheets, and send it forth into the world, is enough to make us ashamed of our species.

The extraordinary bitterness of spirit which Mr Southey manifests towards his opponents is, no doubt, in a great measure to be attributed to the manner in which he forms his opinions. Differences of taste, it has often been remarked, produce greater exasperation than differences on points of science. But this is not all. A peculiar austerity marks almost all Mr Southey's judgments of men and actions. We are far from blaming him for fixing on a high standard of morals, and for applying that standard to every case. But rigour ought to be accompanied by discernment, and of discernment Mr Southey seems to be utterly destitute. His mode of judging is monkish; it is exactly what we should expect from a stern old Benedictine, who had been preserved from many ordinary frailties by the restraints of his situation. No man out of a cloister ever wrote about love, for example, so coldly and at the same time so grossly. His descriptions of it are just what we should hear from a recluse, who knew the passion only from the details of the confessional. Almost all his heroes make love either like seraphim or like cattle. He seems to have no notion of any thing between the Platonic passion of the Glendoveer, who gazes with rapture on his mistress's leprosy, and the brutal appetite of Arvalan and Roderick. In Roderick, indeed, the two characters are united. He is first all clay, and then all spirit; he goes forth a Tarquin, and comes back too ethereal to be married. The only love-scene, as far as we can recollect, in *Madoc*, consists of the delicate attentions which a savage, who has drunk too much of the Prince's metheglin, offers to Goervyl. It would be the labour of a week to find, in all the vast mass of Mr Southey's poetry, a single passage indicating any sympathy with those feelings which have consecrated the shades of Vaucluse and the rocks of Meillerie.

Indeed, if we except some very pleasing images of paternal tenderness and filial duty, there is scarcely any thing soft or humane in Mr Southey's poetry. What theologians call the spiritual sins are his cardinal virtues—hatred, pride, and the insatiable thirst of vengeance. These passions he disguises under the name of duties; he purifies them from the alloy of vulgar interests; he ennobles them by uniting them with energy, fortitude, and a severe sanctity of manners, and then holds them up to the admiration of mankind. This is the spirit of Thalaba, of Ladurlad, of Adosinda, of Roderick after his regeneration. It is the spirit which, in all his writings, Mr Southey appears to affect. 'I do well to be angry,' seems to be the predominant feeling of his mind. Almost the only mark of charity which he vouchsafes to his opponents is to pray for their conversion, and this he does in terms not unlike those in which we can imagine a Portuguese priest interceding with Heaven for a Jew, delivered over to the secular arm after a relapse.

We have always heard, and fully believe, that Mr Southey is a very amiable and humane man; nor do we intend to apply to him personally any of the remarks which we have made on the spirit of his writings. Such are the caprices of human nature. Even Uncle Toby troubled himself very little about the French grenadiers who fell on the glacis of Namur. And when Mr Southey takes up his pen, he changes his nature as much as Captain Shandy when he girt on his sword. The only opponents to whom he gives quarter are those in whom he finds something of his own character reflected. He seems to have an instinctive antipathy for calm, moderate men—for men who shun extremes and who render reasons. He has treated Mr Owen of Lanark, for example, with infinitely more respect than he has shown to Mr Hallam or to Dr Lingard; and this for no reason that we can discover, except that Mr Owen is more unreasonably and hopelessly in the wrong than any speculator of our time.

Mr Southey's political system is just what we might expect from a man who regards politics, not as a matter of science, but as a matter of taste and feeling. All his schemes of government have been inconsistent with themselves. In his youth he was a republican; yet, as he tells us in his preface to these *Colloquies*, he was even then opposed to the Catholic claims. He is now a violent Ultra-Tory. Yet while he maintains, with vehemence approaching to ferocity, all the sterner and harsher parts of the Ultra-Tory theory of government, the baser and dirtier part of that theory disgusts him. Exclusion, persecution, severe punishments for libellers and demagogues, proscriptions, massacres, civil war, if necessary, rather than any concession to a discontented people,—these are the measures which he seems inclined to recommend. A severe and gloomy tyranny—crushing opposition—silencing remonstrance— drilling the minds of the people into unreasoning obedience,—has in it something of grandeur which delights his imagination. But there is nothing fine in the shabby tricks and jobs of office. And Mr Southey, accordingly, has no toleration for them. When a democrat, he did not perceive that his system led logically, and would have led practically, to the removal of religious distinctions. He now commits a similar error. He renounces the abject and paltry part of the creed of his party, without perceiving that it is also an essential part of that creed. He would have tyranny and purity together; though the most superficial observation might have shown him that there can be no tyranny without corruption.

It is high time, however, that we should proceed to the consideration of the work, which is our more immediate subject, and which, indeed, illustrates in almost every page our general remarks on Mr Southey's writings. In the preface, we are informed that the author, notwithstanding some statements to the contrary, was always opposed to the Catholic Claims. We fully believe this; both because we are sure that Mr Southey is incapable of publishing a deliberate falsehood, and because his averment is in itself probable. It is exactly what we should have expected that, even in his wildest paroxysms of democratic enthusiasm, Mr Southey would have felt no wish to see a simple remedy applied to a great practical evil; that the only measure which all the great statesmen of two generations have agreed with each other

347

in supporting, would be the only measure which Mr Southey would have agreed with himself in opposing. He has passed from one extreme of political opinion to another, as Satan in Milton went round the globe, contriving constantly to 'ride with darkness.' Wherever the thickest shadow of the night may at any moment chance to fall, there is Mr Southey. It is not every body who could have so dexterously avoided blundering on the daylight in the course of a journey to the Antipodes.

Mr Southey has not been fortunate in the plan of any of his fictitious narratives. But he has never failed so conspicuously, as in the work before us; except, indeed, in the wretched *Vision of Judgement*. In November 1817, it seems, the Laureate was sitting over his newspaper, and meditating about the death of the Princess Charlotte. An elderly person, of very dignified aspect, makes his appearance, announces himself as a stranger from a distant country, and apologises very politely for not having provided himself with letters of introduction. Mr Southey supposes his visitor to be some American gentleman, who has come to see the lakes and the lake-poets, and accordingly proceeds to perform, with that grace which only long experience can give, all the duties which authors owe to starers. He assures his guest that some of the most agreeable visits which he has received have been from Americans, and that he knows men among them whose talents and virtues would do honour to any country. In passing, we may observe, to the honour of Mr Southey, that, though he evidently has no liking for the American institutions, he never speaks of the people of the United States with that pitiful affectation of contempt by which some members of his party have done more than wars or tariffs can do to excite mutual enmity between two communities formed for mutual friendship. Great as the faults of his mind are, paltry spite like this has no place in it. Indeed, it is scarcely conceivable that a man of his sensibility and his imagination should look without pleasure and national pride on the vigorous and splendid youth of a great people, whose veins are filled with our blood, whose minds are nourished with our literature, and on whom is entailed the rich inheritance of our civilisation, our freedom, and our glory.

But we must return to Mr Southey's study at Keswick. The visitor informs the hospitable poet that he is not an American, but a spirit. Mr Southey, with more frankness than civility, tells him that he is a very queer one. The stranger holds out his hand. It has neither weight nor substance. Mr Southey upon this becomes more serious; his hair

348

stands on end; and he adjures the spectre to tell him what he is, and why he comes. The ghost turns out to be Sir Thomas More. The traces of martyrdom, it seems, are worn in the other world, as stars and ribbands are worn in this. Sir Thomas shows the poet a red streak round his neck, brighter than a ruby, and informs him that Cranmer wears a suit of flames in paradise,—the right hand glove, we suppose, of peculiar brilliancy.

Sir Thomas pays but a short visit on this occasion, but promises to cultivate the new acquaintance which he has formed, and, after begging that his visit may be kept secret from Mrs Southey, vanishes into air.

The rest of the book consists of conversations between Mr Southey and the spirit about trade, currency, Catholic emancipation, periodical literature, female nunneries, butchers, snuff, book-stalls, and a hundred other subjects. Mr Southey very hospitably takes an opportunity to lionize the ghost round the lakes, and directs his attention to the most beautiful points of view. Why a spirit was to be evoked for the purpose of talking over such matters, and seeing such sights—why the vicar of the parish, a blue-stocking from London, or an American, such as Mr Southey supposed his aerial visitor to be, might not have done as well—we are unable to conceive. Sir Thomas tells Mr Southey nothing about future events, and indeed absolutely disclaims the gift of pre-science. He has learned to talk modern English: he has read all the new publications, and loves a jest as well as when he jested with the executioner, though we cannot say that the quality of his wit has materially improved in Paradise. His powers of reasoning, too, are by no means in as great vigour as when he sate on the woolsack; and though he boasts that he is 'divested of all those passions which cloud the intellects and warp the understandings of men,' we think him—we must confess—far less stoical than formerly. As to revelations, he tells Mr Southey at the outset to expect none from him. The Laureate expresses some doubts, which assuredly will not raise him in the opinion of our modern millennarians, as to the divine authority of the Apocalypse. But the ghost preserves an impenetrable silence. As far as we remember, only one hint about the employments of disembodied spirits escapes him. He encourages Mr Southey to hope that there is a Paradise Press, at which all the valuable publications of Mr Murray and Mr Colburn are reprinted as regularly as at Philadelphia; and delicately insinuates, that Thalaba and The Curse of Kehama are among the number. What a contrast does this absurd fiction present to those charming narratives which Plato and Cicero prefixed to their dialogues! What cost in machinery, yet what poverty of effect! A ghost brought in to say what any man might have said! The glorified spirit of a great statesman and philosopher dawdling, like a bilious old Nabob at a watering-place, over quarterly reviews and novels—dropping in to pay long calls—making excursions in search of the picturesque! The scene of St George and St Denys in the Pucelle is hardly more ridiculous. We know what Voltaire meant. Nobody, however, can suppose that Mr Southey means to make game of the mysteries of a higher state of existence. The fact is, that in the work before us, in the *Vision of Judgement*, and in some of his other pieces, his mode of treating the most solemn subjects differs from that of open scoffers only as the extravagant representations of sacred persons and things in some grotesque Italian paintings differ from the caricatures which Carlile exposes in the front of his shop. We interpret the particular act by the general character. What in the window of a convicted blasphemer we call blasphemous we call only absurd and ill-judged in an altar-piece.

We now come to the conversations which pass between Mr Southey and Sir Thomas More, or rather between two Southeys, equally eloquent, equally angry, equally unreasonable, and equally given to talking about what they do not understand. Perhaps we could not select a better instance of the spirit which pervades the whole book than the discussion touching butchers. These persons are represented as castaways, as men whose employment hebetates the faculties and hardens the heart;—not that the poet has any scruples about the use of animal food. He acknowledges that it is for the good of the animals themselves that men should feed upon them. 'Nevertheless,' says he, 'I cannot but acknowledge, like good old John Fox, that the sight of a slaughter-house or shambles, if it does not disturb this clear conviction, excites in me uneasiness and pain, as well as loathing. And that they produce a worse effect upon the persons employed in them, is a fact acknowledged by that law or custom which excludes such persons from sitting on juries upon cases of life and death.'

This is a fair specimen of Mr Southey's mode of looking at all moral questions. Here is a body of men engaged in an employment, which, by his own account, is beneficial, not only to mankind, but to the very creatures on whom we feed. Yet he represents them as men who are necessarily reprobates—as men who must necessarily be reprobates, even in the most improved state of society—even, to use his own phrase, in a Christian Utopia. And what reasons are given for a judgment so directly opposed to every principle of sound and manly morality? Merely this, that he cannot abide the sight of their apparatus —that, from certain peculiar associations, he is affected with disgust when he passes by their shops. He gives, indeed, another reason; a certain law or custom, which never existed but in the imaginations of old women, and which, if it had existed, would have proved just as much against butchers as the ancient prejudice against the practice of taking interest for money, proves against the merchants of England. Is a surgeon a castaway? We believe that nurses, when they instruct children in that venerable law or custom which Mr Southey so highly approves, generally join the surgeon to the butcher. A dissecting-room would, we should think, affect the nerves of most people as much as a butcher's shambles. But the most amusing circumstance is, that Mr Southey, who detests a butcher, should look with special favour on a soldier. He seems highly to approve of the sentiment of General Meadows, who swore that a grenadier was the highest character in this world or in the next; and assures us, that a virtuous soldier is placed in the situation which most tends to his improvement, and will most promote his eternal interests. Human blood, indeed, is by no means an object of so much loathing to Mr Southey, as the hides and paunches of cattle. In 1814, he poured forth poetical maledictions on all who talked of peace with Buonaparte. He went over the field of Waterloo, —a field beneath which twenty thousand of the stoutest hearts that ever beat are mouldering,—and came back in an ecstasy, which he mistook for poetical inspiration. In most of his poems,—particularly in his best poem, *Roderick*,—and in most of his prose works, particularly in the *History of the Peninsular War*, he shows a delight in snuffing up carnage, which would not have misbecome a Scandinavian bard, but which sometimes seems to harmonize ill with the Christian morality. We do not, however, blame Mr Southey for exulting, even a little ferociously, in the brave deeds of his countrymen, or for finding something 'comely and reviving' in the bloody vengeance inflicted by an oppressed people on its oppressors. Now, surely, if we find that a man whose business is to kill Frenchmen may be humane, we may hope that means may be found to render a man humane whose business is to kill sheep. If the brutalizing effect of such scenes as the storm of St Sebastian may be counteracted, we may hope that in a Christian Utopia, some minds might be proof against the kennels and dressers of Aldgate. Mr Southey's feeling, however, is easily explained. A butcher's knife is by no means so elegant as a sabre, and a calf does not bleed with half the grace of a poor wounded hussar.

It is in the same manner that Mr Southey appears to have formed his opinion of the manufacturing system. There is nothing which he hates so bitterly. It is, according to him, a system more tyrannical than that of the feudal ages,—a system of actual servitude,—a system which destroys the bodies and degrades the minds of those who are engaged in it. He expresses a hope that the competition of other nations may drive us out of the field; that our foreign trade may decline, and that we may thus enjoy a restoration of national sanity and strength. But he seems to think that the extermination of the whole manufacturing population would be a blessing, if the evil could be removed in no other way.

Mr Southey does not bring forward a single fact in support of these views, and, as it seems to us, there are facts which lead to a very different conclusion. In the first place, the poor-rate is very decidedly lower in the manufacturing than in the agricultural districts. If Mr Southey will look over the Parliamentary returns on this subject, he will find that the amount of parish relief required by the labourers in the different counties of England, is almost exactly in inverse proportion to the degree in which the manufacturing system has been introduced into those counties. The returns for the years ending in March 1825, and in March 1828, are now before us. In the former year, we find the poor-rate highest in Sussex,—about 20s. to every inhabitant. Then come Buckinghamshire, Essex, Suffolk, Bedfordshire, Huntingdonshire, Kent, and Norfolk. In all these the rate is above 15s. a-head. We will not go through the whole. Even in Westmoreland, and the North Riding of Yorkshire, the rate is at more than 8s. In Cumberland and Monmouthshire, the most fortunate of all the agricultural districts, it is at 6s. But in the West Riding of Yorkshire, it is as low as 5s.; and when we come to Lancashire, we find it at 4s.,—one-fifth of what it is in Sussex. The returns of the year ending in March 1828, are a little, and but a little, more unfavourable to the manufacturing districts. Lancashire, even in that season of distress, required a smaller poor-rate than any other district, and little more than one-fourth of the poor-rate raised in Sussex. Cumberland alone, of the agricultural districts, was as well off as the West Riding of Yorkshire. These facts seem to indicate that the manufacturer is both in a more comfortable and in a less dependent situation than the agricultural labourer.

As to the effect of the manufacturing system on the bodily health, we must beg leave to estimate it by a standard far too low and vulgar for a mind so imaginative as that of Mr Southey—the proportion of births and deaths. We know that, during the growth of this atrocious system—this new misery,—(we use the phrases of Mr Southey,)—this new enormity—this birth of a portentous age—this pest, which no man can approve whose heart is not seared, or whose understanding has not been darkened—there has been a great diminution of mortality—and that this diminution has been greater in the manufacturing towns than anywhere else. The mortality still is, as it always was, greater in towns than in the country. But the difference has diminished in an extraordinary degree. There is the best reason to believe, that the annual mortality of Manchester, about the middle of the last century, was one in twenty-eight. It is now reckoned at one in forty-five. In Glasgow and Leeds a similar improvement has taken place. Nay, the rate of mortality in those three great capitals of the manufacturing districts, is now considerably less than it was fifty years ago over England and Wales taken together—open country and all. We might with some plausibility maintain, that the people live longer because they are better fed, better lodged, better clothed, and better attended in sickness; and that these improvements are owing to that increase of national wealth which the manufacturing system has produced.

Much more might be said on this subject. But to what end? It is not from bills of mortality and statistical tables that Mr Southey has learned his political creed. He cannot stoop to study the history of the system which he abuses—to strike the balance between the good and evil which it has produced—to compare district with district, or generation with generation. We will give his own reason for his opinion—the only reason which he gives for it—in his own words:

We remained awhile in silence, looking upon the assemblage of dwellings below. Here, and in the adjoining hamlet of Millbeck, the effects of manufactures and of agriculture may be seen and compared. The old cottages are such as the poet and the painter equally delight in beholding. Substantially built of the native stone without mortar, dirtied with no white lime, and their long, low roofs covered with slate, if they had been raised by the magic of some indigenous Amphion's music, the materials could not have adjusted themselves more beautifully in accord with the surrounding scene; and time has still further harmonized them with weather-stains, lichens, and moss, short grasses, and short fern, and stone-plants of various kinds. The ornamented chimneys, round or square, less adorned than those which, like little turrets, crest the houses of the Portuguese peasantry; and yet not less happily suited to their place, the hedge of clipt box beneath the windows, the rose-bushes beside the door, the little patch of flower-ground, with its tall hollyocks in front; the garden beside, the bee-hives, and the orchard with its bank of daffodils and snow-drops, the earliest and the profusest in these parts, indicate in the owners some portion of ease and leisure, some regard to neatness and comfort, some sense of natural, and innocent, and healthful enjoyment. The new cottages of the manufacturers are upon the manufacturing pattern—naked, and in a row.

How is it, said I, that every thing which is connected with manufactures presents such features of unqualified deformity? From the largest of Mammon's temples down to the poorest hovel in which his helotry are stalled, these edifices have all one character. Time will not mellow them; nature will neither clothe nor conceal them; and they will remain always as offensive to the eye as to the mind.

Here is wisdom. Here are the principles on which nations are to be governed. Rose-bushes and poor-rates, rather than steam-engines and independence. Mortality and cottages with weather-stains, rather than health and long life with edifices which time cannot mellow. We are told, that our age has invented atrocities beyond the imagination of our fathers; that society has been brought into a state, compared with which extermination would be a blessing;—and all because the dwellings of cotton-spinners are naked and rectangular. Mr Southey has found out a way, he tells us, in which the effects of manufactures and agriculture may be compared. And what is this way? To stand on a hill, to look at a cottage and a manufactory, and to see which is the prettier. Does Mr Southey think that the body of the English peasantry live, or ever lived, in substantial and ornamented cottages, with box-hedges, flower-gardens, bee-hives, and orchards? If not, what is his parallel worth? We despise those *filosofastri*,[1] who think that they serve the cause of science by depreciating literature and the fine arts. But if any thing could excuse their narrowness of mind, it would be such a book as this. It is not strange that when one enthusiast makes the picturesque the test of political good, another should feel inclined to proscribe altogether the pleasures of taste and imagination.

Thus it is that Mr Southey reasons about matters with which he thinks himself perfectly conversant. We cannot, therefore, be surprised to find that he commits extraordinary blunders when he writes on points of which he acknowledges himself to be ignorant. He confesses that he is not versed in political economy—that he has neither liking nor aptitude for it; and he then proceeds to read the public a lecture concerning it which fully bears out his confession.

[1] 'Amateur philosophers'.

'All wealth,' says Sir Thomas More, 'in former times was tangible. It consisted in land, money, or chattels, which were either of real or conventional value.'

Montesinos, as Mr Southey somewhat affectedly calls himself, answers:

'Jewels, for example, and pictures, as in Holland,—where indeed at one time tulip bulbs answered the same purpose.'

'That bubble,' says Sir Thomas, 'was one of those contagious insanities to which communities are subject. All wealth was real, till the extent of commerce rendered a paper currency necessary; which differed from precious stones and pictures in this important point, that there was no limit to its production.'

'We regard it,' says Montesinos, 'as the representative of real wealth; and, therefore, limited always to the amount of what it represents.'

'Pursue that notion,' answers the ghost, 'and you will be in the dark presently. Your provincial bank-notes, which constitute almost wholly the circulating medium of certain districts, pass current to-day. To-morrow, tidings may come that the house which issued them has stopt payment, and what do they represent then? You will find them the shadow of a shade.'

We scarcely know at which end to begin to disentangle this knot of absurdities. We might ask, why it should be a greater proof of insanity in men to set a high value on rare tulips than on rare stones, which are neither more useful nor more beautiful? We might ask, how it can be said that there is no limit to the production of paper-money, when a man is hanged if he issues any in the name of another, and is forced to cash what he issues in his own? But Mr Southey's error lies deeper still. 'All wealth,' says he, 'was tangible and real till paper currency was introduced.' Now, was there ever, since men emerged from a state of utter barbarism, an age in which there were no debts? Is not a debt, while the solvency of the debtor is undoubted, always reckoned as part of the wealth of the creditor? Yet is it tangible and real wealth? Does it cease to be wealth, because there is the security of a written acknowledgment for it? And what else is paper currency? Did Mr Southey ever read a bank-note? If he did, he would see that it is a written acknowledgment of a debt, and a promise to pay that debt. The promise may be violated—the debt may remain unpaid—those to whom it was due may suffer: but this is a risk not confined to cases of paper currency—it is a risk inseparable from the relation of debtor and creditor. Every man who sells goods for any thing but ready money, runs the risk of finding that what he considered as part of his wealth one day is nothing at all the next day. Mr Southey refers to the picture-galleries of Holland. The pictures were undoubtedly real and tangible possessions. But surely it might happen, that a burgomaster might owe a picture-dealer a thousand guilders for a Teniers. What in this case corresponds to our paper money is not the picture, which is tangible, but the claim of the picture-dealer on his customer for the price of the picture, which is not tangible. Now, would not the picture-dealer consider this claim as part of his wealth? Would not a tradesman who knew of it give credit to the picture-dealer the more readily on account of it? The burgomaster might be ruined. If so, would not those consequences follow which, as Mr Southey tells us, were never heard of till paper money came into use? Yesterday this claim was worth a thousand guilders. To-day what is it? The shadow of a shade.

It is true, that the more readily claims of this sort are transferred from hand to hand, the more extensive will be the injury produced by a single failure. The laws of all nations sanction, in certain cases, the transfer of rights not yet reduced into possession. Mr Southey would scarcely wish, we should think, that all indorsements of bills and notes should be declared invalid. Yet even if this were done, the transfer of claims would imperceptibly take place to a very great extent. When the baker trusts the butcher, for example, he is in fact, though not in form, trusting the butcher's customers. A man who owes large bills to tradesmen and fails to pay them, almost always produces distress through a very wide circle of people whom he never dealt with.

In short, what Mr Southey takes for a difference in kind, is only a difference of form and degree. In every society men have claims on the property of others. In every society there is a possibility that some debtors may not be able to fulfil their obligations. In every society, therefore, there is wealth which is not tangible, and which may become the shadow of a shade.

Mr Southey then proceeds to a dissertation on the national debt, which he considers in a new and most consolatory light, as a clear addition to the income of the country.

'You can understand,' says Sir Thomas, 'that it constitutes a great part of the national wealth.'

'So large a part,' answers Montesinos, 'that the interest amounted, during the prosperous time of agriculture, to as much as the rental of all the land in Great Britain; and at present to the rental of all lands, all houses, and all other fixed property put together.'

The Ghost and the Laureate agree that it is very desirable that there should be so secure and advantageous a deposit for wealth as the funds afford. Sir Thomas then proceeds:

'Another and far more momentous benefit must not be overlooked; the expenditure of an annual interest, equalling, as you have stated, the present rental of all fixed property.'

'That expenditure,' quoth Montesinos, 'gives employment to half the industry in the kingdom, and feeds half the mouths. Take, indeed, the weight of the national debt from this great and complicated social machine, and the wheels must stop.'

From this passage we should have been inclined to think, that Mr Southey supposes the dividends to be a free-gift periodically sent down from heaven to the fundholders, as quails and manna were sent to the Israelites; were it not that he has vouchsafed, in the following question and answer, to give the public some information which, we believe, was very little needed.

'Whence comes the interest?' says Sir Thomas.

'It is raised,' answers Montesinos, 'by taxation.'

Now, has Mr Southey ever considered what would be done with this sum if it were not paid as interest to the national creditor? If he would think over this matter for a short time, we suspect that the 'momentous benefit' of which he talks would appear to him to shrink strangely in amount. A fundholder, we will suppose, spends an income of five hundred pounds a-year, and his ten nearest neighbours pay fifty pounds each to the tax-gatherer, for the purpose of discharging the interest of the national debt. If the debt were wiped out—a measure, be it understood, which we by no means recommend—the fundholder would cease to spend his five hundred pounds a-year. He would no longer give employment to industry, or put food into the mouths of labourers. This Mr Southey thinks a fearful evil. But is there no mitigating circumstance? Each of his ten neighbours has fifty pounds more than formerly. Each of them will, as it seems to our feeble understandings, employ more industry, and feed more mouths, than formerly. The sum is exactly the same. It is in different hands. But on what grounds does Mr Southey call upon us to believe that it is in the hands of men who will spend less liberally or less judiciously? He seems to think, that nobody but a fundholder can employ the poor; that if a tax is remitted, those who formerly used to pay it proceed immediately to dig holes in the earth, and bury the sum which the government had been accustomed to take; that no money can set

357

industry in motion till it has been taken by the tax-gatherer out of one man's pocket and put into another man's. We really wish that Mr Southey would try to prove this principle, which is indeed the foundation of his whole theory of finance; for we think it right to hint to him, that our hard-hearted and unimaginative generation will expect some more satisfactory reason than the only one with which he has yet favoured it,—a similitude touching evaporation and dew.

Both the theory and the illustration, indeed, are old friends of ours. In every season of distress which we can remember, Mr Southey has been proclaiming that it is not from economy, but from increased taxation, that the country must expect relief; and he still, we find, places the undoubting faith of a political Diafoirus, in his

Resaignare, repurgare, et reclysterizare.[1]

'A people,' he tells us, 'may be too rich, but a government cannot be so.'

'A state,' says he, 'cannot have more wealth at its command than may be employed for the general good, a liberal expenditure in national works being one of the surest means for promoting national prosperity; and the benefit being still more obvious, of an expenditure directed to the purposes of national improvement. But a people may be too rich.'

We fully admit, that a state cannot have at its command more wealth than *may be* employed for the general good. But neither can individuals, or bodies of individuals, have at their command more wealth than *may be* employed for the general good. If there be no limit to the sum which may be usefully laid out in public works and national improvement, then wealth, whether in the hands of private men or of the government, *may* always, if the possessors choose to spend it usefully, be usefully spent. The only ground, therefore, on which Mr Southey can possibly maintain that a government cannot be too rich, but that a people may be too rich, must be this, that governments are more likely to spend their money on good objects than private individuals.

But what is useful expenditure? 'A liberal expenditure in national works,' says Mr Southey, 'is one of the surest means for promoting national prosperity.' What does he mean by national prosperity? Does he mean the wealth of the state? If so, his reasoning runs thus:—The more wealth a state has the better; for the more wealth a state has, the

[1] Molière, *Le Malade imaginaire*.

more wealth it will have. This is surely something like that fallacy, which is ungallantly termed a lady's reason. If by national prosperity he means the wealth of the people, of how gross a contradiction is he guilty. A people, he tells us, may be too rich—a government cannot—for a government can employ its riches in making the people richer. The wealth of the people is to be taken from them, because they have too much, and laid out in works which will yield them more.

We are really at a loss to determine whether Mr Southey's reason for recommending large taxation is that it will make the people rich, or that it will make them poor. But we are sure, that if his object is to make them rich, he takes the wrong course. There are two or three principles respecting public works, which, as an experience of vast extent proves, may be trusted in almost every case.

It scarcely ever happens, that any private man, or body of men, will invest property in a canal, a tunnel, or a bridge, but from an expectation that the outlay will be profitable to them. No work of this sort can be profitable to private speculators, unless the public be willing to pay for the use of it. The public will not pay of their own accord for what yields no profit or convenience to them. There is thus a direct and obvious connexion between the motive which induces individuals to undertake such a work, and the utility of the work.

Can we find any such connexion in the case of a public work executed by a government? If it is useful, are the individuals who rule the country richer? If it is useless, are they poorer? A public man may be solicitous for his credit: but is not he likely to gain more credit by an useless display of ostentatious architecture in a great town, than by the best road or the best canal in some remote province? The fame of public works is a much less certain test of their utility, than the amount of toll collected at them. In a corrupt age, there will be direct embezzlement. In the purest age, there will be abundance of jobbing. Never were the statesmen of any country more sensitive to public opinion, and more spotless in pecuniary transactions, than those who have of late governed England. Yet we have only to look at the buildings recently erected in London for a proof of our rule. In a bad age, the fate of the public is to be robbed. In a good age, it is much milder—merely to have the dearest and the worst of every thing.

Buildings for state purposes the state must erect. And here we think that, in general, the state ought to stop. We firmly believe, that five hundred thousand pounds subscribed by individuals for rail-roads or canals would produce more advantage to the public than five millions voted by Parliament for the same purpose. There are certain old saws about the master's eye and about every body's business, in which we place very great faith.

There is, we have said, no consistency in Mr Southey's political system. But if there be in it any leading principle, if there be any one error which diverges more widely and variously than any other, it is that of which his theory about national works is a ramification. He conceives that the business of the magistrate is, not merely to see that the persons and property of the people are secure from attack, but that he ought to be a perfect jack-of-all-trades,—architect, engineer, schoolmaster, merchant, theologian,—a Lady Bountiful in every parish,—a Paul Pry in every house, spying, eaves-dropping, relieving, admonishing, spending our money for us, and choosing our opinions for us. His principle is, if we understand it rightly, that no man can do any thing so well for himself, as his rulers, be they who they may, can do it for him; that a government approaches nearer and nearer to perfection, in proportion as it interferes more and more with the habits and notions of individuals.

He seems to be fully convinced, that it is in the power of government to relieve the distresses under which the lower orders labour. Nay, he considers doubt on this subject as impious. We cannot refrain from quoting his argument on this subject. It is a perfect jewel of logic.

'Many thousands in your metropolis,' says Sir Thomas More, 'rise every morning without knowing how they are to subsist during the day; as many of them, where they are to lay their heads at night. All men, even the vicious themselves, know that wickedness leads to misery; but many, even among the good and the wise, have yet to learn that misery is almost as often the cause of wickedness.'

'There are many,' says Montesinos, 'who know this, but believe that it is not in the power of human institutions to prevent this misery. They see the effect, but regard the causes as inseparable from the condition of human nature.'

'As surely as God is good,' replies Sir Thomas, 'so surely there is no such thing as necessary evil. For, by the religious mind, sickness, and pain, and death, are not to be accounted evils.'

Now, if sickness, pain, and death, are not evils, we cannot understand why it should be an evil that thousands should rise without knowing how they are to subsist. The only evil of hunger is, that it produces first pain, then sickness, and finally death. If it did not produce these it would be no calamity. If these are not evils, it is no calamity.

We cannot conceive why it should be a greater impeachment of the Divine goodness, that some men should not be able to find food to eat, than that others should have stomachs which derive no nourishment from food when they have eaten it. Whatever physical effects want produces may also be produced by disease. Whatever salutary effects disease may produce, may also be produced by want. If poverty makes men thieves, disease and pain often sour the temper and contract the heart.

We will propose a very plain dilemma: Either physical pain is an evil, or it is not an evil. If it is an evil, then there is necessary evil in the universe: If it is not, why should the poor be delivered from it?

Mr Southey entertains as exaggerated a notion of the wisdom of governments as of their power. He speaks with the greatest disgust of the respect now paid to public opinion. That opinion is, according to him, to be distrusted and dreaded; its usurpation ought to be vigorously resisted; and the practice of yielding to it is likely to ruin the country. To maintain police is, according to him, only one of the ends of government. Its duties are patriarchal and paternal. It ought to consider the moral discipline of the people as its first object, to establish a religion, to train the whole community in that religion, and to consider all dissenters as its own enemies.

'Nothing,' says Sir Thomas, 'is more certain, than that religion is the basis upon which civil government rests; that from religion power derives its authority, laws their efficacy, and both their zeal and sanction; and it is necessary that this religion be established as for the security of the state, and for the welfare of the people, who would otherwise be moved to and fro with every wind of doctrine. A state is secure in proportion as the people are attached to its institutions; it is, therefore, the first and plainest rule of sound policy, that the people be trained up in the way they should go. The state that neglects this prepares its own destruction; and they who train them in any other way are undermining it. Nothing in abstract science can be more certain than these positions are.'

'All of which,' answers Montesinos, 'are nevertheless denied by our professors of the arts Babblative and Scribblative; some in the audacity of evil designs, and others in the glorious assurance of impenetrable ignorance.'

The greater part of the two volumes before us is merely an amplification of these absurd paragraphs. What does Mr Southey mean by saying, that religion is demonstrably the basis of civil government? He cannot surely mean that men have no motives except those derived from religion for establishing and supporting civil government, that

361

no temporal advantage is derived from civil government, that man would experience no temporal inconvenience from living in a state of anarchy? If he allows, as we think he must allow, that it is for the good of mankind in this world to have civil government, and that the great majority of mankind have always thought it for their good in this world to have civil government, we then have a basis for government quite distinct from religion. It is true, that the Christian religion sanctions government, as it sanctions every thing which promotes the happiness and virtue of our species. But we are at a loss to conceive in what sense religion can be said to be the basis of government, in which it is not also the basis of the practices of eating, drinking, and lighting fires in cold weather. Nothing in history is more certain than that government has existed, has received some obedience and given some protection, in times in which it derived no support from religion,—in times in which there was no religion that influenced the hearts and lives of men. It was not from dread of Tartarus, or belief in the Elysian fields, that an Athenian wished to have some institutions which might keep Orestes from filching his cloak, or Midias from breaking his head. 'It is from religion,' says Mr Southey, 'that power derives its authority, and laws their efficacy.' From what religion does our power over the Hindoos derive its authority, or the law in virtue of which we hang Brahmins its efficacy? For thousands of years civil government has existed in almost every corner of the world,—in ages of priestcraft,—in ages of fanaticism,—in ages of Epicurean indifference,—in ages of enlightened piety. However pure or impure the faith of the people might be, whether they adored a beneficent or a malignant power, whether they thought the soul mortal or immortal, they have, as soon as they ceased to be absolute savages, found out their need of civil government, and instituted it accordingly. It is as universal as the practice of cookery. Yet, it is as certain, says Mr Southey, as any thing in abstract science, that government is founded on religion. We should like to know what notion Mr Southey has of the demonstrations of abstract science. But a vague one, we suspect.

The proof proceeds. As religion is the basis of government, and as the state is secure in proportion as the people are attached to its institutions, it is therefore, says Mr Southey, the first rule of policy, that the government should train the people in the way in which they should go; and it is plain, that those who train them in any other way, are undermining the state.

Now it does not appear to us to be the first object that people should always believe in the established religion, and be attached to the established government. A religion may be false. A government may be oppressive. And whatever support government gives to false religions, or religion to oppressive governments, we consider as a clear evil.

The maxim, that governments ought to train the people in the way in which they should go, sounds well. But is there any reason for believing that a government is more likely to lead the people in the right way, than the people to fall into the right way of themselves? Have there not been governments which were blind leaders of the blind? Are there not still such governments? Can it be laid down as a general rule that the movement of political and religious truth is rather downwards from the government to the people, than upwards from the people to the government? These are questions which it is of importance to have clearly resolved. Mr Southey declaims against public opinion, which is now, he tells us, usurping supreme power. Formerly, according to him, the laws governed; now public opinion governs. What are laws but expressions of the opinion of some class which has power over the rest of the community? By what was the world ever governed, but by the opinion of some person or persons? By what else can it ever be governed? What are all systems, religious, political, or scientific, but opinions resting on evidence more or less satisfactory? The question is not between human opinion, and some higher and more certain mode of arriving at truth, but between opinion and opinion,—between the opinion of one man and another, or of one class and another, or of one generation and another. Public opinion is not infallible; but can Mr Southey construct any institutions which shall secure to us the guidance of an infallible opinion? Can Mr Southey select any family,—any profession—any class, in short, distinguished by any plain badge from the rest of the community, whose opinion is more likely to be just than this much-abused public opinion? Would he choose the peers, for example? Or the two hundred tallest men in the country? Or the poor Knights of Windsor? Or children who are born with cawls, seventh sons of seventh sons? We cannot suppose that he would recommend popular election; for that is merely an appeal to public opinion. And to say that society ought to be governed by the opinion of the wisest and best, though true, is useless. Whose opinion is to decide, who are the wisest and best?

Mr Southey and many other respectable people seem to think that when they have once proved the moral and religious training of the people to be a most important object, it follows, of course, that it is an object which the government ought to pursue. They forget that we have to consider, not merely the goodness of the end, but also the fitness of the means. Neither in the natural nor in the political body have all members the same office. There is surely no contradiction in saying that a certain section of the community may be quite competent to protect the persons and property of the rest, yet quite unfit to direct our opinions, or to superintend our private habits.

So strong is the interest of a ruler, to protect his subjects against all depredations and outrages except his own,—so clear and simple are the means by which this end is to be effected, that men are probably better off under the worst governments in the world, than they would be in a state of anarchy. Even when the appointment of magistrates has been left to chance, as in the Italian Republics, things have gone on better than they would have done, if there had been no magistrates at all, and every man had done what seemed right in his own eyes. But we see no reason for thinking that the opinions of the magistrate are more likely to be right than those of any other man. None of the modes by which rulers are appointed,—popular election, the accident of the lot, or the accident of birth,—afford, as far as we can perceive, much security for their being wiser than any of their neighbours. The chance of their being wiser than all their neighbours together is still smaller. Now we cannot conceive how it can be laid down, that it is the duty and the right of one class to direct the opinions of another, unless it can be proved that the former class is more likely to form just opinions than the latter.

The duties of government would be, as Mr Southey says that they are, paternal, if a government were necessarily as much superior in wisdom to a people, as the most foolish father, for a time, is to the most intelligent child, and if a government loved a people as fathers generally love their children. But there is no reason to believe, that a government will either have the paternal warmth of affection or the paternal superiority of intellect. Mr Southey might as well say, that the duties of the shoemaker are paternal, and that it is an usurpation in any man not of the craft to say that his shoes are bad, and to insist on having better. The division of labour would be no blessing, if those by whom a thing is done were to pay no attention to the opinion of those for whom it is done. The shoemaker, in *The Relapse*, tells Lord Fopping-ton, that his lordship is mistaken in supposing that his shoe pinches. 'It does not pinch—it cannot pinch—I know my business—and I never made a better shoe.' This is the way in which Mr Southey would have a government treat a people who usurp the privilege of thinking. Nay, the shoemaker of Vanburgh has the advantage in the comparison. He contented himself with regulating the customer's shoes, about which he knew something, and did not presume to dictate about the coat and hat. But Mr Southey would have the rulers of a country prescribe opinions to the people, not only about politics, but about matters concerning which a government has no peculiar sources of information, —concerning which any man in the streets may know as much, and think as justly, as a king,—religion and morals.

Men are never so likely to settle a question rightly, as when they discuss it freely. A government can interfere in discussion, only by making it less free than it would otherwise be. Men are most likely to form just opinions, when they have no other wish than to know the truth, and are exempt from all influence, either of hope or fear. Government, as government, can bring nothing but the influence of hopes and fears to support its doctrines. It carries on controversy, not with reasons, but with threats and bribes. If it employs reasons, it does so not in virtue of any powers which belong to it as a government. Thus, instead of a contest between argument and argument, we have a contest between argument and force. Instead of a contest in which truth, from the natural constitution of the human mind, has a decided advantage over falsehood, we have a contest, in which truth can be victorious only by accident.

And what, after all, is the security which this training gives to governments? Mr Southey would scarcely recommend, that discussion should be more effectually shackled, that public opinion should be more strictly disciplined into conformity with established institutions, than in Spain and Italy. Yet we know that the restraints which exist in Spain and Italy have not prevented atheism from spreading among the educated classes, and especially among those whose office it is to minister at the altars of God. All our readers know how, at the time of the French Revolution, priest after priest came forward to declare that his doctrine, his ministry, his whole life, had been a lie,—a mummery during which he could scarcely compose his countenance sufficiently to carry on the imposture. This was the case of a false, or at least a grossly corrupted religion. Let us take, then, the case of all others the most favourable to Mr Southey's argument. Let us take that form of religion, which he holds to be the purest, the system of the Arminian part of the Church of England. Let us take the form of government which he most admires and regrets, the government of England in the time of Charles the First. Would he wish to see a closer connexion between church and state than then existed? Would he wish for more powerful ecclesiastical tribunals? for a more zealous king? for a more active primate? Would he wish to see a more complete monopoly of public instruction given to the Established Church? Could any government do more to train the people in the way in which he would have them go? And in what did all this training end? The Report of the State of the Province of Canterbury, delivered by Laud to his Master at the close of 1639, represents the Church of England as in the highest and most palmy state. So effectually had the government pursued that policy which Mr Southey wishes to see revived, that there was scarcely the least appearance of dissent. Most of the bishops stated that all was well among their flocks. Seven or eight persons in the diocese of Peterborough had seemed refractory to the church, but had made ample submission. In Norfolk and Suffolk all whom there had been reason to suspect had made profession of conformity, and appeared to observe it strictly. It is confessed that there was a little difficulty in bringing some of the vulgar in Suffolk to take the sacrament at the rails in the chancel. This was the only open instance of non-conformity which the vigilant eye of Laud could find in all the dioceses of his twenty-one suffragans, on the very eve of a revolution, in which primate and church, and monarch and monarchy, were to perish together.

At which time would Mr Southey pronounce the constitution more secure; in 1639, when Laud presented this Report to Charles, or now, when thousands of meetings openly collect millions of dissenters, when designs against the tithes are openly avowed, when books attacking not only the Establishment, but the first principles of Christianity, are openly sold in the streets? The signs of discontent, he tells us, are stronger in England now than in France when the States-General met; and hence he would have us infer that a revolution like that of France may be at hand. Does he not know that the danger of states is to be estimated, not by what breaks out of the public mind, but by what stays in it? Can he conceive any thing more terrible than the situation of a government which rules without apprehension over a people of hypocrites,—which is flattered by the press, and cursed in the inner chambers—which exults in the attachment and obedience of its subjects, and knows not that those subjects are leagued against it in a free-masonry of hatred, the sign of which is every day conveyed in the glance of ten thousand eyes, the pressure of ten thousand hands, and the tone of ten thousand voices? Profound and ingenious policy! Instead of curing the disease, to remove those symptoms by which alone its nature can be known! To leave the serpent his deadly sting, and deprive him only of his warning rattle!

When the people whom Charles had so assiduously trained in the good way had rewarded his paternal care by cutting off his head, a new kind of training came into fashion. Another government arose, which, like the former, considered religion as its surest basis, and the religious discipline of the people as its first duty. Sanguinary laws were enacted against libertinism; profane pictures were burned; drapery was put on indecorous statues; the theatres were shut up; fast-days were numerous; and the Parliament resolved that no person should be admitted into any public employment, unless the House should be first satisfied of his vital godliness. We know what was the end of this training. We know that it ended in impiety, in filthy and heartless sensuality, in the dissolution of all ties of honour and morality. We know that at this very day scriptural phrases, scriptural names, perhaps some scriptural doctrines, excite disgust and ridicule, solely because they are associated with the austerity of that period.

Thus has the experiment of training the people in established forms of religion been twice tried in England on a large scale; once by Charles and Laud, and once by the Puritans. The High Tories of our time still entertain many of the feelings and opinions of Charles and Laud, though in a mitigated form; nor is it difficult to see that the heirs of the Puritans are still amongst us. It would be desirable that each of these parties should remember how little advantage or honour it formerly derived from the closest alliance with power,—that it fell by the support of rulers, and rose by their opposition,—that of the two systems, that in which the people were at any time being drilled, was always at that time the unpopular system,—that the training of the High Church ended in the reign of the Puritans, and the training of the Puritans in the reign of the harlots.

This was quite natural. Nothing is so galling and detestable to a people not broken in from the birth, as a paternal, or, in other words, a meddling government,—a government which tells them what to read, and say, and eat, and drink, and wear. Our fathers could not bear it two hundred years ago; and we are not more patient than they. Mr Southey thinks that the yoke of the church is dropping off, because it is loose. We feel convinced that it is borne only because it is easy, and that, in the instant in which an attempt is made to tighten it, it will be flung away. It will be neither the first nor the strongest yoke that has been broken asunder and trampled under foot in the day of the vengeance of England.

How far Mr Southey would have the government carry its measures for training the people in the doctrines of the church, we are unable to discover. In one passage Sir Thomas More asks with great vehemence,

'Is it possible that your laws should suffer the unbelievers to exist as a party?

'Vetitum est adeo sceleris nihil?'[1]

Montesinos answers. 'They avow themselves in defiance of the laws. The fashionable doctrine which the press at this time maintains is, that this is a matter in which the laws ought not to interfere, every man having a right, both to form what opinion he pleases upon religious subjects, and to promulgate that opinion.'

It is clear, therefore, that Mr Southey would not give full and perfect toleration to infidelity. In another passage, however, he observes, with some truth, though too sweepingly, that 'any degree of intolerance short of that full extent which the Papal Church exercises where it has the power, acts upon the opinions which it is intended to suppress, like pruning upon vigorous plants; they grow the stronger for it.' These two passages, put together, would lead us to the conclusion that, in Mr Southey's opinion, the utmost severity ever employed by the Roman Catholic Church in the days of its greatest power ought to be employed against unbelievers in England; in plain words, that Carlile and his shopmen ought to be burned in Smithfield, and that every person who, when called upon, should decline to make a solemn profession of Christianity, ought to suffer the same fate. We do not, however, believe that Mr Southey would recommend such a course, though his language would, in the case of any other writer, justify us in supposing this to be his meaning. His opinions form no system at all. He never sees, at one glance, more of a question than will furnish matter for one flowing and well-turned sentence; so that it would be the height of unfairness to charge him personally with holding a doctrine, merely because that doctrine is deducible, though by the closest and most accurate reasoning, from the premises which he has laid down. We are, therefore, left completely in the dark as to Mr Southey's opinions about toleration. Immediately after censuring the government for not punishing infidels, he proceeds to discuss the question of the Catholic disabilities—now, thank God, removed—and

[1] 'Is, then, no kind of crime forbidden?' (Ovid, *Metamorphoses*.)

defends them on the ground that the Catholic doctrines tend to persecution, and that the Catholics persecuted when they had power.

'They must persecute,' says he, 'if they believe their own creed, for conscience-sake; and if they do not believe it, they must persecute for policy; because it is only by intolerance that so corrupt and injurious a system can be upheld.'

That unbelievers should not be persecuted, is an instance of national depravity at which the glorified spirits stand aghast. Yet a sect of Christians is to be excluded from power, because those who formerly held the same opinions were guilty of persecution. We have said that we do not very well know what Mr Southey's opinion about toleration is. But, on the whole, we take it to be this, that everybody is to tolerate him, and that he is to tolerate nobody.

We will not be deterred by any fear of misrepresentation from expressing our hearty approbation of the mild, wise, and eminently Christian manner, in which the Church and the Government have lately acted with respect to blasphemous publications. We praise them for not having thought it necessary to encircle a religion pure, merciful, and philosophical,—a religion to the evidences of which the highest intellects have yielded,—with the defences of a false and bloody superstition. The ark of God was never taken till it was surrounded by the arms of earthly defenders. In captivity, its sanctity was sufficient to vindicate it from insult, and to lay the hostile fiend prostrate on the threshold of his own temple. The real security of Christianity is to be found in its benevolent morality, in its exquisite adaptation to the human heart, in the facility with which its scheme accommodates itself to the capacity of every human intellect, in the consolation which it bears to the house of mourning, in the light with which it brightens the great mystery of the grave. To such a system it can bring no addition of dignity or of strength, that it is part and parcel of the common law. It is not now for the first time left to rely on the force of its own evidences, and the attractions of its own beauty. Its sublime theology confounded the Grecian schools in the fair conflict of reason with reason. The bravest and wisest of the Cæsars found their arms and their policy unavailing when opposed to the weapons that were not carnal, and the kingdom that was not of this world. The victory which Porphyry and Diocletian failed to gain, is not, to all appearance, reserved for any of those who have in this age directed their attacks against the last restraint of the powerful, and the last hope of the wretched. The whole history of the Christian Religion shows, that she is in far greater danger of being corrupted by the alliance of power, than of being crushed by its opposition. Those who thrust temporal sovereignty upon her, treat her as their prototypes treated her author. They bow the knee, and spit upon her; they cry Hail! and smite her on the cheek; they put a sceptre into her hand, but it is a fragile reed; they crown her, but it is with thorns; they cover with purple the wounds which their own hands have inflicted on her; and inscribe magnificent titles over the cross on which they have fixed her to perish in ignominy and pain.

The general view which Mr Southey takes of the prospects of society is very gloomy; but we comfort ourselves with the consideration that Mr Southey is no prophet. He foretold, we remember, on the very eve of the abolition of the Test and Corporation Acts, that these hateful laws were immortal, and that pious minds would long be gratified by seeing the most solemn religious rite of the Church profaned, for the purpose of upholding her political supremacy. In the book before us, he says that Catholics cannot possibly be admitted into Parliament until those whom Johnson called 'the bottomless Whigs,' come into power. While the book was in the press, the prophecy was falsified, and a Tory of the Tories, Mr Southey's own favourite hero, won and wore that noblest wreath, 'Ob cives servatos.'[1]

The signs of the times, Mr Southey tells us, are very threatening. His fears for the country would decidedly preponderate over his hopes, but for his firm reliance on the mercy of God. Now, as we know that God has once suffered the civilised world to be overrun by savages, and the Christian religion to be corrupted by doctrines which made it, for some ages, almost as bad as Paganism, we cannot think it inconsistent with his attributes that similar calamities should again befall mankind.

We look, however, on the state of the world, and of this kingdom in particular, with much greater satisfaction, and with better hopes. Mr Southey speaks with contempt of those who think the savage state happier than the social. On this subject, he says, Rousseau never imposed on him even in his youth. But he conceives that a community which has advanced a little way in civilisation is happier than one which has made greater progress. The Britons in the time of Cæsar were happier, he suspects, than the English of the nineteenth century. On the whole, he selects the generation which preceded the Reformation

[1] 'For preserving the people.' The reference is to the Duke of Wellington who was Prime Minister when the Catholic Emancipation Act was passed.

as that in which the people of this country were better off than at any time before or since.

This opinion rests on nothing, as far as we can see, except his own individual associations. He is a man of letters; and a life destitute of literary pleasures seems insipid to him. He abhors the spirit of the present generation, the severity of its studies, the boldness of its enquiries, and the disdain with which it regards some old prejudices by which his own mind is held in bondage. He dislikes an utterly unenlightened age; he dislikes an investigating and reforming age. The first twenty years of the sixteenth century would have exactly suited him. They furnished just the quantity of intellectual excitement which he requires. The learned few read and wrote largely. A scholar was held in high estimation; but the rabble did not presume to think; and even the most enquiring and independent of the educated classes paid more reverence to authority, and less to reason, than is usual in our time. This is a state of things in which Mr Southey would have found himself quite comfortable; and, accordingly, he pronounces it the happiest state of things ever known in the world.

The savages were wretched, says Mr Southey; but the people in the time of Sir Thomas More were happier than either they or we. Now, we think it quite certain that we have the advantage over the contemporaries of Sir Thomas More, in every point in which they had any advantage over savages.

Mr Southey does not even pretend to maintain that the people in the sixteenth century were better lodged or clothed than at present. He seems to admit that in these respects there has been some little improvement. It is indeed a matter about which scarcely any doubt can exist in the most perverse mind, that the improvements of machinery have lowered the price of manufactured articles, and have brought within the reach of the poorest some conveniencies which Sir Thomas More or his master could not have obtained at any price.

The labouring classes, however, were, according to Mr Southey, better fed three hundred years ago than at present. We believe that he is completely in error on this point. The condition of servants in noble and wealthy families, and of scholars at the Universities, must surely have been better in those times than that of common day-labourers; and we are sure that it was not better than that of our workhouse paupers. From the household book of the Northumberland family, we find that in one of the greatest establishments of the kingdom the servants lived almost entirely on salt meat, without any bread at all. A

more unwholesome diet can scarcely be conceived. In the reign of
Edward the Sixth, the state of the students at Cambridge is described
to us, on the very best authority, as most wretched. Many of them dined
on pottage made of a farthing's worth of beef with a little salt and
oatmeal, and literally nothing else. This account we have from a contemporary master of St. Johns. Our parish poor now eat wheaten
bread. In the sixteenth century the labourer was glad to get barley,
and was often forced to content himself with poorer fare. In Harrison's
introduction to Holinshed we have an account of the state of our
working population in the 'golden days,' as Mr Southey calls them, of
good Queen Bess.

The gentilitie [says he] commonly provide themselves sufficiently of wheat for
their own tables, whylest their household and poore neighbours in some shires
are inforced to content themselves with rice or barleie; yea, and in time of
dearth, many with bread made eyther of beanes, peason, or otes, or of altogether, and some acornes among. I will not say that this extremity is oft so well
to be seen in time of plentie as of dearth; but if I should I could easily bring my
trial: for albeit there be much more grounde eared nowe almost in everye
place then hath beene of late yeares, yet such a price of corne continueth in
eache towne and markete, without any just cause, that the artificer and poore
labouring man is not able to reach unto it, but is driven to content himself with
horse-corne; I mean beanes, peason, otes, tares, and lintelles.

We should like to see what the effect would be of putting any parish
in England now on allowance of 'horse-corne.' The helotry of Mammon are not, in our day, so easily enforced to content themselves as the
peasantry of that happy period, as Mr Southey considers it, which elapsed
between the fall of the feudal and the rise of the commercial tyranny.

'The people,' says Mr Southey, 'are worse fed than when they were
fishers.' And yet in another place he complains that they will not eat
fish. 'They have contracted,' says he, 'I know not how, some obstinate
prejudice against a kind of food at once wholesome and delicate, and
everywhere to be obtained cheaply and in abundance, were the demand
for it as general as it ought to be.' It is true that the lower orders have
an obstinate prejudice against fish. But hunger has no such obstinate
prejudices. If what was formerly a common diet is now eaten only in
times of severe pressure, the inference is plain. The people must be fed
with what they at least think better food than that of their ancestors.

The advice and medicine which the poorest labourer can now obtain,
in disease or after an accident, is far superior to what Henry the Eighth
could have commanded. Scarcely any part of the country is out of the

reach of practitioners, who are probably not so far inferior to Sir Henry Halford as they are superior to Sir Anthony Denny. That there has been a great improvement in this respect Mr Southey allows. Indeed he could not well have denied it. 'But,' says he, 'the evils for which these sciences are the palliative, have increased since the time of the Druids, in a proportion that heavily overweighs the benefit of improved therapeutics.' We know nothing either of the diseases or the remedies of the Druids. But we are quite sure that the improvement of medicine has far more than kept pace with the increase of disease during the last three centuries. This is proved by the best possible evidence. The term of human life is decidedly longer in England than in any former age, respecting which we possess any information on which we can rely. All the rants in the world about picturesque cottages and temples of Mammon will not shake this argument. No test of the state of society can be named so decisive as that which is furnished by bills of mortality. That the lives of the people of this country have been gradually lengthening during the course of several generations, is as certain as any fact in statistics, and that the lives of men should become longer and longer, while their physical condition, during life, is becoming worse and worse, is utterly incredible.

Let our readers think over these circumstances. Let them take into the account the sweating sickness and the plague. Let them take into the account that fearful disease which first made its appearance in the generation to which Mr Southey assigns the palm of felicity, and raged through Europe with a fury at which the physician stood aghast, and before which the people were swept away by thousands. Let them consider the state of the northern counties, constantly the scene of robberies, rapes, massacres, and conflagrations. Let them add to all this the fact that seventy-two thousand persons suffered death by the hands of the executioner during the reign of Henry the Eighth, and judge between the nineteenth and the sixteenth century.

We do not say that the lower orders in England do not suffer severe hardships. But, in spite of Mr Southey's assertions, and in spite of the assertions of a class of politicians, who, differing from Mr Southey in every other point, agree with him in this, we are inclined to doubt whether they really suffer greater physical distress than the labouring classes of the most flourishing countries of the Continent.

It will scarcely be maintained that the lazzaroni[1] who sleep under the porticos of Naples, or the beggars who besiege the convents of Spain,

1 'Beggars'.

are in a happier situation than the English commonalty. The distress
which has lately been experienced in the northern part of Germany,
one of the best governed and most prosperous districts of Europe, sur-
passes, if we have been correctly informed, any thing which has of late
years been known among us. In Norway and Sweden the peasantry are
constantly compelled to mix bark with their bread, and even this
expedient has not always preserved whole families and neighbour-
hoods from perishing together of famine. An experiment has lately been
tried in the kingdom of the Netherlands, which has been cited to
prove the possibility of establishing agricultural colonies on the waste-
lands of England; but which proves to our minds nothing so clearly as
this, that the rate of subsistence to which the labouring classes are
reduced in the Netherlands is miserably low, and very far inferior to
that of the English paupers. No distress which the people here have
endured for centuries, approaches to that which has been felt by the
French in our own time. The beginning of the year 1817, was a time of
great distress in this island. But the state of the lowest classes here was
luxury compared with that of the people of France. We find in
Magendie's *Journal de Physiologe Experimentale*, a paper on a point of
physiology connected with the distress of that season. It appears that
the inhabitants of six departments, Aix, Jura, Doubs, Haute Saone,
Vosges, and Saone et Loire, were reduced first to oatmeal and potatoes,
and at last to nettles, bean-stalks, and other kinds of herbage fit only
for cattle; that when the next harvest enabled them to eat barley-
bread, many of them died from intemperate indulgence in what they
thought an exquisite repast; and that a dropsy of a peculiar description
was produced by the hard fare of the year. Dead bodies were found on
the roads and in the fields. A single surgeon dissected six of these, and
found the stomach shrunk, and filled with the unwholesome aliments
which hunger had driven men to share with beasts. Such extremity of
distress as this is never heard of in England, or even in Ireland. We are,
on the whole, inclined to think, though we would speak with diffidence
on a point on which it would be rash to pronounce a positive judgment
without a much longer and closer investigation than we have bestowed
upon it, that the labouring classes of this island, though they have their
grievances and distresses, some produced by their own improvidence,
some by the errors of their rulers, are on the whole better off as to
physical comforts, than the inhabitants of any equally extensive
district of the old world. On this very account, suffering is more
acutely felt and more loudly bewailed here than elsewhere. We must take

into the account the liberty of discussion, and the strong interest which the opponents of a ministry always have to exaggerate the extent of the public disasters. There are many parts of Europe in which the people quietly endure distress that here would shake the foundations of the state,—in which the inhabitants of a whole province turn out to eat grass with less clamour than one Spitalfields weaver would make here, if the overseers were to put him on barley-bread. In those new countries in which a civilized population has at its command a boundless extent of the richest soil, the condition of the labourer is probably happier than in any society which has lasted for many centuries. But in the old world we must confess ourselves unable to find any satisfactory record of any great nation, past or present, in which the working classes have been in a more comfortable situation than in England during the last thirty years. When this island was thinly peopled, it was barbarous. There was little capital; and that little was insecure. It is now the richest and the most highly civilized spot in the world; but the population is dense. Thus we have never known that golden age, which the lower orders in the United States are now enjoying. We have never known an age of liberty, of order, and of education, an age in which the mechanical sciences were carried to a great height, yet in which the people were not sufficiently numerous to cultivate even the most fertile valleys. But, when we compare our own condition with that of our ancestors, we think it clear that the advantages arising from the progress of civilisation have far more than counterbalanced the disadvantages arising from the progress of population. While our numbers have increased tenfold, our wealth has increased a hundred fold. Though there are so many more people to share the wealth now existing in the country than there were in the sixteenth century, it seems certain, that a greater share falls to almost every individual, than fell to the share of any of the corresponding class in the sixteenth century. The King keeps a more splendid court. The establishments of the nobles are more magnificent. The esquires are richer, the merchants are richer, the shopkeepers are richer. The servingman, the artisan, and the husbandman, have a more copious and palatable supply of food, better clothing, and better furniture. This is no reason for tolerating abuses, or for neglecting any means of ameliorating the condition of our poorer countrymen. But it is a reason against telling them, as some of our philosophers are constantly telling them, that they are the most wretched people who ever existed on the face of the earth.

We have already adverted to Mr Southey's amusing doctrine about national wealth. A state, says he, cannot be too rich; but a people may be too rich. His reason for thinking this, is extremely curious.

A people may be too rich, because it is the tendency of the commercial, and more especially, of the manufacturing system, to collect wealth rather than to diffuse it. Where wealth is necessarily employed in any of the speculations of trade, its increase is in proportion to its amount. Great capitalists become like pikes in a fish-pond, who devour the weaker fish; and it is but too certain, that the poverty of one part of the people seems to increase in the same ratio as the riches of another. There are examples of this in history. In Portugal, when the high tide of wealth flowed in from the conquests in Africa and the East, the effect of that great influx was not more visible in the augmented splendour of the court, and the luxury of the higher ranks, than in the distress of the people.

Mr Southey's instance is not a very fortunate one. The wealth which did so little for the Portuguese was not the fruit, either of manufactures or of commerce carried on by private individuals. It was the wealth, not of the people, but of the government and its creatures, of those who, as Mr Southey thinks, can never be too rich. The fact is, that Mr Southey's proposition is opposed to all history, and to the phenomena which surround us on every side. England is the richest country in Europe, the most commercial, and the most manufacturing. Russia and Poland are the poorest countries in Europe. They have scarcely any trade, and none but the rudest manufactures. Is wealth more diffused in Russia and Poland than in England? There are individuals in Russia and Poland, whose incomes are probably equal to those of our richest countrymen. It may be doubted, whether there are not, in those countries, as many fortunes of eighty thousand a-year, as here. But are there as many fortunes of five thousand a-year, or of one thousand a-year? There are parishes in England, which contain more people of between five hundred and three thousand pounds a-year, than could be found in all the dominions of the Emperor Nicholas. The neat and commodious houses which have been built in London and its vicinity, for people of this class, within the last thirty years, would of themselves form a city larger than the capitals of some European kingdoms. And this is the state of society in which the great proprietors have devoured the smaller!

The cure which Mr Southey thinks that he has discovered is worthy of the sagacity which he has shown in detecting the evil. The calamities arising from the collection of wealth in the hands of a few capitalists are to be remedied by collecting it in the hands of one great capitalist, who has no conceivable motive to use it better than other capitalists,—the all-devouring state.

It is not strange that, differing so widely from Mr Southey as to the past progress of society, we should differ from him also as to its probable destiny. He thinks, that to all outward appearance, the country is hastening to destruction; but he relies firmly on the goodness of God. We do not see either the piety, or the rationality, of thus confidently expecting that the Supreme Being will interfere to disturb the common succession of causes and effects. We, too, rely on his goodness,—on his goodness as manifested, not in extraordinary interpositions, but in those general laws which it has pleased him to establish in the physical and in the moral world. We rely on the natural tendency of the human intellect to truth, and on the natural tendency of society to improvement. We know no well-authenticated instance of a people which has decidedly retrograded in civilisation and prosperity, except from the influence of violent and terrible calamities,— such as those which laid the Roman Empire in ruins, or those which, about the beginning of the sixteenth century, desolated Italy. We know of no country which, at the end of fifty years of peace and tolerably good government, has been less prosperous than at the beginning of that period. The political importance of a state may decline, as the balance of power is disturbed by the introduction of new forces. Thus the influence of Holland and of Spain is much diminished. But are Holland and Spain poorer than formerly? We doubt it. Other countries have outrun them. But we suspect that they have been positively, though not relatively, advancing. We suspect that Holland is richer than when she sent her navies up the Thames,—that Spain is richer than when a French king was brought captive to the footstool of Charles the Fifth.

History is full of the signs of this natural progress of society. We see in almost every part of the annals of mankind how the industry of individuals, struggling up against wars, taxes, famines, conflagrations, mischievous prohibitions, and more mischievous protections, creates faster than governments can squander, and repairs whatever invaders can destroy. We see the capital of nations increasing, and all the arts of life approaching nearer and nearer to perfection, in spite of the grossest corruption and the wildest profusion on the part of rulers.

The present moment is one of great distress. But how small will that distress appear when we think over the history of the last forty years;— a war, compared with which, all other wars sink into insignificance;—

377

taxation, such as the most heavily taxed people of former times could not have conceived;—a debt larger than all the public debts that ever existed in the world added together;—the food of the people studiously rendered dear;—the currency imprudently debased, and imprudently restored. Yet is the country poorer than in 1790? We fully believe that, in spite of all the misgovernment of her rulers, she has been almost constantly becoming richer and richer. Now and then there has been a stoppage, now and then a short retrogression; but as to the general tendency there can be no doubt. A single breaker may recede, but the tide is evidently coming in.

If we were to prophesy that in the year 1930, a population of fifty millions, better fed, clad, and lodged than the English of our time, will cover these islands,—that Sussex and Huntingdonshire will be wealthier than the wealthiest parts of the West-Riding of Yorkshire now are,— that cultivation, rich as that of a flower-garden, will be carried up to the very tops of Ben Nevis and Helvellyn,—that machines, constructed on principles yet undiscovered, will be in every house,—that there will be no highways but rail-roads, no travelling but by steam,—that our debt, vast as it seems to us, will appear to our great-grandchildren a trifling encumbrance, which might easily be paid off in a year or two,—many people would think us insane. We prophesy nothing; but this we say—If any person had told the Parliament which met in perplexity and terror after the crash in 1720, that in 1830 the wealth of England would surpass all their wildest dreams—that the annual revenue would equal the principal of that debt which they considered as an intolerable burden—that for one man of £10,000 then living, there would be five men of £50,000; that London would be twice as large and twice as populous, and that nevertheless the mortality would have diminished to one-half what it then was,—that the post-office would bring more into the exchequer than the excise and customs had brought in together under Charles II,—that stage-coaches would run from London to York in twenty-four hours—that men would sail without wind, and would be beginning to ride without horses—our ancestors would have given as much credit to the prediction as they gave to *Gulliver's Travels*. Yet the prediction would have been true; and they would have perceived that it was not altogether absurd, if they had considered that the country was then raising every year a sum which would have purchased the fee-simple of the revenue of the Plantagenets—ten times what supported the government of Elizabeth —three times what, in the time of Oliver Cromwell, had been thought intolerably oppressive. To almost all men the state of things under which they have been used to live seems to be the necessary state of things. We have heard it said, that five per cent is the natural interest of money, that twelve is the natural number of a jury, that forty shillings is the natural qualification of a county voter. Hence it is, that though, in every age, every body knows that up to his own time progressive improvement has been taking place, nobody seems to reckon on any improvement during the next generation. We cannot absolutely prove that those are in error who tell us that society has reached a turning point—that we have seen our best days. But so said all who came before us, and with just as much apparent reason. 'A million a-year will beggar us,' said the patriots of 1640. 'Two millions a-year will grind the country to powder,' was the cry in 1660. 'Six millions a-year, and a debt of fifty millions!' exclaimed Swift—'the high allies have been the ruin of us.' 'A hundred and forty millions of debt!' said Junius— 'well may we say that we owe Lord Chatham more than we shall ever pay, if we owe him such a load as this.' 'Two hundred and forty millions of debt!' cried all the statesmen of 1783 in chorus—'what abilities, or what economy on the part of a minister, can save a country so burdened?' We know that if, since 1783, no fresh debt had been incurred, the increased resources of the country would have enabled us to defray that burden, at which Pitt, Fox and Burke stood aghast—to defray it over and over again, and that with much lighter taxation than what we have actually borne. On what principle is it, that when we see nothing but improvement behind us, we are to expect nothing but deterioration before us?

It is not by the intermeddling of Mr Southey's idol—the omniscient and omnipotent State—but by the prudence and energy of the people, that England has hitherto been carried forward in civilisation; and it is to the same prudence and the same energy that we now look with comfort and good hope. Our rulers will best promote the improvement of the people by strictly confining themselves to their own legitimate duties—by leaving capital to find its most lucrative course, commodities their fair price, industry and intelligence their natural reward, idleness and folly their natural punishment—by maintaining peace, by defending property, by diminishing the price of law, and by observing strict economy in every department of the state. Let the Government do this—the People will assuredly do the rest.

114. From an unsigned review, *Fraser's Magazine*

June 1830, i, 584–600

From an article criticizing Macaulay's review of *Colloquies* (No. 113). The article commences with a lengthy attack upon the *Edinburgh Review* and its Whig contributors and upon Macaulay's political and literary career.

Mr. Southey has read much, has written much, and, by his critic's confession, has 'exercised considerable influence on the most enlightened generation of the most enlightened people that ever existed.' Now, this 'most enlightened generation of the most enlightened people that ever existed' have not been led to believe in Mr. Southey's mere assertion, from any persuasion of his being a prophet or an evangelist—they have believed in him, and been influenced by his writings, from the thorough and heartfelt conviction of their truth. Men are not apt to lend their credulity to their fellows merely on the strength of flat and naked positions; and the greater the enlightenment of such men, the stiffer is the stubbornness of their pride and obstinacy in yielding their faith as converts to new promulgations of opinions. If, in process of time, they confess to the influence of any such promulgation, we may be sure that their judgments have been convinced by the argumentative elucidations of the new opinionist. The effect most directly demonstrates the cause. The wisdom, moreover, of every age, is sufficient for that age to which it owes its birth. It may be little or great, faulty or perfect—this in nowise affects our argument. If, by universal consent, or by the consent of the majority, or any considerable party in the community, an individual is allowed the intellectual supremacy, by that very act not only is his equality to his contemporaries, or partial super-excellence over them, acknowledged, but his complete and unqualified superiority over them *must* also be admitted. It does not require any very bright comprehension to understand that the first man of every age has anticipated that age. How stands it, therefore, with Mr. Southey? What is his intellectual position in this 'most enlightened generation?' Even his enemy, Mr. Thomas Babington Macauley, confesses that he has exercised '*considerable* influence.' This phrase holds a self-contradiction. In points of understanding there can be no half measures,—there can be no qualifications —no divisions or subdivisions of beliefs or leanings; it must be entirely, or in nowise. Either a teacher enjoys influence, or he does not. If the former, it must be on given and precisely defined grounds; and again, if so, his influence is absolute over his own sphere of action or domination. It is the same with this intellectual supremacy as with temporal sovereignty—the power of kings is defined, and within that definition it is absolute: were it not so, there would be a constant interference with their actions, and kings would soon find themselves in reality unkinged—or, like our friend Sancho in his grand government of Barataria, who, when he thought himself the lord of 'all he surveyed,' discovered, to his woe, that he was, in his actions, the most circumscribed of mortals. How fares it, then, with our mighty Logician, Macauleides? If our reasoning be worth a rush, his admission as to Mr. Southey's 'influence on the most enlightened generation of the most enlightened people that ever existed,' pulls him one way, whilst his hollow assertion that 'in the mind of Mr. Southey reason has no place at all,' necessarily pulls him in the opposite direction; and supposing that the argumentative Cantab were squatted between two stools, the 'enlightened generation' would draw away one—Mr. Southey's want of 'reason' would draw away the other—and bounce on the ground would come the logician, in the very midst and heyday of his triumphant feats of logomachy. We may conclude this paragraph by quoting Mr. Macaulay's own glittering verbiage against himself:— 'He does not seem to know what an argument is,' and 'two contradictory propositions cannot be undeniable truths.' And thus have we, we trust, used our speech,

> until it has return'd
> His terms of treason doubled down his throat.[1]

So much for the general argument. We will now say a word or two with respect to Mr. Southey in particular.

Mr. Southey is one of the most accomplished scholars of which this country has ever boasted—and accomplished scholarship predicates very pointedly, we think, years of deep study, various reading, thought,

[1] Shakespeare, *Richard II*.

and reflection. General history, moreover, has been Mr. Southey's favourite branch of study—and 'History is Philosophy teaching by example.'. . .

So vast has been his reading, that, we are led to opine, if the truth were known, it would be found that Mr. Southey, the scholar, had forgotten more than Mr. Thomas Babington Macauley, the logician and Cantab, had ever contrived to scrape together into that receptacle for polite education of which we have ventured to make mention at the commencement of this article.

The Laureate has, moreover, been noted as one of the most effectual controversial writers of his day; and as controversy cannot be carried on without argument, and general reputation for any quality is not to be acquired by charlatanism—and as the Laureate has gained a general reputation for his feats as such controversial writer, we need say no more on this subject.

Mr. Thomas Babington Macauley is eternally crowing up his own logical efficiency, and the illogical and common-place arguments of every other individual. Could he persuade the world of these facts, it were well for the Cantab—but, alas! his assertions pass by his auditory even as the idle wind to which they pay not the slightest observance. In reference to Mr. Southey's alleged weakness in argumentation, thus stands the fact:—That the Laureate is not a keen disputant, cannot be denied—that his writings are not stuck full of philosophical knotti-nesses and metaphysical intertwistings, is equally so;—but it is also undeniable, that, in the most beautiful style of which the English language is susceptible, and of which our literature can boast, the theories which his mind has conceived, the actions of past ages which his patience and industry have attained, and those other actions which (his existence having been cast at the period which witnessed the most remarkable circumstances and events that mankind were ever fated to behold) his wondering eyes have witnessed, have been severally noted down and recounted to the world at large, whilst his philan-thropic bosom glowed with the ardent and Christian hope that his fellow-creatures would employ his narratives in practical and bene-ficial adaptation. Such has been the tendency of all Mr. Southey's literary exertions. With such views, therefore, the mode of composition and method of argument which he has employed have been well selected. Mankind are contented to receive instruction in intelligible language, and are fain to turn their backs on the fantastic tricks and incomprehensible cackle of logomachising ganders and self-vaunting pseudo-persifleurs and jargonists—leaving them to the contemplation of their own egregious contortions of body, their own super-exquisite jaw openings and oral crookedness, in the respective mirrors of their own vanity. . . .

'Mr. Southey's political system,' says his critic, 'is just what we might expect from a man who regards politics not as a matter of science, but as a matter of taste and feeling. All his schemes of government have been inconsistent with themselves. In his youth he was a republican; yet, as he tells us in his preface to these *Colloquies*, he was, even then, opposed to the Catholic claims,' &c.—we have already given the whole of the paragraph. In answer, we reply briefly: 1. Although Mr. Southey may regard politics 'not as a matter of science, but as a matter of taste and feeling,' it behoves not Mr. Macauley to bring the charge of inconsistency against the Laureate in particular— but rather against those members of his own House who have wantonly and impudently forfeited their pledged faith to their country— and apostatised and ratted from their own confiding party for a worse motive than defect of taste or misapplication of feeling—FOR BASE WORLDLY EMOLUMENT AND A HIRELING STIPEND.—2. To say of a young man that in his youth he was a republican, is almost the best praise that can be yielded to the purity and goodness of his nature. A ripened judgment is a thing unnatural for youth—and, without a ripened judgment, it is impossible to say to a certainty that republicanism is one of those errant false lights which have worked infinite woe to the world. But it is natural that a youth, even in his youngest years, should, if he be possessed of quick feelings and warmth of heart, have some bias; and it is, further, natural that he should lean towards that, whatever it may be, which is brought nearest to a heart so liable to excitation. Now, the story of republican Rome and republican Greece (in the usual course of study) is forced upon him as a subject for every day's, every hour's consideration, until his imagination becoming inflamed by contemplating the actions of a Miltiades, and Themistocles, and Aristides,—of an Epaminondas, Phocyon, and Thrasybulus,—of a Coriolanus and Cincinnatus,—of a Scipio and Regulus;—he imagines that all blessings and all glory in governments must flow from republics; and, consequently, he is induced to become a warm republican, until a further knowledge of the constitution and essence of happiness induces an alteration in his opinions. Viewing the matter in this light, we are confident that every reader will consider the republicanism of boyhood and early youth as not only venial, but praiseworthy.—

3. Though Mr. Southey be an ultra-Tory, there is no necessity for following precisely along the ruts and in the footmarks made by every other ultra-Tory that ever preceded him.—4. That Mr. Southey bears not mortal enmity to those individuals who have been politically opposed to him, may be proved from his recent *Life of John Bunyan.* The amplest justice has been done to that obstinate, yet honest nonconformist; and the kindness of feeling which he has evinced towards the old offender and scurrilist, Mr. Hone, has drawn upon himself the displeasure of his own party.—5. Democracy does not predicate the removal of religious distinctions. The religion of Rome, and the schools of ancient philosophy, continued in vigour, notwithstanding the existence of democracy.

We now turn to that paragraph wherein is contained Mr. Southey's confession against butchers. And, 1. Because butchers are in an employment which is beneficial to society, is no reason why they, by the wear and tear of that employment, should not be divested of all humanity, as much as coal-heavers are rendered unfit for the society of the Duke of Wellington, or nightmen or scavengers for associating with Sir Robert Peel, or Mr. Dawson, or the Bishop of London.—2. Though 'the certain law or custom' prejudicial to the milky characters of butchers, 'may never have existed but in the imaginations of old women,' still the very inference from its being, by Mr. Macauley's own acknowledgment, habitual to the imaginations of old women— who, Heaven knows, form perhaps a larger portion of the community than the *Athenian* critic will allow—is, that it has somewhat of the character, and therefore somewhat of the truth, of a popular proverb. —3. 'Looking with favour on a soldier' argues not, in respect to Mr. Southey, 'that human blood is by no means an object of so much disgust as the hides and paunches of cattle;' or that he loves the stench of human carnage, because, 'in 1814, he poured forth poetical maledictions on all who talked of peace with Buonaparte.' If this were true of the Laureate, Mr. Pitt, and the late Lord Melville, and his present Majesty, and his immortal father, and the late Lords Liverpool and Castlereagh, and the Duke of Wellington, and Sir Walter Scott, and Mr. Wordsworth, with every man who ever lighted a farthing rushlight in illumination of the glorious successes of our national armies, would severally be fiends of equal magnitude with the quiet, unobtrusive, placable Mr. Southey.—4. The ecstasy which broke forth in *The Poet's Pilgrimage* is very good 'poetical inspiration,' notwithstanding the shallow-pated Mr. Thomas Babington Macauley's naked assertion to the contrary; and if the magpie-tongued criticaster had turned up to the poem, he would have paused, and *perhaps* felt, a secret shame at bringing his atrocious charge against the gentle laker;—first, because his opening motto from Pindar shews that his poetical mind was rhapsodising over the brilliance of national triumph.—Secondly, because the proem would have presented as sweet a family picture as the kindest-hearted of poets ever drew. The man who can without hesitation—nay, with pleasure—participate in the youthful frolics of children, and who, even after having arrived at the maturity of human life, still retains in his bosom the desire for self-improvement, and the unsubdued spark of youthful emulation, is not exactly the individual whose nostrils are to be delighted by the fetid effluvia steaming over a field of slaughtered bodies. . . .

But why should he have singled out Mr. Southey for his fierce and foul vituperation? No one can impugn the harmless tenure of Mr. Southey's life, or his retiring nature (particularly since he refused a seat in that very sapient assembly, of which Mr. Macauley is so bright and particular a star), or the sincerity of his faith, or his earnest wish to further the improvement of his fellow-creatures, or the soundness of his scholarship. Now, for any, or all these reasons, however Mr. Macauley may differ from the Laureate, surely the latter, if the Cantab be a saint, or even a Christian, deserves respectful consideration and fair usage, to say nothing of love, charity, mercy, and forbearance— qualities which, by their beauty of conduct on all occasions, the saints have identified with themselves. But his false reasonings and low abuse of the Laureate prove Mr. Thomas Babington Macauley to be no whit better than the general run of his sinful fellow-creatures. The Laureate has made for himself a fair reputation—the Cantab has made for himself no reputation at all for any thing fair or manly—the moral beggar, therefore, hates his richer neighbour, and that hatred is mani- fested in the exquisite piece of criticism, the beauties of which we have done all that in us lay to shew forth to the admiration of an enraptured world.

115. John Stuart Mill on Southey

October 1831

From a letter to John Sterling, 20–22 October 1831. Reprinted from *The Earlier Letters of John Stuart Mill, 1812–1848*, ed. F. E. Mineka (Toronto, 1963), i, pp. 82–3.

During July and August 1831 Mill visited the Lake District, 'where I saw much splendid scenery, and also saw a great deal both of Wordsworth and Southey'.

I also saw a great deal of Southey, who is a very different kind of man, very inferior to Wordsworth in the higher powers of intellect, & entirely destitute of his philosophic spirit, but a remarkably pleasing & likeable man. I never could understand him till lately; that is, I never could reconcile the tone of such of his writings as I had read, with what his friends said of him: I could only get rid of the notion of his being insincere, by supposing him to be extremely fretful and irritable: but when I came to read his *Colloquies*, in which he has put forth much more than in any other work, of the natural man, as distinguished from the writer aiming at a particular effect, I found there a kind of connecting link between the two parts of his character, & formed very much the same notion of him which I now have after seeing & conversing with him. He seems to me to be a man of gentle feelings & bitter opinions. His opinions make him think a great many things abominable which are not so; against which accordingly he thinks it would be right, & suitable to the fitness of things, to express great indignation: but if he really feels this indignation, it is only by a voluntary act of the imagination that he conjures it up, by representing the thing to his own mind in colours suited to that passion: now, when he knows an individual & feels disposed to like him, although that individual may be placed in one of the condemned categories, he does not conjure up this phantom & feels therefore no principle of repugnance, nor excites any. No one can hold a greater number of the opinions & few have more of the qualities, which he condemns, than some whom he has known intimately & befriended for many years: at the same time he would discuss their faults & weaknesses or vices with the greatest possible freedom in talking about them. It seems to me that Southey is altogether out of place in the existing order of society: his attachment to old institutions & his condemnation of the practices of those who administer them, cut him off from sympathy & communion with both halves of mankind. Had he lived before radicalism & infidelity became prevalent, he would have been the steady advocate of the moral & physical improvement of the poorer classes & denouncer of the selfishness & supineness of those who ought to have considered the welfare of those classes as confided to their care. Possibly the essential one-sidedness of his mind might then have rendered him a democrat: but now the evils which he expects from increase of the power wielded by the democratic spirit such as it now is, have rendered him an aristocrat in principle without inducing him to make the slightest compromise with aristocratic vices and weaknesses. Consequently he is not liked by the Tories, while the Whigs and radicals abhor him.

116. Bulwer-Lytton on Southey

1833

From *England and the English* (2 vols, 1833) by the novelist Edward George Earle Lytton Bulwer-Lytton (1803–73), ii, pp. 59–60.

But the most various, scholastic, and accomplished of such of our literary contemporaries as have written works as well as articles, and prose as well as poetry—is, incontestably, Dr. Southey. *The Life of Nelson* is acknowledged to be the best biography of the day. *The Life of Wesley* and *The Book of the Church*, however adulterated by certain prepossessions and prejudices, are, as mere compositions, characterized by an equal simplicity and richness of style,—an equal dignity and an equal ease. No writer blends more happily the academical graces of the style of last century, with the popular vigour of that which distinguishes the present. His *Colloquies* are, we suspect, the work on which he chiefly prides himself, but they do not seem to me to contain the best characteristics of his genius. The work is overloaded with quotation and allusion, and, like Tarpeia, seems crushed beneath the weight of its ornaments; it wants the great charm of that simple verve which is so peculiarly Southeian. Were I to do justice to Southey's cast of mind—to analyse its properties and explain its apparent contradictions, I should fill the two volumes of this work with Southey alone. Suffice it *now* (another occasion to do him ampler justice may occur elsewhere,) to make two remarks in answer to the common charges against this accomplished writer. He is alleged to be grossly inconsistent in politics, and wholly unphilosophical in morals. I hold both these charges to spring from the coarse injustice of party. If ever a man wrote a complete vindication of himself—that vindication is to be found in Southey's celebrated *Letter* to a certain Member of Parliament; the triumphant dignity with which he puts aside each successive aspersion—the clearness with which, in that *Letter*, his bright integrity shines out through all the mists amidst which it voluntarily passes, no dispassionate man can mark and not admire. But he is not philosophical? —No,—rather say he is not logical; his philosophy is large and learned, but it is all founded on hypothesis, and is poetical not metaphysical.

THE DOCTOR

1834-47

Southey's only attempt at a novel. The first two volumes were published anonymously in 1834. Three further volumes appeared in 1835, 1837 and 1838. Volumes vi and vii were edited by Southey's son-in-law, J. W. Warter, in 1847. Warter also edited a one-volume edition in 1848.

Southey worked on *The Doctor* over a long period. In December 1815 he referred in a letter to 'a notion only half a day old' which he called 'Dr. Dove'. For the first time he alludes to the possibility of publication: 'There is so much of *Tristram Shandy* about it, that I think it will be proper to take the name of Stephen Yorickson Esqre in the title page. . . . So much of it is done, that I shall very probably put it to press in the spring' (Curry, ii, p. 130).

It was obvious from the sale of the first volume that the work would not be a notable financial success and Southey himself claimed that it had 'clearly failed' (*Life*, vi, p. 235).

117. John Gibson Lockhart, unsigned review, *Quarterly Review*

March 1834, li, 68–96

Extracts from the opening and conclusion of his review. For a note on Lockhart see No. 89.

This work has excited more attention than any one belonging, or approaching, to the class of *novels*, which has appeared in England for a considerable number of years; and we are not at all disposed to wonder that such should have been the case. It is broadly distinguished from the mass of books recently published in the same shape and form, both by excellencies of a very high order, and by defects, indicating such occasional contempt of sound judgment, and sense, and taste, as we can hardly suppose in a strong and richly cultivated mind, unless that mind should be in a certain measure under the influence of disease. The author says of one of his characters:—'He was born with one of those heads in which the thin partition that divides great wit from folly is wanting.' The partition in his own head would seem to be a moveable one. A clearer or a more vigorous understanding than he in his better parts exhibits, we have seldom encountered; but two-thirds of his performance look as if they might have been penned in the vestibule of Bedlam. The language, however, even where the matter is most absurd, retains the ease, the strength, and the purity of a true master of English; and there occur, ever and anon, in chapters over which no human being but a reviewer will ever travel for the second time, turns of expression which would of themselves justify us in pronouncing the author of this 'apish and fantastic' nondescript to be a man of genius.

The writer is often a wise one—but his attempts at what is now called *wit* are, in general, unsuccessful: nor can we speak much better of his humour, though he has undoubtedly a few passages which might make Heraclitus chuckle. With these rare exceptions, his jocularity is pedantic and chilling—his drollery wire-drawn, super-quaint,

Whistlecraftish. The *red* letters and mysterious monogram of his title-page—the *purple* German-text of his dedication to *the Bhow Begum Redora Niabarma*—his division of chapters into ante-initial, initial, and post-initial—his inter-chapters—his post-fixed preface, &c, &c.—what are all these things but paltry imitations of the poorest sort of fun in *Tristram Shandy*? All his jesting about bells, and 'the manly and English art' of bell-ringing, (excepting one *Dutch* quotation,) appears to us equally dolorous. As for his bitter sneers at Lord Byron—his clumsy and grossly affected contempt for Mr. Jeffrey—and the heavy mag-niloquence of his own self-esteem—we dismiss them at once in silence. They mark as evidently the disruption of the 'thin partition,' as his prolix babble on the garden-physic of his great-grandmother, the drivelling of the alchemists, and the succession of the mayors of Doncaster—or his right merry and conceited elaboration of one of the dirtiest of all the practical jokes in Rabelais.

If we were not quite serious in our suspicion that *The Doctor* is the work of a man who stands more in need of physic than of criticism, we should have felt it our duty to illustrate, by citations, the justice of the language which we have not hesitated to apply to so great a portion of these volumes. As it is, we willingly spare ourselves a thankless piece of trouble, and our readers a dose or two of dullness—and, indeed, of disgust. Let us henceforth drop a veil upon the moun-tain of dross and rubbish, and keep all our daylight for the gold and gems, which have made it worth the sifting.

One word only as to the outline. The author does not seem to have reflected that Rabelais adopted the broad grotesque of his plan—(and execution also)—because it would have been impossible for any man of that age, above all for a curé of Meudon, to satirize the baseness of French courtiers, and the hypocrisy of Romish priests—in any direct shape; or to have perceived that, after all, the great French humorist would have been infinitely more popular than he is, had he not pushed the system of *rambling* to such an extent as he has done. The same sort of thing might have been the result of a very little reflection on the personal position and character of the author of *Tristram Shandy*,—which work, of course, has been the more immediate prototype of *The Doctor*. Sterne was to the last, what we have no reason to believe that Rabelais was in the more advanced part of his life,—a profligate priest; and his buffoonery of manner was the shield rather than cloak of his licentiousness. Moreover, there is one very important particular in which Sterne's *plan*, with all its wildness, stands contrasted, to its own infinite advantage, against that of his anonymous imitator. The strange farrago of odd, yet often second-hand learning, for the purpose of exhibiting which *Tristram Shandy* was, no doubt, first conceived, is all, by the art of Sterne, poured out dramatically: the character of *My Father* is a most original conception, most happily worked out with a skill which can convert materials, apparently the most incongruous, to the one main design; and the same may be said of *Slop*. *The Doctor* seems to have been framed with exactly the same primary view—that of furnishing a pretext for the clearance of a rich commonplace book; but the author, after a few awkward attempts to avail himself, for this purpose, of the instrumentality of *his* hero's father and tutor, takes the office of showman openly into his own hands—and thenceforth the 'curiosities of literature,' of which *The Doctor* presents certainly a sequence not unworthy of being classed with D'Israeli's charming one, or with that in Southey's *Omniana*, are brought forth, so as hardly to help in any degree the development of any one of the characters in the book.

And who are these characters? First and foremost is Daniel Dove, M.D., late Surgeon-Apothecary in Doncaster—the hero of the book —'The Doctor.' Then there are his father, Daniel Dove the Elder, yeoman of Ingleton; his uncle, William Dove, a half-idiot; his rural pedagogue, Mr. Richard Guy; his old master, the *quondam* Halford of Doncaster, Philip Hopkins; and for heroines we have Dinah, the mother of the doctor, Deborah, his wife, and that wife's mother—of neither of whom, however, the desultory novelist has as yet found leisure to give us more than a few glimpses. Add to these some three or four *real* persons long since defunct, such as Dr. Green, the in his day celebrated quack of Penrith—one or two half insane recluses— and Mr. Rowland Dixon, the proprietor of a gigantic set of puppets, —and suppose descriptions and anecdotes of them and their odd doings swimming rare in a sea of quotations, prose and verse, serious and comic,—Latin, French, *Low*-Dutch—(N.B.—no High-Dutch)— Spanish, Portuguese, and, above all, English and Italian. There is such a total contempt of all the ordinary rules of story-telling, that half a volume is bestowed on the hero's infancy, and we then leap at once to his full-grown manhood. Forthwith the bells ring for his wedding; but ere we have seen the veil lifted from the face of the bride, the bride's mother fixes the author's attention, and *her* love story must take precedence of her daughter's—which last, accordingly, is not half told by the time that volume the second closes. What the author means to make of these heroes and heroines in the eight or eighteen volumes which we presume are yet to come, we can offer no sort of conjecture —no more, we are pretty sure, could the author himself at this hour.

[Quotes selected passages.]

Be this author who he may, the names which conjecture has banded about in connexion with his work imply, all and each of them, a strong impression of the ability and erudition which it evinces. At first, suspicion lighted almost universally, we believe, on the Poet Laureate himself; and certainly the moral, political, and literary doctrines of the book are such, in the main, as might have countenanced such a notion—nor do we hesitate to pay the language of the book the extraordinary compliment of saying that much of it also might have done even Mr. Southey no discredit; but surely, of all the gross errors, both in the conception and in the execution, to which we have already alluded, the least could never have been supposed to have come from him,—unless, perhaps, in some merely juvenile prolusion, casually dug up out of a long-forgotten cabinet; and their catalogue contains some items which even that theory could never have reconciled us to affiliate upon him. Of the real author of the work we happen to know he is ignorant; so we may spare ourselves further speculation on this head.

118. Henry Crabb Robinson on
The Doctor

1836–8

Three extracts from *Henry Crabb Robinson on Books and their Writers* (3 vols, 1938), ed. E. J. Morley.

(a) 23 January 1836

I finished this morning the first volume of *The Doctor*, which I shall be content with for the present. I have no doubt, whatever, that it is by Southey. Even its intolerance I fear does not exclude the idea. Towards the end he says of the Puritans: 'of whom it has long been the fashion to speak with respect instead of holding them up to contempt and infamy and abhorrence, which they have so richly merited'! This disgusts me so much that it has fixed me in the determination not to visit the Doctor [Southey] at Keswick this year. In this book there are beautiful serious chapters. The characters of the idiot and of the two Daniels are delightfully executed. The humour is coarse and the tone of the opinions harsh and sectarian with a sort of effort at good humour and kindness. Among the indications of its coming from Southey is the profusion of Spanish literature and old English odd citations. The only German book mentioned is one I gave him several years ago—all the *opinions religious and political are his.* [ii, p. 483.]

(b) 10 September 1837

I read through the second volume of *The Doctor*, having read (and already forgotten) the first volume at Wordsworth's a year and half ago. I was amused by the book in spite of merely tedious topographical detail about Doncaster, and though I was disgusted by the illiberal spirit and no slight portion of cant scattered throughout. The transition from the grave to comic scenes is in Wordsworth's eyes abrupt and uncomfortable, and he, as well as myself, thinks the comic passages much less pleasing than the serious. In the first two volumes, the Doctor certainly excites no interest. He is the theme of perpetual praise, but the author must ask for credit that his hero deserves this praise. The reader would not find it out for anything that he himself says and does. I think it, after all, by no means certain that Southey is the author, and do not wish to consider him as such on account of an unamiable tone running through the whole, and Southey is a most amiable man. [ii, p. 537.]

(c) 31 December 1838
Reading Southey's *Doctor*, volume three: it is pretty light reading. But oh! how void of thought, or, rather, how *thin* the thought compared with Carlyle's book[1]—at least, I find the third volume diffuse almost to tiresomeness. [ii, p. 560.]

119. Thomas Carlyle meets Southey

1835

This very evocative description of Southey occurs in a letter of 27 February to Alexander Carlyle. Reprinted from *Letters of Thomas Carlyle 1826–1836*, ed. C. E. Norton, ii, p. 284.

Southey is lean as a harrow; *dun* as a tobacco-*spluchan*;[2] *no* chin (I mean the smallest), *snubbed* Roman nose, vehement brown eyes, huge *white* head of hair; when he rises,—all legs together. We had considerable talk together: he is a man positive in his own Tory Church of England way; well informed, rational; a good man: but perhaps so striking for nothing as for his excitability and irritability, which I should judge to be pre-eminent even among Poets. We parted kindly; and might be ready to meet again. He lives at Keswick (in Cumberland there); thinks the world is sinking to ruin, and writes diligently.

[1] Robinson had been reading Carlyle's *History of the French Revolution*.
[2] 'Tobacco-pouch'.

120. George Ticknor, reunion with Southey

3 September 1835

From Ticknor's *Life, Letters, and Journals* (2 vols, 1876), ii, pp. 434–5, recounting a visit to Southey in Keswick. Ticknor had first met Southey in 1817 (see No. 82). The two men subsequently corresponded at infrequent intervals.

We came here by invitation to pass the evening with Southey, but we accepted the invitation with some hesitation, for Mrs. Southey has been several months hopelessly deranged, and is supposed now to be sinking away. . . . He received us very kindly, but was much moved when he showed me his only son, and reminded me that I had last seen him hardly three weeks old, in his cradle in the same room.

Southey was natural and kind, but evidently depressed, much altered since I saw him fifteen years ago, a little bent, and his hair quite white. He showed me the materials for his edition of Cowper and the beginning of the *Life*; the last work, he says, he shall ever do for the booksellers. Among the materials was the autograph manuscript of *John Gilpin*, and many letters. . . . He read us, too, about three cantos of his *Oliver Newman*,—the poem on American ground,—some of it fine, but the parts intended to be humorous in very bad taste. He showed me as many curious and rare manuscripts and books as I could look at, and told me that he means now to finish his history of Portugal and Portuguese literature; and if possible write a history of the Monastic Orders. If he does the last, it will be bitter enough. He says he has written no *Quarterly Review* for two years, and means to write no more; that reviews have done more harm than good, etc. In politics I was surprised to find him less desponding than Wordsworth, though perhaps more excited. He says, however, that Ireland will not be tranquillized without bloodshed, admits that Sir Robert Peel is not a great man, and that England is now desperately in want of really great minds to manage its affairs. His conversation was very various, sometimes quite remarkable, but never rich or copious like Wordsworth's, and never humorous or witty. It was rather abundant in matters of fact, and often in that way quite striking and effective.

121. Evaluation by Henry Crabb Robinson

29 January 1839

Extract from *Henry Crabb Robinson on Books and their Writers* (3 vols, 1938), ed. E. J. Morley, ii, pp. 566–7.

Looked over last night and this morning the new edition of Southey's works for the sake of the new matter—in prefaces. I found nothing in it to excite a desire to read again the poems I formerly read, or those I am unacquainted with—I have always thought more highly of Southey's prose works than his poems; but, believing him as a thinker to be either quite wrong or only partially right on all the great points of religion and politics, I cannot possibly rank him very highly. Still, he is a most excellent man and of great general ability and a beautiful stylist in prose.

122. Herman Merivale on Southey's poetry, *Edinburgh Review*

January 1839, lxviii, 354–76

From his unsigned review of the *Poetical Works* (1838).

Merivale (1806–74) was the eldest son of John Herman Merivale (see No. 53). He was a barrister who contributed regularly to the *Edinburgh Review* between 1832 and 1874. In later life he was successively Under-Secretary of State for the Colonies and for India.

There is a species of poetry which appears to belong exclusively to a period of advanced civilisation, and of which, indeed, it is impossible to conceive the existence without it. It is that of which the character consists in the imitation of nature, not as she appears in actual converse with man, or observation of external things, but as she is reflected in books. There are three worlds, so to speak, in each of which all men, of whose occupations literature forms a very serious part, may be said to live by turns—the world of real life—the world of imagination or fancy—the world of ideas and reflections derived from reading. Now, the second of these, which is the proper region of the poet, derives its substance and colouring chiefly from the first or the third, according to the character of the man, influenced by that of the age in which he lives. To the non-student, real life, with its manifold fields of observation, appears fresh and distinct; the ideas drawn from books are few and faint. In the studious man—that is, the *bona fide* slave of books, of whose waking hours more than half are spent in the strong application of the mind to literary subjects—the very reverse takes place. The colouring of external things grows to him fainter and fainter; his mind becomes more and more unable accurately to seize and define them; the past or the distant, seen through the medium of books, acquires daily more vividness, and becomes at last almost his only reality; unless his mind be forcibly drawn back to more natural objects by the influence of circumstances. Such a bookworm, if he turns poet, may be rich in description, pathetic or humorous, and accurate in delineation of character; but his compositions will always be remarkable for some of that air of artifice which seems almost inevitable in copies—studies, not from nature, but from pictures.

Let us contrast the different modes in which the thoughts and images acquired from reading are employed by poets to whom it is only an auxiliary, and those who use it as a principal source of their inspiration. It is difficult for us to realize to ourselves the progress of a mind such as that of Shakspeare, especially under such circumstances of life as his scanty biography reveals to us. But thus much is plain—that his faculties of observation must have been keen and active, used with the utmost interest, and affording the truest enjoyment; and that his imagination, creative as it is, must have constantly revelled in the production of images and sketches of things far beyond the ordinary limits of nature, yet derived from archetypes seen by him in nature, and never sinning against her fitness and proportion. In the course of his desultory reading he falls with avidity on those narratives of discovery in which the public took such intense delight in that age of eager, half-informed curiosity; the relation of Sir George Somers's trip to the Bermudas; the abridgement of Magellan's voyage in Master Robert Eden's *History of Travaile*, which tells us of a certain 'very tractable and pleasant gyant' whom the Portuguese navigator encountered on some desolate coast, and of the 'great devyll Setebos,' on whom the aforesaid giant and his fellows continually called. He finds a story ready to his hand in the pages of Turbervile—one of the authors whom, in his indolence, he is accustomed to consult, to save the labour of inventing a plot for the Globe or the Rose. The result is the *Tempest*—that most graceful of all compounds of human interest and supernatural agency. But how much of this exquisite production is really owing to the studies of its writer? A frame-work—the names and titles of a few personages—and a few hints for the construction of a magical island, and its fiendish aborigines. The rest is all his own—from Ariel, half-incorporated with the element whence he derives his name, to the veriest sons of earth, Trinculo and his sottish confederate, —all are the creatures of his wonderful imagination, or of a perception of dramatic truth more wonderful still.

How different from this is the process by which a modern poet of the studious order manufactures a poem out of the second-hand materials of his inspiration! We will suppose him endowed with a powerful fancy, and an especial taste for that portion of the marvellous which borders on the grotesque. He plunges into the learning of remote and half-romantic ages—the antiquities of Mexico, for instance, and the narratives of the companions of Cortes—or the stores of Eastern fable collected by Sale, D'Herbelot, and other Orientalists, whose praiseworthy labours had till then served for little other purpose than to furnish us with commentaries on the *Arabian Nights' Entertainments*. He seizes greedily on the matters most suitable to his taste and purpose; and little labour is required to construct a story by way of thread to string together these choice extracts of his commonplace book. If he alters a description or scene from his originals, or amplifies it, which last is more commonly the case, he does so, not by interweaving it with pictures of real things drawn from his own perception, but by tacking to it other minute fragments of his book-learning. He wants characters; but he has none of that dramatic power which can create them; they, too, must be sought for within the walls of his library. He makes them, to suit the necessity of his fiction, Homeric, or Miltonic, or Chivalric—any thing, in short, but real human beings. All this he may adorn with that exalted moral sentiment which heightens poetry; and which, because it appeals to and excites the nobler part of our nature, is often itself mistaken for poetical feeling; and with all the assistance which rhetoric and prosody can furnish. And in this way he may construct a *Madoc* or a *Thalaba*—and dozens more of such poems, if his faculties hold out; for the vein is inexhaustible.

It may, perhaps, be thought that we are here running into much unnecessary refinement on the simple distinction between original and imitative poetry. But this is not our meaning. Originality consists, not so much in the source from whence the materials used by a poet are drawn, as in his mode of using them. Virgil is by no means an original poet; yet he is a natural one. A strong sense of the beauty of external nature breathes through his poems; it is described with all the freshness of actual observation; but, from his own taste, and that of his time, he has clothed his feelings in the phraseology of Greek writers. Ben Jonson, on the other hand, is very far from being a natural writer; his inspiration is wholly redolent of books. Scarcely a character or a trait seems drawn from the life as observed by himself; yet is he original, because a peculiar vein of thought, essentially his own, runs through his compositions. The first derives his matter (a portion of it at least) from nature, but colours it with tints procured from others. The

400

latter draws his matter from books, but the colouring is proper to himself.

This last character appears to us applicable to Southey likewise. Although a very artificial writer, he is nevertheless an original one. His mannerism both of thought (if we may be allowed the use of such an expression) and of diction is very marked, but it belongs to no school. He is never an imitator, seldom even a plagiarist. In the preface to the edition before us, he has set down, very fairly as it appears, the amount of obligation of which he is conscious to brother poets, both of old and modern date. The reader will probably think that he has even overrated it. Notwithstanding the immense extent of his reading, it is singular how little the tone of sentiment, or even the language, of his favourite authors seems to have amalgamated with his own. There is something in his nature which does not easily admit of a mixture with the currents which it is constantly receiving. Probably no writer of our time, for example, has anything like the same extent of acquaintance with early English poetry. Yet, except in one exquisite little piece (the Lines on the 'Holly Tree,' too well-known for insertion here), we cannot at this moment remember any attempt on his part to imitate the species of composition with which he is most familiar. Books are absolutely necessary to set him a-thinking; but he rarely borrows the thoughts or the style which he finds in them.

We trust that, in contrasting the creation of such a masterpiece as the *Tempest* with the manufacture of a Southeian Epic, we shall not be understood to indulge in an invidious trick of criticism;—comparing our subject with the incomparable, and then pronouncing it deficient as measured by that gigantic standard. Our object was merely to convey as clearly as possible our ideas respecting that class of poets to which our author especially belongs; although it is our honest opinion, that in that class he ranks deservedly high. . . .

Nevertheless, it often appears to the reader of Southey as if he rather wanted the leisure than the faculty for the development of the finer shades of the poetical character. His inconceivable rapidity of composition hurries him onward, without giving him time to refine the current of his thoughts. His only mode of evincing his satisfaction with a favourite idea, or a striking description, is to amplify. Every corner of the picture must be filled up, and every part of it brought out into the same staring prominence. It is observable that this unpleasing peculiarity is not confined to isolated passages or portions of his works. Each of his long narrative poems is nothing more than a prolix *capriccio* on one single note in the poetical gamut. With the most eccentric combinations of groupes, scenes and personages, there is no variety of style or of ideas. *Thalaba* and *Kehama* are tales of prodigy and mythology; and they consist, accordingly, of nothing but prodigies. No repose—no descent from the clouds to the earth (except in a very few detached episodes) is allowed to the reader. He is inclined to feel like the Arabian hero himself, tired of the unearthly society in which he moves—

> Every where magic! how his soul
> Longed after human intercourse!

and to thank Dr. Southey's propitious stars, which have prevented him from executing the formidable intention declared in one of his prefaces, of 'exhibiting the most remarkable forms of mythology which have at any time obtained among mankind, by making each the groundwork of a narrative poem!' Conceive a Negro Thalaba, waging implacable warfare with Mumbo Jumbo—or twenty books of blank verse on the prayer-mill establishment of the Calmucks! *Madoc* and *Roderick*, on the other hand, are free from the supernatural, and chiefly conducted in the method of dialogue or narrative;—a dangerous experiment for one whose talent is essentially undramatic. And here the characters prose and preach so unremittingly, that the reader is reduced to wish for the company of an Afrite or a Glendoveer by way of relief.

This monotony is no doubt a necessary result of the astonishing fertility of one who is said to have burnt more verses, between his twentieth and thirtieth year, than any other living bard has written in all his days. Were the productions of our author confined to poetry alone, he would fill a respectable place on the shelves even in this prolific age, as the ten closely printed volumes before us evince. But when to this is added the mass of prose which he has contributed to our literature, and the prodigious though desultory studies which he has gone through, in the process of 'reading up' the several subjects on which he has exercised his pen, his exertions border on the incredible. Those of Voltaire, and even of Scott, both of whom, comparatively speaking, drew from their own imagination and fancy the materials of their voluminous writings, sink to nothing in the comparison. His life has been one incessant course of literary production. The fertile field of his genius has never been left to itself for a single season, to recover strength by such abandonment. On the contrary, it has been wrought from his earliest years under a perpetual system of rotation;—exhausting crops of history, ethics, and polemics, alternating with the lighter produce of poetry, criticism, and biography. Arthur Young himself could not have more cordially abhorred a fallow. . . .

Of the greater poems of our author, *Thalaba* continues by far the favourite with us. Nowhere has he lavished so abundantly his singular powers of gorgeous description; and although, as usual, his best passages are often weakened by tedious amplification, yet the nature of the subject, and the Arabian sources from which it is drawn, seem to render the vice less palpable than in other instances. There is a sustained spirit and rapidity of action throughout, very different from the heavy march of his other epics; and the wild measure in which it is composed—though we should be sorry to meet with it in the hands of an imitator—lends itself to the dream-like changes of the scenery and subject with unusual effect. To our mind, portions of the first seven cantos—particularly the description of the ruins of Babylon, in the fifth —and almost the whole of the last three—are not only the very highest efforts of their author of his serious vein, but hold no mean rank in the English poetry of the present century. The character of Thalaba is the connecting bond of the whole; and, wanting as Dr Southey is in the faculty of giving dramatic truth to his personages, it is singular how much of interest attaches to the adventures of this superhuman hero, whose only characteristics are unvarying piety, unfaltering courage, and absolute unity of purpose—light without shade of any description. Next to *Thalaba* stands, in our estimation, *Roderick*, although a poem of a widely different character: it has much of pathos, much of a stern moral sublimity,—the rough materials of a noble poem; but, alas! it is much easier to admire than to read it. *Madoc* wants interest both in the conception and the details, although some of the poetry would have graced a better chosen subject. *The Curse of Kehama* is perhaps the most unequal of the whole. It contains some of the most brilliant and some of the sweetest passages in all his compositions. The lines on love ('They sin, who tell us love can die'), more frequently called to mind, perhaps, than any thing else their author has written, are alone sufficient to immortalise it; although an imitation (rare with him) of the manner of Scott. Yet, after all, the work is an unsuccessful attempt to turn to poetical use the dullest and coldest of idolatries. It is, besides, too often a spiritless copy of *Thalaba*; and it argues both such careless haste in the execution, and barrenness of dramatic conception, that even minute points in the story are repetitions of passages in the older poem. For example, the interview of Kehama and Ladurlad, in the eighteenth canto, is the counterpart of that between Mohareb and Thalaba in prison. The scene of merriment which vexes Ladurlad when revisiting his own desolate home, exactly answers to the marriage procession which Thalaba encounters under similar affliction. The Hindoo peasant and his daughter form throughout far too close a parallel to Moath and Oneiza. All the laboured shiftings of the story, the distresses, escapes, and adventures of its most uninteresting *dramatis personæ*, remind us of nothing so much as the events of a Christmas pantomime—the Rajah and his dead son Arvalan, in the garb of Pantaloon and Clown, chasing the Hindoo Columbine and her betrothed Harlequin the Glendoveer through all manner of stage transformations, and balked at every turn, with a competent allowance of the thwacks and kicks which theatrical justice annually awards to those celebrated rovers. Those who think differently, may doubtless find good grounds for their opinion in Dr Southey's new preface to this poem; in which, with the true instinct of an author, who always stands on his defence on the weakest point of his poetical position, he gives abundant reasons why it ought to have been excellent. 'No poem,' says he, 'could have been more deliberately planned, or more carefully composed.'

It was in an unfortunate hour for Dr Southey's genius that the opportunity was afforded him of inditing the next series of his poems —his *Laureate Odes*, and their kindred compositions. Possessed as he has been from his earliest youth with a strong desire to dictate orthodoxy to mankind—whether after the creed of Wat Tyler, or that of Sir Thomas More—nothing could have given a more unlucky impulse to the spirit of preaching than the possession of the sort of poetical pulpit thus afforded him. Enfranchised from the servile tenure of former laureates, and permitted to commute their annual rent of odes for such occasional payments as it might suit his fancy to disburse, he voluntarily subjected himself to much severer service than any of his predecessors had undergone. They were usually content, in time of peace, with repeating soft panegyrics on the personal and moral graces of their illustrious patrons and all their kindred: in time of war, with such vague invocations of the Deity of battles, and such gentle solicitations of the Goddess of peace, as they might hazard without committing themselves either in a political or military point of view. He, conceiving that his office formed part of the general police establishment of the empire, treated us to paraphrases of the oaths of allegiance and supremacy, the proclamation against vice and immorality, and the

greater part of the gazettes of the last war; with a running commentary
of anathema against all such as contravened the former and under-
valued the latter. By this bold but mistaken usurpation of a new
province, where they only succeeded in provoking smiles, he laid
himself open to much severer treatment at the hands both of friends
and enemies. We have no wish to repeat—it is impossible to retract—
our old remarks on the bad taste, the egotism, the dulness of these now
almost forgotten productions. There is one, however, which deserves
to be rescued from the fate of its companions—the 'Funeral Song for
the Princess Charlotte,' which now first appears in their number. It
was first published, we believe, some years ago in one of the 'Annuals'.
This was indeed a subject on which the dullest laureate who ever
swallowed sack, could scarcely have failed to be impressive. Yet even
here the poet has shown that want of taste and finish which disfigures
so many of his happiest efforts. There is no moral connexion between
the thoughts which the chronicled sepulchres of St George's Chapel
call up in his mind: nothing to point and apply them to the mournful
solemnity of the day. There are spirited lines on Edward IV. and his
battles of the Roses—

> Cressy was to this but sport,
> Poitiers but a pageant vain,
> And the victory of Spain
> Seemed a strife for pastime meant,
> And the work of Agincourt
> Only like a tournament—
> Half the blood which there was spent
> Had sufficed to win again
> Anjou and ill-yielded Maine,
> Normandy and Aquitaine—

But what have they—or the misfortunes of the 'murdered monarch'—
or the deeds of 'hateful Henry,' to do with the fate of that young
'Flower of Brunswick,' by whose hearse the poet is standing? Nothing
whatever, except that she is charged to carry to the two first the news
of the battle of Waterloo; while the last, being expressly exempted
from the benefit of any communication with her, seems brought in by
way of gratuitous insult. Had a Whig poet, just at that time, taken
the liberty of mentioning Henry VIII. in such terms and such company,
he would certainly have exposed himself to the infliction of a page or
two of rebuke in the Laureate's next preface—if not an ex officio
information into the bargain.

But the true character of Southey (as is the case with most authors whose power resides rather in the intellect than the imagination) is not to be sought in his greater poems, nor in the set tasks of his laureate workmanship. These are elaborate studies—exercises of literary skill. The spirit of the poet is to be found in his minor pieces, the more vigorous and less trained offspring of his genius. First and foremost among these are his ballads. In them he is really an original and a creative writer. We speak not so much of his performances in the line of chivalrous romance, although these are assuredly not without their excellence. Queen Orraca and Don Ramiro were Scott's two favourites among the ballads of his friend belonging to this class—his is no trifling authority on such a subject—and the peculiarly solemn tone of the first, and the freshness and energy of the second, explain and justify his preference. Few more picturesque passages are to be found in the whole range of modern ballad poetry, than the opening stanzas of the latter; few more spirited than the address of Aldonza to the Moorish King, versified as it is, almost word for word, from the old Portuguese chronicler—

O Alboazar! then quoth she,
Weak of heart as weak can be—
Full of revenge and wiles is he.
Look at these eyes beneath that brow—
I know Ramiro better than thou!
Kill him, for thou hast him now:
He must die, be sure, or thou.
Hast thou not heard the history
How, to the throne that he might rise,
He plucked out his brother Ordono's eyes?
And dost not remember his prowess in fight,
How often he met thee and put thee to flight,
And plundered thy country for many a day:
And how many Moors he has slain in the strife,
And how many more carried captive away?
How he came to show friendship—and thou didst believe him!
How he ravish'd thy sister—and wouldst thou forgive him?
And hast thou forgotten that I am his wife,
And that now by thy side I lie like a bride,
The worst shame that can ever a Christian betide?

But they both want the true ballad interest. The stories, like many of their author's, are scarcely intelligible of themselves; and when painfully unravelled by the help of the notes, they only excite the reader's wonder at their oddity, and the quaintness of the taste which could have selected them. On the whole, though Southey did much towards introducing the noble Spanish ballad to English taste, Mr Lockhart, his imitator, has surpassed him in point of execution. But the ballads to which we would refer, as the productions of all others most characteristic of his genius, are those of a comic or semi-serious character, where he plays with the marvellous;—those of which saints, monks, and devils, are the uniform heroes. There is an odd raciness about these productions which it is impossible to describe, and difficult to compare to any thing else in existence. It seems as if the author had toiled all his life in the mines of strange and obsolete knowledge, to extract—not the useful, for which he has a thorough aversion—nor the poetical, for which he has perhaps no especial sensibility—but the grotesque and fantastic. His view of supernatural humour is as completely his own as that of Callot or Hoffmann. 'Take my word for it, sir,' said Mr Edgeworth, on perusing them, 'the bent of your genius is for comedy.' His extravagances are not only inimitable, but they are scarcely intelligible to the mass of readers; they require a special education; nor can any one justly relish a genuine joke of the Laureate, who has not a competent acquaintance with the *Breviary* and the *Golden Legend*. And so evident is the enjoyment with which the author himself dwells upon them, that we have often suspected, when perusing these *pia hilaria*,[1] and still more the multitudinous essays, notes, and reviews which he has enriched with the same recondite learning, that the superstitions which he ridicules have a strong and inexplicable hold on his understanding. We do not mean that he believes in the virtues of relics, or the horns and hoofs of the fiend. But such strange food penetrates into a system predisposed for its reception. Dealers in burlesque ghost stories are generally those who have a lurking credulity about apparitions. Even so we doubt whether, under a different dispensation, his favourite monstrosities would not have wrought on his faith as much as they now tickle his fancy. In another age, he would have lent himself with a fearful joy to all the wild suspicions which were engendered in the public mind against obnoxious sects or individuals. He would have firmly believed in the Baphomet-worship and child-sacrifices of the Templars. His name would have appeared as attesting witness to well authenticated tales of witchcraft, demoniacal possession, and vampirism. He would have entertained no doubt that the Jews at their merry-makings crucify children and pierce the Host with

[1] 'Serious jokes'.

their swords; and that they have a peculiar odour in their misbelieving state, which immediately leaves a converted Hebrew at the moment of baptism. Orthodox in the extreme, we doubt whether he would even have shrunk from the practical corollary of these propositions as to the Templars, witches, and Jews aforesaid. There is a certain organ of destructiveness at work in his composition, notwithstanding all the counteracting influences of a most amiable character;—witness the peculiar gusto with which the Saracens are slaughtered all through the twenty books of Don *Roderick*—and the magicians in *Thalaba*—and the 'short way with Bonaparte,' so calmly recommended to the Allies by the Pilgrim to Waterloo. Nay, some have detected hints of even darker propensities in various parts of his works. More timid critics than ourselves have remarked, not without horror, the evident taste with which he lingers over the anthropophagous performances of the Indians of Brazil.

123. Reminiscences by Thomas De Quincey

1839

From *Tait's Edinburgh Magazine*, 1839, vi, 453–64, 513–17. Extracts from De Quincey's series of articles entitled 'Lake reminiscences, from 1807 to 1830. By the English Opium-Eater: no. iv, William Wordsworth and Robert Southey; no. v, Southey, Wordsworth, and Coleridge.'

It was about seven o'clock when I reached Southey's door; for I had stopped to dine at a little public-house in Threlkeld, and had walked slowly for the last two hours in the dark. The arrival of a stranger occasioned a little sensation in the house; and, by the time the front door could be opened, I saw Mrs Coleridge, and a gentleman whom I could not doubt to be Southey, standing, very hospitably, to greet my entrance. Southey was, in person, somewhat taller than Wordsworth, being about five feet eleven in height, or a trifle more, whilst Wordsworth was about five feet ten; and, partly from having slenderer limbs, partly from being more symmetrically formed about the shoulders than Wordsworth, he struck one as a better and lighter figure, to the effect of which his dress contributed; for he wore pretty constantly a short jacket and pantaloons, and had much the air of a Tyrolese mountaineer. On the next day arrived Wordsworth. I could read at once, in the manner of the two authors, that they were not on particularly friendly, or rather, I should say, confidential terms. It seemed to me as if both had silently said—we are too much men of sense to quarrel, because we do not happen particularly to like each other's writings: we are neighbours, or what passes for such in the country. Let us shew each other the courtesies which are becoming to men of letters; and, for any closer connexion, our distance of thirteen miles may be always sufficient to keep us from *that*. In after life, it is true—fifteen years, perhaps, from this time—many circumstances combined to bring Southey and Wordsworth into more intimate terms of friendship: agreement in politics, sorrows which had happened to both alike in their domestic relations, and the sort of tolerance for different opinions in literature, or, indeed, in anything else, which advancing years and experience are sure to bring with them. But, at this period, Southey and Wordsworth entertained a mutual esteem, but did not cordially like each other. Indeed, it would have been odd if they had. Wordsworth lived in the open air: Southey in his library, which Coleridge used to call his wife. Southey had particularly elegant habits (Wordsworth called them finical) in the use of books. Wordsworth, on the other hand, was so negligent, and so self-indulgent in the same case, that as Southey, laughing, expressed it to me some years afterwards, when I was staying at Greta Hall on a visit—'To introduce Wordsworth into one's library, is like letting a bear into a tulip garden.' . . .

Returning to Southey and Greta Hall, both the house and the master may deserve a few words more of description. For the master, I have already sketched his person; and his face I profess myself unable to describe accurately. His hair was black, and yet his complexion was fair: his eyes I believe to be hazel and large; but I will not vouch for that fact: his nose aquiline; and he has a remarkable habit of looking up into the air, as if looking at abstractions. The expression of his face was that of a very acute and an aspiring man. So far, it was even noble, as it conveyed a feeling of a serene and gentle pride, habitually familiar with elevating subjects of contemplation. And yet it was impossible that this pride could have been offensive to any body, chastened as it was by the most unaffected modesty; and this modesty made evident and prominent by the constant expression of reverence for the great men of the age, (when he happened to esteem them such,) and for all the great patriarchs of our literature. The point in which Southey's manner failed the most in conciliating regard, was, in all which related to the external expressions of friendliness. No man could be more sincerely hospitable—no man more essentially disposed to give up even his time (the possession which he most valued) to the service of his friends. But there was an air of reserve and distance about him—the reserve of a lofty, self-respecting mind, but, perhaps, a little too freezing—in his treatment of all persons who were not amongst the *corps* of his ancient fireside friends. Still, even towards the veriest strangers, it is but justice to notice his extreme courtesy in sacrificing his literary employments for the day, whatever they might be, to the duty (for such he made it) of doing the honours of the lake, and the adjacent mountains.

Southey was at that time, (1807) and has continued ever since, the most industrious of all literary men on record. A certain task he prescribed to himself every morning before breakfast. This could not be a very long one, for he breakfasted at nine, or soon after, and *never* rose before eight, though he went to bed duly at half-past ten; but, as I have many times heard him say, less than nine hours' sleep he found insufficient. From breakfast to a latish dinner (about half after five or six) was his main period of literary toil. After dinner, according to the accident of having or not having visitors in the house, he sate over his wine; or he retired to his library again, from which, about eight, he was summoned to tea. But, generally speaking, he closed his *literary* toils at dinner; the whole of the hours after that meal being dedicated to his correspondence. This, it may be supposed, was unusually large, to occupy so much of his time, for his letters rarely extended to any length. At that period, the post, by way of Penrith, reached Keswick about six or seven in the evening. And so pointedly regular was Southey in all his habits, that, short as the time was, all letters were answered on the same evening which brought them. At tea he read the London papers. It was perfectly astonishing to men of less methodical habits, to find how much he got through of elaborate business by his unvarying system of arrangement in the distribution of his time. We often hear it said, in accounts of pattern ladies and gentlemen, (what Coleridge used contemptuously to style *goody* people,) that they found time for everything; that business never interrupted pleasure; that labours of love and charity never stood in the way of courtesy or personal enjoyment. This is easy to say—easy to put down as one feature of an imaginary portrait: but I must say, that in actual life I have seen few such cases. Southey, however, *did* find time for every- thing. It moved the sneers of some people, that even his poetry was composed according to a predetermined rule; that so many lines should be produced, by contract, as it were, before breakfast; so many at such an other definite interval. And I acknowledge, that so far I went along with the sneerers, as to marvel exceedingly how that *could* be possible. But if, *a priori*, one laughed and expected to see verses corresponding to this mechanic rule of construction, *a posteriori* one was bound to judge of the verses as one found them. Supposing them good, they were entitled to honour, no matter for the previous reasons which made it possible that they would *not* be good. And generally, however un- dubitably they *ought* to have been bad, the world has pronounced them good. In fact they *are* good; and the sole objection to them is, that they are too intensely *objective*—too much reflect the mind, as spreading itself out upon external things—too little exhibit the mind, as intro- verting itself upon its own thoughts and feelings. This, however, is an objection, which only seems to limit the range of the poetry—and all poetry *is* limited in its range: none comprehends more than a section of the human power. Meantime the prose of Southey was that by which he lived. The *Quarterly Review* it was by which, as he expressed it to myself in 1810, he '*made the pot boil.*' About the same time, possibly as early as 1808, (for I think that I remember in that journal an account of the Battle of Vimiera,) Southey was engaged by an Edinburgh publisher, [Constable, was it not?] to write the entire historical part of the *Edinburgh Annual Register*, at a salary of £400 per annum. Afterwards, the publisher, who was intensely national and, doubtless, never from the first cordially relished the notion of importing English aid into a city teeming with briefless barristers and variety of talent, threw out a hint that perhaps he might reduce the salary to £300. Just about this time I happened to see Southey, who said laughingly—'If the man of Edinburgh does this, I shall *strike* for an advance of wages.' I presume that he *did* strike, and, like many other 'operatives,' without effect. Those who work for lower wages during a strike are called *snobs*, the men who stand out being *nobs*. Southey became a resolute nob; but some snob was found in Edinburgh, some youthful advocate, who accepted £300 per annum, and thenceforward Southey lost this part of his income. I once possessed the whole work; and in one part, viz. the *Domestic Chronicle*, I know that it is executed with a most culpable carelessness—the beginnings of cases being given without the ends, the ends without the beginnings—a defect but too common in public journals. The credit of the work, however, was staked upon its treatment of the current public history of Europe, and the tone of its politics in times so full of agitation, and teeming with new births in every year, some fated to prove abortive, but others bearing golden promises for the human race. Now, whatever might be the talent with which Southey's successor performed his duty, there was a loss in one point for which no talent of mere execution could make amends. The very prejudices of Southey tended to unity of feeling: they were in harmony with each other, and grew out of a strong moral feeling, which is the one sole secret for giving interest to an historical narration, fusing the incoherent details into one body, and carrying the reader fluently along the else monotonous recurrences and un-meaning details of military movements. Well or ill directed, a strong moral feeling, and a profound sympathy with elementary justice, is that which creates a soul under what else may well be denominated, Miltonically, 'the ribs of death.' Now this, and a mind already made up even to obstinacy upon all public questions, were the peculiar qualifications which Southey brought to the task—qualifications not to be bought in any market, not to be compensated by any amount of mere intellectual talent, and almost impossible as the qualifications of a much younger man. As a pecuniary loss, though considerable, Southey was not unable to support it; for he had a pension from Government before this time. . . .

Of Southey, meantime, I had learned, upon this brief and hurried visit, so much in confirmation or in extension of my tolerably just preconceptions, with regard to his character and manners, as left me not a very great deal to add, and nothing at all to alter, through the many years which followed of occasional intercourse with his family, and domestic knowledge of his habits. A man of more serene and even temper could not be imagined; nor more uniformly cheerful in his tone of spirits; nor more unaffectedly polite and courteous in his demeanour to strangers; nor more hospitable in his own wrong—I mean by the painful sacrifices, which hospitality entailed upon him, of time, so exceedingly precious that, during his winter and spring months of solitude, or whenever he was left absolute master of its distribution, every half hour in the day had its peculiar duty. In the still 'weightier matters of the law,' in cases that involved appeals to conscience and high moral principle, I believe Southey to be as exemplary a man as can ever have lived. Were it to his own instant ruin, I am satisfied that he would do justice and fulfil his duty under any possible difficulties, and through the very strongest temptations to do otherwise. For honour the most delicate, for integrity the firmest, and for generosity within the limits of prudence, Southey cannot well have a superior; and, in the lesser moralities—those which govern the daily habits, and transpire through the manners—he is certainly a better man—that is, (with reference to the minor principle concerned,) a more *amiable* man —than Wordsworth. He is less capable, for instance, of usurping an undue share of the conversation; he is more uniformly disposed to be charitable in his transient colloquial judgments upon doubtful actions of his neighbours; more gentle and winning in his condescensions to inferior knowledge or powers of mind; more willing to suppose it possible that he himself may have fallen into an error; more tolerant of avowed indifference towards his own writings, (though, by the way, I shall have something to offer in justification of Wordsworth upon this charge;) and, finally, if the reader will pardon a violent instance of anti-climax, much more ready to volunteer his assistance in carrying a lady's reticule or parasol. As a more *amiable* man, (taking that word partly in the French sense, partly also in the loftier English sense,) it might be imagined that Southey would be a more eligible companion than Wordsworth. But this is not so; and chiefly for three reasons which more than counterbalance Southey's greater amiability: *first,* because the natural reserve of Southey, which I have mentioned before, makes it peculiarly difficult to place yourself on terms of intimacy with him; *secondly,* because the range of his conversation is more limited than that of Wordsworth—dealing less with life and the interests of life—more exclusively with books; *thirdly,* because the style of his conversation is less flowing and diffusive—less expansive— more apt to clothe itself in a keen, sparkling, aphoristic form—conseqently much sooner and more frequently coming to an abrupt close. A sententious, epigrammatic form of delivering opinions has a certain effect of *clenching* a subject, which makes it difficult to pursue it without a corresponding smartness of expression, and something of the same antithetic point and equilibration of clauses. Not that the reader is to suppose in Southey a showy master of rhetoric and colloquial swordplay, seeking to strike and to dazzle by his brilliant hits or adroit evasions. The very opposite is the truth. He seeks, indeed, to be effective, not for the sake of display, but as the readiest means of retreating from display, and the necessity for display: feeling that his station in literature and his laurelled honours make him a mark for the curiosity and interest of the company—that a standing appeal is constantly turning to him for his opinion—a latent call always going on for his voice on the question of the moment—he is anxious to comply with this requisition at as slight a cost as may be of thought and time. His heart is continually reverting to his wife, viz., his library; and that he may waste as little effort as possible upon his conversational exercises—that the little he wishes to say may appear pregnant with much meaning—he finds it advantageous, and, moreover, the style of his mind naturally prompts him, to adopt a trenchant, pungent, aculeated form of terse, glittering, stenographic sentences—sayings which have the air of laying down the law without any *locus penitentiæ*[1] or privilege of appeal, but are not meant to do so: in short, aiming at brevity for the company as well as for himself, by cutting off all opening for discussion and desultory talk, through the sudden winding up that belongs to a sententious aphorism. The hearer feels that 'the record is closed;' and he has a sense of this result as having been accomplished by something like an oracular laying down of the law *ex cathedra*; but this is an indirect collateral impression from Southey's manner, and far from the one he meditates or wishes. An oracular manner he does certainly affect in certain dilemmas of a languishing or loitering conversation; not the peremptoriness, meantime, not the imperiousness of the oracle is what he seeks for, but its brevity, its dispatch, its conclusiveness. Finally, as a fourth reason why Southey is less fitted for a genial companion than Wordsworth, his spirits have been, of late years, in a lower key than those of the latter. The tone of Southey's animal spirits was never at any time raised beyond the standard of an ordinary sympathy; there was in him no tumult, no agitation of passion; his organic and constitutional sensibilities were healthy, sound, perhaps strong—but not profound, not excessive. Cheerful he was, and animated at all times; but he levied no tributes on the spirits or the feelings beyond what all people could furnish. One reason why his bodily temperament never, like that of Wordsworth, threw him into a state of tumultuous excitement, which required intense and elaborate conversation to work off the excessive fervour, was, that, over and above his far less fervid constitution of mind and

[1] 'Place for repentance'.

body, Southey rarely took any exercise; he led a life as sedentary, except for the occasional excursions in summer, (extorted from his sense of kindness and hospitality,) as that of a city tailor. And it was surprising to many people, who did not know by experience the prodigious effect upon the mere bodily health of regular and congenial mental labour, that Southey should be able to maintain health so regular, and cheerfulness so uniformly serene. Cheerful, however, he was, in those early years of my acquaintance with him; but it was manifest to a thoughtful observer, that his golden equanimity was bound up in a threefold chain, in a conscience clear of all offence, in the recurring enjoyments from his honourable industry, and in the gratification of his parental affections. If any one chord should give way, there (it seemed) would be an end to Southey's tranquillity. . . . Southey, like Gibbon, was a miscellaneous scholar; he, like Gibbon, of vast historical research; he, like Gibbon, signally industrious, and patient, and elaborate in collecting the materials for his historical works. Like Gibbon, he had dedicated a life of competent ease, in a pecuniary sense, to literature; like Gibbon, he had gathered to the shores of a beautiful lake, remote from great capitals, a large, or, at least, sufficient library; (in each case, I believe, the library ranged, as to numerical amount, between seven and ten thousand;) and, like Gibbon, he was the most accomplished *litterateur* amongst the erudite scholars of his time, and the most of an erudite scholar amongst the accomplished litterateurs. After all these points of agreement known, it remains as a pure advantage on the side of Southey—a mere *lucro ponatur*—that he was a poet; and, by all men's confession, a respectable poet, brilliant in his descriptive powers, and fascinating in his narration, however much he might want of

The vision and the faculty divine.[1]

It is remarkable amongst the series of parallelisms that have been or might be pursued between two men, both had the honour of retreating from a parliamentary life; Gibbon, after some silent and inert experience of that warfare; Southey, with a prudent foresight of the ruin to his health and literary usefulness, won from the experience of his nearest friends.

I took leave of Southey in 1807, at the descent into the vale of Legbesthwaite, as I have already noticed. One year afterwards, I became a permanent resident in his neighbourhood; and, although, on

[1] Wordsworth, *The Excursion*.

various accounts, my intercourse with him was at no time very strict, partly from the very uncongenial constitution of my own mind, and the different direction of my studies, partly from my reluctance to levy any tax on time so precious and so fully employed, I was yet on such terms for the next ten or eleven years, that I might, in a qualified sense, call myself his friend.

124. Wordsworth's epitaph

1843

Inscription on the monument to Southey in Crosthwaite Church.

Ye vales and hills, whose beauty hither drew
The poet's steps and fixed him here, on you
His eyes have closed! and ye, loved books, no more
Shall Southey feed upon your precious lore,
To works that ne'er shall forfeit their renown
Adding immortal labours of his own—
Whether he traced historic truth, with zeal
For the state's guidance or the church's weal,
Or fancy, disciplined by studious art,
Informed his pen, or wisdom of the heart,
Or judgments sanctioned in the patriot's mind
By reverence for the rights of all mankind.
Wide were his aims, yet in no human breast
Could private feelings find a holier nest.
His joys, his griefs, have vanished like a cloud
From Skiddaw's top; but he to Heaven was vowed
Through a life long and pure; and Christian faith
Calmed in his soul the fear of change and death.

125. Lord Shaftesbury on Southey's character

24 March 1843

Entry in Shaftesbury's diary, reprinted from E. Hodder, *The Life and Work of the Seventh Earl of Shaftesbury* (3 vols, 1886), i, p. 262. A letter from Shaftesbury to Southey in 1829 marked the beginning of a friendship which lasted until Southey's death. Southey's writings exercised a considerable influence on Shaftesbury.

After three years of mental eclipse Robert Southey has been gathered to his fathers; I loved and honoured him; that man's noble writings have, more than any other man's, advanced God's glory and the inalienable rights of our race. He was essentially the friend of the poor, the young, and the defenceless—no one so true, so eloquent, and so powerful.

126. Wordsworth on Southey and Coleridge

5 October 1844

From a letter to Isabella Fenwick. Reprinted from *The Letters of William and Dorothy Wordsworth, 1841–50,* ed. E. de Selincourt (1939), p. 1231.

Now I do believe . . . that no man can write verses that will live in the hearts of his Fellow creatures but through an over powering impulse in his own mind, involving him often times in labour that he cannot dismiss or escape from, though his duty to himself and others may require it. Observe the difference of execution in the Poems of Coleridge and Southey, how masterly is the workmanship of the former, compared with the latter; the one persevered in labour unremittingly, the other could lay down his work at pleasure and turn to anything else. But what was the result? Southey's Poems, notwithstanding the care and forethought with which most of them were planned after the material had been diligently collected, are read once but how rarely are they recurred to! how seldom quoted, and how few passages, notwithstanding the great merit of the works in many respects, are gotten by heart.

127. Joseph Cottle on Southey in early life

1847

From *Reminiscences of Samuel Taylor Coleridge and Robert Southey* (1847). This is a revised edition of Cottle's *Early Recollections, Chiefly Relating to the Late Samuel Taylor Coleridge, During His Long Residence in Bristol* (2 vols, 1837).

Cottle (1770–1853) was a Bristol bookseller and minor poet. He published early volumes of poetry by Southey, Coleridge and Wordsworth. Southey read Cottle's volumes in July 1837, describing the work as 'Recollections of so many things which had better have been forgotten' (*Life*, vi, p. 335).

(a) Description of Cottle's first meeting with Southey, 1794
One morning shortly after, Robert Lovell called on me, and introduced Robert Southey. Never will the impression be effaced, produced on me by this young man. Tall, dignified, possessing great suavity of manners; an eye piercing, with a countenance full of genius, kindliness, and intelligence, I gave him at once the right hand of fellowship, and to the moment of his decease, that cordiality was never withdrawn. I had read so much of poetry, and sympathized so much with poets in all their eccentricities and vicissitudes, that, to see before me the realization of a character, which in the abstract most absorbed my regards, gave me a degree of satisfaction which it would be difficult to express.

(b) Account of a course of historical lectures delivered by Southey in Bristol, 1795 (cf. No. 3):
These lectures of Mr. Southey were numerously attended, and their composition was greatly admired; exhibiting as they did a succinct view of the various subjects commented upon, so as to chain the hearers' attention. They at the same time evinced great self-possession in the lecturer; a peculiar grace in the delivery; with reasoning so judicious and acute, as to excite astonishment in the auditory that so

419

young a man should concentrate so rich a fund of valuable matter in lectures, comparatively so brief, and which clearly authorized the anticipation of his future eminence. From this statement it will justly be inferred, that no public lecturer could have received stronger proofs of approbation than Mr. S. from a polite and discriminating audience.

128. John Anster, unsigned review, *North British Review*

February 1850, xii, 371–410

From the opening of the review of the *Life and Correspondence.* The review was continued in *North British Review*, May 1850, xiii, 225–63.

Anster (1793–1867), translator of Goethe, was Regius Professor of Civil Law in the University of Dublin from 1850. He contributed to the *North British Review* from 1847 on Irish affairs and literary subjects.

For a period of more than fifty years the writings of Southey were among those which, in England, most contributed to create or to modify public opinion. His first published poem was written in the year 1791; and from the date of its publication till the close of his life, there was not, we believe, a year in which he did not hold communication with the minds of others, in almost every form which a retired student can employ. Literature was not alone his one absorbing passion, but it was also his professional occupation. Southey, when speaking of Spenser, describes him as

> Sweetest bard, yet not more sweet
> Than pure was he, and not more pure than wise;
> High-priest of all the Muses' mysteries.

At the same altar, and with the same purity of heart, and with the same wisdom, he too served. It may seem to be regretted, that they who serve the altar have to live by the altar; but to the necessity in which he found himself, of working out a livelihood by unwearied industry in the occupations to which the higher instincts of his nature called him, we no doubt owe much of what is most genial in the works of this true poet. To this alone—such at least seems the probability—was it owing that he became a prose writer at all, for none of his prose writings have that unity of purpose and design which distinguishes the works of pure imagination; and yet there can be no doubt that, as a prose writer, he is one of the most graceful in our language. It is, however, as a poet that we think Southey must be most remembered. It is not depreciating Goldsmith's unequalled prose works, to say, that it is as a poet he takes highest rank. Had he not been a poet, he could not have written those prose works, and so with Southey. Dispose, however, of this question as the reader may, the earlier portion of his biography with which we have to deal will compel us rather to think of him in that character in which he first appeared before the public. Through both his poems and his prose works, his individual character so distinctly appears, that it would be scarce possible to mistake a page of his writing for that of any other man. He has not avoided imitation. On the contrary, his early poems are too often echoes of Cowper and Akenside: and the quaintnesses which appear more conspicuously in his prose works, are in kind identical with those of Fuller and Sir Thomas Browne. We feel that he is writing in the midst of his books; and that his essays on topics of present interest are always affected by his throwing his mind into the way of thinking of an age that has passed away. Still there is everywhere a definiteness and decision of purpose, which is that which constitutes true originality; and *his* thoughts it is which are expressed in a dialect which he feels to be common property, and of which he as little remembers how each particular phrase or cadence has been formed, as we can determine how we have learned the words of the language we speak. Everywhere, even in his earliest writings, his own mind makes itself distinctly felt. Of this the strongest evidence is, that where its expression is not subdued by the higher tones of elevated poetry, we have always an under-current of quiet humour that exhibits a man happy himself, or, if unhappiness comes, who feels himself blameless for what he cannot avert, and who is disposed at all times to view surrounding things in a spirit of kindliness.

129. John Henry Newman on Southey's epics

22 March 1850

From a letter to J. M. Capes. Reprinted from *The Letters and Journals of John Henry Newman*, ed. C. S. Dessain, xiii, pp. 449–50. Newman is commenting upon a review of Southey's *Life and Correspondence* submitted for the *Rambler*. He referred again to 'Southey's beautiful poem of Thalaba' in his *Apologia*.

I don't quite agree in the critic's view of Southey's poems. *Thalaba* has ever been to my feelings the most sublime of English Poems—I don't know Spenser—I mean *morally* sublime. And his poems generally end, not with a marriage, but with death and future glory. The versification of *Thalaba* is most melodious too—many persons will not observe they are reading blank verse. To single out particular passages as 'They sin who tell us etc' (in *Kehama*) is surely to evince an insensibility of the real merit of such poems—they are epics, not a string of sonnets or epigrams. You will be amazed at this outbreak. Also, it is news to me (but it may be *true*) that Southey was so soon popular. I thought he had been laughed at with Wordsworth for years. I heard of him first (which proves nothing) when the *Rejected Addresses* came out in the winter of 1812–13. Then I read *Kehama* and got it well nigh by heart. Of course a boy may easily confuse his first knowledge with the first popularity of an author. Still, I can't help thinking Southey's poems were not read *at once* like Scott's. I recollect hearing Scott's *Lay of the Last Minstrel* read out as early I suppose as 1809?

130. Charlotte Brontë on Southey

12 April 1850

Extract from a letter to William Smith Williams. Reprinted from *The Brontës: Their Lives, Friendships and Correspondence,* ed. T. J. Wise and J. A. Symington (4 vols, Oxford, 1932), iii, pp. 98–9. Charlotte Brontë had recommended Southey's poetry—'the greater part at least of his, some is certainly exceptionable'—in a letter to Ellen Nussey, 4 July 1834. During the winter of 1836/7 she corresponded briefly with Southey when she solicited his opinion of some of her poems.

The perusal of Southey's Life has lately afforded me much pleasure; the autobiography with which it commences is deeply interesting and the letters which follow are scarcely less so, disclosing as they do a character most estimable in its integrity and a nature most amiable in its benevolence, as well as a mind admirable in its talent. Some people assert that Genius is inconsistent with domestic happiness, and yet Southey was happy at home and made his home happy; he not only loved his wife and children *though* he was a poet, but he loved them the better *because* he was a poet. He seems to have been without taint of worldliness; London, with its pomp and vanities, learned coteries with their dry pedantry rather scared than attracted him; he found his prime glory in his genius, and his chief felicity in home-affections. I like Southey.

131. Walter Savage Landor,
Fraser's Magazine

December 1850, xlii, 647–50

An open letter to Southey's son, Charles Cuthbert, editor of his *Life and Correspondence*. Although Landor (1775–1864) and Southey were contemporaries at Oxford they did not meet until 1808, when they became close friends. In 1798 Southey had reviewed enthusiastically Landor's *Gebir*, published anonymously. In a letter to Anna Seward in 1808 he referred to *Gebir* as 'the only contemporary poem to which I am, as a poet, in the slightest degree indebted' (Curry, i, p. 476). Throughout their lives the two men provided each other with considerable encouragement. Southey appears as a speaker in two of Landor's *Imaginary Conversations*.

It is not because I enjoyed your father's friendship, my dear sir, that I am now about to send you my testimony to his worth. Indeed that very friendship, and the frequent expression of it in his letters for more than forty years, have made me hesitate too long before the public.

Never in the course of my existence have I known a man so excellent on so many points. What he was as a son, is now remembered by few; what he was as a husband and a father, shows it more clearly than the best memory could represent it. The purity of his youth, the integrity of his manhood, the soundness of his judgment, and the tenderness of his heart, they alone who have been blest with the same qualities can appreciate. And who are they? Many with one, some with more than one, nobody with all of them in the like degree. So there are several who possess one quality of his poetry; none who possess the whole variety.

For poetry there must be invention, energy, truth of conception, wealth of words, and purity of diction. His were indeed all these, excepting one; and that one often came when called for—I mean, energy. This is the chief characteristic and highest merit of Byron; it is also Scott's, and perhaps more than equally. Shelley is not deficient in it; nor is Keats, whose heart and soul are sheer poetry, overflowing from its fermentation. Wordsworth is as meditative and thoughtful as your father, but less philosophical; his intellect was less amply stored; his heart was narrower. He knew the fields better than men, and ordinary men better than extraordinary. He is second to your father alone, of all poets, ancient or modern, in local description. The practice of the ancients has inculcated the belief that scenery should be rare and scanty in heroic poetry. Even those among them who introduce us into pastoral life are sparing of it. Little is there in Theocritus, hardly a glimpse in Moschus or Bion: but Virgil has more and better of (what is called) *description*, in his *Æneid* than in his *Eclogues* or *Georgics*. The other epic poets, whatever the age or country, are little worth noticing, with the single and sole exception of Apollonius. I am inclined to think there is more of beautiful and appropriate scenery in *Roderick* alone, than the whole range of poetry, in all its lands, contains. Whatever may be the feeling of others in regard to it, I find it a relief from sanguinary actions and conflicting passions, to rest awhile beyond, but within sight. However, the poet ought not at any time to grow cool and inactive in the field of battle, nor retire often, nor long.

The warmest admirers of Wordsworth are nevertheless so haunted by antiquity, that there are few among them, I believe, who would venture to call him, what I have no hesitation in doing, the superior both of Virgil and of Theocritus in description. And description, let it be remembered, is not his only nor his highest excellence. Before I come to look into his defects, I am ready to assert that he has written a greater number of good sonnets than all the other sonneteers in Europe put together: yet sometimes in these compositions, as in many others of the smaller, he is expletive and diffuse; which Southey never is. Rural and humble life has brought him occasionally to a comparison with Crabbe. They who in their metaphors are fond of applying the physical to the moral, might say perhaps that Wordsworth now and then labors under a diarrhœa; Crabbe under a constipation; each without the slightest symptom of fever or excitement. Immeasurably above Crabbe, and widely different, less graphic, less concise, less anatomical, he would come nearer to Cowper, had he Cowper's humour. This, which Wordsworth totally wanted, your father had abundantly. Certainly the commentator who extolled him for *universality*, intended no irony, although it seems one. He wanted not only universality, but variety, in which none of our poets is comparable to Southey. His humour is gentle and delicate, yet exuberant. If in the composition of Wordsworth there had been this one ingredient, he would be a Cowper in solution, with a crust of prose at the bottom, and innumerable flakes and bee-wings floating up and down loosely and languidly. Much of the poetry lately, and perhaps even still, in estimation, reminds me of plashy and stagnant water, with here and there the broad flat leaves of its fair but scentless lily on the surface, showing at once a want of depth and of movement. I would never say this openly, either to the censurers or the favorers of such as it may appear to concern. For it is inhumane to encourage enmities and dislikes, and scarcely less so to diminish an innocent pleasure in good creatures incapable of a higher. I would not persuade, if I could, those who are enraptured with a morrice-dancer and a blind fiddler, that those raptures ought to be reserved for a Grisi and a Beethoven, and that if they are very happy they are very wrong. The higher kinds of poetry, of painture, and of sculpture, can never be duly estimated by the majority even of the intellectual. The marbles of the Parthenon and the Odes of Pindar bring many false worshippers, few sincere. Cultivation will do much in the produce of the nobler arts, but there are only a few spots into which this cultivation can be carried. Of what use is the plough, or the harrow, or the seed itself, if the soil is sterile and the climate uncongenial?

Remarks have been frequently and justly made on the absurdity of classing in the same category the three celebrated poets who resided contemporaneously and in fellowship near the Lakes. There is no resemblance between any two of them in the features and character of their poetry. Southey could grasp great subjects, and completely master them; Coleridge never attempted it; Wordsworth attempted it, and failed. He has left behind him no poem, no series or collection of his, requiring and manifesting so great and diversified powers as are exhibited in *Marmion*, or *The Lady of the Lake*, in *Roderick*, or *Thalaba*, or *Kehama*. His *Excursion* is a vast congeries of small independent poems, several very pleasing. Breaking up this unwieldy vessel, he might have constructed out of its materials several eclogues; craft drawing little water.

Coleridge left unfinished, year after year, until his death, the promising *Christabel*. Before he fell exhausted from it, he had done enough to prove that he could write good poetry, not enough to prove that he could ever be a great poet. He ran with spirit and velocity a short distance, then dropped. Excelling no less in prose than in poetry, he raised expectations which were suddenly overclouded and blank, undertook what he was conscious he never should perform, and declared he was busily employed in what he had only dreamt of. Never was love more imaginary than his love of Truth. Not only did he never embrace her, never bow down to her and worship her, but he never looked her earnestly in the face. Possessing the most extraordinary powers of mind, his unsteadiness gave him the appearance of weakness. Few critics were more acute, more sensitive, more comprehensive; but, like other men, what he could say most eloquently he said most willingly; and he would rather give or detract with a large full grasp, than weigh deliberately.

Conscience with Southey stood on the other side of Enthusiasm. What he saw, he said; what he found, he laid open. He alone seems to have been aware that criticism, to be complete, must be both analytical and synthetic. Every work should be measured by some standard. It is only by such exposition and comparison of two, more or less similar in the prominent points, that correctness of arbitriment can be attained. All men are critics; all men judge the written or unwritten words of others. It is not in works of imagination, as you would think the most likely for it, but it is chiefly in criticism that writers at the present day are discursive and erratic. Among our regular bands of critics there is almost as much and as ill-placed animosity on one side, and enthusiasm on the other, as there is among the vulgar voters at parliamentary elections, and they who differ from them are pelted as heartily. In the performance of the ancient drama there were those who modulated with the pipe the language of the actor. No such instrument is found in the wardrobe of our critics, to temper their animosity or to direct their enthusiasm. Your father carried it with him wherever he sat in judgment; because he knew that his sentence would be recorded, and not only there. Oblivion is the refuge of the unjust; but their confidence is vain in the security of that sanctuary. The most idle and ignorant hold arguments on literary merit. Usually the commencement is, '*I think with you, but,*' &c., or '*I do not think with you.*' The first begins with a false position; and there is probably one, and more than one, on each side. The second would be quite correct if it ended at the word *think*; for there are few who can do it, and fewer who will. The kindlier tell us that no human work is perfect. This is untrue: many poetical works are. Many of Horace, more of Catullus, still more of Lafontaine; if indeed fable may be admitted as poetry by coming in its garb and

equipage. Surely there are several of Moore's songs, and several of
Barry Cornwall's, absolutely perfect. Surely there are also a few small
pieces in the Italian and French. I wonder, on a renewed investigation,
to find so few in the Greek. But the fluency of the language carried
them too frequently among the shallows; and even in the graver and
more sententious the current is greater than the depth. The Ilissus is
sometimes a sandbank. In the elegant and graceful arrow there is often
not only much feather and little barb, but the barb wants weight to
carry it with steadiness and velocity to the mark. Milton and Cowper
were the first and last among us who breathed without oppression on
the serene and cloudless heights where the Muses were born and educated. Each was at times a truant from his school; but even the lower of
the two, in his *Task*, has done what extremely few of his preceptors
could do. Alas! his Attic honey was at last turned sour by the leaven of
fanaticism. I wish he and Goldsmith, and your father, could call to
order some adventurous members of our poetical yacht-club, who are
hoisting a great deal of canvas on a slender mast, and 'unknown regions
dare explore' without compass, plummet, or anchor. Nobody was
readier than Southey to acknowledge that, in his capacity of laureate,
he had written some indifferent poetry; but it was better than his
predecessor's or successor's on similar occasions. Personages whom he
was expected to commemorate looked the smaller for the elevation of
their position; and their naturally coarse materials crumbled under
the master's hand. Against these frail memorials we may safely place
his *Inscriptions*, and challenge all nations to confront them. We are
brought by these before us to the mournful contemplation of his own
great merits lying unnoticed; to the indignant recollection of the many
benefices, since his departure, and since you were admitted into holy
orders, bestowed by chancellors and bishops on relatives undis-
tinguished in literature or virtue. And there has often been a powerful
call where there has been a powerful canvasser. The father puts on the
colours of the candidate; and the candidate, if successful, throws a
scarf and a lambskin over the shoulder of the son. Meanwhile, the son
of that great and almost universal genius, who, above all others, was
virtually, truly, and emphatically, and not by a vain title, Defender of
the Faith,—defender far more strenuous and more potent than any
prelatical baron since the Reformation; who has upheld more efficiently,
because more uprightly, the assaulted and endangered constitution of
the realm than any party-man within the walls of the Parliament-house;
who declined the baronetcy which was offered to him and the seat to

which he was elected;—he leaves an only son, ill-provided for, with a family to support. Different, far different, was his conduct in regard to those whom the desire of fame led away from the road to fortune. He patronized a greater number of intellectual and virtuous young men, and more warmly, more effectually, than all the powerful. I am not quite certain that poets in general are the best deserving of patronage: he however could and did sympathize with them, visit them in their affliction, and touch their unsoundness tenderly. Invidiousness seems to be the hereditary ophthalmia of our unfortunate family; he tended many laboring under the disease and never was infected. Several of those in office, I am credibly informed, have entered the fields of literature; rather for its hay-making, I presume, than for its cultivation. Whatever might have been the disadvantages to your father from their competition, will, I hope, be unvisited upon you. On the contrary, having seen him safe in the earth, probably they will not grudge a little gold-leaf for the letters on his gravestone, now you have been able to raise it out of the materials he has left behind. We may expect it reasonably; for a brighter day already is dawning. After a quarter of a million spent in the enlargement of royal palaces and the accommodation of royal horses; after a whole million laid out under Westminster Bridge; after an incalculable sum devoted to another Tower of Babel, for as many tongues to wag in; the Queen's Majesty has found munificent advisers, recommending that the entire of *twenty-five pounds annually* shall be granted to the representative of that officer who spent the last years of his life, and life itself, in doing more for England's commerce than Alexander and the Ptolemies did for the world's. He quelled the terrors of the desert, and drew England and India close together.

132. John Gibson Lockhart and Whitwell Elwin, *Quarterly Review*

December 1850, lxxxviii, 197–247

From the conclusion of their unsigned review of the *Life and Correspondence.* Elwin (1816–1900) was an Anglican clergyman and editor of Pope. He contributed to the *Quarterly Review* from 1843 to 1885 and edited the periodical from 1854 to 1860. For Lockhart see No. 89.

Many men are endowed with mental gifts, who want the talent to turn them to account—who are unable to cut and polish the diamonds they find. Southey was a skilful workman. His materials were grouped in admirable order, and he imparted to a narrative his own intelligence. The reflections were seldom profound, but neither were they trivial, and they usually embodied some natural feeling which appealed to the better sympathies of mankind. His pure and perspicuous style combined the charm of ease with the finish of art. Passages of transcendant power he rarely attempted even amidst the buoyancy of youth—never afterwards; but his works abound in those which are forcible and felicitous, lively and thoughtful, humorous also and satirical. Somebody compared Coleridge to a muddy torrent, sonorous but not transparent; Southey's delight was in clearer and stiller waters. He was only turbid when playfulness degenerated into fooling. An acute sense of the ridiculous, unchastized by the salutary monitions of a free social existence, enabled him, even at the firmest period of intellectual dignity, to find mirth in dreary nonsense; and when, writing from behind a mask, he gave unlimited scope to his wildest fancies in *The Doctor*, he marred its many beauties by conceits which have not contributed to his character for wisdom or wit.

To be concise was among the excellences which he proposed to himself, and one to which he long conceived he had attained. 'Wiredrawing,' he said, 'he had never learnt to perform.' But compression requires more time and thought than his habits could possibly allow; and except in occasional sentences, brevity was not among the merits of his style. He was however more diffuse in what he told than in his manner of telling it. His propensity was to accumulate where it should have been his business to select, and he wearied less patient and inquisitive minds by the multitude of trifling details. 'Woe be to him,' exclaims Voltaire, 'who says everything that can be said!' However circuitous the road, his pleasure in the journey continued to the end. Sir Isaac Newton re-wrote his Chronology seventeen times for the sole purpose of making it shorter. Southey's last copy was pretty sure to cover the most paper. It was for his advantage to be confined within narrow limits. The Essays which he penned grudgingly added more to his reputation—even by his own confession—than the more dignified performances in which he pleased himself and foresaw deathless fame. *The Life of Nelson*—the most popular of his productions—was an imposed task, of which the publisher prescribed the size as well as the subject. He afterwards related that his materials would have extended to ten times the bulk, and had he been allowed a larger dish he would certainly have served up the milk with the cream.

His favourite pursuit was ecclesiastical history; but it was the Roman Catholic part of it which he had chiefly studied, with a view to his projected—alas! only projected—work on the monastic orders. In the religious history of England he was far from deep. His *Book of the Church*, though excellent in execution, is found in these days of revived inquiry to be superficial and incomplete. It makes a nearer approach to an elegant abridgment of Fox's Martyrs than to a general view of the Established Church. His special religious biographies are not obnoxious to the charge of want of research. The most enthusiastic Methodist could hardly desire a minuter narrative of the rise and progress of his sect than Southey has preserved in *The Life of Wesley*. For the rest of the world the minuteness is its fault. The story is well and impartially told, but clogged with digressions and the off-scourings of the subject. In the parts which relate to Wesley the monument is felt to be too large for a hero who was the agent of great effects without being singularly great himself. Adventitious circumstances added much of celebrity to the *Life of Kirke White*. White was a plant of premature and sickly growth. His poems are smooth, feeble, and vapid, with no originality, and little of anything. He owed his notoriety to his evangelical principles and the countenance of Southey. When a man of letters, whose testimony seemed the more impartial that he was opposed to their opinions, adopted their disciple and attested his genius, the religious party—proud of the distinction—united their acclamations and ratified the decree. Southey did what he professed—told White's history with simplicity and taste; and evangelical enthusiasm repaid his extravagant admiration of the Remains by excessive panegyrics on the attendant Life. Neither bark singly would have floated far. *The Life of Cowper*, in which piety and real poetry were combined, must have presented a theme after Southey's heart. In itself the career was melancholy and monotonous. The hermit's letters, however, describe its petty vicissitudes with such sportive grace, that he has interested the world in all which concerned him from the workings of his mysterious malady down to the glazing of his cucumber frames. Southey was excellent at stringing pearls. He has culled with judgment the passages which reflect Cowper's amiable existence, and connected them with dexterity. These extracts make up two-thirds of the *Life*. The portion which is original is pleasant reading, but shows a falling off both in force and finish from his earlier biographies. His estimate of Cowper's writings is meagre and vague,—a common fault of his literary criticism. He seems suddenly to pull himself up when on the point of saying something really discriminating.

The History of the Brazils was a bold experiment upon the perseverance of the public. The scene was remote, the action wanted unity, the characters were contemptible, the events destitute of grandeur or romance. The utmost rigour in choosing the particulars, and art in grouping them, were requisite to conquer these inherent defects. Never was Southey so blind to the truth that 'Nature has meal and bran.' For a circumstance to have happened was reason sufficient why it should be told. He broke up a history, already too disjointed, by wanton episodes, and persisted in congregating facts without significance, and enterprises without result, till he sank the vessel with the weight of the cargo. The mind sickens over the obscure conflicts of savage warfare, the minute topography of petty cities, and the dry descriptions of the products of Brazil. There is little animation in the narrative to enliven the dulness of the materials, and no luminous deductions of policy and science to add to their importance. That the work is creditable to Southey's research, that it contains curious facts, that there are many pages of classic composition (though the style is not in his happiest vein), is what all would take for granted. Any one who opens the book must regret the application of such talent and industry to the disinterring a mountain of mouldering bones that he might bury them again. The necessity to attempt an epitaph has alone emboldened us to disturb the sanctity of the tomb.

The *History of the Peninsular War* is a more remarkable instance that a large amount of good writing will sometimes fail to make a good book. Here then was abundant interest in the subject, but the narrative flags. Military topics were unsuited to Southey. His language is devoid of that martial impetuosity which stirs the blood like the sound of the trumpet; nor does he make up in accuracy what is wanting in spirit. Soldiers pronounce that he is unlucky in his conceptions of their craft— that he misses the point of actions and the purpose of campaigns; and even civilians must observe that a battle of his consists of separate onsets without connexion or plan. But everything is tolerable compared to the abstracts of parliamentary debates, and the old habit of rendering tedious what belonged to his theme by the addition of what did not. A siege is the signal to relate the origin and fortunes of the town, to talk of its cathedrals and monasteries, its pretended relics and the wonders they wrought. He must have gone to the Peninsula itself for his model, and emulated chroniclers such as Sandoval, who commences the History of Charles V. by deducing his genealogy from Adam and Eve. Excellent as are portions of Southey's record, the interest goes on decreasing with the progress, and what pleased at the beginning gets too flat to be endured.

The Naval History of England, though published in a more popular form, had even less success; nor, in spite of many striking pages, can we say that the public was unjust.

The Letters of Don Manuel Espriella on England, published in 1807, showed a great advance from the *Peninsular Letters* of 1796; the style is now quite Southeian, and the subjects treated are in great part those which to the end most fixed his attention. The pictures of English life in the middle sphere are true and graceful; but it is evident that he had seen very little of higher society. What is not least interesting is the contrast which his statements often present to the actual condition of matters after the lapse of only forty years; for example, the imaginary Don hears with astonishment that some London newspapers circulate 5000 copies daily;—Portman Square, 'on the outskirts of the town,' is approached 'on one side by a road unlit, unpaved, inaccessible to carriages';—and clergymen are wholly indistinguishable from other gentlemen by anything in their style of dress. The *Colloquies on the Progress and Prospects of Society* contain a wider and more solemn exposition of Southey's views on the evils of our social state. Alas! he is not seldom more successful in detecting disease than in prescribing remedies. Richelieu and Father Joseph were arranging a campaign.

'There,'—said Joseph, putting his finger upon the map,'there the troops must cross the river.'—'You forget,' replied the Minister, 'that your finger is not a bridge.' Few theorists, in their paper plans, have the scrupulous regard to consequences which distinguished my Uncle Toby when, demolishing his fortifications in obedience to the conditions of peace, he forbore to commence by a breach in the ramparts, because, if the French were treacherous, the garrison would be left exposed. The charm of the *Colloquies* is the same as in so many of Southey's writings—the graceful expression of sentiments which find an echo in every uncorrupted heart. The privilege to be colloquial has encouraged him to be even more paraphrastic than ordinary, or many of the passages would be among the best he has penned. The idea of summoning Sir Thomas More to be the leader in the dialogue was not over-felicitous. He is as much the pupil as the master of Montesinos; or, rather, he leaves behind him his supernatural wisdom and fills his pitcher at Southey's cistern. We believe we shall not be singular in venturing to say that his articles on similar topics in this *Review* are calculated to inspire a higher notion of him as a practical reformer. He was the better for writing under a degree of check, and feeling that he must carry *in limine*[1] the assent of a more arithmetical mind. The subject of pauperism had engaged him from a very early period—it fills a large space in *Espriella*. The cognate one of General Education was considered with equal care and philanthropy, and handled with equal fulness and elegance. In fact, Southey gave the first effective impulse to not a few of the most marked ameliorations of recent years.

His verse, like his prose, was injured by prolixity. His idea of poetry was almost the same that the old actor had of Hercules, when he insisted that he should be represented tall and thin, without the pithy massiveness assigned him by vulgar tradition. This disposition to linger over his theme—to prolong his notes till the sweetness of the melody is lost in the weariness of monotony—he had caught from Spenser, whom from youth to age he loved and studied above all the masters of song. The *Tale of Paraguay*—written in Spenser's stanza— shows with what fatal fidelity he copied this defect of his original. Pope used to say that poets lost half the credit they deserved, from the world being ignorant how much judgment rejected of what genius conceived. Southey was an unsparing blotter of verse, but crossed out less than he put in. 'Much,' he says, speaking of the revision of *Thalaba*, 'was pruned off, and *more* was ingrafted.' 'I am correcting *Madoc*,' he

1 'At the threshold'.

writes to William Taylor, 'with merciless vigilance—shortening and shortening—distilling wine into alcohol.' Yet a few months later, when he had gone through 1800 lines of the MS., he announced to his brother that they had grown to 2530. He was never sufficiently sensible that in the currency of Parnassus two-and-forty sixpences are not equivalent to a guinea.

This diffuseness assumes various forms. In the *Tale of Paraguay* he repeats an idea half a dozen times over, as if aiming to display the richness of a stage wardrobe, which for every actor has a profusion of dresses. In his minor poems the besetting error is mostly shown by pursuing a conception through its minutest ramifications, or in devoting stanza upon stanza to the expression of trifles not worthy to be expressed. His larger poems abound in passages beautiful in themselves, but utterly misplaced. He is for ever stopping to expatiate upon scenes, and declaim upon ethics, when it would have pleased the reader to see the action proceed and quicken its pace. His language, in all his verse, is usually the opposite of terse and condensed. He has Doric simplicity, but wants Doric strength. He relates that he read Cowper's *Odyssey* to cure his poetry of its 'wheyishness.' This he did on the principle that to live with the talkative is the way to learn silence, which proves his having at last become aware of the fault, though he never overcame it.

His first epic was a juvenile production, which his maturer judgment on the whole condemned—and perhaps we have already said more than enough about it. *Madoc* he believed (as we have seen) would stand and flourish, but acknowledged the story to be uninteresting and the passion deficient. The greater part, in truth, is a cento of travels, and little raised above prose in thought, or even in phrase. Battles and combats abound, but want the fire and animation which agitate and hurry on the mind. None of the characters have the strongly-marked traits which create an intense sympathy, and make them live in the memory. They are personifications of virtues and vices rather than women and men. The virtuous, who are the majority, preach with a monotony of moral sentiment, and act with a monotony of heroic devotion, more insipid than winning. But a reperusal reveals numerous beauties which escaped our notice while cutting open leaf after leaf—touches of nature and tenderness, strokes of eloquence, and, above all, fine specimens of descriptive power. He is only not in the very highest class of descriptive poets, because he descends to particulars where it had been better to give a few bold strokes, and by them enable the imagination to fill up the details;—and because, by the elaborate distinctness with which he isolates his picture, he betrays the artifice of a mind not itself thoroughly heated. Coleridge, we remember, contrasted him in this respect with Homer, to whom he so often likened himself. 'The modern artist,' said he, 'takes you into a gallery where brilliant canvasses are carefully arranged in costly frames—the divine ancient carries the key of a rolling panorama.'

Roderick was a great improvement upon *Madoc*. There is still a meagre fable, of which the catastrophe is foreseen; a loitering narrative, unseasonable description, an excess of pulpit eloquence, a too prevailing uniformity of tone and conduct; but there is far more passion, and for once a character which arrests attention. Roderick is the poem, and the other personages merely touch us through their relation to him. The worst defect is the total disregard of the spirit of the age, and of the contending factions, which should have coloured the story as the dye the woof, and would have made it picturesque in the extreme. The historic outline apart, and the Epic is redolent of England in the nineteenth century instead of Spain in the eighth.

The two lyrical tales—*Thalaba* and *Kehama*—were portions of a scheme for making each of the principal mythologies the basis of a poem. His purpose was not to display the influence of different creeds upon the actions of men, but to develop the wild absurdities of the mythologies themselves. Neither was historic accuracy a part of his plan. He avowedly rejected what he pleased, exalted what he took, and added much in the same exaggerated strain. He infused the soul of Christianity into the skeleton of heathenism. Instead of their natural fruits these false religions produce the virtues of the poet's faith; grapes grow on thorns and figs on thistles. No skill could overcome the vices inherent in the design, which was the offspring of private predilection, and not of a consideration of what would interest mankind. The book of Revelations was his favourite part of the Bible when a boy, and whatever bore a resemblance to the visions of the Apocalypse had a charm for his fancy.

Upon a foundation so unpromising he reared what is probably his masterpiece in verse. The story of *Thalaba* will not bear criticism; it must be judged by the poetry to which it gives birth; and this, taken as a whole, is the most vigorous, elastic, and picturesque that ever came from his pen. The scenes he creates show a strong, if not a luxuriant imagination; and the unadorned language equally proclaims that a command of imagery, which depends on a facility of detecting resemblances, was not among his gifts. If it had been in the fountain it would have flowed in the aqueduct. What little ornament of this class lies scattered through his poetry is trite and commonplace.

Kehama has admirable passages, but they bear a slender proportion to those which are feeble and grotesque. It would be difficult to define the limits of supernatural machinery—to say where it begins to revolt the imagination which it aims to lead captive. But Southey was himself aware that the subject of *Kehama* was beyond the sphere of general sympathy, and the wonder is that it could engage his own. Sancho Panza hung an entire night by the roots of a bush which grew on a declivity, and discovered when day broke that his feet were within a couple of inches of the ground. The situation would have seemed awful to any who partook his delusion, and supposed him suspended over a precipice;—it only amuses us whom Cid Hamet has made aware of the fact. A Hindoo might very possibly think the marvels of *Kehama* sublime.

Southey's feeling of the fitness between the verse and story of *Thalaba* seems really well founded, but his management of his lyrics is open to objection. He has carried his irregularity to such an extent that the ear continually misses the repetition of the metre; and in poetry, as in music, a recurrence of similar rhythm is essential to harmony. The transitions too are as violent as they are frequent. He repeatedly passes in the middle of a sentence from a solemn measure to jig and singsong, and shocks by the incongruity of the parts, where his intention, no doubt, was to charm by variety. In place of the undulations of hill and dale we have the jolts of a rugged road. The melody is often exquisite, but it is fitful and ill combined. *Kehama* exhibits the same disposition to push liberty to licence. The author's decision that 'its metre united, *in a manner peculiar to itself*, the advantages of rhyme with the strength and freedom of blank verse,' will appear strange to any one who compares the far greater strength and freedom of Dryden's tales with entire sections of *The Curse of Kehama*, which are little removed above nursery jingle. In another particular he was somewhat capricious;—he interposed throughout his poems lines which either no other mouth could make musical, or no other ear would approve.

The sublimities of religion were not the only attractions for him in theological themes. He had a particular love for all the perversities of belief and practice which have disgraced mankind. The lying legends of fraud, and the fantastic freaks of fanaticism, were sought with avidity and retailed with glee. These pious aberrations were provocatives to mirth, and incidents and language too sacred for such use are tricked out in sportive rhymes for the amusement of the world. One piece of profanity should not be cured by another. But Southey in his gravest moods trod hallowed ground with a daring step. In his *Vision of Judgement* he assumed the office of the Creator, and pronounced decisions which are veiled from every mortal eye. The grounds upon which he admits his elect to heaven are as mistaken as the attempt. Wolfe is there for his generalship, Handel for his music, Reynolds for his painting, Chatterton for his poetry. He always spoke of his own latter end without any of the qualifications which become a creature who must make it a continual suit to God that he will bear with infirmities and pardon offences. For the rest, in spite of some happy lines at the commencement, this ambitious attempt to naturalise the Homeric metre was not generally admired. He says, however, that his 'compeers' were of a different opinion, and expressly dwells on the satisfaction which 'women, as far as he could learn, took in the new rhythm'. The good ladies of Cat's Eden were lenient critics of ill-represented spondees and monotonous cæsura.

The best of his minor pieces are those in which the subject is made subservient to moral feelings. A few specimens are of most admirable excellence—the *Holly Tree* and the Lines on his Bookroom, for example —many are elegant and graceful; the bulk of them he wished in later years had been committed to the flames instead of the press. His caution nevertheless did not increase with age. The youngest child of his Muse was always a favourite however deformed, and it is amusing to observe the constant expression of his entire satisfaction with newly-composed poems which he afterwards found it expedient to re-write. Nothing he sent into the world at the beginning of his career can be more rude, bald, and pointless, than *All for Love* and *The Pilgrim to Compostella*, which he published in the mellow evening of his days. They are the rinsings of the cask when the wine was drawn out.

He contributed largely to the intellectual pleasure of his country, and not a little, we think, to its social and œconomical improvement; but it had been better for his fame if his lot had been cast, not on 'this England and this Now,' but a comfortably furnished cell in a Bene-dictine monastery some two centuries earlier. Then—besides that, after living easily amidst a proud and an applauding corporation, he must assuredly have been canonized in due season—his writings would have been reverentially collected into a range of folios, and no editorial care would have been thought too much for their illustration. In our steam-paced age, and elbowed by writers more in unison with its impatient vivacities, all his solid and elegant endowments could win for him at best a secondary place in the eyes of men: and we doubt that any future era would welcome a complete edition of his works. It is, however, impossible that partial reprints should not from time to time be called for: we incline to think that even now an authentic collection of his poems—all the occasional ones being included in their original form and in strictly chronological order—would be acceptable to the public; and that a judicious critic might make such a selection from his published prose as would fill at least a dozen very saleable octavos. Even in his Histories many of the passages that were tiresome to the eager contemporary as interrupting the narrative, are in themselves both beautiful and curious, and would form rich *Omniana*. Of his letters we have spoken at sufficient length: here we anticipate not abridgment but expansion. They present one of the most interesting portraitures of the literary character that mankind are ever likely to contemplate, and, as respects the better inner life, a lesson of true and loveable virtue and purity which never was or will be surpassed. *Multa pars vitabit Libitinam.*[1]

---

[1] 'A great part will survive the grave.' (Horace, *Odes*, III, xxx.)

133. William Bodham Donne,
Edinburgh Review

April 1851, xciii, 370–402

From his unsigned review of the *Life and Correspondence*. Donne (1807–82), a regular reviewer, was appointed Deputy Examiner of Stage Plays in 1849 and Examiner in 1857. From 1852 to 1857 he was Librarian of the London Library.

The present seems a fitting place for a few general observations upon Southey's station in English poetry. If there were ever, formally, a Lake-school, he did not belong to it; since he disliked the *Lyrical Ballads*, and it was friendship for Wordsworth which seems to have reconciled him to the *Excursion*. As little did he appertain to the order of bards, of whom Byron was the coryphæus,[1]—passion and Southey being irreconcilable terms. He was probably correct in calling 'Spenser' his 'master,' although the interval between them was as wide as the interval between Titian and West. Both, indeed, were poets of quantity: delighting in what Lydgate calls 'the long processes of an auncyent tale.' But in Spenser space is a shifting and gorgeous panorama, vivid in hue, majestic in form, and populous with chivalrous and mystic groups. Whereas in Southey amplitude of proportion too often resembles a wintry landscape, from which motion and colour are absent, and the outline alone remains of suspended life and luxuriance. Of still life Southey, indeed, is occasionally a skilful painter; but he was too dispassionate in himself, and too unversed in men's works and ways to inform his pictures with dramatic energy. His bad agents are all gloom; his good agents are all seraphic; his lovers are either merely sensual, or merely spiritual and metaphysical; the virtues of his heroes excite no sympathy; the vices of his criminals awaken no horror. Like characters in the old mysteries, they are speaking allegories, and not real persons.

[1] 'Leader'.

Yet we would recommend the youthful poetic aspirant to study Southey's poems; not indeed as he would study the masters of the great ancient and modern schools, but for the sake of their inexhaustible supplies of poetic materials. No writer, if we except Milton, has hived so much from the stores of books, or has displayed happier skill in discovering veins of imaginative ore even in the most rugged and unlikely soils. The materials, it is true, often surpass the workmanship. Mr. Fox was said to listen attentively to learned but ineffective speeches, in order that he might speak them over again. And although *Madoc* and *Kehama*, will never be re-written, their *disjecta membra*[1] may become serviceable under some more adroit combination. To the defects which we have noted, Southey's omnivorous appetite for reading doubtless contributed. Nearly all his poems are as much works of research as of imagination. His notes are more entertaining than the text, and sometimes as poetical. The very objectivity of his mind—a mind averse from introversion, and strenuous rather than susceptible,— favoured an undue accretion of its contents from books alone. He set to work upon an epic poem as many painters prepare themselves for an historical picture. They study archæology; they dive into black letter; they visit scenes of battle or of council; and they produce a brilliant masquerade. In like manner, in his longer poems, Southey assigns authorities for his characters, his costume, his similes, and his episodes, till the wonder is that, working on such a plan, so much of his work should have been so good. Of his ballads we deem much more highly than of his epics. Their needful brevity constrained his habitual gyrations. Yet even in his ballads ease and spontaneity are too often wanting; the legend and the chronicle are too apparent; they savour more of the library than the minstrel; and we turn for relief to Campbell and Scott.

Southey himself, half-humorously and half-gravely, avows his propensity to be voluminous. 'Is it not a pity,' he says, 'that I should not execute my intentions of writing more verses than Lope di Vega, more tragedies than Dryden, and more epic poems than Blackmore? The more I write, the more I have to write. I have a Helicon kind of dropsy upon me, and "crescit indulgens." '[2] He omitted to remark that Dryden's plays are nearly forgotten, that Blackmore's epics procured him a niche in the *Dunciad*, and that not fifty men in Europe have read a quarter of Lope di Vega's plays. In his nineteenth year Southey had held an *auto-da-fé* upon at least 15,000 verses; he plunged early into the

---

[1] 'Scattered fragments'.   [2] 'It grows by indulging itself'. (Horace, *Odes*, II, ii.)

Italian epic poets; he waded, as few men have done, through the
Araucana; and one of his literary aspirations was to complete the
Faëry Queen. He composed verses at his morning toilette, in his solitary
walks, on his occasional journeys; he poured them forth like unpre-
meditated conversation; he transcribed with the diligence of a Bene-
dictine monk. Shelley called him a great improvisatore. The morning
after he had completed *Kehama*, he was ready to begin *Roderick*. Poetry,
he remarks, softens the heart: '*Madoc* was essential to his happiness;'
'no man ever tagged rhyme without being the better for it.' But
although in prose the more men write, the better probably they will
write, it is not so with verse. 'Poetry,' says Milton, 'is solemn, sensuous,
and severe;' and these are qualities earned only by excision, selection,
and concentration. The taste of the reading public at the beginning of
the present century affords indeed a cause, if not a justification, of this
excess in quantity. In 1802, the greatness of a poet was thought to
depend upon a certain cubic amount of verse. Glover's *Leonidas* and
Klopstock's *Messiah* were not quite obsolete. Collins, and Gray, and
Burns had not written enough for a diploma of the first order. A
similar propensity displayed itself at one time in Roman literature; and
the later Roman epics are the least read, and perhaps the least readable,
of the verse which survived and scarcely survived, to modern times.
It would be unjust to compare Southey with the post-Augustan
writers, except perhaps with Valerius Flaccus. He has much more
vigour and variety, and is much less tedious. Yet we doubt whether,
in another generation, *Madoc* will be better known than *Silius Italicus*,
or *Kehama* be more frequently cited than the *Thebaid*. . . .

Periodical writing had indeed been at all times Southey's sheet
anchor. He pays it himself the homely compliment, that 'it made the
pot boil.' The *Edinburgh Annual Register* had yielded him for a time an
annual income of £400; and when he ceased to conduct its historical
department, the *Quarterly Review* made up for its loss. But although
Southey was well inclined to think highly of his poetical and historical
compositions,—so much so indeed as to compare *Madoc* with the
Odyssey, and the *History of Brazil* with Herodotus!—he was equally
disposed to underrate his contributions to periodical literature. His
letters frequently express a poignant regret that these ephemeral tasks
should engross so much of his time. In case abstinence from this
'drudgery,' for such he terms it, would have ensured the completion
of his grander historical projects—the histories of the Monastic Orders,
of Portugal, and of English Literature—we should cordially echo his

regret; and, as it is, we deeply lament that national or royal bounty should not have enabled him, while he had yet the power, to accomplish designs so well suited to his genius, and so likely to have remained 'possessions for ever.' But we cannot regret that Southey should have added, by his enforced labour, so many beautiful chapters to the current and more consumable literature of his age. As a critic, indeed, he ranks below Lessing and the Schlegels. He was less analytic than Coleridge, less discriminating than Mr. Hallam, and less pictorial than Mr. Macaulay. But he possessed, in an unusual degree, the requisites for periodical composition. His clear, masculine, and harmonious style, it is superfluous to commend. His universal reading enabled him to adorn every subject that he treated. He passed from one topic to another with the versatility of an advocate passing from the Crown Court to Nisi Prius; and his fancy was never more happily employed than in enlivening the themes of another, whether dull and superficial, or lively and well informed, with his own pithy analogies or humorous allusions. To the *Quarterly Review* alone he furnished, in the course of thirty years, nearly a hundred articles. His aid and reputation are well known to have contributed most materially and in many respects most justly to the early success and permanent celebrity of that journal.

The friends of Southey proposed or attempted many schemes for the improvement of his worldly circumstances. But every successive scheme proved either impracticable or unadvisable. Some we have already noticed. In 1809 he applied for the stewardship of the Derwentwater estates belonging to Greenwich Hospital. Their proximity to Greta Hall, and the annual salary of the office, £700, were obvious recommendations. But, upon inquiry, the duties of the stewardship were wholly unsuited to his habits and pursuits. 'The place of residence varied over a tract of country of about eighty miles.' This was too roving a commission for one whose tap-root was so firmly fixed to one spot. And the steward was expected to be 'a perfect agriculturist, land-surveyor, mineralogist, and lawyer.' Now of farming Southey knew as much as Virgil or 'honest Tusser,' could teach him; he had probably never measured his own garden by any other gauge than long strides; he did not know granite from oolite; and he had long shaken hands with law. 'For my own part,' writes Mr. Grosvenor Bedford, after recounting the Protean functions of the steward, 'I would rather live in a hollow tree all the summer, and die when the cold weather should set in, than undertake such an employment.' The situation of librarian to the Advocates' Library at Edinburgh, with a salary of £400 a-year, and with the prospect of an increase, was offered him in 1818; but this, as well as a proposal to take part in the political management of *The Times* newspaper, were declined by him,—the one, because it would have obliged him to live in a great city, the other, because it would have tied him down to a certain line of opinions, to both of which he was equally averse. Southey, indeed, was not an easy man to serve or suit. His constitutional cheerfulness rendered him comparatively indifferent to preferment; while his love of home, and his inveterate habits of study, indisposed him to change and removal. 'The truth is,' he said, 'that I have found my way in the world, and am in that state of life to which it has pleased God to call me, and for which it has pleased Him to qualify me. At the same time my means are certainly so straitened that I should very gladly obtain an addition to them, if it could be obtained without changing the main stream of my pursuits.' By the university of Oxford he was clothed with the highest honour which that learned body can bestow upon a layman—the title of Doctor—of which he made no use, and which 'put nothing in his purse.' Two other distinctions, of which men of more ambition or of less simplicity and independence would have been proud, he refused —a baronetcy, as inconsistent with his means, and a seat in Parliament, as incompatible with his pursuits. The laureateship, which was conferred on him principally through the intervention of Sir Walter Scott, was a more substantial boon, since it enabled him, by a fresh life-insurance, to make further provision for his family; and the subsequent pension, so gracefully granted and received, at the hands of Sir Robert Peel, might have been a national benefit, had it been given earlier. There is, perhaps, no country in Europe so deficient as England in appropriate provisions for literary men who are not connected with the universities, or who have not taken refuge in the Church. Of literature itself the State takes little or no cognisance. It is difficult for contemporaries to gauge its merits; it is still more difficult for a government to apportion its rewards.

For one who travelled late in life, and whom it was so difficult to detach from home, Southey travelled extensively, at least at a time when as yet railways were not, and the diligence and post-waggon retained their aboriginal tardiness. The records of his 'trips' are so agreeable, that we cannot help wishing that 'to travel and tell his travels had been more of his employment.' He was among the crowd of English who hurried to the Continent in 1815; and the *Poet's Pilgrimage to Waterloo* is one of the fruits of his first journey. He had watched the fluctuations of the mighty struggle between Europe and England, and finally between Europe and Napoleon, with all the ardour of his temperament, and hailed its unexpected termination with unbounded and indiscriminating joy. For his prophecies of a triumphant issue he took more than due credit: the inexorable end came to pass indeed, not, however, so much by the standing up of kings, as by the banding together of nations. With the immediate results of the Great Peace he appears to have been altogether dissatisfied. The world did not revert entirely to the year 1788; and therefore Southey complained that the revolutionary serpent was not killed, but only scotched. Throughout his remarks upon the social and political state of England at this time,—from 1816 and for several years afterwards,—upon the measures of government as well as upon the tactics of opposition,—we can discern little sagacity, little sound information, and even less tolerance and comprehensiveness, than we could imagine possible in a spectator so intelligent and so much in earnest. He indulged in a species of pastoral dream about the superior honesty and happiness of the 'felices agricolæ:'[1] he feared and hated manufactures: he was opposed to freedom of commerce: he identified dissent with disaffection: he sighed for the Church of Laud and for the policy of Burleigh and the Tudors. Yet what else could be expected from one whose days were passed with the dead, and who, according to his biographer, 'long as he had resided at Keswick, knew scarcely any thing of the persons among whom he lived.' These remarks must not be thought ungracious: our opinions upon Southey's social and political theories have often been unreservedly expressed; and, in support of them, we appeal to the contrast between his essays upon subjects he understood and his essays upon subjects on which he only felt. Let readers, who distrust our judgment, compare his papers in the *Quarterly Review*, upon 'Monastic Institutions,' 'Cemeteries,' and the 'Copyright Act,' with his papers on 'The Manufacturing System,' 'Parliamentary Reform,' and 'the Rise and Progress of Disaffection,' and he [*sic*] will admit—unless we greatly err—that, in political controversy, he had, in Milton's expressive phrase, 'the use only of his left hand.'

Southey's literary reputation rendered him a welcome and an honoured visitant in whatever quarter his continental excursions were directed; but nowhere was he more welcome than in Holland, and in no family more completely domesticated than in that of Bilderdijk the poet. Mrs. Bilderdijk had translated *Roderick* into her native language,

[1] 'Happy farmers'.

and made its author famous in the Low Countries. Her husband—like Southey himself—was, in his domestic circle, full of life, spirits, and enthusiasm; and, as there is some resemblance in the character of their poetry, so there was a close accordance in the general opinions of the brother bards. An accident, which put a stop to Southey's journey in 1825, and consigned him to the sofa instead of the diligence and packet-boat, tended directly to foster their new friendship. He became an inmate in Bilderdijk's house; was nursed by his fair and accomplished translator; and, in the blooming promise and home-education of her son Lodowijk, saw reflected the image of his own hearth. The learned stores of the hospitable Verbeyst—whose Rhenish was as good as any, and whose beer was the best in the world—furnished the library at Keswick with many ponderous and important recruits; while the letters from Leyden in 1825 are as delightful a picture of a scholar on his travels, as is his general correspondence of his daily life in Cumberland.

We have already alluded to the early working out of Southey's poetical vein; so contrary to the experience of greater poets. After the publication of *Roderick*, in 1814, he produced nothing of moment in poetry, and the Corpus Southeianum—for so his collected epics might be called—was obscured by the more fervid and genial brilliance of Byron and Moore, of Shelley and Wordsworth. But Southey's poetic spring was succeeded by a long and fruitful season of prose writings; of which some few were comparatively still-born, but many of them survive and will probably last as long as the English language. In his *Life of Nelson*, first published in 1813, he opened, in our opinion, the true vein of his genius—Biography; and, if we were required to perform for his works a service similar to that which the priest and barber rendered to the library of Don Quixote, we would at once rescue from the purgatory flames his *Lives of Nelson, Wesley,* and *Cowper.* Southey was naturally too voluminous to be safely entrusted with a subject of ample verge and margin. The narrower limits of biography were salutary for his genius. They compelled him to be brief, without denying him the privilege of short excursions and legitimate ornament. His diction too, smooth and rhythmical as it was, was also in a still higher degree colloquial. In anecdotes he delighted, and he told them well: he read character—at least the characters of the dead—acutely, and he delineated it perspicuously; his command of illustrative matter was unbounded, and he framed his portraitures with it most skilfully. On these accounts, had he executed his design of continuing Warton's

History of English Poetry, he would in all respects, except epigrammatic vigour, have probably surpassed Johnson's *Lives of the Poets*. This is on the supposition,—first, that his continuation would have been made on other principles than those which Mackintosh justly censures as having misled him in his *Specimens of the later English Poets,*— and, next, that his code of anti-Johnsonian criticism would have been reduced within the bounds of reason. Of Southey's three historical works, the *Narrative of the Peninsular War* has long been dead, if, indeed, it can be said to have lived at all. It was constructed on Raleigh's and Howell's plan of perpetually stopping progress to discuss the origin of every place or circumstance he had occasion to introduce. His *Book of the Church* will always be read with pleasure for its style, but cannot be trusted for its assertions. Had it been as impartial as it is picturesque, it would be one of the most delightful of manuals. But the temper in which it is written will satisfy those alone who are predetermined to think Laud in the right, and the Puritans and Long Parliament in the wrong. The *History of Brazil* is a performance of far higher merit than either of the fore-mentioned works. Its subject alone is a drawback upon its popularity, for few persons have any special motive for study-ing the records of a Portuguese settlement in three quarto volumes. The materials on this occasion were collected by his uncle, Herbert Hill, were themselves unrivalled in value, and were accessible at the time to none but the historian. His whole heart was in this book: it was an episode in his long-cherished History of Portugal: and the labour of love was discharged with unwonted vigour and alacrity. In his account of the Brazils no political antipathies disturb the genial current of his fancy. He revels in glowing descriptions of the marvels of tropical nature, the picturesque features of savage life, and the chivalrous adventures of the European settlers. The *Colloquies* and *The Doctor* combined display the twofold aspect of Southey's character—its earnest and its sportive side. The earlier of these works has been de-scribed by Mr. Macaulay in a former number of this Journal. The latter, besides its odd learning and Shandean turn of speculation, exhibits in the character of the Doves, and in a most graceful love-story, powers which, more sedulously cultivated, might have enrolled their author in the goodly company of British novelists.

447

134. Walter Bagehot on Southey

1853

Extract from 'Shakespeare the Man', contributed by Bagehot (1826–77) to the *Prospective Review* in 1853 and reprinted in *Literary Studies* (1879). Bagehot's generally unflattering view of Southey, indicated in this passage, is somewhat modified in his later essay on Henry Crabb Robinson, where he refers briefly to Southey as 'the great master' of a prose style of 'effectual simplicity'.

The reason why so few good books are written, is that so few people that can write know anything. In general an author has always lived in a room, has read books, has cultivated science, is acquainted with the style and sentiments of the best authors, but he is out of the way of employing his own eyes and ears. He has nothing to hear and nothing to see. His life is a vacuum. The mental habits of Robert Southey, which about a year ago were so extensively praised in the public journals, is the type of literary existence, just as the praise bestowed on it shows the admiration excited by it among literary people. He wrote poetry (as if anybody could) before breakfast; he read during breakfast. He wrote history until dinner; he corrected proof sheets between dinner and tea; he wrote an essay for the *Quarterly* afterwards; and after supper by way of relaxation composed *The Doctor*—a lengthy and elaborate jest. Now what can anyone think of such a life—except how clearly it shows that the habits best fitted for communicating information, formed with the best care, and daily regulated by the best motives, are exactly the habits which are likely to afford a man the least information to communicate. Southey had no events, no experiences. His wife kept house and allowed him pocket-money, just as if he had been a German professor devoted to accents, tobacco, and the dates of Horace's amours. And it is pitiable to think that so meritorious a life was only made endurable by a painful delusion. He thought that day by day, and hour by hour, he was accumulating stores for the instruction and entertainment of a long posterity. His epics were to be in the hands of all men, and his *History of Brazil* the 'Herodotus of the South American Republics.' As if his epics were not already dead, and as if the people who now cheat at Valparaiso care a *real* who it was that cheated those before them. Yet it was only by a conviction like this that an industrious and caligraphic man (for such was Robert Southey), who might have earned money as a clerk, worked all his days for half a clerk's wages, at occupation much duller and more laborious.

135. Nathaniel Hawthorne on Southey

1855

From *The English Notebooks of Nathaniel Hawthorne*, ed. R. Stewart (1941). During July 1855 Hawthorne visited Southey's former home, Greta Hall in Keswick, and his monument and grave in Crosthwaite Church.

As for Southey himself, my idea is, that few better or more blameless men have ever lived, than he; but he seems to lack color, passion, warmth, or something that should enable me to bring him into close relation with myself.

136. 'A cold man', Samuel Rogers on Southey

1856

From *Recollections of the Table-Talk of Samuel Rogers*, ed. A. Dyce (1856), pp. 208–9. The poet Rogers (1763–1855) was offered the Laureateship on Wordsworth's death in 1850 but declined it.

In all his domestic relations Southey was the most amiable of men; but he had no general philanthropy; he was what you call *a cold man*. He was never happy except when reading a book or making one. Coleridge once said to me, 'I can't *think* of Southey, without seeing him either mending or using a pen.' I spent some time with him at Lord Lonsdale's, in company with Wordsworth and others; and while the rest of the party were walking about, talking, and amusing themselves, Southey preferred sitting solus in the library. 'How *cold* he is!' was the exclamation of Wordsworth—himself so joyous and communicative.

137. Southey as essayist and reviewer

1856

From an anonymous article entitled 'A Quartet of Quarterly Reviewers' in *Bentley's Miscellany*, xl, 320–4.

It was review-writing that brought grist to the Keswick mill, however; review-writing was Southey's bread-winner, and therefore must be pursued as a trade, though never so irksome; it was his staff of life, and as such must be used in daily exercise, and not exchanged for a broken reed like epic poesy or ambitiously designed history, on which if a man like Southey lean, sure he is to pierce his hand, or worse. So he had to cultivate the quarterlies on economic principles and with periodical punctuality, instead of cultivating the muses on a little oat-meal. He was ill at ease under the yoke; but gall and fret him as it might, it must be borne. He kicked against the pricks, but they kept him in the right way, and urged him onwards whither he would not. All the time spent on 'articles' for Albemarle-street he accounted so much time lost; lost from those colossal poems which, in his heart of hearts (truly the heart is deceitful above all things), he believed to contain a full solution of the problem,

> What shall I do to be for ever known,
> And make the age to come my own?

Review-writing was an accursed obstacle to a yearly-renewed lease of immortality; for it prevented his producing *per annum*, as he felt himself willing and able to do, an epic as long every whit as *Madoc*, as fluent as *Thalaba*, as fanciful as *Kehama*. 'My history as an author,' he complains to W. S. Landor, 'is not very honourable to the age in which we live. By giving up my whole time to worthless work in reviews, magazines, and newspapers, I could thrive, as by giving up half my time to them, I contrive to live. In the time thus employed every year I could certainly produce such a poem as *Thalaba*, and if I did I should starve.' This is what Coleridge calls, in the *Biographia*

Literaria, Southey's 'generous submission to tasks of transitory interest, or such as *his* genius alone could make otherwise.'

In 1827, overtures were made to our willy-nilly Reviewer to write for the *Foreign Quarterly*. Willingly, he (no doubt unwillingly) answered—*as* willingly as for John Murray (an equivocal assent), 'at the same price.' The free will was directed by fate; for fate compelled Southey to write reviews, in order to make both ends meet at Greta Hall; but only money could make the mare go, on so weary, stale, flat, but then *not* unprofitable, a route. Hence, when the managers of the *Foreign Quarterly* attempted to (what Southey calls) 'wheedle' him into giving them an article for their first number at ten guineas a sheet —he waxed wroth. Well, then, they would screw up their price to fifty pounds for the article. Would that do? Not at all: Southey answered them in no mealy-mouthed or soft-nibbed penmanship, that he wrote such things literally for lucre, and for nothing else, and that if they had screwed their price up to the sticking point, he certainly should not lower his to meet it. 'This,' he told Henry Taylor, 'brought an apology for tradesmanlike dealing, and a hope that I would be pleased to accept the £100.' How essential it was to the poet's exchequer and home department, that *he* at least should conduct these negotiations in a tradesmanlike spirit, may be inferred from a fragment in his correspondence with G. C. Bedford in the following year, where he writes: 'Now from the said public my last year's [1827] proceeds were,—for the *Book of the Church* and the *Vindiciæ*, per John Murray, *nil*; and for all the rest of my works in Longman's hands, about £26,'—'so that if it were not for reviewing, it would be impossible for me to pay my current expenses.'

Southey was a jibbing horse in the *Quarterly* team. He had a dislike to the driver, who had the whip-hand of him, and sometimes touched him on the raw. In 1822, and afterwards, he was quite disposed to take part in an opposition Review, to the extent even of editing it, if proper terms could be come to, which they never could. When Gifford died, and himself was passed over by John Murray, Southey's hope was to secure the Albemarle-street editorship for John (now Mr. Justice) Coleridge, with whom he could work more harmoniously than with the deceased despot. But to his intense chagrin, the berth was assigned to Lockhart, under whom Southey worked grudgingly and of necessity, noway as a cheerful giver. His personal antipathy to Lockhart is freely enough expressed in the series of his letters last published. Murray, of course, got deeper than ever in his bad books.

'Murray,' he tells his uncle Hill, in 1825, 'has not written to me since the change of administration, feeling, no doubt, whenever he thinks of me in connexion with that subject, like a dog when he has his tail between his legs. He has got himself sufficiently into disgrace with all parties concerned.' In 1827 he complains of 'the cavalier behaviour of Lockhart,' which, he says, made him think it very likely that he must withdraw from the *Review*. And in 1835 he writes, that Lockhart and Murray between them have contrived to affront him to the point of secession: 'The story is not worth telling; it was a piece of disrespectful ill-usage, which I resent not upon either Lockhart or Murray, but upon the *Review* personified,'—a *façon de parler*[1] with a good meaning, morally rather than critically speaking—a charitable construction, and there an end.

Before he seceded, however, Southey had contributed to the *Quarterly* a prodigious variety of articles, written in that conscientious spirit of industrious research, and with that unlaboured grace of style, *simplex munditiis*,[2] which made him so important an ally, and hence so constant a communicant to the Tory oracle. First and last he wrote upon themes so various that they seem to be the epitome of the age, in matters political, economical, and literary.

---

[1] 'Manner of speaking'.   [2] 'Simple in its elegance'.

138. Southey's character: a tribute from Thackeray

1860

From *The Four Georges* by William Makepeace Thackeray, first published in the *Cornhill Magazine* in four parts during 1860. Extract from part IV: 'George the Fourth', *Cornhill Magazine*, October 1860, ii, 385–406.

I will take another man of letters, whose life I admire even more,—an English worthy, doing his duty for fifty noble years of labour, day by day storing up learning, day by day working for scant wages, most charitable out of his small means, bravely faithful to the calling which he had chosen, refusing to turn from his path for popular praise or princes' favour;—I mean *Robert Southey*. We have left his old political landmarks miles and miles behind; we protest against his dogmatism; nay, we begin to forget it and his politics: but I hope his life will not be forgotten, for it is sublime in its simplicity, its energy, its honour, its affection. In the combat between Time and Thalaba, I suspect the former destroyer has conquered. Kehama's curse frightens very few readers now; but Southey's private letters are worth piles of epics, and are sure to last among us, as long as kind hearts like to sympathize with goodness and purity, and love and upright life. 'If your feelings are like mine,' he writes to his wife, 'I will not go to Lisbon without you, or I will stay at home, and not part from you. For though not unhappy when away, still without you I am not happy. For your sake, as well as my own and little Edith's, I will not consent to any separation; the growth of a year's love between her and me, if it please God she should live, is a thing too delightful in itself, and too valuable in its consequences, to be given up for any light inconvenience on your part or mine. . . . On these things we will talk at leisure; only, dear, dear Edith, *we must not part!*'

This was a poor literary gentleman. The First Gentleman in Europe had a wife and daughter too. Did he love them so? Was he faithful to them? Did he sacrifice ease for them, or show them the sacred examples of religion and honour? Heaven gave the Great English Prodigal no such good fortune. Peel proposed to make a baronet of Southey; and to this advancement the king agreed. The poet nobly rejected the offered promotion.

'I have,' he wrote, 'a pension of £200 a year, conferred upon me by the good offices of my old friend C. Wynn, and I have the laureateship. The salary of the latter was immediately appropriated, as far as it went, to a life insurance for £3,000, which, with an earlier insurance, is the sole provision I have made for my family. All beyond must be derived from my own industry. Writing for a livelihood, a livelihood is all that I have gained; for, having also something better in view, and never, therefore, having courted popularity, nor written for the mere sake of gain, it has not been possible for me to lay by anything. Last year, for the first time in my life, I was provided with a year's expenditure beforehand. This exposition may show how unbecoming and unwise it would be to accept the rank which, so greatly to my honour, you have solicited for me.'

How noble his poverty is, compared to the wealth of his master! His acceptance even of a pension was made the object of his opponents' satire: but think of the merit and modesty of this State pensioner; and that other enormous drawer of public money, who receives £100,000 a year, and comes to Parliament with a request for £650,000 more!

139. George Borrow on Southey

1862

Chapter 27 of *Wild Wales* (1862) includes a short description of a visit to the ruined castle above Beaumaris Bay in Anglesey, 'a favourite residence of the celebrated Owain Gwynedd, the father of the yet more celebrated Madoc, the original discoverer of America'.

I repeated all the Bardic lines I could remember connected with Madoc's expedition, and likewise many from the *Madoc* of Southey, not the least of Britain's four great latter poets, decidedly her best prose writer, and probably the purest and most noble character to which she has ever given birth.

140. Lewis Carroll parodies Southey

1865

This poem, which Alice recites to the Caterpillar in chapter 5 of *Alice's Adventures in Wonderland*, is a skilful parody of 'The Old Man's Comforts, and How He Gained Them'. Southey's poem is printed first.

THE OLD MAN'S COMFORTS,

AND HOW HE GAINED THEM.

You are old, Father William, the young man cried,
 The few locks which are left you are grey;
You are hale, Father William, a hearty old man,
 Now tell me the reason, I pray.

In the days of my youth, Father William replied
 I remember'd that youth would fly fast,
And abused not my health and my vigour at first,
 That I never might need them at last.

You are old, Father William, the young man cried,
 And pleasures with youth pass away;
And yet you lament not the days that are gone,
 Now tell me the reason, I pray.

In the days of my youth, Father William replied,
 I remember'd that youth could not last;
I thought of the future, whatever I did,
 That I never might grieve for the past.

You are old, Father William, the young man cried,
 And life must be hastening away;
You are cheerful, and love to converse upon death,
 Now tell me the reason, I pray.

I am cheerful, young man, Father William replied,
  Let the cause thy attention engage;
In the days of my youth I remember'd my God!
  And He hath not forgotten my age.

(PARODY)

'You are old, father William,' the young man said,
  'And your hair has become very white;
And yet you incessantly stand on your head—
  Do you think, at your age, it is right?'

'In my youth,' father William replied to his son,
  'I feared it might injure the brain;
But, now that I'm perfectly sure I have none,
  Why, I do it again and again.'

'You are old,' said the youth, 'as I mentioned before,
  And have grown most uncommonly fat;
Yet you turned a back-somersault in at the door—
  Pray what is the reason of that?'

'In my youth,' said the sage, as he shook his grey locks,
  'I kept all my limbs very supple
By the use of this ointment—one shilling the box—
  Allow me to sell you a couple?'

'You are old,' said the youth, 'and your jaws are too weak
  For anything tougher than suet;
Yet you finished the goose, with the bones and the beak—
  Pray, how did you manage to do it?'

'In my youth,' said his father, 'I took to the law,
  And argued each case with my wife;
And the muscular strength, which it gave to my jaw,
  Has lasted the rest of my life.'

'You are old,' said the youth, 'one would hardly suppose
  That your eye was as steady as ever;
Yet you balanced an eel on the end of your nose—
  What made you so awfully clever?'

'I have answered three questions, and that is enough,'
Said his father. 'Don't give yourself airs!
Do you think I can listen all day to such stuff?
Be off, or I'll kick you down stairs!'

141. Thomas Carlyle's reminiscences of Southey

January–March 1867

From the appendix to Carlyle's *Reminiscences*, ed. J. A. Froude
(2 vols, 1881), ii, pp. 309–29. This appendix was written during
the period from January to March 1867.

When it was that I first got acquainted with Southey's books, I do not
now recollect, except that it must have been several years after he had
been familiar to me as a name, and many years after the public had
been familiar with him as a poet, and poetically and otherwise didactic
writer. His laureateship provoked a great deal of vulgar jesting; about
the 'butt of sack,' etc.; for the newspaper public, by far the greater
number of them radically given, had him considerably in abhorrence,
and called him not only Tory, but 'renegade,' who had traitorously
deserted, and gone over to the bad cause. It was at Kirkcaldy that we
all read a 'slashing article' (by Brougham I should now guess, were it
of the least moment) on Southey's *Letters to W. Smith, M.P.* of Norwich, a small Socinian personage, conscious of meaning grandly and
well, who had been denouncing him as 'renegade' (probably contrasting the once *Wat Tyler* with the now laureateship) in the House of
Commons; a second back stroke, which, in the irritating circumstances
of the *Wat* itself (republished by some sneaking bookseller) had driven
Southey to his fighting gear or polemical pen. The pamphlet itself we
did not see, except in review quotations, which were naturally the

shrillest and weakest discoverable, with citations from *Wat Tyler* to accompany; but the flash reviewer understood his trade; and I can remember how we all cackled and triumphed over Southey along with him, as over a slashed and well slain foe to us and mankind; for we were all Radicals in heart, Irving and I as much as any of the others, and were not very wise, nor had looked into the *per contra* side. I retract now on many points, on that of 'Barabbas' in particular, which example Southey cited as characteristic of democracy, greatly to my dissent, till I had much better, and for many years, considered the subject.

That bout of pamphleteering had brought Southey much nearer me, but had sensibly diminished my esteem of him, and would naturally slacken my desire for farther acquaintance. It must have been a year or two later when his *Thalaba, Curse of Kehama, Joan of Arc*, etc. came into my hands, or some one of them came, which awakened new effort for the others. I recollect the much kindlier and more respectful feeling these awoke in me, which has continued ever since. I much recognise the piety, the gentle deep affection, the reverence for God and man, which reigned in these pieces: full of soft pity, like the wailings of a mother, and yet with a clang of chivalrous valour finely audible too. One could not help loving such a man; and yet I rather felt too as if he were a shrillish thin kind of man, the feminine element perhaps considerably predominating and limiting. However, I always afterwards looked out for his books, new or old, as for a thing of value, and in particular read his articles in the *Quarterly*, which were the most accessible productions. In spite of my Radicalism, I found very much in these Toryisms which was greatly according to my heart; things rare and worthy, at once pious and true, which were always welcome to me, though I strove to base them on a better ground than his,—his being no eternal or time-defying one, as I could see; and time in fact, in my own case, having already done its work then. In this manner our innocently pleasant relation, as writer and written for, had gone on, without serious shock, though, after *Kehama*, not with much growth in quality or quantity, for perhaps ten years.

It was probably in 1836 or 7, the second or third year after our removal to London, that Henry Taylor, author of *Artevelde* and various similar things, with whom I had made acquaintance, and whose early regard, constant esteem, and readiness to be helpful and friendly, should be among my memorabilia of those years, invited me to come to him one evening, and have a little speech with Southey, whom he

judged me to be curious about, and to like, perhaps more than I did.
Taylor himself, a solid, sound-headed, faithful man, though of morbid
vivacity in all senses of that deep-reaching word, and with a fine
readiness to apprehend new truth, and stand by it, was in personal
intimacy with the 'Lake' sages and poets, especially with Southey; he
considered that in Wordsworth and the rest of them was embodied all
of pious wisdom that our age had, and could not doubt but the sight
of Southey would be welcome to me. I readily consented to come,
none but we three present, Southey to be Taylor's guest at dinner, I
to join them after—which was done. Taylor, still little turned of
thirty, lived miscellaneously about, in bachelor's lodgings, or sometimes for a month or two during 'the season' in furnished houses,
where he could receive guests. In the former I never saw him, nor to
the latter did I go but when invited. It was in a quiet ground-floor,
of the latter character as I conjectured, somewhere near Downing
Street, and looking into St. James's Park, that I found Taylor and
Southey, with their wine before them, which they hardly seemed to
be minding; very quiet this seemed to be, quiet their discourse too; to
all which, not sorry at the omen, I quietly joined myself. Southey was
a man towards well up in the fifties; hair grey, not yet hoary, well
setting off his fine clear brown complexion; head and face both
smallish, as indeed the figure was while seated; features finely cut; eyes,
brow, mouth, good in their kind—expressive all, and even vehemently
so, but betokening rather keenness than depth either of intellect or
character; a serious, human, honest, but sharp almost fierce-looking
thin man, with very much of the militant in his aspect,—in the eyes
especially was visible a mixture of sorrow and of anger, or of angry
contempt, as if his indignant fight with the world had not yet ended in
victory, but also never should in defeat. A man you were willing to
hear speak. We got to talk of Parliament, public speaking and the like
(perhaps some electioneering then afoot?) On my mentioning the
candidate at Bristol, with his 'I say ditto to Mr. Burke'—'Hah, I myself
heard that' (had been a boy listening when that was said!) His contempt for the existing set of parties was great and fixed, especially for
what produced the present electoral temper; though in the future too,
except through Parliaments and elections, he seemed to see no hope. . . .

I think the party must have soon broken up. I recollect nothing
more of it, except my astonishment when Southey at last completely
rose from his chair to shake hands; he had only half risen and nodded
on my coming in; and all along I had counted him a lean little man;

but now he shot suddenly aloft into a lean tall one, all legs, in shape and stature like a pair of tongs, which peculiarity my surprise doubtless exaggerated to me, but only made it the more notable and entertaining. Nothing had happened throughout that was other than moderately pleasant; and I returned home (I conclude) well enough satisfied with my evening. Southey's sensitiveness I had noticed on the first occasion as one of his characteristic qualities; but was nothing like aware of the extent of it till our next meeting

This was a few evenings afterwards, Taylor giving some dinner, or party, party in honour of his guest; if dinner I was not at that, but must have undertaken for the evening sequel, as less incommodious to me, less unwholesome more especially. I remember entering, in the same house, but upstairs this time, a pleasant little drawing-room, in which, in well-lighted, secure enough condition, sat Southey in full dress, silently reclining, and as yet no other company. We saluted suitably; touched ditto on the vague initiatory points; and were still there, when by way of coming closer, I asked mildly, with no appearance of special interest, but with more than I really felt, 'Do you know De Quincey?' (the opium-eater, whom I knew to have lived in Cumberland as his neighbour). 'Yes, sir,' said Southey, with extraordinary animosity, 'and if you have opportunity, I'll thank you to tell him he is one of the greatest scoundrels living!' I laughed lightly, said I had myself little acquaintance with the man, and could not wish to recommend myself by that message. Southey's face, as I looked at it, was become of slate colour, the eyes glancing, the attitude rigid, the figure altogether a picture of Rhadamanthine rage,—that is, rage conscious to itself of being just. He doubtless felt I would expect some explanation from him. 'I have told Hartley Coleridge,' said he, 'that he ought to take a strong cudgel, proceed straight to Edinburgh, and give De Quincey, publicly in the streets there, a sound beating—as a calumniator, cowardly spy, traitor, base betrayer of the hospitable social hearth, for one thing!' It appeared De Quincey was then, and for some time past, writing in *Blackwood's Magazine* something of an autobiographic nature, a series of papers on the 'Lake' period of his life, merely for the sake of the highly needful trifle of money, poor soul, and with no wish to be untrue (I could believe) or hurt anybody, though not without his own bits of splenetic conviction, and to which latter, in regard of Coleridge in particular, he had given more rein than was agreeable to parties concerned. I believe I had myself read the paper on Coleridge, one paper on him I certainly read, and had been the reverse of tempted by it to look after the others; finding in this, e.g., that Coleridge had the greatest intellect perhaps ever given to man, 'but that he wanted, or as good as wanted, common honesty in applying it;' which seemed to me a miserable contradiction in terms, and threw light, if not on Coleridge, yet on De Quincey's faculty of judging him or others. In this paper there were probably withal some domestic details or allusions, to which, as familiar to rumour, I had paid little heed; but certainly, of general reverence for Coleridge and his gifts and deeds, I had traced, not deficiency in this paper, but glaring exaggeration, coupled with De Quincean drawbacks, which latter had alone struck Southey with such poignancy; or perhaps there had been other more criminal papers, which Southey knew of, and not I? In few minutes we let the topic drop, I helping what I could, and he seemed to feel as if he had done a little wrong; and was bound to show himself more than usually amicable and social, especially with me, for the rest of the evening, which he did in effect; though I quite forget the details, only that I had a good deal of talk with him, in the circle of the others; and had again more than once to notice the sin-gular readiness of the blushes; amiable red blush, beautiful like a young girl's, when you touched genially the pleasant theme; and serpent-like flash of blue or black blush (this far, very far the rarer kind, though it did recur too) when you struck upon the opposite. All details of the evening, except that primary one, are clean gone; but the effect was interesting, pleasantly stimulating and surprising. I said to myself, 'How has this man contrived, with such a nervous system, to keep alive for near sixty years? Now blushing under his grey hairs, rosy like a maiden of fifteen; now slaty almost, like a rattle-snake or fiery serpent? How has he not been torn to pieces long since, under such furious pulling this way and that? He must have somewhere a great deal of methodic virtue in him; I suppose, too, his heart is thoroughly honest, which helps considerably!' I did not fancy myself to have made personally much impression on Southey; but on those terms I accepted him for a loyal kind of man; and was content and thankful to know of his existing in the world, near me, or still far from me, as the fates should have determined. For perhaps two years I saw no more of him; heard only from Taylor in particular, that he was overwhelmed in misery, and imprudently refusing to yield, or screen himself in any particular. Imprudently, thought Taylor and his other friends; for not only had he been, for several continuous years, toiling and fagging at a collective edition of his works, which cost him a great deal of incessant labour; but far worse, his poor wife had sunk into insanity, and moreover he would not, such his feeling on this tragic matter, be persuaded to send her to an asylum, or trust her out of his own sight and keeping! Figure such a scene; and what the most sensitive of mankind must have felt under it. This, then, is the garland and crown of 'victory' provided for an old man, when he survives, spent with his fifty years of climbing and of running, and has what you call won the race!

It was after I had finished the *French Revolution*, and perhaps after my Annandale journey to recover from this adventure, that I heard of Southey's being in town again. His collective edition was complete, his poor wife was dead and at rest; his work was done, in fact (had he known it), all his work in the world was done; and he had determined on a few weeks of wandering, and trying to repose and recreate himself, among old friends and scenes. I saw him twice or thrice on this occasion; it was our second and last piece of intercourse, and much the more interesting, to me at least, and for a reason that will appear. My wild excitation of nerves, after finishing that grim book on *French Revolution*, was something strange. The desperate nature of our circumstances and outlooks while writing it, the thorough possession it had taken of me, dwelling in me day and night, keeping me in constant fellowship with such a 'flamy cut-throat scene of things,' infernal and celestial both in one, with no fixed prospect but that of writing it, though I should die, had held me in a fever blaze for three years long; and now the blaze had ceased, problem *taliter qualiter*[1] was actually done, and my humour and way of thought about all things was of an altogether ghastly, dim-smouldering, and as if preternatural sort. . . .

Such being my posture and humour at that time, fancy my surprise at finding Southey full of sympathy, assent and recognition of the amplest kind, for my poor new book! We talked largely on the huge event itself, which he had dwelt with openly or privately ever since his youth, and tended to interpret, exactly as I, the suicidal explosion of an old wicked world, too wicked, false and impious for living longer; and seemed satisfied and as if grateful, that a strong voice had at last expressed that meaning. My poor *French Revolution* evidently appeared to him a good deed, a salutary bit of 'scriptural' exposition for the public and for mankind; and this, I could perceive, was the soul of a great many minor approbations and admirations of detail, which

[1] 'In whatever manner'.

he was too polite to speak of. As Southey was the only man of eminence that had ever taken such a view of me, and especially of this my first considerable book, it seems strange that I should have felt so little real triumph in it as I did. . . .

Truly I can say for myself, Southey's approbation, though very privately I doubtless had my pride in it, did not the least tend to swell me; though, on the other hand, I must own to very great gloom of mind, sullen some part of it, which is possibly a worse fault than what it saved me from. I remember now how polite and delicate his praises of me were; never given direct or in over measure, but always obliquely, in the way of hint or inference left for me; and how kind, sincere and courteous, his manner throughout was. Our mutual considerations about the *French Revolution*, about its incidents, catastrophes, or about its characters, Danton, Camille, etc., and contrasts and comparisons of them with their (probable) English compeers of the day, yielded pleasant and copious material for dialogue when we met. Literature was hardly touched upon: our discourse came almost always upon moral and social topics. Southey's look, I remarked, was strangely careworn, anxious, though he seemed to like talking, and both talked and listened well; his eyes especially were as if filled with gloomy bewilderment and incurable sorrows. He had got to be about sixty-three, had buried all his suffering loved ones, wound up forty years of incessant vehement labour, much of it more or less ungenial to him; and in fact, though he knew it not, had finished his work in the world; and might well be looking back on it with a kind of ghastly astonishment rather than with triumph or joy! . . .

Southey and I got to speaking about Shelley (whom perhaps I remembered to have lived in the Lake country for some time, and had started on Shelley as a practicable topic). Southey did not rise into admiration of Shelley either for talent or conduct; spoke of him and his life, without bitterness, but with contemptuous sorrow, and evident aversion mingled with his pity. To me also poor Shelley always was, and is, a kind of ghastly object, colourless, pallid, without health or warmth or vigour; the sound of him shrieky, frosty, as if a ghost were trying to 'sing to us;' the temperament of him spasmodic, hysterical, instead of strong or robust; with fine affections and aspirations, gone all such a road:—a man infinitely too weak for that solitary scaling of the Alps which he undertook in spite of all the world. At some point of the dialogue I said to Southey, 'a haggard existence that of his.' I remember Southey's pause, and the tone and air with which he answered, 'It is a haggard existence!' His look, at this moment, was unusually gloomy and heavy-laden, full of confused distress;—as if in retrospect of his own existence, and the haggard battle it too had been . . . .

The last time I saw Southey was on an evening at Taylor's, nobody there but myself; I think he meant to leave town next morning, and had wished to say farewell to me first. We sat on the sofa together; our talk was long and earnest; topic ultimately the usual one, steady approach of democracy, with revolution (probably explosive) and a finis incomputable to man; steady decay of all morality, political, social, individual; this once noble England getting more and more ignoble and untrue in every fibre of it, till the gold (Goethe's composite king) would all be eaten out, and noble England would have to collapse in shapeless ruin, whether for ever or not none of us could know. Our perfect consent on these matters gave an animation to the dialogue, which I remember as copious and pleasant. Southey's last word was in answer to some tirade of mine against universal mammon-worship, gradual accelerating decay of mutual humanity, of piety and fidelity to God or man, in all our relations and performances, the whole illustrated by examples, I suppose; to which he answered, not with levity, yet with a cheerful tone in his seriousness, 'It will not, and it cannot come to good!' . . .

Southey I used to construe to myself as a man of slight build, but of sound and elegant; with considerable genius in him, considerable faculty of speech and rhythmic insight, and with a morality that shone distinguished among his contemporaries. I reckoned him (with those blue blushes and those red) to be the perhaps excitablest of all men; and that a deep mute monition of conscience had spoken to him, 'You are capable of running mad, if you don't take care. Acquire habitudes; stick firm as adamant to them at all times, and work, continually work!'

This, for thirty or forty years, he had punctually and impetuously done; no man so habitual, we were told; gave up his poetry, at a given hour, on stroke of the clock, and took to prose, etc. etc.; and, as to diligence and velocity, employed his very walking hours, walked with a book in his hand; and by these methods of his, had got through perhaps a greater amount of work, counting quantity and quality, than any other man whatever in those years of his; till all suddenly ended. I likened him to one of those huge sandstone grinding cylinders which I had seen at Manchester, turning with inconceivable velocity (in the condemned room of the iron factory, where 'the men die of lung disease at forty,' but are permitted to smoke in their damp cellar, and think that a rich recompense!)—screaming harshly, and shooting out each of them its sheet of fire (yellow, starlight, etc. according as it is brass or other kind of metal that you grind and polish there)— beautiful sheets of fire, pouring out each as if from the paper cap of its low-stooping-backed grinder, when you look from rearward. For many years these stones grind so, at such a rate; till at last (in some cases) comes a moment when the stone's cohesion is quite worn out, overcome by the stupendous velocity long continued; and while grinding its fastest, it flies off altogether, and settles some yards from you, a grinding-stone no longer, but a cartload of quiet sand.

142. John Dennis on Southey's prose

1876

From the conclusion of the chapter on Southey in Dennis's *Studies in English Literature* (1876). The essay was first published anonymously in the *Cornhill Magazine*, October 1873, xxviii, 468–83.

Dennis, literary critic and historian, edited several literary texts and was, for a time, editor of the *Reader*. After analysing the defects of Southey's poetry, Dennis turns to a discussion of his prose works.

As a poet, Southey cannot be classed with the great English masters; as a prose writer, his manly, simple, flexible style may be regarded as a model. In reading his books, the attention is not immediately drawn to the form of the composition, as in the case of such mannerists as Lord Macaulay and Mr. Carlyle, but when it is examined it will be found to fulfil admirably the purpose of the writer.

'The reason why so many persons write ill,' he said, 'is because they think it necessary to write a style something different from the common speech.' Southey was in no danger of falling into an error of this kind. He used the simplest words to express his thoughts, and it is never possible to mistake his meaning. No modern writer states facts more clearly or more honestly, but the judgment which he draws from his facts is often curiously perverse. The power of forming a wise judgment was not one of Southey's intellectual privileges. Like his friend Landor, he had the peculiarity, as Mr. Forster has pointed out, of putting the imagination and passions in the place of reason, and of thinking thus and thus by the mere force of his will and pleasure. 'It was not ill said by an acute observer who knew them both, that their fault was not that of blindness to the truth so much as that of indifference to give it welcome unless as a discovery or possession of their own.' This is true, we think, but true in a larger degree of Landor than of his friend. Southey had strong feelings, and reached his decisions by their help. He had not time to think out a subject calmly, and he was far too impetuous to judge of any serious question impartially. That the opinions of his early and ardent youth were not those of his mature manhood, can excite no wonder. Most men of original power pass through one or more mental revolutions before they find rest for the intellect and the heart, and to this rule Southey formed no exception. His fault lay in his unwillingness to grant to others the freedom of which he had made such ample use himself; but his integrity, so often questioned in his lifetime, may now be regarded as unimpeachable. 'He has convinced me,' wrote a shrewd observer, 'of the perfect exemption of his mind from all dishonourable motives in the change which has taken place in his practical politics and philosophy;' and the publication of Southey's correspondence has confirmed the judgment of Crabb Robinson.

There are some illustrious men who are never rash in speech, and who speak and write to their intimate friends with the most circumspect wisdom. They rarely make a mistake, or commit an absurdity; their propriety is exquisite, and when they die it may be safe to produce their correspondence without much editorial supervision. Southey was not one of these men; he wrote often rashly and thoughtlessly, and his hasty words, which expressed in many instances a momentary prejudice or feeling, have had the misfortune to be preserved in print. 'In days of old,' he once wrote, as if anticipating the injury that would be done him, 'when an author was dead and buried, *Requiescat in Pace* might have been written on his tombstone: but those days are past, and he must expect now to be dissected and embalmed, to have his rags presented as relics, and to be canonized by his devotees.' The 'rags' have been zealously flaunted by Southey's 'devotees;' but there is some comfort in the thought that, thanks to the mode of presentation, they have failed to attract attention.

It cannot be denied, moreover, that reckless opinions are to be often found in his published works as well as in his correspondence, and thus it has come to pass that the most trustworthy of writers is at the same time the least satisfactory of guides. Thus, for instance, Southey does not scruple to assert in print that the political economists 'are to the Government of this country such counsellors as the magicians were to Pharaoh; whosoever listens to them has his heart hardened:' and he terms *The Wealth of Nations* 'a tedious and hard-hearted book, greatly overvalued even on the score of ability.' He denounces our manufacturing system as a pest to society, which debases all who are engaged in it; he declares that 'the Protestant cause sustained more injury from the English Puritans than from all the efforts of Spain and Austria combined, and of France also, when France put forth its strength against it;' and that the Puritans should be held up 'to contempt and infamy and abhorrence.' Again and again the liberal-minded reader is moved to something like contempt, or aroused to fierce anger, by the extravagant and narrow opinions put forth by Robert Southey. And yet Southey could write, expressing herein a feeling of which many of us must have been conscious. 'I have an instinctive horror of bigotry. When Dissenters talk of the Establishment they make me feel like a High Churchman, and when I get among High Churchmen I am ready to take refuge in Dissent.' On some points, it is but fair to add, Southey was in advance of his age. He writes wisely in many places of the imperative necessity of a national education, and he was one of the first to press upon the public the services that might be rendered by Protestant sisters-of-mercy and by ladies properly trained as hospital nurses.

In the Preface to the collected edition of his poems, Southey remarks that it was the greatest of all advantages to him to have lived more than half his life in retirement, conversing with books rather than men; but the reader who follows the poet's career will probably arrive at a precisely opposite conclusion. 'Beware that you be not swallowed up in books,' wrote John Wesley, and this assuredly was in many respects the misfortune of his biographer. 'He was never happy,' said Rogers, 'except when making or reading a book;' and so inveterate was this love of solitary study, that in society Southey, feeling that he had little conversational power, would 'roll himself up like a hedgehog.' Solitude may have many advantages, but it is scarcely calculated to produce breadth of thought or freedom from prejudice; and Southey, brooding tenderly and constantly over the wealth of his own mind, was not likely to discover its deficiencies. He needed collision with other intellects; but this salutary contact with his fellows he disliked, and, as much as possible, avoided.

If we reckon his *Quarterly Review* articles, Southey produced in all nearly two hundred volumes, in itself a small library. Many of these works are more likely to be consulted than to be read; while some on which the writer set most count must stand, it is to be feared, on the shelves which contain (to use Lamb's familiar epithet) the books that are not books. Southey's *magnum opus*, *The History of Portugal*, was destined never to be finished; but a portion of this vast undertaking, *The History of Brazil*, was accomplished to the entire satisfaction of the historian, who said that ages hence it will be found among those works which are not destined to perish, and be to the Brazilians, when they shall have become a powerful nation, what the work of Herodotus is to Europe. The prophecy cannot be contradicted, but it may fairly be questioned; and when we remember how many prophecies Southey made in his life-time, which have already turned out to be delusions, it is not unreasonable to conjecture that this also will prove a blunder. *The History of Brazil* was an enormous achievement, but it was labour ill-bestowed; and Sir Walter Scott characterizes it wisely, when he says, in writing to the author, 'A more faithless and worthless set than both Dutch and Portuguese I have never read of, and it requires your knowledge of the springs of human action and your lively description of "hair-breadth 'scapes" to make one care whether the hog bites the dog or the dog bites the hog.'

Still less satisfactory in its results was the toil bestowed by Southey on his *History of the Peninsular War*, a work which has been since accomplished with consummate ability by a military historian. The Duke of Wellington spoke of Southey's *History* as wholly inadequate, and as displaying gross ignorance, which was likely enough in matters of military detail; and here too, as in so many of his works, he wasted his strength and wearied the reader's patience by a display of useless erudition. Well would it have been for Southey's fame had he attended to the wise axiom of Dryden, which that great poet, by the way, often forgot himself: 'An author is not to write all he can, but only all he ought.'

The truth is, and scores of instances might be cited in proof of it, that the Poet-Laureate, with all his ingenuity and learning and perseverance, and with a literary ability that might have enabled him to put what he knew in an agreeable form, missed the mark again and again. He could not, for the life of him, distinguish between the topics to which he was specially attracted and the subjects likely to interest the public; he even thought that he had power to command attention whether his readers wished to attend or not. Sometimes he hit, as it were, by accident on a theme which was fitted for popularity. *The Life of Nelson* is as beautiful a specimen of biography as we possess in the language, and for this fascinating work we are indebted, in a measure, to the publisher as well as to the author. Southey, though rebelling against the imposition, was happily restricted within narrow limits. He could have made the book, he said, ten times as long, and there can be no doubt that if he had had his way he would have done so and have spoilt it.

His love of digression, of ingenious trifling, and of exhibiting in a half-serious, half-grotesque fashion, the results of his prodigious acquisitions, is notably exhibited in *The Doctor*, a book which charms and annoys the reader by turns. 'How beautiful!' he exclaims, on reading one page: 'How horribly wearisome!' he sighs out, on turning to the next. On the whole, perhaps the fatigue predominates over the pleasure, although there are moods of happy indolence in which this medley of humour, nonsense, and wisdom may prove a grateful opiate. It has been said with some truth of Mr. Trollope's singularly clever novels, that they may be taken up at almost any time with pleasure, and laid down again without serious regret, and perhaps a similar criticism may be passed upon *The Doctor*. In its best chapters it is eminently good, but it will *keep*, and no anxiety is felt to follow continuously the writer's footsteps. Open on any page, and some beautiful thought, or quaint suggestion, or amusing anecdote will attract attention; but the reader is not allured on by what he reads, and deems it but little consequence on which page he may alight. We said that *The Doctor* may, to certain persons and at certain times, prove an agreeable sedative; but just as there are people who become excited instead of soothed by opium, so there are readers, we suspect, whom this strange book will irritate almost beyond endurance. The preface to Wordsworth's *Excursion* gave William Blake, the poet-artist, a stomach complaint, which nearly killed him; *The Doctor,* with its impertinent digressions and its perpetual movement towards a point it never attains, might produce a nervous attack.

The great charm of Southey's style, and his consummate skill as a biographer, are perhaps best displayed in *The Life of Wesley*; but here, too, his want of logical power is everywhere apparent. The facts which he states with scrupulous fidelity often palpably contradict the inferences he draws from them. Nor is this all; for the opinion of the writer, as given on one page, is sometimes entirely opposed to the opinion he utters on another, and at variance with his known principles. His intuitions are often right, his deliberate judgment, if such it may be called, is frequently wrong. Southey acknowledges that he could not stand severe thought, and indeed he was too busy a man in his profession to be a profound thinker.

Southey's contributions to the literature of English poetry are not many, but they are so able that it is to be deplored he did not carry out his intention of continuing the *History* left so imperfect by Warton. His knowledge of the subject was immense, and he might have produced a narrative full of critical and biographical interest and written in the purest English, which would have formed a text-book for students. His *Life of Cowper,* although in parts a little languid and diffusive, shows how admirably Southey could write about poets and poetry; but in this department of literature, as in others, he appears to have expended much comparatively useless strength. This was partly owing to his singular kindness of heart, which led him again and again to befriend those who needed help and deserved it. Southey, for example, by his friendship for Kirke White while living, and by the publication of his *Remains* after his decease, produced an interest in that young poet, which, to judge from the poems he left behind him, was far beyond his deserts. *The Lives of Uneducated Poets* is another work, written with a benevolent object, which, if looked at apart from the kindly purpose of the writer, must be regarded as waste labour; but while we regret that the claims upon Southey prevented him oftentimes from accomplishing the work for which he was most fitted, it is pleasant at the same time to remember how ready he ever was to sacrifice personal aims to generous and self-denying labours.

> Only the actions of the just
> Smell sweet, and blossom in their dust.[1]

---

[1] James Shirley, *The Lady of Pleasure.*

With these actions the life of Southey was crowded and ennobled. He said many a bitter thing in his day, made rash statements, uttered opinions of men and measures which will not bear a moment's examination; but he never knowingly did an unjust act, or shirked an obvious duty. To use a homely saying, his heart was all along in its right place; and if, as a politician and theologian, he sometimes indulged in what may be called feminine passion, the life he lived was one of the manliest, and is even more worthy of a place in the memory of Englishmen than his great literary achievements.

143. Gerard Manley Hopkins on the versification of *Thalaba*

1878

From *The Correspondence of Gerard Manley Hopkins and Richard Watson Dixon*, ed. C. C. Abbott (1935), p. 13. In a letter to Dixon, 5 October 1878, Hopkins discusses the versification of Milton's *Samson Agonistes*. Dixon replied: 'I never heard of anything more ridiculous than comparing the *Samson* and *Thalaba*.'

It is amazing that so great a writer as Newman should have fallen into the blunder of comparing the first chorus of the *Agonistes* with the opening of *Thalaba* as instancing the gain in smoothness and correctness of versification made since Milton's time—Milton having been not only ahead of his own time as well as all aftertimes in verse-structure but these particular choruses being his own highwater mark. It is as if you were to compare the Panathenaic frieze and a teaboard and decide in the teaboard's favour.

144. Edward Dowden on Southey

1879

Dowden's *Southey* (1879) in the English Men of Letters Series was the first attempt to provide a rounded assessment of Southey's life and work. The final chapter, reprinted here, offers a thoughtful and sensitive survey of his literary achievement.

SOUTHEY'S WORK IN LITERATURE

Southey's career of authorship falls into two chief periods—a period during which poetry occupied the higher place and prose the lower, and a period during which this order was reversed. His translations of romantic fiction—*Amadis of Gaul, Palmerin of England,* and *The Cid*—connect the work of the earlier with that of the latter period, and serve to mark the progress of his mind from legend to history and from the fantastic to the real. The poet in Southey died young, or, if he did not die, fell into a numbness and old age like that of which an earlier singer writes:—[1]

> Elde that in my spirit dulleth me,
> Hath of endyting all the subtilité
> Welnyghe bereft out of my remembraance.

After thirty Southey seldom cared to utter himself in occasional verse. The uniformity of his life, the equable cheerfulness maintained by habits of regular work, his calm religious faith, his amiable Stoicism left him without the material for lyrical poetry; and one so honest and healthy had no care to feign experiences of the heart which were not his. Still he could apply himself to the treatment of large subjects with a calm continuous energy; but as time went on his hand grew slack, and wrought with less ease. Scarcely had he overcome the narrative poet's chief difficulty, that of subduing varied materials to an unity of design, when he put aside verse and found it more natural to be historian than poet.

[1] Chaucer, *The Complaint of Venus.*

474

The poetry of sober feeling is rare in lyrical verse. This may be found admirably rendered in some of Southey's shorter pieces. Although his temper was ardent and hopeful, his poems of pensive remembrance, of meditative calm, are perhaps the most characteristic. Among these his *Inscriptions* rank high. Some of those in memory of the dead are remarkable for their fine poise of feeling, all that is excessive and transitory having been subdued; for the tranquil depths of sorrow and of hope which lie beneath their clear, melodious words.

Southey's larger poetical works are fashioned of two materials, which do not always entirely harmonize. First, material brought from his own moral nature; his admiration of something elevated in the character of man or woman—generosity, gentleness, loyalty, fortitude, faith. And secondly, material gathered from abroad; mediæval pomps of religion and circumstance of war; Arabian marvels, the work of the enchanters and the genii; the wild beauties and adventure of life amid New-world tribes; the monstrous mythology of the Brahman. With such material the poet's inventive talent deals freely, rearranges details or adds to them; still Southey is here rather a *finder* than a *maker*. His diligence in collecting and his skill in arranging were so great that it was well if the central theme did not disappear among manifold accessories. One who knows Southey, however, can recognize his ethical spirit in every poem. Thalaba, as he himself confessed, is a male Joan of Arc. Destiny or Providence has marked alike the hero and the heroine from mankind; the sheepfold of Domremi, and the palm-grove by old Moath's tent, alike nurture virgin purity and lofty aspiration. Thalaba, like Joan, goes forth a delegated servant of the Highest to war against the powers of evil; Thalaba, like Joan, is sustained under the trials of the way by the sole talisman of faith. We are not left in doubt as to where Southey found his ideal. Mr. Barbauld thought Joan of Arc was modelled on the Socinian Christ. He was mistaken; Southey's ideal was native to his soul. 'Early admiration, almost adoration of Leonidas, early principles of Stoicism derived from the habitual study of Epictetus, and the French Revolution at its height when I was just eighteen—by these my mind was moulded.' And from these, absorbed into Southey's very being, came Thalaba and Joan.

The word *high-souled* takes possession of the mind as we think of Southey's heroic personages. Poetry, he held, ought rather to elevate than to affect—a Stoical doctrine transferred to art, which meant that his own poetry was derived more from admiration of great qualities, than from sympathy with individual men or women. Neither the quick and passionate tenderness of Burns, nor the stringent pathos of Wordsworth, can be found in Southey's verse. No eye probably ever shed a tear over the misery of Ladurlad and his persecuted daughter. She, like the lady in *Comus*, is set above our pity and perhaps our love. In *Kehama*, a work of Southey's mature years, the chivalric ardour of his earlier heroes is transformed into the sterner virtues of fortitude and an almost despairing constancy. The power of evil, as conceived by the poet, has grown more despotic; little can be achieved by the light-winged Glendoveer—a more radiant Thalaba—against the Rajah; only the lidless eye of Seeva can destroy that tyranny of lust and pride. *Roderick* marks a higher stage in the development of Southey's ethical ideal. Roderick too is a delegated champion of right against force and fraud; he too endures mighty pains. But he is neither such a combatant, pure and intrepid, as goes forth from the Arab tent, nor such a blameless martyr as Ladurlad. He is first a sinner enduring just punishment; then a stricken penitent; and from his shame and remorse he is at last uplifted by enthusiasm on behalf of his God and his people into a warrior saint, the Gothic Maccabee.

Madoc stands somewhat away from the line of Southey's other narrative poems. Though, as Scott objected, the personages in *Madoc* are too nearly abstract types, Southey's ethical spirit dominates this poem less than any of the others. The narrative flows on more simply. The New-world portion tells a story full of picturesque incident, with the same skill and grace that belong to Southey's best prose writings. Landor highly esteemed *Madoc*. Scott declared that he had read it three times since his first cursory perusal, and each time with increased admiration of the poetry. Fox was in the habit of reading aloud after supper to eleven o'clock, when it was the rule at St. Ann's Hill to retire; but while *Madoc* was in his hand, he read until after midnight. Those, however, who opened the bulky quarto were few; the tale was out of relation with the time; it interpreted no need, no aspiration, no passion of the dawn of the present century. And the mind of the time was not enough disengaged to concern itself deeply with the supposed adventures of a Welsh prince of the twelfth century among the natives of America.

At heart, then, Southey's poems are in the main the outcome of his moral nature; this we recognize through all disguises, Mohammedan, Hindoo, or Catholic. He planned and partly wrote a poem—*Oliver Newman*—which should associate his characteristic ideal with Puritan principles and ways of life. The foreign material through which his ethical idea was set forth went far, with each poem, to determine its reception by the public. Coleridge has spoken of 'the pastoral charm and wild streaming lights of the *Thalaba*.' Dewy night moon-mellowed, and the desert-circle girdled by the sky, the mystic palace of Shedad, the vernal brook, Oneiza's favourite kidling, the lamp-light shining rosy through the damsel's delicate fingers, the aged Arab in the tent-door,—these came with a fresh charm into English narrative poetry eighty years ago. The landscape and the manners of Spain, as pictured in *Roderick*, are of marked grandeur and simplicity. In *Kehama* Southey attempted a bolder experiment, and although the poem became popular, even a well-disposed reader may be allowed to sympathize with the dismay of Charles Lamb among the monstrous gods: 'I never read books of travels, at least not farther than Paris or Rome. I can just endure Moors, because of their connexion as foes with Christians; but Abyssinians, Ethiops, Esquimaux, Dervises, and all that tribe I hate. I believe I fear them in some manner. A Mohammedan turban on the stage, though enveloping some well-known face, . . . does not give me unalloyed pleasure. I am a Christian, Englishman, Londoner, Templar. God help me when I come to put off these snug relations, and to get abroad into the world to come.'

Though his materials are often exotic, in style Southey aimed at the simplicity and strength of undefiled English. If to these melody was added, he had attained all he desired. To conversations with William Taylor about German poetry—certainly not to Taylor's example— he ascribes his faith in the power of plain words to express in poetry the highest thoughts and strongest feelings. He perceived in his own day the rise of the ornate style, which has since been perfected by Tennyson, and he regarded it as a vice in art. In early years Akenside had been his instructor; afterwards he owed more to Landor than to any other master of style. From *Madoc* and *Roderick*—both in blank verse—fragments could be severed, which might pass for the work of Landor; but Southey's free and facile manner, fostered by early reading of Ariosto, and by constant study of Spenser, soon reasserts itself; from under the fragment of monumental marble, white almost as Landor's, a stream wells out smooth and clear, and lapses away never dangerously swift nor mysteriously deep. On the whole, judged by the highest standards, Southey's poetry takes a midmost rank; it neither renders into art a great body of thought and passion, nor does it give faultless expression to lyrical moments. But it is the out-put of a large and vigorous mind, amply stored with knowledge; its breath of life is the moral ardour of a nature strong and generous, and therefore it can never cease to be of worth.

Southey is at his best in prose. And here it must be borne in mind that, though so voluminous a writer, he did not achieve his most important work, *The History of Portugal*, for which he had gathered vast collections. It cannot be doubted that this, if completed, would have taken a place among our chief histories. The splendour of story and the heroic personages would have lifted Southey into his highest mood. We cannot speak with equal confidence of his projected work of second magnitude, *The History of the Monastic Orders*. Learned and sensible it could not fail to be, and Southey would have recognized the more substantial services of the founders and the brotherhoods; but he would have dealt by methods too simple with the psychology of religious emotions; the words enthusiasm and fraud might have risen too often to his lips; and at the grotesque humours of the devout, which he would have exhibited with delight, he might have been too prone to smile.

As it is, Southey's largest works are not his most admirable. *The History of Brazil*, indeed, gives evidence of amazing patience, industry, and skill; but its subject necessarily excludes it from the first rank. At no time from the sixteenth to the nineteenth century was Brazil a leader or a banner-bearer among lands. The life of the people crept on from point to point, and that is all; there are few passages in which the chronicle can gather itself up, and transform itself into a historic drama. Southey has done all that was possible; his pages are rich in facts, and are more entertaining than perhaps any other writer could have made them. His extraordinary acquaintance with travel gave him many advantages in narrating the adventures of early explorers; and his studies in ecclesiastical history led him to treat with peculiar interest the history of the Jesuit Reductions.

The *History of the Peninsular War* suffers by comparison with the great work of Sir William Napier. That heroic man had himself been a portion of the strife; his senses singularly keen were attuned to battle; as he wrote, the wild bugle-calls, the measured tramp, the peals of musketry, the dismal clamour sounded in his ears; he abandoned himself again to the swiftness and 'incredible fury' of the charge. And with his falcon eye he could discern amid the shock or formless dispersion, wherever hidden, the fiery heart of victory. Southey wrought in his library as a man of letters; consulted sources, turned over manuscripts, corresponded with witnesses, set his material in order. The passion of justice and an enthusiasm on behalf of Spain give unity to his work. If he estimated too highly the disinterestedness and courage of the people of the Peninsula, the illusion was generous. And it may be that enduring spiritual forces become apparent to a distant observer, which are masked by accidents of the day and hour from one who is in their midst.

History as written by Southey is narrative rendered spiritual by moral ardour. There are no new political truths, he said. If there be laws of a nation's life other than those connected with elementary principles of morality, Southey did not discover these. What he has written may go only a little way towards attaining the ultimate ends of historical study, but so far as it goes it keeps the direct line. It is not led astray by will-o'-the-wisp, vague-shining theories that beguile night wanderers. Its method is an honest method as wholesome as sweet; and simple narrative if ripe and sound at first is none the less so at the end of a century.

In biography, at least, one may be well pleased with clear and charming narrative. Here Southey has not been surpassed, and even in this single province he is versatile; he has written the life of a warrior, of a poet, and of a saint. His industry was that of a German; his lucidity and perfect exposition were such as we rarely find outside a French memoir. There is no style fitter for continuous narrative than the pedestrian style of Southey. It does not beat upon the ear with hard metallic vibration. The sentences are not cast by the thousand in one mould of cheap rhetoric, nor made brilliant with one cheap colour. Never dithyrambic, he is never dull; he affects neither the trick of stateliness nor that of careless ease; he does not seek out curiosities of refinement, nor caress delicate affectations. Because his style is natural it is inimitable, and the only way to write like Southey is to write well.

'The favourite of my library, among many favourites;' so Coleridge speaks of *The Life of Wesley*, 'the book I can read for the twentieth time, when I can read nothing else at all.' And yet the school-boy's favourite, *The Life of Nelson*, is of happier inspiration. The simple and chivalric hero, his splendid achievements, his pride in duty, his patriotism, roused in Southey all that was most strong and high; but his enthusiasm does not escape in lyrical speech. 'The best eulogy of Nelson,' he says, 'is the faithful history of his actions; the best history that which shall relate them most perspicuously.' Only when all is over, and the captain of Trafalgar lies dead, his passion and pride find utterance:—'If the chariot and the horses of fire had been vouchsafed for Nelson's translation, he could scarcely have departed in a brighter blaze of glory.' From Nelson on the quarter-deck of the *Victory*, to Cowper caressing his tame hares, the interval is wide; but Southey, the man of letters, lover of the fireside, and patron of cats, found it natural to sympathize with his brother poet. His sketches of literary history in *The Life of Cowper* are characteristic. The writer's range is wide, his judgment sound, his enjoyment of almost everything literary is lively; as critic he is kindly yet equitable. But the highest criticism is not his. Southey's vision was not sufficiently penetrative; he culls beauties, but he cannot pluck out the heart of a mystery.

His translations of romantic fiction, while faithful to their sources, aim less at literal exactitude than at giving the English reader the same pleasure which the Spaniard receives from the originals. From the destruction of Don Quixote's library Master Nicholas and the curate spared *Amadis of Gaul* and *Palmerin of England*. Second to Malory's grouping of the Arthur cycle *Amadis* may well take its place. Its chivalric spirit, its wildness, its tenderness and beauty are carefully preserved by the translator. But Southey's chief gift in this kind to English readers is *The Cid*. The poem he supposed, indeed, to be a metrical chronicle instead of a metrical romance—no fatal error; weaving together the best of the poem, the ballads and the chronicle, he produced more than a mere compilation. 'I know no work of the kind in our language,' wrote Coleridge, 'none which, uniting the charms of romance and history, keeps the imagination so constantly on the wing, and yet leaves so much for after reflection.'

Of Southey's political writings something has been said in a former chapter. Among works which can be brought under no general head, one that pleased the public was *Espriella's Letters*, sketches of English landscape, life, and manners, by a supposed Spanish traveller. The letters, giving as they do a lively view of England at the beginning of the present century, still possess an interest. Apart from Southey's other works stands *The Doctor*; nowhere else can one find so much of his varied erudition, his genial spirits, his meditative wisdom. It asks for a leisurely reader content to ramble everywhere and no whither, and still pleased to take another turn because his companion has not yet come to an end of learning, mirth, or meditation. That the author of a book so characteristic was not instantly recognized is strange. 'The wit and humour of *The Doctor*,' says Edgar Poe, a keen critic, 'have seldom been equalled. We cannot think Southey wrote it.' Gratitude is due to Doctor Daniel Dove from innumerable 'good little women and men,' who have been delighted with his story of *The Three Bears*. To know that he had added a classic to the nursery would have been the pride of Southey's heart. Wide eyes entranced and peals of young laughter still make a triumph for one whose spirit, grave with a man's wisdom, was pure as the spirit of a little child.

Bibliography

This short select bibliography is confined to works which list or discuss the nineteenth-century criticism of Southey. Place of publication is London unless otherwise stated.

BERNBAUM, ERNEST, *Guide through the Romantic Movement* (2nd edition, New York, 1949): includes a chapter on Southey's achievement with notes on some contemporary and later assessments.

CARNALL, GEOFFREY, *Robert Southey and His Age: The Development of a Conservative Mind* (Oxford, 1960): this important study of the growth of Southey's political ideas contains much information about contemporary attitudes to him.

CARNALL, GEOFFREY, *Robert Southey* (1964): pamphlet in the British Council's Writers and Their Work series. Includes a short bibliography listing the most important biographical and critical studies.

CARNALL, GEOFFREY, 'Robert Southey', in *The New Cambridge Bibliography of English Literature, vol. III: 1800–1900*, ed. George Watson (Cambridge, 1969): the most comprehensive listing yet published.

CURRY, KENNETH, 'Robert Southey', in *The English Romantic Poets and Essayists: A Review of Research and Criticism*, ed. C. W. Houtchens and L. H. Houtchens (revised edition, New York, 1966): the best narrative survey of criticism and scholarship.

HALLER, WILLIAM, *The Early Life of Robert Southey, 1774–1803* (New York, 1917): discusses Southey's early literary career in relation to contemporary influences and criticism.

HAYDEN, JOHN O., *The Romantic Reviewers 1802–1824* (1969): discusses Southey's reception by the periodical press and lists reviews of his works to 1824.

HOADLEY, FRANK TALIAFERRO, 'The controversy over Southey's *Wat Tyler*', *Studies in Philology*, xxxviii (1941), 81–96: the best account of the progress of the quarrel.

SIMMONS, JACK, *Southey* (1945): the standard biography. Contains much information about the reception of Southey's works.

Index

The index is arranged in three sections:
  I. Southey's writings. Includes all references to volumes published by Southey and significant references to individual short poems.
  II. Southey: topics & characteristics. Lists aspects of Southey's work, personality and reception.
 III. General. Includes personal names and titles of periodicals. Literary works are indexed under the names of their authors.

I. SOUTHEY'S WRITINGS

II. SOUTHEY: TOPICS AND CHARACTERISTICS

prose writing, variety of forms attempted 2, 14

rapidity of composition *see* haste in composition
reflection, RS deficient in 18, 27, 30
religion and theology, attitudes to 18, 19, 29, 154–5, 161, 272–83, 309–13, 361–70, 437–8, 445
reviewer *see* essayist and reviewer
Roman Catholic Emancipation *see* Catholic Emancipation

scholarship *see* erudition
sisterhoods, RS advocates 29, 469
slave-trade, attitude to 319
social commentator 2, 19–20, 29, 123–124, 333–85, 445

supernatural subjects *see* mythological subjects

tenderness 9, 105, 177, 181, 213–14
theology *see* religion and theology
translator 2, 22, 96–8, 128, 320, 474, 480

versification 2, 5, 6, 13, 42, 64, 65, 67, 78–80, 95, 104, 108–9, 114, 136, 145, 176–7, 182, 192, 197, 201–3, 204–5, 223, 284, 286–9, 296, 317, 324, 437, 438
vindictiveness in poems 9, 191
violence in works 30, 31, 106, 351, 408

war, attitude to 42, 196, 210–13, 351
wit *see* humour and wit

III. GENERAL

Aikin, John 4, 41–2, 54–5
Akenside, Mark 421
Allchin, A. M. 29
Analytical Review 4, 47–8
Annual Anthology 102, 197
Annual Review 22, 115–16
Anster, John 27, 420–1
Anti-Jacobin 5, 55–60, 194, 267
Antijacobin Review & Magazine 17
Ariosto, Ludovico 477
Aristotle 103
Augustan Review 10, 208–9, 222–3

Bagehot, Walter 27–8, 448–9
Baldwin & Cradock (publishers) 26
Barlow, Joel 257
Beaumont, Lady 101
Beaumont, Sir George 100
Bedford, Grosvenor Charles: on RS 8, 22, 179–82; friendship with RS 9, 13, 21, 117, 272, 290, 333, 443, 452
Benbow, William 326–7
Bentley's Miscellany 451–3
Bernbaum, Ernest 30, 483
Bilderdijk, Katharina Wilhelmina 445–446
Bilderdijk, Willem 445–6
Black Dwarf 239–40
Blackmore, Sir Richard 118
Blackwood's Edinburgh Magazine 19, 266, 279–83, 323

Bonaparte *see* Napoleon Bonaparte
Borrow, George 456
Bowles, William Lisle 45
Bowles, Caroline 26
Brinton, Crane 29
British Critic 8, 11, 17, 38, 63–4, 97–8, 173–4, 183–6, 204–5, 310–11
British Review 9, 190–3
Brontë, Charlotte 27, 423
Brougham, Henry, Lord 12, 248
Browne, Sir Thomas 421
Bulwer-Lytton, Edward George Earle Lytton 15, 387–8
Bunyan, John 22, 62
Burke, Edmund 265, 342
Burns, Robert 45, 476
Burton, Robert 331
Butler, Charles 309
Byron, George Gordon, Lord: on RS 1, 12, 13–14, 21, 130–1, 157, 242, 261–5, 266–71, 290–2, 295–302; references 195, 280, 320, 326, 424, 440, 446

Cabinet 127
Campbell, Thomas 137, 195, 262, 270–1, 280, 324–5, 441
Canning, George 55, 247
Capes, J. M. 422
Carlile, Richard 285, 368
Carlyle, Alexander 395

INDEX

Carlyle, Thomas: on RS 28, 395, 459–467; compared with RS 395, 467
Carnall, Geoffrey 20, 29, 483
Carroll, Lewis 457–9
Castlereagh, Robert Stewart, Lord 222, 247, 251, 263
Changeling, The (poem) 13, 243–5
Chatterton, Thomas 22
Chew, S. C. 30
Christian Observer 188–9
Churchill, Charles 270
Cibber, Colley 198, 218, 221, 344
Clarendon, Edward Hyde, Earl of 281–3
Clarkson, Mrs Thomas 286
Cobban, Alfred 29
Cobbett, William 240, 249
Cole, Henry 328
Coleridge, John Taylor: on RS 8, 183–6; friendship with RS 16, 452
Coleridge, Samuel Taylor: on RS 4, 15, 21, 22, 49–50, 51–3, 128–9, 251, 258–61, 338, 436, 450, 451–2, 477, 479, 480; compared or contrasted with RS 1, 3, 6, 38, 45, 69, 280, 320, 331, 418, 426–7, 430, 443; personal relations with RS 4, 13, 19, 24, 29, 37, 40, 246, 247, 261; RS on *Lyrical Ballads* 20–1, 440; references 45–6, 160, 183, 268–70, 342, 408–9, 411, 462–3
Conder, Josiah 11–12, 210–14
Cornhill Magazine 454–5, 467–73
Cornwall, Barry 428
Cottle, Joseph: on RS 419–20; relations with RS 4, 24, 40, 132, 175, 419; references 49, 53, 272
Courier 13, 19, 194, 246, 247, 290, 326
Cowper, William: RS as editor of 22, 26, 396, 432, 446, 472, 480; RS compared or contrasted with 45, 46, 69, 94, 195, 325, 421, 425, 428, 435
Crabbe, George 262, 270–1, 425
Critical Review: on RS 4, 6, 10, 17, 37, 43–5, 91–5, 113–14, 134–7, 171–2, 194–6, 206–7; RS as contributor to 20, 24; reference 176
Croker, John Wilson 169, 194, 247, 251
Curry, Kenneth 28, 29, 483

Dante 132, 135
Davy, Humphry 128

Dennis, John 467–73
De Quincey, Thomas 408–16, 462–3
Dicey, A. V. 29
D'Israeli, Isaac 392
Dixon, Richard Watson 473
Donne, John 69
Donne, William Bodham 27, 440–7
Dowden, Edward 28, 474–81
Dryden, John 39, 63, 116, 120, 136, 169, 199, 221, 223, 268, 270, 437, 470
Dwight, Timothy 257

Eclectic Review 7, 10, 11, 14, 17, 106–8, 138–45, 148–50, 174, 198–203, 210–214, 307, 324–6
Edinburgh Annual Register 25, 137, 411–12, 442
Edinburgh Review: on RS 1, 6, 7, 19, 27, 68–90, 96–7, 121–4, 159, 161, 215–18, 268, 341–79, 398–408, 440–447; references 25, 196, 248, 266, 271, 380
Eldon, John Scott, Lord 231
Eliot, John 256
Elwin, Whitwell 27, 430–9
European Magazine and London Review 11
Examiner 12, 13, 219–22, 233–5, 246–253, 311–13

Fenwick, Isabella 418
Ferriar, John 102–4
Foreign Quarterly Review 26, 452
Foster, John 138–45
Fraser's Magazine 380–5, 424–9
Frere, John Hookham 55
Fuller, Thomas 331, 421

General Review of British and Foreign Literature 111–12
George III, King 13, 222, 284–302, 331
George IV, King 196, 217, 220, 454–5
Gibbon, Edward 303, 415
Gifford, William 21, 55, 179, 183, 247, 270–1, 452
Gittings, Robert 31
Godwin, William 155
Goldsmith, Oliver 270, 421, 428
Gordon, George Huntly 334
Gray, Thomas 269
Grigson, Geoffrey 30–1
Guide 328